THE LONTAR ANTHOLOGY OF INDONESIAN POETRY

THE LONTAR ANTHOLOGY OF INDONESIAN POETRY

The Twentieth Century in Poetry

edited by

John H. McGlynn
Dorothea Rosa Herliany
Deborah Cole

University of Hawai'i Press
HONOLULU

First published in Indonesia by:
The Lontar Foundation
Jl. Danau Laut Tawar No. 53
Jakarta 10210 Indonesia
www.lontar.org

Published in North America by:
University of Hawai'i Press
2840 Kolowalu St.
Honolulu, HI 96822
www.uhpress.hawaii.edu

22 21 20 19 18 17   6 5 4 3 2 1

Library of Congress Cataloging-in-Publication Data

Names: McGlynn, John H., editor. | Herliany, Dorothea Rosa, 1963- editor |
    Cole, Deborah (Deborah L.), editor. | Lontar Foundation (Jakarta, Indonesia)
Title: The Lontar anthology of Indonesian poetry : the twentieth century in
    poetry / edited by John H. Mcglynn, Dorothea Rosa Herliany, Deborah Cole.
Description: Honolulu : University of Hawai'i Press ; Jakarta : Lontar
    Foundation, [2017] | Includes bibliographical references.
Identifiers: LCCN 2017018173| ISBN 9780824875039 (hardcover alk. paper) |
    ISBN 9780824875046 (pbk. alk. paper)
Subjects: LCSH: Indonesian poetry—20th century—Translations into English. |
    LCGFT: Poetry.
Classification: LCC PL5086.5.E5 L66 2017 | DDC 899/.2211208—dc23
LC record available at https://lccn.loc.gov/2017018173

This publication was made possible by the generosity of the Henry Luce Foundation.
Funding for translation was provided by
the Ministry of Education and Culture of the Republic of Indonesia.

Editorial Board:	John H. McGlynn, Dorothea Rosa Herliany, Deborah Cole
Guest Editors:	Agus R. Sarjono, Eka Budianta, Joko Pinurbo, Radhar Panca Dahana
Advisors:	Rida K Liamsi, Siti Nuraini, Todung Mulya Lubis, Toeti Heraty
Editorial Manager:	Wikan Satriati
Editorial Assistants:	Aris Kurniawan, Aris Masruri Harahap, Ariyantri Eddy Tarman, Esthi Winarni
Design:	DesignLab
Layout:	Cyprianus Jaya Napiun

Contents

II. 1942–1949: The Japanese Occupation and the Indonesian Revolution

An Uneasy Revolution by Radhar Panca Dahana

III. 1950–1966: Creating National Unity

IV. 1966–1970: Order and Harmony

V. 1971–1989: Development

VI. 1990s: Opposition

VII. 1998–2000: A New Age of Reform

Stripping Away the False and Leaving It Behind by Eka Budianta 483

Publisher's Note

The *Lontar Anthology of Indonesian Poetry* presents a selection of some of the best examples of Indonesian poetry written in the twentieth century. There have been other anthologies of Indonesian poetry, to be sure, but with 324 poems by 184 authors, this anthology has the distinction of being more comprehensive and representative in nature than any other collection. While we hope the anthology will appeal to all readers of poetry, this volume is primarily intended for use in the study and teaching of Indonesian literature in translation. Other goals include giving voice to Indonesian authors on the international stage; introducing Indonesian literature to a wider international audience; presenting to foreign readers the events and ideas that have influenced and shaped both the development of Indonesian literature and the nation as a whole during the twentieth century; and, in that way, building greater understanding of Indonesia abroad.

LAIP provides readers with a portrait of twentieth-century Indonesia as seen through the lens of its poetry. Each section of the book embodies the particular and changing zeitgeist of the decades of the last century as they were articulated and negotiated by Indonesian voices. The work's two organizing themes, "plurality and continuity," provide a frame within which many of the important topics of the last century—for example, decolonization and the emergence of national consciousness; the deconstruction of ethnic and gendered identities; and the environmental and social effects of modernization—were experienced and expressed by the inhabitants of the Indonesian archipelago.

Unlike all previous anthologies of Indonesian poetry in translation, which are limited in scope either because the poems were selected according to the preferences of a particular editor or because the selected works were limited to those that were widely known and easily available, LAIP represents a complete range of poetic expression published in Indonesian during the twentieth century. In addition to poems written by all major poets, this anthology also includes poems by many authors who have been successful locally but whose work has not previously been introduced to national or global audiences. In most cases their work was not published in the country's main publishing centers, which are generally located on the island of Java. This anthology is unique because the poems were selected based on both their literary merit and also their ability to contribute to the representation of the diversity of Indonesian experiences during the twentieth century—rather than whether a poet is well known or has been previously widely received.

Through the publication of LAIP and as a complement to the Lontar anthologies of Indonesian drama and short stories, Lontar is clearing a space for the non-specialist and specialist alike to explore the trajectories of a nation and its people through its poetry, which continues to act as the barometer of Indonesian literary life.

Publication of *The Lontar Anthology of Indonesian Poetry* (and companion anthologies of Indonesian short stories and drama from the twentieth century also published by Lontar) would not have been possible without the generous support of the Henry Luce Foundation. To the staff and the decision makers at the Henry Luce Foundation, especially Helena Kolenda, Program Director for Asia, Lontar will be forever grateful. As the director of publications at Lontar and a co-editor of this anthology, during the preparation of this anthology it was my pleasure to have worked with scores of authors, translators, researchers and other personnel. Special thanks must go to my co-editors, Deborah Cole and Dorothea Rosa Herliany, whose dedication to this book project never waned; to Lontar staff members, especially Tuti Zairati, the foundation's finance director, and Wikan Satriati, managing editor; and to Aris Kurniawan, special project assistant. I would also like to thank the book's guest editors, well-known poets Agus R. Sarjono, Eka Budianta, Joko Pinurbo and Radhar Panca Dahana, each of whom contributed incisive introductory texts, and advisory board members and senior poets Rida K Liamsi, Siti Nuraini, Todung Mulya Lubis and Toeti Heraty, whose thoughts about the world of Indonesian poetry were always insightful. I will always be grateful to my North America–based editorial team of poetry editor Helen Guri, project editor Meg Taylor and copy editor Ruth Gaskill, whose skill, craft and efficiency are unmatched. My final thanks, however, are reserved for the team of remarkable translators who were involved in the production of this monumental anthology and whose names are listed in the publication credits at the back of this book.

John H. McGlynn

Preface

O f all the literary genres that might be translated from Indonesian into English, poetry is arguably the most essential, enjoying as is it does a status far and above that of all other genres, even the novel, which is viewed in most Western countries as the premier form of literature. Such is not the case in Indonesia where poetry is the country's most commonly circulated literary genre, taught in public schools and accessible to the public through newspapers, magazines, radio, television, films and poetry readings. Portable and widely accessible, the genre reflects and embodies the significant ideological changes that occurred during the twentieth century. In arguing for the necessity of poetic representations of history in public discourse, the poet Goenawan Mohamad once cited Octavio Paz: "Poetry is that other voice. Not the sound of history or anti-history, but instead the sound which in history always expresses something different."[1] This anthology widens and sharpens our view of Indonesia and Indonesian.

As a genre, Indonesian poetry emerged during the twentieth century and records the nation's linguistic, literary and political history. Originally created by elites writing in Malay, the archipelago's lingua franca for more than a millennium, poetry (*puisi* in Indonesian) is inseparable from the birth of the nation in 1945. The development of Malay into Bahasa Indonesia, first proposed in 1928 by members of the Youth Congress, accomplished linguistic unity in a country where some five hundred languages are still spoken today. This process owed its success in no small part to the poets who purposefully manipulated both the language itself and a variety of formal poetic structures to test the grammatical limits of Indonesian as well as to widen the social expectations of their readers. During the postwar era, with wider access to Western texts and control of print production after the Dutch and the Japanese left the archipelago, poets began to mass distribute poems printed in Indonesian for the general reading public. Thus, more than any other literary genre, poetry has helped to shape an Indonesian national consciousness.

---

[1] Octavio Paz, as cited by Goenawan Mohamad, "Paz," in *Catatan Pinggir 4* (Jakarta: PT Pustaka Utama Grafiti, 1995), 259.

In facilitating cultural and intellectual exchange between Indonesia and the English reading world, this anthology is truly unique. Unlike all previous collections of Indonesian poetry in translation, which are limited in scope either because the poems were selected according to the preferences of a single editor or drawn from sources that were widely known or easily accessible, this collection represents the complete range of poetry published in Indonesian during the twentieth century. Alongside poems written by the major poets, the reader will find poems by many locally successful authors whose work has been previously unknown to national or global audiences, often because it was published far from the country's main literary centers on the island of Java. This is the only poetry anthology in English that takes as its organizing principle the question, "How do Indonesians themselves want to be read by the rest of the world?"

A team of Indonesian poets and literary scholars worked with the editors to select the poems they felt would best represent Indonesia. The team included four leading Indonesian poets and literary scholars, Agus R. Sarjono, Eka Budianta, Joko Pinurbo and Radhar Panca Dahana, who served as guest editors. They also contributed essays to introduce readers to the literary and historical context during each of the major time periods. In selecting poems for inclusion, the team considered formal innovation and historical relevance as well as the representation of local specificity, universal experience, and engagement with issues of global concern. The team also agreed on the following goals for the anthology:

1.   To gather together a wider segment of Indonesian poets than has ever been presented before (considering factors such as class, ethnicity, gender and ideology).

2.   To introduce Indonesian poetry to a wide international audience and foster inter-cultural understanding in academic and public discourse through the translation of globally significant literary texts into English.

3.   To paint a picture of the significant ideas and events that shaped Indonesian history through poetry written during the twentieth century.

Not unlike other literary texts, poetry offers readers the ability to imagine worlds and alternative solutions to problems beyond the reach of diplomatic or scientific discourse. The problems addressed by writers in Indonesia during the twentieth century often emerged, and were identified, as tensions in everyday life between the modern and the traditional, and between the individual and society. It was poetry's unique capacity to represent and embody these tensions, in part through formal strategies that navigated between the written and the oral, that has given this genre its power, value and high status in contemporary Indonesian society. This anthology is the first comprehensive attempt to translate the many and varied ways that Indonesian poets have continued to represent and interrogate these tensions in their multiple and evolving forms.

We hope that you will enjoy this collection of delightful, poignant, creative and thought-provoking texts and that, as you discover in these poems both the startlingly familiar and the wonderfully strange, you will fall in love with Indonesia.

John H. McGlynn
Dorothea Rosa Herliany
Deborah Cole

Different But Still United

by Radhar Panca Dahana

To speak of Indonesian poetry in the second half of the twentieth century leads inevitably to the question: was Indonesian literature—modern Indonesian literature—born in the early part of the century? Identifying its origins is important, for this forms the basis of our understanding of the poetry—its desires and aims, the thoughts it gives rise to, how language and form have been chosen. But this question of when modern Indonesian literature originated continues to be debated. There is no one authority whose views are accepted by a majority of critics, scholars or even literary activists in Indonesia. Instead, there are nearly a dozen dissenting opinions about when modern Indonesian literature originated.

One of these critics, Bakrie Siregar, considered the period of 1918–1919 to be the starting point of modern Indonesian literature, with the publication of *Student Hidjo* (published in English under the title *A Student Named Hijo*) by Mas Marco Kartodikromo (1890–1935) and the collection of poetry *Sair Rempah-Rempah* (Poems of Spices).[1] Sabarudin Ahmad and Zuber Usman[2] argued that Indonesia's new, or modern, literature appeared as far back as the time of Abdullah bin Abdulkadir Munsyi (1796–1854). On the other hand, three other figures—Umar Junus, J.S. Badudu and Zaidan Hendy—thought that the modern period should date to the publication of the literary magazine *Pujangga Baru* in 1933. With total confidence, Umar Junus wrote, "The new Indonesian literature clearly made its appearance in 1933."[3]

Another widely supported view—advanced by Nugroho Notosusanto, Hans Bague (H.B.) Jassin, Ajip Rosidi, Usmar Effeny and Andries (A.) Teeuw, among others—contended that Indonesia's modern literature got underway in 1920,

---

[1] Bakrie Siregar, *Sedjarah Sastera Indonesia 1* (Jakarta: Akademi Sastera dan Bahasa "Multatuli," 1964).

[2] Zuber Usman, *Kesusasteraan Baru Indonesia* [New Literature of Indonesia] (Jakarta: Gunung Agung, 1957), 1–8.

[3] Umar Junus, "Istilah dan Masa Waktu 'Sastra Melayu' dan 'Sastra Indonesia'" [Terms and Chronologies of "Malay Literature" and "Indonesian Literature"], *Medan Ilmu Pengetahuan* I, no. 3 (July 1960): 256.

distinguished in particular by the publication of Merari Siregar's novel *Azab dan Sengsara* (Pain and Suffering). In the realm of poetry, this new literature began with "Bahasa, Bangsa" (Language, Nation), written by seventeen-year-old Mohammad Yamin and printed in the magazine *Jong Sumatra* (Young Sumatra) in its inaugural edition in February 1921.

This latter view, particularly as it was articulated by two major figures in the history of Indonesian literary criticism and research—H.B. Jassin and A. Teeuw—has been widely accepted by critics and scholars of Indonesian literature right up to the present day. The arguments put forward by A. Teeuw, in particular, are frequently cited. But the question of when Indonesian literature "began" is still open to debate.

Period of Collapse

In researching the history of Indonesian literature, A. Teeuw divided the early period of Indonesia's modern literature into two phases, the 1920s and the 1940s—that is, the period before and the period after the revolution. His reasoning in pinpointing the birth of modern Indonesian literature is less than completely clear, especially in his well-regarded book *Sastra Baru Indonesia* (1980), which was followed by an English edition, *Modern Indonesian Literature* (1994).

In this book, Teeuw stresses in several places that the "innovation" and "modernism" of Indonesian literature after the 1920s was marked by differences in "feelings" and "ideas" from the work that came before.[4] But he does not identify the feelings and ideas that are supposedly so different between these two periods. At the very least, he equivocates. Mohammad Yamin's poem, "Bahasa, Bangsa"—which Teeuw cites as an example—has a title that suggests new feelings and ideas; namely, ideas about one language and a new nation, Indonesia. As it turns out, however, the poem was written about Sumatra and the Malay world, as opposed to the more inclusive concept of Indonesia.

Teeuw asserts that Indonesia's modern literature is distinguished by a "basic framework that is Indonesian in nature," but the evidence he offers does not support this. The same sense of contradiction holds for the following phase, the postwar period (1945 and afterwards), the dating of which leads to more doubt. For Teeuw, 1942 is a more accurate date for the shift than 1945, for 1942 was the year of the "collapse of the Dutch East Indies empire," and the 1945 proclamation of Indonesian independence was merely the logical outcome of that earlier event. But then he states that the '45 Generation (known in Indonesia as Angkatan '45) "were still not the creators of a truly modern Indonesian literary tradition."[5]

---

[4] A. Teeuw, *Sastra Baru Indonesia* [New Literature of Indonesia] (Ende: Nusa Indah, 1980), 15.
[5] Ibid., 16.

For Teeuw, the beginning of a phase or era must be evidenced by "newness" in the "collapse" of the old. He states that the gulf separating prewar writing from writing of the revolutionary period is far wider than that separating prewar writing from traditional Malay literature. Teeuw's thinking is in line with a belief shared by many Indonesian critics—that in the periodization and origin-setting of Indonesian literature there must be a demarcation of a "newness," in the sense that the new period constitutes a destruction of, or rupture from, old methods and systems, replacing them with methods and systems that are either new, or thought to be new.

History, though, does not always move forward in such a clearly defined, Marxist process. "Newness" does not immediately initiate new phases, periods, eras or societies. In cultural development—language and literature, for example— change can come gradually. Newness is accruing every second, continuously, as an integral part of the growth and development of how we communicate with language and express ourselves in literature. As with the literature, determining when the Indonesian language was first formed—pinpointing a rupture or the creation of new morphologies or semantics—is impossible. Both language and literature derive from a process that is ongoing.

This process can be illustrated by the origins of English, a language that began with one of the Celtic ethnic groups in the southern part of the British Isles and evolved when—between the fifth and seventh centuries—other tribes moved in from the western part of what is now Germany to colonize the land. In doing so, they swallowed up the local language and formed what eventually developed into English. But at the outset this identity was not "English," since it derived from the words *Engla Land* or *Angle Land* (the present day Angeln, a place in northern Germany where the *Englise* language was spoken). There was no rupture that demarcated Year One of the English language. Its starting point came not with an assault at the top, but occurred over a long period of time—from 600 to 1150—during which Old English flourished. The great literary work *Beowulf* was written in Old English, an early form of the language that has become absolutely impossible to understand or speak for just about anyone in England today.

Correspondingly, it is mistaken, even misleading, to say that Indonesian— Bahasa Indonesia—began when it was decreed to be the official language in the People's Council (Volksraad) of the Dutch East Indies in 1918, or after the Youth Oath (Sumpah Pemuda) in 1928. No matter where a national language originates, it needs a very long time—not merely eighty or a hundred years—to fully develop. And as with Old English, we would not understand, nor be able to read or pronounce, the original version.

I feel a similar situation went on with the French language. This second "official" global language actually began with a Celtic ethnic group, just as in England, though this particular people lived in a western coastal region of present-day France. Then, subjugation by Rome, notably under Julius Caesar, resulted in 95 percent of French vocabulary deriving from Latin. But the final formation of this Romance language resulted from an invasion in the third century by Germanic peoples, who called the people to their south "Franks," meaning "freemen." This word later became, variously, French, Frankish, Franceis/Francesc or, in present-day France, Français.

During the Middle Ages, English and French were strongly influenced by each other, as well as by other languages. A similar process occurred in the history of the Indonesian language. Based on Malay—the official state language of the kingdom of Sriwijaya in the seventh century, and evident in the oldest inscriptions of the sixth century—Indonesian flourished beyond its ethnic source as a lingua franca. This language of politics, trade and social life matured by allowing foreign and local influences to penetrate it easily, without concern for "ownership" and without denying the presence of other regional languages.

New Data

When reading the poems that open this anthology—poems that are widely seen as marking the beginning of Indonesia's modern literature, language and national consciousness—it is worth considering the discussion above. Applying a date to the idea of Indonesian national identity and consciousness is "politics as usual," in accordance with textbooks issued by the government. But in actual fact, new data support a different interpretation of our national reality. The idea of nationhood—which in Indonesia is officially thought to have commenced in 1908 with the establishment of Boedi Oetomo (which, it should be noted, was actually a Javanist organization)—actually started much earlier with Islamic students and Indonesian religious scholars who studied in Egypt and the Middle East.

According to Abaza and Azra, Islamic students—including such modernist figures as Muhammad Abduh (1849–1905) and Jamâl al-Din al Afghâni (1838–1897)—flooded the schools and universities in the Middle East through the nineteenth century and became well acquainted with the concepts of modernity, nationhood and independence.[6] They transmitted these new ideas to their countries of origin through such publications as *Suara al-Azar* and *Pilihan Timur*,

---

[6] According to Mona Abaza, the phenomenon of *santri*, that is, Islamic students studying in the Middle East, started at the beginning of the seventeenth century, especially at the modernist teacher-training schools in Cairo (Al-Azhar), Mekah, Medinah, or in the Hadramaut. See further: Abaza, Mona, *Islamic Education, Perception and Exchanges: Indonesian Students in Cairo*, her thesis for the Department of Sociology, Sociology of Development, at Bielefeld University, Germany. See also: Asyumardi Azra, "Melacak Pengaruhdan Pergeseran Orientasi Tamatan Cairo" [The Shift in Orientation of Cairo Graduates], *Studia Islamika*, vol. 2, no. 3 (1995): 199–219.

calling for, as written in one editor's memorandum, unity—for "all our people, whether in Java or Sumatra, or in Borneo, or in the Malay Peninsula . . ."[7]

At the end of the nineteenth century, intellectual groups, including theosophical ones, in Surakarta and other places began thinking about modernity and freedom, so that when—*before* the establishment of Boedi Oetomo in 1908—Wahidin Sudirohusodo lectured about freedom, literature, nationhood and independence, he had an audience for his ideas. Because of this history, the poems written during these two early periods acted as loudspeakers or amplifiers for ideas that had already long existed. The prevailing view of critics—that everything started around this time—actually ends up stultifying this history and depriving it of its dynamism and cultural roots.

Taking a broader view allows us to understand the context more fully when, for example, we encounter works from an early phase (1920–1942) that do not reflect the ideas about language, culture or the Indonesian nation we have been told to expect. The greatest figure of this period, the poet Amir Hamzah, is positioned as "merely" the heir—albeit the best one—of the formal, stylistic and socio-cultural problems of Malay literature. Nonetheless, saying this in no way denies the importance of the position of this early poetry in the course of the history of this country.

We just have to accept that all the poems coming from this period made their own contribution in forming, developing and enriching language, literature and poetry, upon which in later days was conferred the name "Indonesian."

United into the Future

In conclusion I would like to touch on the artistry and aesthetics of the poems themselves. I intentionally passed over this dimension in order to better illuminate the situational and contextual issues of the periods under discussion. To dwell on aesthetic and artistic choices, which are very individual in nature, would be to evade the basic aim of this introduction: to reflect on a real world, the world of a particular time, as it is preserved in the poetry in this anthology. Furthermore, I am writing this introduction with the understanding that the poems here have already gone through a rigorous editorial selection process.

It is, of course, fascinating to discuss the various issues particular to poetry—form, rhyme, alliteration, structure, diction, and so forth—all of which can serve to clarify a writer's purpose and line of thought. However, let such discussion be part of another publication. What this anthology clearly hopes to achieve is an offering of poetry that can help the reader get to know Indonesia, its society, culture and even its physical and spiritual turbulence—its dreams.

---

[7] Azra, "Melacak Pengaruh dan Pergeseran Orientasi Tamatan Cairo," 209.

From the periods discussed in this introduction, we can gain at least a little knowledge about one aspect of Indonesian society, particularly in the period before and after the war: the process that formed this country and people has from the beginning been rendered chaotic by sharp differences of opinion. This in turn bequeathed a particular heritage on following generations, a legacy that clings to us even in the present. Nevertheless, the main lesson of that process, also evidenced to this day, is that no matter how intense the differences and conflicts, and even no matter, perhaps, how deep the traumas inflicted, the poets and literary community, as well as Indonesian society at large, are united by a compact of the heart, a compact that destines them to stay united no matter what the future brings.

1920-1942
THE EMERGENCE
OF A NATIONAL
CONSCIOUSNESS

Introduction to the 1920–1942 Period

Outer and Inner Worlds

Radhar Panca Dahana

The early years of this period were marked by publications of literary works in "High" or Riau Malay by Balai Pustaka, a publishing house set up by the Dutch colonial government as a part of its "ethical policy" to improve the ability of the colonial subjects who spoke Dutch to become colonial employees, or at least to absorb colonial culture. Netherlands East Indies politics at the start of the twentieth century had created the Commissie voor de Inlandsche School en Volkslectuur (Commission for the People's Reading and Education) in 1908. Over time, the work of this commission increased in volume—among other things, its mission was expanded to curb the growth of "unauthorized reading material" produced by Indigenous or Peranakan Chinese publishers and to repress the spread of new ideas about freedom and independence. In 1917 the name of the commission was changed to Kantoor voor de Volkslectuur (Office of the People's Reading), which subsequently became better known as Balai Pustaka (Hall of Fine Books).

Balai Pustaka, although it had a significant influence on the flowering of Indonesian literature, at least in the view of A. Teeuw,[1] did not give sufficient free rein to *pribumi* (indigenous) writers to express their thoughts and aspirations concerning freedom and independence. An instrument of propaganda of the colonial government (as its director, Dr. D.A. Rinkes, himself made clear), Bali Pustaka aimed to block the expanding market of "book merchants whose intentions were less than pure." This reasoning caused a number of works by *pribumi* writers to be edited, cut, rewritten or even denied a publication permit, as was the case with Armijn Pane's novel *Belenggu* (Shackles).

In fact, feelings of unity and nationhood, as well as the desire for independence, had grown quite strong, especially since the birth of the first modern mass movement, *Sarekat Islam* (Islamist Union), in 1912, and the first political organization, Indische Partij (Indies Party) one year prior. The

---

[1] A. Teeuw, *Sastra Baru Indonesia* [New Literature of Indonesia] (Ende: Nusa Indah, 1980), 31.

earliest radical ideas about the struggle for independence also appeared at this time (especially within communist circles), as expressed in the literary works of such writers as Semaoen and Roestam Effendi. So, in fact, Bakrie Siregar's conclusions are correct. In addition to the influence of Dutch writers (especially those who were members of Tachtigers, also known as the 1880 Generation or Angkatan '80) and writers from other European countries and North America, the influence of Marxist writers (such as Maxim Gorki in Russia and Lu Xun in China) on Indonesian literary works should not be overlooked. There were strong influences from all over the world in these early days.

In his inaugural address as honorary professor of the faculty of literature at the University of Indonesia in 1975, the authoritative critic H.B. Jassin gave a series of examples of how Indonesian writers, since the beginning of the twentieth century, quite intensely mingled with and were influenced by scientists and writers from around the world.[2] This influence was not simply in terms of technique and composition, but also in terms of attitudes to life and ways of thinking. Roestam Effendi's *Bebasari*, for example, was acknowledged by its author as having been influenced by William Shakespeare, despite apparent differences in form. Beginning with Merari Siregar, widely considered the creator of modern Indonesian literature, and continuing up to Achdiat Kartamiharja in the 1940s and 1950s, and Iwan Simatupang and Rendra in the 1960s and 1970s, Indonesian writers were readers, observers and translators of world literature. Names like Sophocles, Ibsen, Strindberg, Malraux, Gide, Joyce, Pasternak, Sartre, Merleau-Ponty, Mallarmé, Saroyan and Camus were familiar within and beyond the discussion forums of Indonesian writers. Sigmund Freud's writings clearly had a deep influence on Armijn Pane's *Belenggu* and on Mochtar Lubis's *Jalan Tak Ada Ujung* (Road Without End). Hegel influenced Sutan Takdir Alisjahbana, who was on staff at Balai Pustaka, in formulating several hypotheses and theses. The existentialism and absurdism of that age influenced Chairil Anwar and many other poets. And so on and so forth.

From elsewhere, Rabindranath Tagore, India's great figure of letters who won the Nobel Prize in 1913, also significantly influenced Indonesian writers, just as he influenced many other Nobel Prize winners, from William Butler Yeats to Pablo Neruda and Octavio Paz. Sanusi Pane was one of the Indonesian literary figures who got to know Tagore quite well. He even visited Tagore's ashram in India and accompanied Tagore on a trip to Java. It seems likely that Pane was influenced by Tagore's spiritual, idealistic views, including the ideas the Bengali writer had about nationalism, which he wrote about beginning around 1915.

---

[2] Subsequently published; see H.B. Jassin, *Sastra Indonesia sebagai Warga Sastra Dunia* [Indonesian Literature as a Citizen of World Literature] (Jakarta: Gramedia, 1983), 3–19.

These examples demonstrate that the world of Indonesian literature was not as narrow as critics such as A. Teeuw, for example, thought. Teeuw considered Dutch language and culture as the primary window through which Indonesian writers saw the world. Though Dutch was the primary official language at that time, many Indonesian intellectuals and writers—by attending academic programs or, in most cases, by teaching themselves—had also mastered other foreign languages, such as English, French and German. By the beginning of the 1940s Dutch influence had faded so drastically that the writer and journalist Rosihan Anwar described Dutch as a minor language: "We are familiar enough with the works of French, English and American writers. We only know the names of the young Dutch writers."[3]

Thus, the idea of a cultural rupture occurring in 1942 with the end of the Dutch East Indies power cannot be supported by the actual reality of writers at the time. The technological advances in transportation and communication that began in the early twentieth century were within easy reach of the community of *pribumi* writers, as reflected in a number of their works during this period. These advances provided writers with access to the latest information about the world, including developments in science, art, politics, economics and so on.

Although not strongly reflected in this anthology, the global events of the early twentieth century—including the establishment of the Republic of China in 1911, which brought an end not only to the Qing dynasty but to imperial rule; the First World War (1914–1918); the Bolshevik Revolution in Russia (1917); and the Great Depression in the 1930s—would not have escaped the notice of these writers, inspiring them and influencing their thinking and artistic expression. The twentieth century was marked by the realization that the world was no longer a simple place, nor one that could be romanticized. New findings in physics, chemistry and mathematics—especially by Einstein with his Theory of Relativity (1905) and the General Theory of Relativity (1915), and of course the Quantum Theory, whose momentum was accelerated by Max Planck (1900)— provided a global understanding that the present-day world was complex, perhaps ineffably so. And there was another aspect to this realization: no people or person could avoid these developments. Everyone was involved, whether influenced or influencing. A new spirit of global interdependency was beginning to be felt as the foundation for ideas in all fields, in politics as well as literature.

Youth and the Ideology of Language in Literature

In the 1920s, the majority of this wave of Indonesian poets were still adolescents. When in 1921 Mohammad Yamin wrote the poem "Language, Nation," which

---

[3] Teeuw, *Sastra Baru Indonesia*, 177.

5

was published in *Jong Sumatera*, a Dutch-language journal, when he was only seventeen years old. At this young age he not only knew Dutch but could also quote Goethe in the original German. Yamin's poetry about the island of his birth, Sumatra, glows with anticipation for the idea of a "nation."

> Sumatra, beloved land of my birth
> from my childhood and youth
> until earthen walls envelop me
> I shall never forget my language.
> O youth, remember, Sumatra's distress
> without a language, the nation disappears.

With the last line of this poem, Yamin seems to be initiating a long, tough discussion among his fellow writers and intellectuals about nation, literature, culture and the imagining of a new identity, one called "Indonesian." Although this early poem by Yamin—and also his first collection, *Tanah Air* (Motherland), which was published one year later—still sees "nation" as Sumatra and "language" as the Malay, the culture that Yamin hails from, the moral force of his struggle to find and defend a national identity is palpable.

The political enthusiasm of this adolescent, no matter how local, is inseparable from, and may even have been inspired by, the zeal of young people in other parts of Indonesia—or, in fact, other parts of the world—who enlivened the first half of that century with a spirit of revolt against the old world. These mobilized youths were everywhere, from North Africa and India to South America. The atmosphere of struggle for a native identity, as well as a growing consciousness of oppression, was widespread in the early twentieth century, quite apart from the war and the extraordinary advances in science and the arts.

In the poem below, written when its author was about sixteen, we can sense the rebellious spirit of another young intellectual: Mohammad Hatta, who, not quite a decade later, would become one of the most important figures in the Indonesian independence movement. Like Yamin's poem, the work appeared in the November 1921 edition of *Jong Sumatera*:

God's Image

> Look east—the gorgeous colors
> Dawn breaks, day approaches
> The sun shoots out sharp brightness
> A smiling vision for all the senses.

Breezes waft down from heaven
Permeating the land, small branches quiver
Wildlife leap from their dens
To see God's image in beauty absolute.

The brightness of lapis lazuli has passed
The stars disappear one by one
Zuhari's light turns to gloom.

Animals receive nature's invocation
Hearts now gladdened, ineffably
By the riches of God the Most Holy

This apparently simple poem is filled with Hatta's awe of God's bounty in the natural world. His spirited, youthful energy comes through clearly in such phrases as "the sun shoots out sharp brightness" and "a smiling vision," as well as in the image of "permeating the land" so that "small branches quiver" and things "leap from their dens." Then with unadorned sincerity he describes "hearts now gladdened, ineffably" by natural phenomena. These same hearts we now know will soon join in building a country.

The spirit of revolt, of breaking free from the strictures of the old and seeking a new life, was an imperative adopted naturally and intelligently by young people of this period. For Minangkabau adolescents like Yamin and Hatta, such a spirit was of course already embedded in their culture. In Minangkabau culture, men do not feel they truly exist, nor are acknowledged as men, until they *merantau*—travel out into the world to seek their fortune, carve out a new path, gain knowledge and establish a livelihood. This tradition dates back to Datuk Perpatih nan Sabatang—the legendary founding ancestor of the Minang people—who, because of his rebellious spirit, "merantau-ed" and became the teacher of the Greek philosopher Aristotle and subsequently an advisor to Alexander the Great. This tradition of merantau was also demonstrated by the Padri, Muslim clerics who traveled to the Holy Land of Arabia during the first half of the nineteenth century, bringing back Wahhabi interpretations of the Quran that instigated radical change in the Minang realms.

Malay youths of all ethnicities (Minang, Riau, Deli, Aceh and so forth) took their history and traditions with them when they went to Java's major cities—Batavia, Yogya, Surabaya, Bandung and Solo—to continue their education or merely try their luck. Rubbing shoulders with people of Javanese, Peranakan Chinese and mixed Dutch descent, as well as with the Dutch themselves, these youths, especially those in Batavia, encountered global news and world literature.

7

Their experiences prompted them to reflect on culture and language and to think ever more deeply about freedom and independence.

These themes were among the most heatedly discussed in literary life. Several of the poets included in this anthology speak of the role of language in literature. These efforts to articulate the importance of language in national and individual identity-making, illustrated in the Yamin poem "Language, Nation" cited above, were complemented by struggles to find new literary forms to embody the new Indonesian voice. For example, Roestam Effendi's poem "Not I, the Storyteller" opens with these two stanzas:

Not I, the storyteller
Skilled in composing *syair* verse
Not I, the state's servant
Bound by expert rules

Rules of grammar, I reject
The linked verse of the old *seloka*
I disavow and discard
For my own song must follow my heart.

This poem, carried in the first issue of the literary magazine *Pujangga Baru* in 1933, shows us how language becomes a motivation for striving toward nationhood. And this brand of linguistic nationalism is displayed even more strongly by Mozasa in his poem "My Language."

Neither lowly nor humble, this language of mine
nor is it stilted, rather it smiles
wonderful, splendid—happy, it roars
agile, adept—it nimbly explores.

O glorious, patronizing brother
extolling the submission of the language of others
high praise for tongues from over There.
Come with me to a garden that flourishes
our language we'll caress and nourish
our gratitude soaring through the air.

Language (and literature) would ultimately be viewed as a precondition for the birth of a nation. It became an ideology for some poets, especially those who were known for their critical essays. The Malay language was central to this ideology, because over the centuries, by nature and nurture, it had achieved a wide reach and was the tongue in which these writers could best express themselves. Yamin, one of the earliest and most vocal exponents of this line of thinking, stressed, "I am confident that the Malay language will gradually emerge as the language of general society or the language of unity for the Indonesian nation, and that Indonesian culture in the ages to come will spring from that language."[4]

The Malay language (Bahasa Melayu) is referred to here not in a narrow sense or as belonging to one specific group. The position had been strictly taken in literary circles that this Bahasa Melayu was in no way the Bahasa Melayu that had been officially recognized by the Dutch colonial government and, specifically, by Balai Pustaka. Nor was it the variant of Malay known as Low Malay or Bazaar Malay, the Malay used by creole groups. As Armijn Pane, a literary figure who had joined Balai Pustaka, wrote "It is the language of unity, not the Malay language used in Deli, Riau, or any regions at all, but the language of general culture and civilization, which people desire, that is, Bahasa Indonesia."[5]

Sutan Takdir Alisjahbana (STA), founder of *Pujangga Baru* and also a member of the Balai Pustaka staff, asserted the same thing as Armijn, that "The advances of Indonesia's language of unity need not be strongly tied to Riau/classic Malay."[6] Moreover, Indonesia's language of unity, which for STA was "a linking language that for centuries grew slowly within the world of Southeast Asians," would in its next development inevitably leave behind its root language, where "energy, time, circumstance, and volatile situations ought to be accepted as positive factors," making it eminently suitable to fulfill its role as Indonesia's language of unity. When "Javanisms" or "Betawisms" appeared, these would not be considered dangers to this language. For STA, such local influences, together with foreign influences, would enrich this new language, "and make it well and truly fit to accomplish its task as Indonesia's language of unity, the supporter of Indonesian culture."[7]

At this point, early in modern Indonesia's history, the question of language was closely associated with national consciousness. Directly or indirectly, those who wrestled with language—the writers and littérateurs—were aware of their influence and responsibility in the great effort to achieve independence. Literature (along with language) and politics were blood brothers who had to work in cooperation, using their individual strengths to achieve the common goal of nationhood.

---

[4] Ibid., 41.

[5] *Pujangga Baru*, 1933, 7.

[6] *Pujangga Baru*, 1957, 24.

[7] Ibid.

Concerning Religion, Love and *Adat*

In addition to the themes of language, literature and nationhood, there are at least four other themes that are prominent in this era's poetry: daily life, the love lives of young people, the clash of *adat* (customary law) with new ways of living, as well as—in the work of several religious poets such as J.E. Tatengkeng, Sanusi Pane, Amir Hamzah and Armijn Pane—the theme of spirituality.

Religious themes, in this case Christian ones, are rather dominant in Tatengkeng's works. Islam, on the other hand, plays a more muted, spiritual role in poetry, particularly in the works of Amir Hamzah. Sanusi Pane searches for the roots of Indonesian spirituality by, among other things, comparing it to spirituality in India and searching for it in a treasure trove of old books from the ancient kingdoms (especially Mataram, Kediri and Majapahit), including such classics as the *Pararaton* or *Nāgarakrtâgama* (also referred to as *Negara Kertagama*).

Regardless of their particular religious or spiritual enthusiasms, these poets are strongly interested in change. Not just from tradition or *adat*, but also from their contemporary situations within Dutch-style colonialism. This is evident in Md. Yati's "At the Demak Mosque," which ends with the following two stanzas:

> I am constantly regaled with memories of times long gone
> when the wali waged their struggle
> to erase Buddhism and spread Islam.
> O, my guide . . . O, my guide . . . !
> Guide to those who spread Islam through Java,
> I see what you have done in every era;
> Islamic history arrayed,
> a friendly reminder to mankind
> for this generation, this century.
> A model for pioneers—
> we are ever so ready to fight!

Religious or spiritual conviction did not yet, at the time this poem was written, appear to be a strong factor pushing society—the poets at least—to struggle against colonialism for independence. Nonetheless, the implications of hope and a new life still radiated strongly. Although religion didn't create mass fanaticism, it still played an important role in daily life. What is interesting is that religion was not trapped in jargon or artificial attributes—bogus markers for a person's or a group's faith. Religion was not at that point being manipulated for sectarian interests, as various groups are doing at present, generating a sort of controlled fanaticism.

In the poems of this era, questions of spirituality are endowed with the beauty of both understanding and expression. These values seem to seep into the words, into the person reading, and into human behavior. They exist in a very personal region, not trapped in slogans. How gentle is the religious feeling displayed by Tatengkang, for example, in this excerpt from his "Sunday Morning Invitation":

> I heard a soft sound
> Ringing through the air
> The leaves and the branches
> The bell in a nearby steeple.

> It said:
> I call the living
> I weep for the dead[8]
> Do not close the door of your heart
> Allow Me to come in . . .
> Come into my heart
> My Lord and My God.

Not many poetic expressions of this period speak specifically of faith and God's oneness. Almost as a rule, the problems of belief and the Islamic faith are tightly bound up with other problems: concerns of daily life and issues specific to the times. The poems of Amir Hamzah, for instance (or those by A.M. Daeng Mijala, or, generally, those by poets of religious nuance), link this dimension to questions of love, *adat* and traditional lifestyles in conflict with new ones.

In several parts of this country, the clash between *adat* and modern life was actually not new. Especially in big cities like Medan, Batavia, Semarang, Surabaya or Makassar, harsh colonialist and capitalist practices that began with the interim Bonapartist colonial government under Governor General Herman Willem Daendels led to clashes with *adat*. Conflicts that were generally about rebelling against or reforming traditional systems grew more intense at the beginning of the twentieth century, at the same time that ideas about freedom, independence and nationalism were spreading.

These issues, among others, are on display in the work of Amir Hamzah, a poet from Langkat, North Sumatra, who was considered by H.B. Jassin to be the greatest poet of this period and by A. Teeuw as "the final poet of Malay literature with a world-class quality."[9] Two collections of his poems, *Buah Rindu*

---

[8] *Kukui apang biahe, Lulungkang u apang nate.* Written on the bell of the Tahuna church, Sangihe, North Sulawesi.

[9] A. Teeuw, *Sastra Baru Indonesia*, 123.

(Fruits of Longing) and, in particular, *Nyanyi Sunyi* (Songs of Silence), constitute the pinnacle, in Hamzah's work, of aesthetic strength and beauty of rhyme and diction. Especially notable are the expressions of his innermost feelings in the conflict between, on the one hand, his spiritual and intellectual eagerness for a new life (and also for his sweetheart in Java) and, on the other, his responsibility as an *adat* leader and as the prospective *bendahara* (a vizier-like position) of the rajah of Langkat.

We can sense all of this conflict in several of Hamzah's poems that became so famous as to be widely memorized: "Padamu Jua" (For You Only), "Berdiri Aku" (I Stand) and "Buah Rindu" (Fruits of Longing). How the rhythm and choice of words can make readers vanish into the inner world of the writer, as if we too are caught up in problems of the heart. Just meld into his poem, "For You Only," his very best, which I feel I would have to reproduce here in its entirety to do it justice. But for a more comprehensive picture of the innermost life of this poet and prince of Langkat and his violent death, the following poem is in order:

I Stand

In silent twilight, I stand
As seagulls swiftly skim the sea foam
Mangroves stoop to losen their tops
And jellyfish surface, tentacles aflare.

The wind returns to cool the earth
To gild the bay in a sheath of gold
Silently racing to the mountain peak
Swirling over the jungle floor.

A rainbow, dipping its hem in the water
Rises up with its colorful pattern
An eagle tucks its wings and waits
Dazed by the procession of colors.

In the face of this most-perfect beauty
Longing and melancholy disturb my heart
I long to feel a measure of peace
To taste a life with certain direction.

Amir Hamzah's poems address the themes of love and conflict with *adat*. His own life reflected these issues: he had to meet the demands of *adat*, hold his lofty position in the kingdom of Langkat and marry a girl chosen by his father (the daughter of the rajah), while his heart and thoughts were anchored in Batavia, and also in Solo, which was where he completed middle school, and where a Javanese girl locked away his heart.

In the work of several poets such as Asmara Hadi, Hamidah, Armijn Pane and Intojo, as well as in most of Mohammad Yamin's poems, there is an entanglement with similar problems—something that is not really surprising if we consider the fact that these poets were still wrestling with their youth and with romantic desires.

What is interesting about the poems of this era is the attention paid by several poets to quotidian problems and everyday reality— themes that are not common in more traditional poems. In effect, poems become a form of news— raising the problems of beggars (as Ali Hasjmy did) or describing the world of prostitutes (as Armijn Pane did) or the difficulties of workers (as A.M. Daeng Mijala did). Poetry offers a vivid picture of the atmosphere at the time, making the bitterness of humanity all the more striking.

Such poems of everyday life show how close to modern reality Indonesian poetry has been from the beginning of its development and how politically contextual it was, in the jargon of communist writers then and later. A communist poet such as Roestam Effendi (in this anthology) is, sadly, less concerned with showing the contemporary dimension. Although he was forced to flee abroad after the communist rebellion of 1926, this was still a time when literature and culture in Indonesia were not shattered by ideological trends or political interests—a state of affairs that began at the end of the 1950s and climaxed in the 1960s.

Language, Nation

Mohammad Yamin

1921

Small and of tender age
the child sleeps in his mother's lap.
His mother sings songs and lullabies
gives praise as is right and proper
rocks him in love night and day
a cradle, the land of his ancestors.

Born into a nation with its own language
surrounded by family and relations
he grows in the wisdom of the Malay land
knows both joy and sorrow
is imbued with a sense of solidarity
by the beauty and melody of his language.

In laughter and in tears
in happiness, calamity, and danger
we breathe so that we may live
language is an extension of our soul.
Wherever Sumatra is, there is my nation.
Wherever Sumatra is, there is my language.

Sumatra, beloved land of my birth
from my childhood and youth
until earthen walls envelop me
I shall never forget my language.
O youth, remember, Sumatra's distress
without a language, the nation disappears.

Not I, the Storyteller

Roestam Effendi

1925

Not I, the storyteller,
Skilled in composing syair verse,
Not I, the state's servant,
Bound by experts' rules.

Rules of grammar, I reject,
The linked verse of the old seloka,
I disavow and discard
For my own song must follow my heart.

So very hard it is to convey,
The stirrings inside my soul,
So soft, so slow, the gentle pulse,
Rhythm is ordered by sense of time.

Often, for a moment, I must stop,
When inspiration fails to come,
Often it is difficult to weave my verse,
For lack of images.

Not I, the singer of tales,
Able to birth packets of pantun,
Not I, the creator of the new,
I listen only to the gentle flow.

Tears

Roestam Effendi

1925

Friends aplenty, a family complete,
enjoying a joke in a world without care,
but when the sorrowful heart struggles to breathe,
where do we go to share our despair?

Mother and Father, the family all near,
somewhere to take life's troubles and pain,
but all they can do is lend us an ear;
they don't understand our sadness, our strain.

There are no words of comfort
when we are in the grip of grief.
Because none can plumb the depths
of the oceans of emotion within us.
It's only the tears, when we are alone,
that can ever relieve the ordeals we endure.

Poem

Sanusi Pane

1931p

Where is the value of a poem?
It is not in its meaning,
in its form, elegant words
sought, considered, selected.

First a question comes from the heart,
then the poem is read through,
and here the magic
reminds one to reflect upon wisdom.

When composing, the poet feels
words streaming forth
from within, not from a search.

This must return within the reader.
As a reflection in a mirror,
it must shake the depths of the soul.

Lotus

Sanusi Pane

1931p

For Ki Adjar Dewantara

In a garden in my country
 Grows a lotus blossom;
 Exquisite charming secreted flower
Unseen by those who pass by.

It is rooted in the heart of the world,
 Laksmi generates glistening leaves;
 Although neglected,
This lustrous lotus blossom illuminates.

Go forth, O Joyful Lotus
Radiant in Indonesia's garden,
 Although the gardeners are few.

Although you are not seen,
Although you are not appreciated,
 You join in shepherding the Era.

Putting the Children to Sleep

Yogi (Abdul Rivai)

1931p

In a rice field, in the jungle,
In a hut—very humble—
Lives a farmer, his wife and children.
They thank God for all He's given.

Far from the village and other homes,
The rice field stands quite alone.
For most people, land rights are rare,
Must make them anxious, living there.

With the fate that God bestows,
I wandered in that jungle land.
How I arrived, I do not know,
On the edge of a field of coiled rattan.

The sun's at its zenith,
The heat is crushing.
My body, exhausted,
Waits sheltered in shadows.

The cock keeps on crowing,
Red fowl in the jungle deep.
Gibbons swing on roots, hanging,
And clouds parade by, love is for keeps.

In the stillness at the edge of that field of rice,
I think back on a farmer's life;
From the hut a voice's echo rings,
A mother sits rocking as she sings.

Sleep, my child, gift of God,
Sleep in the woven rattan cradle;
My rocking child is a pound of gold,
Laid down in the hut, all alone.

Sleep, darling, Mother rocks you,
No need to cry when Mother leaves.
Father and Mother work the fields
To satisfy our children's needs.

Sleep my child, my native gold,
On the lap of the wind that gently blows.
Remember your blessings—not riches untold—
Wrapped in a sheet, swaddled in its folds.

Live in the fields, on "communal" land;
On the mountainside the body stands.
My child, as long as you live,
Don't forget your home in the village.

O, my child, my darling,
Little one sleep in your swing.
It's for you the birds in the woods are singing,
While the wind in leaves does the fanning.

Sleep while the monkeys in the forest scream;
Their thunderous howls will lull you to sleep.
Dream in the light of the full moon,
In your mother's lap, yearning.

Remember Mother, remember Father,
Remember the fate of those who farm;
Destiny is in the hands of the Cosmos,
A life surrendered first and foremost.

Hey my child, grow quickly—
Soon a teen, then a youth.
You may become Mother's assistant;
To the hut, fields and land, a servant.

At the Demak Mosque

Md. Yati
1934

From far off
the pinnacle atop Bintara Mosque can be seen,
waving a greeting to traveling merchants
who come to see the sights.

I ruminate on devotion
to Allah, creator of the universe,
when I stop for some time at Bintara Mosque,
treasure of the *wali*[1] of long ago.

This mosque is truly old.
Centuries of time revealed,
and still it stands sturdy,
the art of my ancestors.

I am constantly regaled with memories
of times long gone
when the *wali* waged their struggle
to erase Buddhism and spread Islam.

O, my guide... O, my guide... !
Guide to those who spread Islam through Java,
I see what you have done in every era;
Islamic history arrayed,
a friendly reminder to mankind
for this generation, this century.
A model for pioneers—
we are so ready to fight!

---

[1] *Wali* refers to those who first brought Islam to Java.

Sangihe Fisherman

Jan Engelbert Tatengkeng

1934p

Covered by the sky and stars
Moonlight dotting the waves
Small drops of dew falling
You wait for the fish to come.

Why are you thinking,
What are you thinking about?
Why do you sing in a soft voice,
Why do you close your eyes?
What are you wondering,
Why do you look towards the shore?

Oh, I understand.
I can see a small fire burning
At the foot of the mountain
That is what you are looking at
It stirs your heart.

Oh, I see a cord
Which no visible eyes can know
Connecting your hearts
The hearts of two sailors
On the sea of love…

Sunday Morning Invitation

Jan Engelbert Tatengkeng

1934p

As I sat in my room
Playing with a flower
I picked the day before
For a friend

I heard a soft sound
Ringing through the air
The leaves and the branches
The bell in a nearby steeple.

It said:

I call the living
I weep for the dead[1]
Do not close the door of your heart
Allow Me to come in…
    Come into my heart
    My Lord and My God.

---

[1] *Kukui apang biahe, Lulungkang u apang nate.* Written on the bell of the Tahuna church, Sangihe, North Sulawesi.

The Tranquility of Nothing

Armijn Pane

1935

Who knows what pushes me towards new life,
leaving behind the old humiliation.

Each time I'm seduced by a gleaming blessing,
I am quickly plunged back into the blackest affliction.

Yet something always urges me to appeal to hope.
I still feel no wariness in seeking out the light.

Though each time I forget the moonlight is fleeting,
I find myself abandoned in the darkest night.

And isn't that the way of every single nation,
when a shining hope seems to draw new life?

Don't people try out all their new machinations,
only to discover suffering was biding its time?

Do you know the lives of your heart and thoughts exist?
Is there any use in fighting to change the nature of what is?

Is it good to try to move the masses?
To make changes, not knowing which might perish or persist?

Can you see the good in quieting your hands,
closing your thoughts, navigating towards nothing?

Can you see the good in abolishing demands,
erasing yourself in the tranquility of Nothing.

Parting

Fatimah Hasan Delais (Hamidah)

1935p

Parting is so hard
Leaving a love wrenches the heart
Whether seated or standing the feeling's the same
Where might consolation be found?

Going here and there in search of peace
Recalling the love of one's life
The troubled heart longs for comfort
Yet the voice will not sing a soothing song.

How is it possible to sing
When your soul is pierced by thorns
And heart and mind are in travail?

How is it possible to find joy
When one is completely alone
And happy memories have quickly gone?

Diamond Eyes

Armijn Pane

1936

A gliding taxi sounded its horn
Heading for the beach or a cheerful place
Clouds swam in the moonlight
There was the glittering sound of a woman's laugh

In a port city I saw you
Sitting silent and alone with your hands in your lap
Despite your thick makeup your age showed
I sat down, you moved away

I sipped coffee with milk
You sat serene with your hands in your lap
I peeled a banana, not because I was hungry
But suddenly I realized you had not eaten

I pretended to be interested
I invited you to eat some rice
While I ate I entertained you
Your eyes sparkled pure diamond

Humanity

Or. Mandank

1936

If I speak
it is not because I am a god
but because I feel
I have some truth to tell.
Perhaps someone
    will be strengthened
    or made happy;
    he might know what to do
    or be helped to think.

If he is worried
he should not bother
about who is speaking
but consider what is being said
because no one is better
than anyone else.
We are all human beings

and so am I.

Weeding the Rice Fields

Yogi (Abdul Rivai)

1936

As the sun slowly rises
A young girl weeds the fields
She sings as she plucks the weeds
Sweet songs full of love.

Her voice floats in the air
So sweet and soft
Sitti is gentle with the rice
Her duties are many.

A distant voice calls
The sound of a bamboo flute
A song of longing
Reaching out to the beloved.

The girl is startled
The music is for her
Her heart beats more quickly
She is caught in its spell.

When the young man arrives
The maiden blushes
There is a smile on her face
As she looks at the rice.

He too is shy
Struck by Amor's arrows
Their hearts struggle with their feelings
Their lives are in God's hands.

The Soul's Lament

Hamidah

1936p

When I see
jasmines
brushed with dew, covered with pearls,
my memories take on many hues

I remember
a palm plantation
filled with perfume, wave after wave,
spread by the gentle winds

My body
relaxes,
thoughts wash over me, refreshing me
with enchanted visions of bygone days

I see the flowers
in my mother's garden,
gently bent, swaying softly,
caressed by wondrous jewels

I am aware,
my soul quivers,
my inner stirrings, profound emotions,
give her form in my garden of verse

A garland
of my deepest feelings,
the emotions flow, take form in words,
in the night of my darkest grief

I listen to the wind whispering
bearing a message from her tomb,
"Blossom, my darling young child.
Spread your fragrance throughout the world
and be happy."

My Language

Mozasa
1937

I write rhymes, I lyricize,
set love loose, passionize,
whisper sadness shriek delight,
with language I break hematite.

To the swaying fields of rice I sing,
their lilting stalks heavy with gold
I call to a bird free on the wing,
in the language of my ancestors of old.

Neither lowly nor humble, this language of mine,
nor is it stilted, rather it smiles
wonderful, splendid—happy it roars,
agile, adept— it nimbly explores.

O, glorious, patronizing brother,
extoling the submission of the language of others,
high praise for tongues from over There.
Come with me to a garden that flourishes,
our language we'll caress and nourish,
our gratitude soaring through the air.

Laborer

A.M. Daeng Mijala

1937p

I sit at my table
Keeping my records
Coffee in, sugar out
Buy kapok, sell copra.

I start in the morning
Work all through the day
I never feel tired
I like what I do.

Nothing is mine.
It belongs to the boss.
I own my labor
Body and mind.

I'm tired at home.
My wife makes me work…

*

I'm paid once a month
I have bills to pay
The money is mine
It makes my head spin.

Take with the left hand
Pay out with the right
Credit, I'm happy
Debit, I'm sad.

The years go by
A laborer's fate never changes
His hands are full all day
Nothing is his own.

My wife loves me
We share our lives…

For You Only

Amir Hamzah

1937p

Wasted and worn
All my love is gone
And now, as before
I return home to You.

You are a candle burning
At a window in the dark
In patience and faithfulness
Calling me slowly home.

I have but one love
Yet I too am mortal
Desiring touch
Desiring form.

Where you are
Form does not exist
Voices so indistinct
Words alone enchant my heart.

You are jealous
You are cruel
I am the prey in your talons
Released then snatched back.

Bewildered, half mad
My love returns home to you
It is you who fan my desire
A maiden behind a veil.

Your love is silent
In waiting, alone
Time passes—it's not my turn
The day dies—but never you...

Swept Away

Amir Hamzah
1937p

Swept away,
I've been swept away, my love!
Reach out your hand to help.
'Tis only silence around me!
No soothing voice, no breeze to cool my heart,
    only water, carrying me down.
I thirst for your love, yearn for your whisper,
    will die of your silence.
The sky closes in, the water lets go, I drown.
I drown in the night,
the water pressing me down from above,
the earth refusing to lift me.
I'm dying, my love, I'm dying!

A New Vitality

Asmara Hadi

1937p

I feel a new vitality
The world is beautiful
The age inspires me
An age of struggle

Once I was sad
I wandered in the darkness
Now I am happy
On fire with struggle

My heart beats with joy
I feel like a hero
I have only one duty
Surrender to the cause.

Contemplating the Power of a Child

Hamidah

1937p

A child cries, his sobs are heaving;
Enduring pain, his body writhes.
His mother sits there, never leaving;
His father weeps with sniffling cries.

A child flinches, enduring pain;
His hands grasp and his legs flail.
Mother sees his withered strain,
Rubs soothing salves to no avail.

A child moans without ceasing;
He gasps and chokes and coughs up blood.
Mother watches as he stops breathing;
His very spirit seems suffocated.

Oh, Child! Part of our very soul.
Oh, Darling! Mother's precious heart.
Mama and Papa would never be consoled
If our sweet darling should die first.

May you recover, my cherished treasure,
Force the sickness from your frame.
Mother sees his spirit hover,
His eyes grow dim, his vision wane.

Oh, child, Mother's one and only!
His soul flutters and then flies past.
Mother sees it go, her heart pounds wildly
As faith, lodged in his body, is lost.

New Emotions

Intojo

1937p

Times change!
Nature evolves!
Songs of life fill the sky.
We human beings
are blessed
with body, soul and all we need.
Let us work
together,
bring light to darkness.
Let us behave
in new ways,
let the buds bloom.
Let us develop
all of our EMOTIONS.
Feel in a new way, live in harmony.

Today's Generation

Asmara Hadi

1938p

On the top of fantasy mountain
I stand, and from there
look down to the place where
today's generation struggles on the fields of time,

creating a new splendor:
songs of the beauty in Indonesia,
later to serve as mementos
of their time in this world.

My spirit shouts, overjoyed
to see the flag fluttering in the wind,
like happiness overflowing
in brightly shining gold.

Like a fleet of airplanes,
indescribable joy shakes the air—
that's the way of today's generation,
a world full of voices.

And in my soul I know so well:
today's generation is assured victory.
It will leave its mark and trail
in a bright and lasting history.

In Agreement

Selasih

1940

Perhaps taking different paths,
    maybe holding different points of view,
we somehow reach agreement in the end.

It was you who taught me
    to look in another direction,
there, far to the north
    where the experts socialized.

Obviously, I knew what you were really saying:
    "Perhaps you might like to emulate that."
I didn't nod, yet I did hear the call,
    and I looked, studied, and observed.

There you can find the perfect example:
    a people clever in their use of language.
As we here are deficient in most everything,
    it's fitting to emulate other countries.

You are for me one half of my soul.
    Do not be anxious or sad;
I'm not averse to doing what you say,
    but my soul hearkens to the north.

You don't think me able
    to travel and leave this island behind
because of my limited knowledge, I know,
    forged as I was by the day and age.

You cannot stop the feeling in me,
    which will always remain in memory,
stirring emotions through words,
    expressing the spirit of my soul.
I didn't think I would ever be able to imitate
    the whisper of my mother in my cradle.

My love, I permit you to go.
　　I will follow you with my gaze;
you will not be gone for all that long.
　　And when you return, you will not bear much weight,
because I know the destination you seek
　　is the perfection of the soul of your nation.

I will stay, holding on to the things that Mother left.
　　I'll hold on with all my strength,
but the desire to go, to be with you,
　　is because of the bond between our souls.
In your travels I pray that you will always remember me,
　　that your gaze will always find this island.

In the end, you say you will return
　　with a flood of riches from your travels.
My grip on the rope will loosen,
　　and the old will be one with the new.

I am sure that you cannot imagine
　　a unity of language being achieved.
Do not flinch in taking up a challenge
　　when the result will be good for the people.

Beggar

Ali Hasjmy

1940p

"Give me some alms, O sir,
I've not eaten since morning.
Help me, noble sir—
a sip of water, a mouthful of rice.

"Look, sir, at our fate.
No home, no family,
we did not buy the clothes on our backs.
The whole way along we beg and beg.

"Look, sir, our fortune—
no hut, no rice fields,
bathed by rain and the heat of day,
constantly suffering along the way.

"It's not our mothers' fault.
Our misery is our own doing.
It's fate, it's fortune
to live in misery day to day.

"O, sir, do not mock us
if alms are not given.
Our bodies have suffered enough—
do not hurt us anymore...

I Stand

Amir Hamzah

1941p

In silent twilight, I stand
As seagulls swiftly skim the seafoam
Mangroves stoop to loosen their tops
And jellyfish surface, tentacles aflare.

The wind returns to cool the earth
To gild the bay in a sheath of gold
Silently racing to the mountain peak
Swirling over the jungle floor.

A rainbow, dipping its hem in the water
Rises up with its colorful pattern
An eagle tucks its wings and waits
Dazed by the procession of colors.

In the face of this most-perfect beauty
Longing and melancholy disturb my heart
I long to feel a measure of peace
To taste a life with certain direction.

Object of Longing

Amir Hamzah

1941p

Death, now please do come to me
Release me from my misery
You are the one I cling to
In this time of utter darkness.

The magpie's song is not at all sweet
In the mind of this young Malay man
The owl's hoot is not one of longing
Not in my ears, as it once was.

Please, I beg, make the clouds move
Those that now cover earth's tapestry
And hang motionless over the hut
Of this wretched nomad from Langkat.

For an instant my eyes signal
To you above, the clouds overhead
In which foreign land do you now travel?
In which country will you be able to survive?

Convey my longing to the one I love
Whisper my praises to that lovely maid
As if I myself were embracing her
Swaddle her legs in soft gold color.

I hear, Mother, Selindung is far away
That same place where a girl sits waiting
How can one ever touch the mountain
If the arm lacks length to reach it?

Mighty eagle, king of the sky
Come to the ground if only for a moment
I want to ask you just one question
Have you chanced to see the woman I speak of?

I have greeted the clouds
Queried all the animals
I have given praise to death
But cannot find the woman I love!

Heading for the Open Seas

Sutan Takdir Alisjahbana

1946p

For the New Generation

We have left you,
calm lake, sheltered
from storms
by the forests and mountains.
We have awoken
from our pleasant dreams.

The waves chase each other
under the broad blue sky.
The winds laugh
as they sweep the beaches
and race the clouds
up the tall cliffs.

Our souls are restless,
ready for struggle.
We can no longer
hide our emotions
behind the hills.
We want to be free,
to throw off whatever binds us.

Thunder in the distance.
Pearls of lightning scatter.
The sound is the sound of victory.
We are happy, we are sad,
the shouting is all around us.

It is hard to make progress.
We are knocked down,
hit in the head, desolate and confused.

But we do not need
what is gone
and we will not grieve
the peace we once knew.

We have left you,
calm lake, sheltered
from storms
by the forests and mountains.
We have awoken
from our pleasant dreams.

Dreams and Life

H.B. Jassin

1942

Have you ever dreamed of
finding silver and gold—
you held it tight in your fist,
afraid you might lose it someone might steal it,
then when you woke up,
you had nothing in your pocket, not even a cent?
Have you seen people
gathering wealth in this world,
working hard greedy for overflowing riches,
then…
they were carried to their graves
wrapped in a shroud?
Friend, compare
Dreams and Life, tell me which one is true.
We can keep nothing from either of them.

Poisonous Words

Suman HS
1946p

In the beginning I told him,
"I'm old, no longer beautiful.
I'm wealthy, that's true,
but I'm sure that doesn't interest you."

> He said, "As long
> as you have your health.
> I don't want wealth.
> I want you for myself
> Please don't deny me."

I whispered to him,
"We are not really right.
You are young and handsome,
I am well past my prime."

> He told me it didn't matter
> He would never do me wrong.
> An older wife knows how to cook,
> she can teach a man to sing.

Who wouldn't be fooled
by such a sweet young man?
He seemed a good catch,
the perfect match.

> I gave him my body.
> Do—darling—whatever you choose.
> My wealth—honey—is yours to use.
> After all—precious—I am your wife,
> I cannot refuse.

My God, I was astonished
at how quickly my wealth vanished.
He didn't like my company.
He didn't care about me.

He loved my money.
Now I see—
when that was gone
so was he.

A voice in the night
describes my plight.
He was needy.
I was greedy.

1942-1949
**THE JAPANESE
OCCUPATION AND
THE INDONESIAN
REVOLUTION**

Introduction to the 1942–1949 Period

An Uneasy Revolution

Radhar Panca Dahana

This short period was truly the most tempestuous in the history of the Indonesian republic—a period of revolution and the war for independence. It began with the Japanese occupation and continued until the Japanese forces were driven out by colonial armies, coinciding with the end of the Second World War. The year 1942 is widely seen as when the revolution started, in light of the tremendous changes that occurred: the arrival of the Japanese and the destruction of the entire Dutch colonial order by a new form of systematic colonialism. This was colonialism not only in a military, political and economic sense, but it also deeply affected culture and the arts. The Japanese government deliberately effected a radical transformation of cultural institutes—that had originally used the Dutch system—to make them serve, and be subservient to, Japanese ideology and culture, complete with the government's obsession with "Greater East Asia," or *Asia Timur Raya* as it was known in Indonesia.

To bring about this transformation, the occupying government introduced the Sendenhan, a cultural propaganda team. In August 1942 the Japanese institutionalized the propaganda effort into an independent department, the Sendenbu (Propaganda Service Office), which was divided into administrative, news and press, and propaganda sections. To strengthen the Sendenbu, the Japanese government specifically established the Keimin Bunka Shidoso (Cultural Center), which had three stated aims: first, to promote Indonesia's traditional arts; second, to educate and train Indonesian artists; and third, to introduce and disseminate Japanese culture.

Of course, the real aim of this institute was to make all artistic production in this country suitable to, and even driven by, Japan's grand objective, shrewdly formulated as the Great East Asia Co-Prosperity Sphere. Very tight selection was made in terms of aesthetics, which led to a deterioration in artistic production and discouraged the involvement of the public in cultural works. Still, this did

53

nothing to prevent the emergence of young writers and adolescents, who, fresh and full of vitality, used their skills and intelligence to surpass their predecessors.

During this brief period there was indeed a general marker—one used by most of those who observe and research literature—for the birth of a generation and a movement, the '45 Generation (Angkatan '45) or the Gelanggang ("Forum") Generation. The year 1949 was when Asrul Sani published the so-called Gelanggang Testimonial of Beliefs, which may be considered the ideological basis or worldview of his generation. This Testimonial of Beliefs provides us with clear evidence that the writers of that time were bound up in, and very well informed about, events of the outside world. Ultimately, the efforts of the Japanese occupying government to prune, graft and shape Indonesian culture and arts were ineffective—in part because its tenure was so short, only three and a half years.

Global events, such as the rise of Hitler, the Second World War, the atomic bombings of Hiroshima and Nagasaki, the rise of independence movements, and the emergence of new philosophical currents and artworks filled with rebellion became the inspiration for this generation. The birth of the United Nations and of cultural thinking that attempted to surmount the East-West divide—a divide which, among other things, had been a subject of debate in the "Polemics on Culture" (Polemik Kebudayaan) of the previous period—inspired the artists of Indonesia to consider the deepening interdependency among humans. That, truly, the cultures of this world exist and develop in an inescapable continuity. Or, to put it more precisely, the political and economic divisions on the world map need not end up segregating cultural work. West and East, North and South must seek out the factors that connect them, and strengthen these. Each side, without exception, had the responsibility to protect the other ones and to cultivate the existence and survival of this cultural work.

Thus, it is not surprising that the contents of the Gelanggang Testimonial—written by one of the best poets, dramatists and essayists of that time, a young man in his twenties, Asrul Sani—imply a sense of moral drive, as the following excerpt shows:

> We are the legitimate heirs of world culture, and we carry this culture forward in our own way. We were born from the masses, and an understanding of the people is for us a hodgepodge collection from which healthy new worlds can be born.
>
> . . . Indonesian culture is a coming together of all sorts of stimuli from voices resounding out of all corners of the earth that we then hurl back from our own throats.

For us, the Revolution is placing new values on the worn-out ones that must be demolished. In this way, we are of the view that the revolution in our own motherland is not yet finished.[1]

Together with Rivai Apin and especially Chairil Anwar, Asrul became a sort of ideological leader of this '45 Generation (a term coined by Rosihan Anwar in the magazine *Siasat* on January 9, 1949). These three writers realized their rebellion against the old order by publishing an anthology, *Three Against Fate* (*Tiga Menguak Takdir*), a punning euphemism for their rejection of the views of Sutan Takdir Alisjahbana ("Takdir" means "fate"), who was considered representative of the prewar literary firmament.

Besides these three writers, this generation gave rise to other names that in later days would be inscribed with gold ink in the history books of Indonesian and world literature: Idrus, Sitor Situmorang, Pramoedya Ananta Toer, Usmar Ismail, Mochtar Lubis and even the communist Bakrie Siregar. Pramoedya received such world acclaim that he was nominated several times for the Nobel Prize for Literature. But the peak of appreciation for him occurred after the 1960s, especially following his disputes with the Cultural Manifesto circle in the mid-1960s and his political detention by the Soeharto regime.

In the 1940s, the real star was Chairil Anwar, a poet who, despite not being especially prolific, was considered to be the leader of this generation based on his essays and poetry. The 1942–1949 period stood out as the time when Chairil, whose short life ended in 1949 when he was only twenty-seven years old, was most productive.

As a poet who was crazy for information about the world, and who worked in close proximity to political life and its players, Chairil demonstrated an amazing intellectual and artistic passion. He possessed an inner force that reached out to grasp the entire world, so that with it he could oppose whatever he saw as being stuck in the local sphere. This included the writers who were published in *Pujangga Baru*; he felt they did not pursue the real moral issues of the age, preoccupied as they were with their own personal questions, trapped in art for art's sake.

In his 1945 essay "Hoppla," Chairil pointed out, "If we face backward we find that *Pujangga Baru* was established in 1933, at the same time that Hitler seized power in Germany, but this magazine has published only one rather

---

[1] A. Rosidi, *Asrul Sani: Surat-surat Kepercayaan Gelanggang* [Asrul Sani: Documents of the Gelanggang Testimonial] (Jakarta: Pustaka Jaya, 1997), 3–4.

superficial article about fascism."[2] In fact, this accusation wasn't altogether true: literary figures before Chairil had been emotionally linked to the problems of the world, including fascism. However, Chairil dismissed their engagement as inadequate, shouting, "Hoppla! Jump to it! Light the pure flame, the flame of solidarity of nations that shall never be extinguished."

The words "solidarity of nations" in Chairil's appeal fit with what was at that time a general global tendency—countries had agreed to form the League of Nations in 1920 and later the United Nations in 1945. For Chairil this had become a choice with ideological meaning. With it he rejected the mutually hostile ideological camps that appeared at the time of Polemics on Culture in the 1930s. In one camp, Sutan Takdir Alisjahbana had advocated that Indonesian culture turn toward Western civilization and take it as a point of reference. On the opposite side, Sanusi Pane and his allies tended to side with the wisdom of the East, or, more precisely, an amalgamation or harmony between East and West.[3]

In Chairil's view, the resolution of problems, from the local to the global, had to be organized multilaterally. For this Minangkabau poet, this conviction was very strong. Articulating his beliefs in poetic language inspired not only many of his readers, but also his fellow writers. And for his part, Chairil dedicated the bulk of his compositions to an individual or a group of some kind. An example of this is his passionate "We're Ready" ("Siap Sedia"—not included in this anthology), which he directs "To My Generation." I excerpt a part of it here:

In time your blood's flow will stop,
But we will soon find others
To continue forging a Prosperous People.

Friends, my friends,
We rise with an awareness,
Infusing even our bones with light.
Friends, my friends,
Let's lift our sword to the Bright World![4]

A strong inner life, terrific passion and well-crafted poems have made Chairil Anwar the poet most remembered by Indonesian society to this day.

---

[2] H.B. Jassin, *Chairil Anwar Pelopor Angkatan 45* [Chairil Anwar, Pioneer of the 1945 Generation] (Jakarta: Gunung Agung, 1956), 121.

[3] Achdiat K. Miharja, *Polemik Kebudayaan* [Polemics on Culture] (Jakarta: Pustaka Jaya, 1977).

[4] Original text from H.B. Jassin, *Sastra Indonesia sebagai Warga Sastra Dunia* [Indonesian Literature as a Citizen of World Literature] (Jakarta: Gramedia, 1983), 51; translation by John H. McGlynn.

The Revolution and Its Critics

Generally speaking, Chairil's passion comes across strongly if we compare it with the poetry of the preceding period, much of which was romantic and even melancholy. Certainly the revolutionary period played a part in this difference. Many of the poets of this period expressed what was happening in their hearts and minds when it came to the revolution. One of the best-known poems in this vein is "Prayer," also written by Chairil Anwar and dedicated "to the firm believer."

My God
Even in my confusion
I still call Your name

Although it's truly difficult
to completely remember You

Your light, hot and pure
is now a candle's flicker in the silent dark

My God
I've lost all form
broken

My God
I am wandering in an alien land

My God at Your door, I knock
I cannot turn back

Although there were poets who used unadorned and straightforward language to criticize the revolution while it was underway, many poets chose ambiguous words and relied on double entendre to convey their messages.[5] Boen S. Oemarjati, in his 1972 Leiden University dissertation *Chairil Anwar: The Poet and His Language*, tried to clarify these ambiguous linguistic tendencies through a study of Chairil's poetry, an endeavor which, although criticized by some, was approved by H.B. Jassin.[6]

---

[5] For an example, see the poem "Seventy Milyun Sudah Bersatu/Kepada UNO!/ Coba Tinjaukan ke Indonesia!" (Seventy Million Have United/To the UNO!/Consider Indonesia!) by the poet Basjah Talsya in the Indonesian edition of this anthology.

[6] Jassin, *Sastra Indonesia sebagai Warga Sastra Dunia*, 215.

Many poems from this period are critical reflections on the revolution itself: its aims, its methods and the people involved in it. A number of poets expressed doubt about the outcomes of the revolution and lack of faith in its proponents, among a variety of other criticisms. An example of this can be seen in Dullah's poem "For Fifteen Friends":

What's the difference anymore
between the millions of people
"inside" beaten half to death
and those "outside" dying of thirst.

Happiness is only in dreams
on blue-green nights
free from locked doors
gazing at dark green valleys.

And when morning comes
doves perch upon *tekik* trees
the body accepts again its part
as a sacrifice in the nation's struggle.

For some writers in this period, the revolution spilled blood for a freedom that may not have been worth it. Here is Supii Wishnukuntjahja's poem "Arrogance":

The wheels turn
and no one cares.
Who? How many
have died on the roads?
It is fate, the masses
are powerless,
soon lost, soon gone,
leaving nothing behind!

There were poets who saw the revolution as necessary and their role in it as indispensable. S. Rukiah, a writer whose socialist sympathies are evident in her work, writes in her poem "Unable":

Do you wish for freedom?
And justice as well?

Then go and leave this place behind.
There is no more time
to moan or to be sad.

Unable, you say?
For fear of misery?

My dear soul,
as long as the stain on this world remains
there will be little room for movement
in mankind's pursuit of Freedom and Justice!

Thus ideological clashes could not really be avoided, not only in politics, but also in literary expression. As the poems in this anthology demonstrate, the revolution—the struggle for independence—provoked doubt, unease and sharp criticism. The poem "Crazy" by Nursjamsu Nasution illustrates how these changes shifted people's worldview and created a sense of being untethered:

"I am a crazy poet! I am a crazy poet!"
Walking forward, looking straight ahead,
ignoring pedicabs, cars, and trams,
staggering and stumbling, drunk on thoughts.
Sleeping with my head hidden under the pillow
to ease the buzzing and ringing.
Sitting sinking into sobs,
jumping up running, pounding my temples.
Dead desires come to haunt.
Widening my eyes in front of the mirror,
pointing at myself, hurling insults:
"Hey, wicked! Hey, crazy!"

I don't know why, but I have become like this.

These are genuine intuitive flinches, twitches, honest expressions of the heart that helped the revolution to mature.

The Inner World and Other Themes

These "intuitive flinches" and honest expressions of the heart are an internal theme that, quite apart from the revolution as an external event, enliven the poets' voices in this period. The personal sphere could also be seen to represent the "inner atmosphere" of society at large during a given period. In addition to Chairil and several names mentioned above, poets such as Maria Amin, Nursjamsu, Usmar Ismail, Dullah, Amal Hamzah, and Anas Ma'ruf expressed in verse their own inner worlds based on the lived reality of the times.

The upheavals in this hidden world not only give us a sense of the national spirit and moral enthusiasms of the times, but they also distinguish the poetry of this period from that of earlier periods in the history of Indonesian literature. For example, the poems of this period seem to have been more strongly influenced by the philosophy and ideology of the Tachtigers group in Holland, also known as the Movement of 1880, than by their own predecessors in the Indies.

As many have observed, the Tachtigers writers held that "art is passion." This was a view influenced by the aesthetic concepts and individualist attitudes of such poets as Keats and Shelley in England and Baudelaire and Flaubert in France, which held true for some of the Indonesian poets of the 1920s, such as J.E. Tatengkeng. However, with the establishment of *Pujangga Baru*, the Tachtigers writers came under sharp criticism. The individualist principles they espoused were judged too extravagant for their Indonesian counterparts.[7]

Although the wartime literati may not have leveled specific criticisms against the Tachtigers group, the philosophical trend toward lived and poetic attitudes that defended the rights and existence of the individual was especially pronounced. The influence of works in the fields of sociology, psychology and anthropology, as well as the currents of existentialism and surrealism, had a profound impact on the literary world. We discover with ease, in the work of almost every poet writing then, personal expressions and disclosures of the innermost self that reflect the collective world by painting the conditions of society. This constitutes a "mass psychological portrait" of the Indonesian people in a time of revolution.

Of interest in this collection is the set of poems by Asrul Sani, which progress from "A Letter from Mother" to "Confession," as though illustrating a child's process of departure from his village and beloved mother. He decides to struggle and not return, until finally he embarks on a search whose climax is spiritual, that of "a traveler [who] searches for God," and whose ending completes the traveler's devotion (the final part of "Confession"):

If there is a consequence it is the dagger earlier at his side
now planted in his own chest
And thus the final word is not mine
Consequences come of their own accord.

---

[7] Jassin, *Sastra Indonesia sebagai Warga Sastra Dunia*; Teeuw 1978[not in the biblio], 67–70.

This set of poems by Asrul lends its unique colors to the rainbow of poetic forms and content that existed during the Japanese period and the struggle for independence. During these periods, poetry was more thematically diverse, more subtle in content and closer to reality than it had previously been. This may have been the result of poets mixing more widely with world literature, art and the new sciences—all of which strengthened intellectual perspectives and made poets more able to distance themselves from reality, thereby encouraging a more objective kind of reflection about what was happening all around.

In this environment, new themes came thronging in. As well as taking on subjects that were explicitly ideological and political, poets reflected on themes that were still, at a global level, in the early stages of discussion. These included issues of gender (in the poetry of Siti Nuraini, for example) and transference ("Daytime in M.A.," by P. Sengodjo), as well as such traditional themes as the daily lives of ordinary people, love, conflicts with *adat* (customary law), and religion. All provide a strong foundation for the birth of even richer and stronger works in the periods to come. Poetry was strongly intertwined with the lived reality of the times—a reality that made the poets and their works gain proximity to, and wide acceptance within, the public sphere.

The Sea

Amal Hamzah

1943

I am standing on the beach
Gazing out across the sea.
The waves come home, break and breach;
Yearning drops cling to the sand's knee.

Waves come in, rolling and tumbling
Then swiftly return home to the depths.
I am astonished and left here pondering
How like the play of time this is.

My heart is truly just the same
Surging and breaking on the beach.
Currents of pleasure turn into pain;
It is so hard to find a feeling of peace...

A Reflection of Life

Amal Hamzah

1943

Just after dawn
Leaving for the office
I catch sight of a man
Scavenging in a trash bin, looking for rice.

At first glance I feel sorrow
My own body feels poor and low
Amidst the riches of a great land
Workers become vagrants.

But then I get a better look at his body
He seems perfectly hale and hearty
Suffering no handicap or injury.

My heart grows angry:
Someone like that doesn't need compassion
In this world of Allah, full of good fortune
He lives by being lazy.

Prayer

Chairil Anwar

1943

to the firm believer

My God
Even in my confusion
I still call Your name

Although it's truly difficult
to completely remember You

Your light, hot and pure
is now a candle's flicker in the silent dark

My God

I've lost all form
broken

My God

I am wandering in an alien land

My God
at Your door, I knock
I cannot turn back

I

Chairil Anwar

1943

When my time comes
I want no one to mourn
Not even you

Forget the sniveling and sobs

I am an untamed beast
Driven from its herd

Even if bullets pierce my flesh
I will attack in rage

I will take the pain and poison
Away in flight
Until the stinging and smarting stop

And I will be even more indifferent

I want to live a thousand years!

The New Humanity

Sutan Takdir Alisjahbana

1944

I love to look far into the distance, from the edge of the vast ocean
    or the top of a high mountain.
I am standing in the middle of a wide field, open as far as the eye can see,
    covered by a canopy of spreading clouds.
My heart overflows, my blood rushes, I am possessed of enormous energy.
God made humanity to rule the world: with eyes to pierce through barriers,
    ears to catch distant sounds, legs to conquer all obstacles, hands to reach
    beyond the heavens.

And it is only fear that turns us into weak caterpillars, bound by thousands of
    cords, unable to move.
Our inability to discern the secrets of the world and our fear of death is
    hallowed by religion. Our reluctance to think and to examine ourselves is
    called belief.
Our refusal to take responsibility is hidden behind the idea of fate, our fear of
    progress is covered by the splendid cloak of custom.
Closed to the possibilities inherent in the world, we live in our own cocoons.
The world promises the humble caterpillar great honor and glory and this is also
    true of humanity, the greatest of all creatures: we are fully equipped with
    all we need but are bound by our own ignorance and poverty.
We are being punished for neglecting the possibility of manifesting the divine
    glory we carry within ourselves.

From Dusk to Dusk

(a fragment)

Usmar Ismail

1944

For A

Tragic

The clouds are spooky and grim
the wind lets out a moan
stuck against a palm tree
drenched by the dusk rain.

The overcast sky is ripped open
dark, blind souls fall
violating the Fair and Lovely day!

Struggle

The bright day turns bleak
covered in gloomy clouds
blown about by absence.
The wind begins to howl
storming into the struggle
as the sun and clouds
fight over their position...

So I begin my plunge
into a life full of disappointments.
War rages outside
and inside my chest
this struggle between sun and clouds
will wrestle on.

Dark room

We fumbled about in a dark room
the air as still and silent as a tomb.
Outside, the bright day went black
the earth and sky grew overcast
a veil unfurled from the sky
blocking almost all else from sight.

Why is day suddenly night?
The morning sun has set
the flower bud will still bloom
but it is no longer new.
Why has the iron stopped
coaxing fire from this rock?

Sunken ship

I am almost drifting away
dragged by murky water.
Scattered pieces of wood
splintered from a shipwreck
are carried by rasping, bubbling water
down to blind shells.

Doggedly I wrap my arms
around a plank
ripped from the wall of a ship
that is sinking into the deep
bottomless ocean.

Serenade Interrompue

M.A. Djoehana

1945

"Preludes," live premier Claude Achilles Debussy

>   Night
>   dark night
>   ambushed

I feel constrained, my sight is blurred,
My hand is still writing!
but the letters are muddled:

No,
the ink flows, but the paper is dissolving
... or my eyes are completely clouded?

>   how can this darkness be breached
>   but suddenly—
> as if I see a red light
> reddish-red, yellow, blood red . . .

Ah, perhaps someone is laughing?
That is fine!
Even I come to smile.
In fact: was it I who said that?

>   "Brother, clever one,
>   this is fire, the fire of hell"

Question

M.A. Djoehana

1945

Why did you say that:
I always await it
now...

why do I await it:
my heart does not want to wait
but...

I turn my head
look to the back, to the side, to the front
but the day is quiet, exceedingly quiet

I clench my hand
I hit the mirror, shattering the silence
but I am stunned to see drops of blood:

drop by drop
my consciousness drains
"What is it?" I ask, I ask,
I ask, I ask . . .

"Is it me who asks?"

Lost Love

Aoh Kartahadimadja

1946

A soft breeze blows.
Lost in thought
the wanderer stares
at the light dancing on the water.

Only one star
all alone
flickering gently
oblivious in the sky.

My heart, my heart
finds no comfort in the breeze
the murmuring brook
or the single star
shining in the sky—
ready to lead the sailor home
across the vast ocean.

Twilight at a Small Harbor

Chairil Anwar

1946

for Sri Ayati

This time no one's looking for love
in the warehouses, in the shacks, or in the tales
of poles and rigging. Boats and ships not at sea
distend themselves in hopes of finding berth.

Drizzle hastens darkness. An osprey's wings
brush the gloom, the swish of day's end rapidly swimming
towards the temptations of future ports. Nothing moves;
the sand and sea asleep, the waves dead and gone.

There's nothing else. I'm alone. Walking,
combing the cape with the suppressed hope
of at once arriving at its tip and bidding farewell
from the fourth strand, embracing that final sob.

Our Nation's Flag Is Red and White

Talsya

1946

Red is for the blood that bathed the earth
The fallen body of my ancestor
White is for his bandages
He died a martyr, shrouded in blood

Red is for the blood that covered his body
That continually flowed through his veins
White is for his pure young heart
Forever in love with the motherland

Red is the color of the innocent afternoon
Of the nature that sheltered my birth
White is the color of the jasmine
A symbol of Indonesia's beauty

Our nation's flag is red and white
Symbol of our sovereignty
Red is the courage and skill of our soldiers
White is purity... *Merdeka!*
Liberty! Forever!

Common Folk

Sanusi Pane

1946p

We walk for centuries,
Through dark, deep ravines,
Not hoping not longing,
Not thinking not loving.

God has forgotten us,
The common folk, children of suffering,
We work ourselves to the bone
While people laugh.

If You truly exist,
O God, then why
Are we chained in prison
Even though we are innocent?

Pool of Youth

Walujati

1946p

In shimmering golden yellow
The pool of my youth lies visible:
Clear and calm as if watching
The comely girl approach...

    In laughter and gaiety, she bathes
    The water bubbles with the play of her hand
    From her loosened tresses, gay flowers fall
    To join in the water's dance.

The lake is now full of waves
And my clear water has turned murky
From the games of the beautiful girl.

    If the young woman were to go home
    The water would be calm, muddied no more,
    And all the commotion would cease

But,
Even if that were so—

    To see the girl slowly go
    Her swaying hips disappear
    I would scream and break the silence:
    "Will you come and play again?"

For 15 Friends

Dullah
1947

The light outside is dim
choking the frozen room
white walls turn grey
iron bars cast shadows.

Just say it's a prison
a place known for torture
but hasn't this whole wide world
become a terrifying prison?

What's the difference anymore
between the millions of people
"inside" beaten half to death
and those "outside" dying of thirst.

Happiness is only in dreams
on blue-green nights
free from locked doors
gazing at dark green valleys.

And when morning comes
doves perch upon *tekik* trees
the body accepts again its part
as a sacrifice in the nation's struggle.

Muhammadiyah Madrasah

Mahatmanto

1947

I left this building
years ago.
Now I return
and open the door with a creak.
A gentle breeze wafts in, rustles
the old paper calendar,
which hasn't been changed;
termites have reached the rafters,
spider webs
on windows with no shutters.

Two or three slugs
stick to frames on the walls—
paintings of mine from years past.
It's not that the slugs are searching for art
spying at my creations! Just...
eating the moss on the glass.

> Ah . . .
> the teachers are long gone,
> having abandoned the students long ago,
> gone to struggle, gone to fight . . .
> but where have they all fallen?

Arrogance

Supii Wishnukuntjahja

1947

The trucks fly past,
scattering dust.

The bushes blink, the weeds shake,
mouths gape, trembling,
but the trucks run wild,
run, run, never stopping.

The wheels turn
and no one cares.
Who? How many
have died on the roads?
It is fate, the masses
are powerless,
soon lost, soon gone,
leaving nothing behind!

... now

I have climbed a mountain,
I can see all around me
how far away
everything is
down there.
If I thought I was
above everything
in the world,
I might feel proud,
very proud.

A car speeds by below,
and I am hidden in the long grass,
no one can see me.
Then I realize
how small and insignificant
I really am.

Seaman's Party

M. Balfas

1948

Kabul
stopped at the edge of the sea.
The rainclouds abound with opiates!
I ran from distant mountains
wanting to sail but it didn't happen
because the waves were flat.

The seaman arrives
he knows the secrets of the sea

that the crazy party
penetrates blind walls
the dead return to life.

Come, come
we will make a story:
a typhoon hits the waves
the sea and the sky unite
the fairies dance together
on the ship
in the morning we stop with the sea foam.

This time eternity does not exist.
This child is made to age quickly!

Row, row, row
farther
there is a more beautiful nymph!
In the end the ship is only wood
its own pieces
searching for dreams
and a compassionate heart in the morning water;
white suit full of vomit
on the tongue of the receding waves.
Dissolution of the soul:
underclothes clinging to the body.

The Last Man

Rivai Apin

1948

for Chairil Anwar

I give up all I own:
the now and the future. For a long bench
in a bright room growing dark at twilight
and a lit cigarette in the hand.

The days I now turn into temples of the past.
Occassionally I smile and laugh to myself.

Deadened days bury me
in objects now decayed and dirty,
but, after the final yawn, I fear
my head will be aslant and my mouth agape
    with my teeth hanging heavily from my gums
regret will issue forth. New days merely mock the past.

Calm Waters

Samiati Alisjahbana

1948

The water is calm, just minor ripples.
A fallen leaf, nudged by the wind,
follows the water's current.
A dragonfly slowly alights
and on the leaf leisurely sails.
The winged mariner atop its prow
calmly passes and goes...

If only the soul could be so calm,
in acquiescence to the situation,
not making a bother, not protesting the silence,
as if satisfied, satisfied with this alone.
Always and ever, forever like that,
even as the muddy base thickens.

Night Scream

Nursjamsu Nasution

1948p

The night train's whistle screams
Moaning to the heavens...
Beset by life's suffering
My struggling nation screams
Moaning to the heavens...

The powerful engine pushes through the darkness;
The wheels spin on their rails
Heading onward to the final station.
Your impassioned faces push through the darkness;
Fight, my nation, for your DREAM,
Keep heading onward, toward Freedom!

Crazy

Nursjamsu Nasution

1948p

Roaring with laughter,
dancing a crazy jig.
Lamenting, shrieking to the sky.
Collapsing onto my back, hit by a scream,
then sitting bolt upright, violently demanding,
"Who dares oppose me!?"
Singing in ear-splitting shrieks,
"I am a crazy poet! I am a crazy poet!"
Walking forward, looking straight ahead,
ignoring pedicabs, cars, and trams,
staggering and stumbling, drunk on thoughts.
Sleeping with my head hidden under the pillow
to ease the buzzing and ringing.
Sitting sinking into sobs,
jumping up running, pounding my temples.
Dead desires come to haunt.
Widening my eyes in front of the mirror,
pointing at myself, hurling insults:
"Hey, wicked! Hey, crazy!"

I don't know why, but I have become like this.

Unable

S. Rukiah

1948p

Do you weep, my soul?
Perhaps…
But not for your lamentations
nor your complaints.
It's useless
for you to cry.

Do you wish for freedom?
And justice as well?

Then go and leave this place behind.
There is no more time
to moan or to be sad.

Unable, you say?
For fear of misery?

My dear soul,
as long as the stain on this world remains
there will be little room for movement
in mankind's pursuit of Freedom and Justice!

The Light Will Die

S. Rukiah

1948p

Indeed, we stand between morning and night
and sometimes see a thousand stars in the sky
or a woman of arrant heart, playing the piano
and singing for a man's love.

Just say that this world is a sweet place
and people delight to read tales of virtue
not knowing that when what remains of a body is bones,
that when the light dies in the nighttime rain,
that when hearts bitterly ask for promises to be kept,
we might read in the Bible the sentence:
"God is indeed great, yet we will never be able
       to understand Him."

Angrily, we return to a dusty road
where beggars plead for a penny or less
and little children wrestle over a toy
while the sun casts drawn-out shadows
upon the earth
and still we are uncertain,
"Will there be the moon and stars tonight?"

When love dies
hot blood turns cold
and we halt this journey into night
to play in drawn-out shadows on the ground
and feel our hearts bitterly asking for promises kept
for years we stand between morning and night
and pay no mind to the scream that pierces the sky
"Tomorrow the light will die!
Tomorrow the light will die!"

Let's just say this world is a sweet place
and that people delight to read tales of virtue
but the woman of arrant heart still plays the piano
and sings for a man's love.

Life's Deceit

S. Rukiah

1948p

Before the mirror
I makeup my face
and under the light of a forty-watt bulb
the smile on my lips
blossoms with love!

I powder my skin
turn my lips a bright red
and wrap a green scarf
around my shoulders.

Before the mirror
I see my self-potrait
and in it, exposed,
my human deceit.

Tonight I am beautiful
beneath the glow
of the streetlights
but when the moon disappears
and the fickle stars fade
I too will wane
without a doubt
and my smile will change
and blossom with venom!

A symbol of the world
is life's deceit
and fooling oneself completely!

I Hear the Azan

Usmar Ismail

1948p

To the Defenders of Our Homeland

I hear your call to prayer at dawn,
Praising God and wishing for protection.
Your voice scatters seeds I know will grow—
Now, it is you who ushers in the era's exaltation.

Throughout my body that was cold and weak,
Warming blood flows fluid once again.
In my chest I feel the quiver of a common dream—
Now, through you, our hopes are growing certain.

I hear the shout of the trumpet as it plays,
Beckoning thee to a faithful place, obliging me
To stand straight and tall with a common aim—
Now, it is you who attains sure victory.

And how could I not have faith?
I feel your feelings, plunge deep into your hurt.
I know that living or dead I still have worth.
This time, brother, we fulfill the devotion in our hearts!

Light in a Glass

Siti Nuraini

1949

Yesterday's twilight was barely different from today's,
just fewer sounds and voices, perhaps, and the smell of incense
permeating a small home out of earshot of the stifled cries
of a woman who has just now lost her newborn child
and a sun unwilling to offer the last of its love
for faith in a human child, and a twilight
in which the wind takes a deep breath, it, too, sensing
the futility of pleas, words, and prayers
even as a mosque's drum dares to beat loudly,
as if to fill the weariness of this day and this heart,
beating alone—calling to those who don't want to hear its sound.
What is the use now of all the flowers of love and the feelings
that have dried and turned black with the clumps of soil
thrown into the hole in the ground along with the prayer for the dead
and the vast amount of hope that once willingly defied
and arrogantly denied the verdict of death.
A dry season has come with the dusk
and erected a place to live in the doorway
of this house of sorrow and a mother's broken heart.
But, finally, the night, which still can love, enfolds both
with an abundance of affection and takes them to
a kingdom, one pleasant and light, where sorrow has no place.
In the softness of a new morning, a woman now forgotten
stoops to pick a strand of flowers from the black ground left as a sign
while memories of the hundreds of notes of affection
now reside silently in her solitary heart.

Yesterday's twilight was no different from today's
with the beauty of the sun slowly fading,
with a small child singing happily upon a lap
and with light trapped in a just-used glass.

A Woman

Siti Nuraini

1949

Secrets hearkening in the distance,
a woman peers out her window,
an odd feeling in her heart; she snaps
into pieces the dried twig in her hand.

Her loving soul is an open lake,
another world for a different life.
Love and desire course at the lake's base
yet never rise to the water's surface.

As birds fly off into the night,
her home fades in silence's embrace.
Standing in the doorway, she shivers,
then hastily slams the door shut
and covers her face going inside.

Between Karawang and Bekasi

Chairil Anwar
1949p

We who lie between Krawang and Bekasi
cannot cry "Freedom" or take up arms anymore,
but who is unable to hear us roar
or see us still marching with stalwart hearts?

We speak to you in the stillness of a silent night
when the chest feels empty and the wall clock ticks.

We died young. All that's left is dirt-covered bones.
Remember us, do remember us.

We did all that we could
yet our work is unfinished, barely begun.

We gave our lives but the work is unfinished.
Who can reckon the value of four or five thousand lives?

We are but scattered bones
which now belong to you.
It is you who decide their value:
whether we died for freedom, victory, hope
or for nothing at all.

We do not know, cannot say.
You are the ones who must now speak.

We speak to you in the stillness of a silent night
when the chest feels empty and the wall clock ticks.

Remember us, do remember us,
carry on, carry on our lives.
Protect those who lead us now:
Bung Sukarno, Bung Hatta, and Bung Syahrir.

Now that we are corpses
give meaning to our lives;
defend the frontier between reality and dreams.

Remember us, do remember us,
whose only remains are earth-covered bones,
the thousands of us who lie between Krawang and Bekasi.

---

[1] This poem is based on or was inspired by the poem "The Young Dead Soldiers" by Archibald MacLeish.

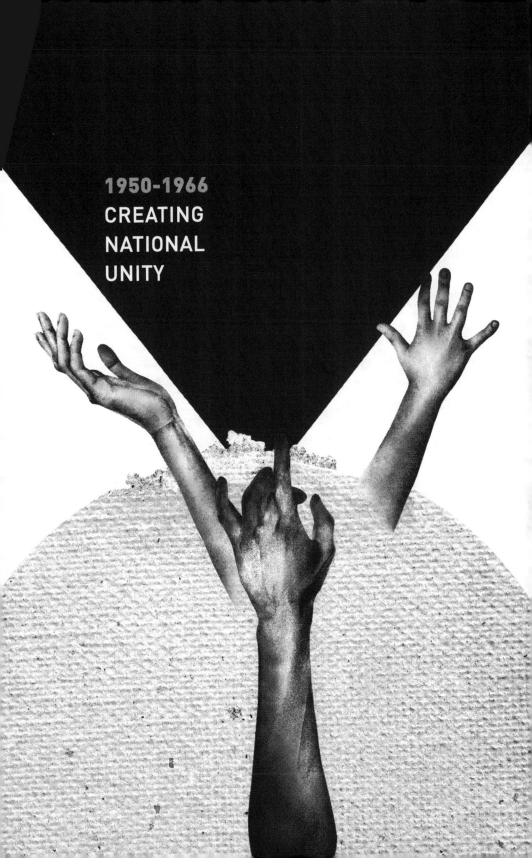

1950-1966
CREATING
NATIONAL
UNITY

Introduction to the 1949–1966 Period

Recognizing Ourselves, Building a Nation

Radhar Panca Dahana

P oets of the revolutionary period, which immediately preceded this one, had expected that poetry in Indonesia would become more innovative, richer in character and more sensitive to the realities of the day than the poetry that had come before. Instead, the 1949–1966 period led to accusations of retrogression—a state of affairs that in literary circles was referred to as an impasse.

Various writers—beginning with Sutan Takdir Alisjahbana and continuing with Tamar Djaja, Yogaswara, Gajus Siagian and finally Nugroho Notosusanto—were critical of the literary climate. A foundation for cultural communication in the Netherlands, STICUSA (Stichting voor Culturele Samenwerking), organized a conference in Amsterdam on June 26, 1953, to discuss the widespread apathy in Indonesian literature. At the conference Sutan Takdir Alisjahbana declared, "These [Indonesian] writers are living in a spiritual vacuum. They've left behind the old, [but] haven't yet discovered a new world." Pramoedya Ananta Toer, already a well-known writer at the time, accused various literary institutions, including the conference organizer, of "only fertilizing the growth of a salon intelligentsia who are detached from their own lives."[1]

In an article written in 1957, Pramoedya Ananta Toer attempted to clarify his position, citing Sutan Takdir Alisjahbana, who had said, "Over these thirty years, the pendulum of Indonesian literature has been hurled from tradition's shackles at the one end to the anarchism of individualism at the other, and what's saddening is that no matter how great the leap, it cannot surpass the West, which has had the past three to four centuries of its own history to traverse.[2]

---

[1] Pramoedya Ananta Toer, "Mencari Sebab Kemunduran Kesusasteraan Indonesia Modern Dewasa Ini" [Seeking the Reasons for the Present-Day Decline of Modern Indonesian Literature] in *Duta Suasana*, 2nd ed. (25), 1953, 14–15.

[2] Pramoedya Ananta Toer, "Apathy; Fatigue; Crisis," in *Siasat* II (515/516), 1957, 34–36.

What Sutan Takdir Alisjahbana described and Pramoedya Ananta Toer tried to convey was that Indonesian culture in general was suffering from an increasingly acute existential haze stemming from the recent wars, both at the local level (the revolutionary war) and globally (the Second World War). The life-and-death struggle of war—which occurred on the heels of a period of literature focused on the question of identity and produced works that were filled with explosions and adventure, both philosophical and physical—created confusion, which only intensified over time.

This state of dissatisfaction, even self-criticism, actually became a global "literary epidemic" during the period after the Second World War. In Britain, dissatisfaction was directed at local literature, which was considered trapped in aestheticism and enmeshed in politics. Dylan Thomas, among others, saw such literature as a form of romanticism that did not contribute anything to actual contemporary life.

In the face of the devastating wounds of war, literature was widely seen as inconsequential nonsense. Various pessimistic, apathetic and even nihilistic views arose, especially in Germany, where the Second World War was seen as a blunder impossible to apologize for, let alone be forgiven. When postwar German writers weren't exploring themes of religion and modernity—which had been rejected by the Third Reich—they were testing ideas from elsewhere, such as French existentialism.

The moralistic and aesthetic trends in literature only served to camouflage writers' inability to address critical political and economic questions in the country that had lost the war. Writers such as Heinrich Böll and Günter Grass saw the postwar world as filled with injustice—an idea that was shared by literary circles in the United States, the country that had won the war. That war—no matter who had nominally won—resulted in trauma, particularly for the lower classes. Only the wealthy had profited from the war.

Although individual nations responded quite differently in the postwar period, generally speaking there was a sense of dissatisfaction, regret and even, on some level, cultural crisis. In Indonesia, this crisis materialized as social disorientation and dislocation, with writers becoming less and less able to clarify their role in the midst of existential grappling at both the regional and global level.

The sense of crisis in the literary world reflected broader issues in Indonesian culture, and in the worlds of politics, law and the economy. During the 1950s and the early years of the 1960s, Indonesian history was filled with debates over the systemic forms of state administration at all levels. Political experiments were undertaken with systems of governance. These debates occurred, too, with the imposition of a legal system that struggled to reconcile "modern law" (that is, Anglo-Saxon law), customary law (*adat*) and colonial law, which was based on the Dutch Continental system. In the economy, there were fierce struggles among the economic orders that were oriented variously to socialism, Pancasila economics and liberal capitalism.

As had been the case in Germany and Great Britain, many works of literature, including poetry, tried to conceal the anxiety brought on by this chaotic situation with expressions and diction that were solely oriented to aestheticism, beauty and romanticism. This was the tendency that Pramoedya called "salon intelligentsia," a term meant to convey that Indonesian writers in this period were insufficiently concerned with contemporary social realities.

Several other prominent writers shared Pramoedya's concerns. Anas Ma'ruf, in his article "Fungsi Sosial Seniman" (The Social Function of the Artist)[3] stressed that each writer, as an artist, must be brave enough to be responsible, in all their works, to everyone. Influenced by the French naturalist philosopher Hippolyte Taine (1828–1893), Ma'ruf wrote in another article that the responsibility of the writer meant "the responsibility to welcome the following questions: What tasks have been accomplished in trying to realize the ideals of literature or the broader ideals of culture? And what was literature's relationship with the natural world around it, with things great and small, things that possessed life or did not?"[4]

Ma'ruf's views were widely held in literary circles during this period, and these views were well suited to contemporary perspectives in literary theory— that all literary works must be linked to the values of their age and the values that were yet to come.[5] This concept was then formalized as the basis of ideals and even working principles for writers' organizations, which flourished from the middle to the end of this period.

The period 1950–1966 was one in which all the elements of Indonesian nationhood moved with the ambition to complete the work of the generations that came immediately before—that is, both the '45 Generation (the war generation) and the generation before that, the so-called Pujangga Baru Generation of the 1930s. The task was to clarify the identity of this nation that they had bravely proclaimed themselves to be a part of.

Tragically, however, these efforts ended in failure. Not only did this generation fail to elucidate Indonesian identity, but its members sank into endless conflict. This period may be remembered mainly for the political wrestling matches that occurred among the elites, who were segregated to an astonishing, unprecedented

---

[3] Anas Ma'ruf, in *Nasional*, no. 1 (27), 1950, 16.

[4] Anas Ma'ruf, "...and the 1945 Generation," *Nasional*, no. 1, 1950, 16.

[5] Rene Wellek and Austin Warren, *Teori Kesusasteraan* [Theory of Literature], trans. Melani Budianta (Jakarta: Gramedia, 1990).

degree. For example, the introduction of parliamentary democracy in 1950 gave birth to tens and even hundreds of political parties, making it impossible for any decision of the many government cabinets to be affirmed with any unanimity.

The experiment of democratic politics under the leadership of President and Supreme Commander Sukarno had no slight impact on Indonesia's literary life. Segregation, whether based on ideology, religion or political orientation, also occurred in literary circles. The traumatic process of finding oneself and the general loss of orientation combined to create cultural circles that mirrored the political cleavages at the top.

Krishnananda attempted to categorize artists and writers of the post-1945 as belonging to one of three groups: "nativists" (with figures like Ki Hadjar Dewantara, H.B. Jassin and Bahrum Rangkuti); "rationalists" (Sutan Takdir Alisjahbana, Anas Ma'ruf, S. Rukiah, Pramoedya Ananta Toer, Achdiat Karta Miharja and Idrus); and "universalists" (Chairil Anwar, Trisno Sumardjo, Asrul Sani, Rivai Apin, Rosihan Anwar and Gadis Rasjid).[6]

Arief Budiman, writing in the following period, divided the literary community of this same post-1945 generation into four groupings, by politics: Lekra (Lembaga Kebudayaan Rakyat; Institute for People's Culture); Manikebu (Manifes Kebudayaan; Cultural Manifesto); cultural institutes formed by political parties, such as LKK (Lembaga Kreatifitas Kemanusiaan; Institute of Humanistic Creativity) and Lesbumi (Lembaga Seniman Budayawan Muslimin Indonesia; Indonesian Muslim Society of Art and Culture); and groups that merely sympathized with, but were independent from, the first three (with activists like Ajip Rosidi and Trisno Sumardjo).[7]

In his research, Muhammad Adi Nugraha identified at least nine groups on the basis of political orientation. These included Lekra, associated with the Indonesian Communist Party (PKI); Lesbumi, associated with the Nadhlatul Ulama Party (NU); Lembaga Kebudayaan Nasional (Institute of National Culture), associated with the Indonesian Nationalist Party; Leski (Institute of Islamic Culture and Arts), associated with Perti (Association of Islamic Schools); LKASM, associated with the Socialist Party (PSI); LKKI (the Institute of Indonesian Catholic Culture), associated with the Catholic Party; Lesbi (Institute of Indonesia Arts and Culture), associated with the Indonesian Party; HSBI (Himpunan Seni Budaya Islam; Community of Islamic Arts and Culture);

---

[6] Krishnananda, "Aliran-aliran Kebudayaan Indonesia" [Indonesia's Cultural Currents] in *Star Weekly*, no. 5 (247), 1950, 23–24.

[7] Arief Budiman, "Politik dalam kesusastraan Indonesia: Sebuah Gambaran Singkat" [Politics in Indonesian Literature: An Overview] in *Kebebasan, Negara, Pembangunan: Kumpulan Tulisan 1965–2005* (Jakarta: Freedom Institute, 2006), 137.

and LSBM (Lembaga Seni Budaya Mahasiswa; Institute of Student Arts and Culture).[8]

These literary splinter groups were quite conspicuous and had an impact on the sectarian categorization of the writers, their political orientation and culture, and the methods and aims of their work. They also differentiated writers in terms of how they viewed the cultural and political visions of their predecessors. Everyone had an opinion concerning the '45 Generation, especially about Chairil Anwar, the main exponent of its views. Some saw that war generation as merely a continuation of the 1930s Generation, while others defended its moral convictions,[9] and still others declared it dead.[10]

But of all these various voices clamoring at their microphones, perhaps it was Lekra and Pramoedya Ananta Toer whose voices resounded the loudest. As mentioned earlier, Pramoedya tried to whip up solidarity and literary partisanship among the "little" people, the ordinary people of the nation. This line of thinking brought him close to the ideas of the Marxists and the Communist political movement, the PKI—an inclination that was shared by other prominent writers and artists of the period, beginning with Idrus, Rivai Apin and Bakrie Siregar, and continuing right up to S. Rukiah and the painter Affandi.

In the mid-1950s, Pramoedya Ananta Toer considered all the writers, including those in Lekra, to be spectators who observed the people from too great a social distance. "Lekra and these newest writers," he once said, "are still just tourists. The problems of the peasants—that is, the impoverished people in a specifically Indonesian sense of the term—are not their problems."[11]

Pramoedya's opinions, always sharply stated like this, eventually elicited a strong reaction from a group of artists and writers who, in the mid-1960s, grouped together as the Manifesto Kebudayaan (Cultural Manifesto). Their nickname "Manikebu" was popularized by Lekra, the group's political enemy. The so-called Manikebu[12] group, in a statement signed by twenty writers and essayists (including H.B. Jassin, Wiratmo Soekito, Trisno Sumardjo, Zaini, Soe Hok Djin alias Arief Budiman, Goenawan Mohamad and Taufiq Ismail), rejected the dominant position of the day—namely, to advance the idea that

---

[8] Muhammad Adi Nugraha, *Sejarah Lembaga Kebudayaan Nasional dalam Kesusastraan Indonesia* [The History of Institutes of National Culture in Indonesian Literature], thesis, 2012, Depok: Faculty of Culture, Universitas Indonesia, 127.

[9] Like Anas Ma'ruf in his article cited above, ibid.

[10] Jogaswara, "Angkatan 45 Sudah Mampus" [The 1945 Generation Has Kicked the Bucket], in *Spektra* I (15), 1949, 12–13.

[11] Pramoedya Ananta Toer, "Tendensi Kerakyatan dalam Kesusasteraan Indonesia Terbaru" [Democratic Tendencies in the Newest Indonesian Literature], in *Star Weekly* II (574), 1956, 5–6.

[12] In Indonesian, *mani kerbau* means "water buffalo semen."

politics was in command of national change. For the Manikebu group, politics was only one cultural sector among many; it had to develop in parallel with others, synergistically, for the nation to flourish.

In his article defending Manikebu, Goenawan Mohamad, a prominent voice in this movement, was even more explicit: "Cultural workers are not the subordinates of the politicians, nor is it the other way around."[13] Even more bluntly, Goenawan Mohamad stated his bias in favor of socialist ideology: "Socialism as an historical tendency in the twentieth century promises the freedom that cultural workers wish for as the voice of a universal humanistic conscience, and therefore, we Indonesian workers have chosen socialism to represent our ideals."[14]

For his part, Wiratmo Soekito, who was considered the thinker behind an early draft of the manifesto, analyzed the position of Indonesian culture in the world arena by stressing that in Indonesia, culture "is motivated by a national identity that strives to free itself from foreign control and meddling, but not seclude itself from the society of nations."[15] And in both a rejection and an accusation of Lekra, Wiratmo opposed the adage "the end justifies the means" in cultural endeavors.

Conflict between these groups came increasingly into the open, creating tensions in Indonesian literature that extended into the following periods. Political involvement was later seen within all literary circles as a specter that threatened not only freedom of expression but the economic security of any writer. The precedent set by this conflict became a bitter lesson in the history of Indonesian literature.

There has been much analysis of the events that occurred around the end of this period. Wijaya Herlambang's Queensland University thesis, which was published in 2013, reveals facts that are both interesting and alarming: that the military, with their threatening weapons, and the intelligence agencies, both foreign and local, played a significant role in the upheavals in literary life of this period.[16] He details how these organizations created opposing camps whose legacies, including threats of revenge, are still influential, right up to the publication of this anthology.

---

[13] Goenawan Mohamad, "Sejarah Lahirnya Manifes Kebudayaan" [The History of the Birth of the Cultural Manifesto], 1963, in *Sastra*, 3rd ed., (9/10), 30–31.

[14] Ibid.

[15] Wiratmo Soekito, "Penjelasan Manifes Kebudayaan" [Explanation of the Cultural Manifesto], 1963, in *Sastra*, 3rd ed. (9/10), 28–29.

[16] See Wijaya Herlambang, *Kekerasan Budaya Pasca 1965* [Cultural Violence Post-1965] (Jakarta: Marjin Kiri, 2013).

The Missing Self

The poets chosen to represent this period address a world that seemed to have lost its external points of reference, its footing and its orientation. This was the case not only because everything that was old had been left behind—as established by Sutan Takdir Alisjahbana in the early period[17]—but also due to the sustained trauma of the war, as well as opposition to the lived attitudes and literary styles of the new writers. All of this made it very difficult to confront new challenges. What Henk Maier characterizes as a lack of coherency or narrative, the absence of a central theme or plot, explains, in short, the inability of Indonesian literature to produce anything that might be called a Bildungsroman.[18]

Chaos, confusion and loss of self are dominant themes in this anthology, as is the theme of "journey." The motif of the lost child recurs, and many poems tell of someone in search of authenticity, individual or national. The verse of Sitor Situmorang may best represent this figure of the lost child on a journey, rite of passage or adventure. His renowned poem "The Lost Child" ends on a bitter note:

> Late at night the mother quits her chores
> The father, long before, has begun to snore
> On the sandy shore, waves hiss and foam
> Knowing the prodigal son has not come home

By contrast, Ajip Rosidi's poem "Return of the Lost Child" has a happy ending. Here, a mother who has exhausted all earthly and spiritual means for finding her child, who mysteriously disappeared, seems to find a reunion, though whether this reunion is earthly or spiritual remains unclear:

> "I'm weak, Mother.
> I'm hungry and thirsty.
> The palace has vanished
> and so has my father."
> She came home, came home,
> the human child,

---

[17] *loc. cit.*, 1.

[18] Henk Maier, "Suara gagal dan Pintu yang Berderit, Tulisan Pramoedya Ananta Toer dalam Bahasa Melayu" [Stammer and the Creaking Door: The Writings of Pramoedya Ananta Toer in Malay], in Keith Foulcher and Tony Day, eds., *Sastra Indonesia Modern: Kritik Postkolonial* [Modern Indonesian Literature: Post-colonial Criticism], revised edition, translated by Koesalah Soebagyo Toer and Monique Soesman (Jakarta: Yayasan Obor Indonesia and KITLV, 2008), 85–88.

because of her mother's love.
She came home, home,
saved by the shawl
of her mother's love.

One possible ending in the adventure of a child who has left behind his mother's womb—whether this womb is biological, social or cultural—is that the child does not return as hoped, disappearing into the outer world, the "other" world that exists beyond the ken of his mother. It may be that physically the parent reunites with the child, but culturally they no longer know each other.

This aspect of the journey theme appears in poems that focus on another dominant theme: the self, the inner or personal life. Many of the poems in this anthology are concerned with the inner world, and, together with poems that depict the journey theme, they show how identity—whether personal, communal or national—becomes a critical question in this period.

The clarification of identity becomes sublime when a critical mass of spiritual doubt commences such a search. The problems of divinity and belief—of the traditional kind—lead to existential doubts. Poets and their verse in this period march like spiritual, cultural and also social pilgrims bearing the burden of questions, doubt, confusion and incompetence in translating the purpose of the age. The young writers of this period—such as Arifin C. Noer, Budiman S. Hartojo and Taufiq Ismail—were among the main representatives in this long line of poet-pilgrims. A fervent religious sensibility in most of their work branches in two, ending either in disbelief or in unshakeable certainty.

Taufiq Ismail, who wrote at the end of this period, is an example of a poet whose work is infused with the symbols of his religion, Islam. In the end he stopped writing poems dealing with social questions, which were popular during the student upheaval in 1966. To this day, Taufiq makes Islam the driving force behind his poetic output. He is also a popular songwriter; Taufiq's songs are performed by a well-known band, Music Bimbo (Hardjakusumah brothers).

Drowning in Politics

Taufik Ismail was one of the best-known spokespeople of the so-called 1966 Generation. This term describes a group of young people who were politically active during the mid-1960s, allied for the most part with the Armed Forces of Indonesia (ABRI), and with Soeharto as the supreme leader. The term was also a label—a stigma at times—in the history of Indonesian literature. Writers clamored for change, shouted out their opposition to the Sukarno regime, and defended anything they considered "universal humanism" as being the high points of history.

Whether label or stigma, the 1966 Generation and its surrounding controversies gave only a small taste of a political atmosphere that became much harsher at the close of that decade. As mentioned above, the political segregation that reached a high point in the application of liberal democracy under Sukarno induced a splintering of cultural and literary forces, which were themselves in constant flux.

The disputes of Manikebu and Lekra grew more intense until Soeharto's New Order was established, giving the advantage to Manikebu, which had supported Soeharto from the start. Manikebu succeeded in dealing a blow to Lekra when a number of Lekra figures were imprisoned without trial while others fled abroad. Apart from the clashes between these two camps, liberal and communist, writers remained in their respective political cages, whether for protection or to tie their literary ideas to the ideological power of a political party.

At that time, literature was in crisis, subject to political repression. Sukarno outlawed Manikebu, and Soeharto in his turn muzzled Lekra. Literary life was filled with salvos of slogans, jargon and all manner of propaganda—words associated with political power. "There were a thousand slogans but zero poems," as Goenawan Mohamad famously described the situation.

This collection gives considerable space to the poetry of those writers who lived in exile, mostly the Lekra refugees. Virtually all of them attacked Soeharto's new regime, directly and explicitly, even harshly, almost without nuance. An example of this directness is A. Kohar Ibrahim's "You Appear":

You appear to be free
in your conniving and stupidity.
But no!
You conceal yourself behind Duplicity!

You appear to be strong
in your arrogance and pride.
But no! You rule from a palace built on millions of lives!

You appear to be pious
But no!
The only things you worship are money and power!

To hell with you. To hell with you.
To hell!

No one would have missed the intent of this image, "You rule from a palace built on millions of lives!" The very same accusation was made by numerous researchers and scholars about the slaughter of 2 million (though some say 500,000) PKI supporters when the New Order first took power.

Perhaps what Goenawan Mohamad said was true, that even poems like this one reeked of scorched slogans. Clear-cut language, diction that reflected opposition, even curses did indeed dominate in the circle of the exiled Lekra poets. Magusig O. Bungai declared his opposition using the imagery of *adat* (customary law) and ethnicity in the poem "Scatter Rice, Salt and Ash": "but do not weep o my villagers / these tribes and this nation will never surrender."

The poem ends with:

the soldiers of this republic have killed, have pillaged
    all the houses in the town

they have banished us, your young hornbills, from the forests
where we were born
do not stifle your traditions, but take heart, children of *Sahawong*
and all the tribes
it's better that we sever heads, respect ourselves,
our homes will not be sold

Years after these events, several of the exiled poets produced work that deeply pondered the meaning of power, exile, and nationhood. Some poets tried to distance themselves from the bitterness of the events that had forced them into exile. Rivai Apin, a prominent exiled poet of the '45 Generation, embraced pacifism. His suffering in war and ideological conflict made him reflect profoundly on the condition of defeat for the many to empower the few. As he wrote in his poem "Going Home on Holiday":

The flowers in the woven bag
are beautiful, so very beautiful—
Say no to war! Eradicate the danger of war!

This desire to end, even "eradicate," the danger of war inspired numerous cultural movements that began to sprout in almost every part of the world, flourishing rapidly in the United States. The appearance of the flower generation was followed by various movements opposing capitalism. In the years that followed, pacifist messages were heard from young artists across the globe: Bob Dylan, Basquiat, John Lennon and others.

In newly independent developing countries, in addition to the constricting traumas of colonialism and war, the new trauma of internal ideological conflicts created suffering and fragmentation in artistic circles. The tragedy of this, confronted by poets such as Kuslan Budiman in the following period, was the involvement of foreign interests who used diplomacy, money and the military to interfere with ideological struggles for power at the local level.

For his doctoral dissertation at the University of Queensland, Wijaya Herlambang researched the division of artists into two major factions whose influence, by the close of this period, had spread to all areas of culture. The Lekra communist poets were on one side, and the Manikebu bearers of liberalism on the other. Although each side accused the other of foreign backing, it was quite obvious that each was heavily controlled, respectively, by the Soviet Union and the United States, the two world powers that were the main actors in the Cold War.

Herlambang clearly depicts how Indonesian artists, writers and poets in this period became propaganda tools of the liberal ideology of the U.S. in its efforts to halt the spread of communist ideology. This movement—at once covered up and supported by leading intellectuals like Soemitro Djojohadikusumo, Mochtar Lubis, Soedjatmoko and Wiratmo Soekito—actually commenced in the mid-1950s, and at the end of the period discussed here stirred up ideas of intellectual freedom and freedom of expression as the antitheses of Sukarno's PKI-supported ideological slogans.

A high point was reached when Wiratmo succeeded in raising major support from well-known young artists for signing the Cultural Manifesto. As Herlambang has shown, eventually these young people were used by the Soeharto-controlled New Order and, with the young poet Goenawan Mohamad in the vanguard, they emerged victorious in the ideological and cultural wars against communist influences, which were then totally eradicated.[19]

The idea of liberty, the ideological basis of liberalism, flowed through the works of poets who became staunch supporters of Manikebu and defenders of the new regime. Among these was Taufiq Ismail, who wrote "Morning, September 2, 1965" (not included in this anthology) in only three short lines:

Love of liberty
Is forbidden love
Today

---

[19] See Wijaya Herlambang, *Kekerasan Budaya Pasca 1965*.

105

While the other distinguished leader, Goenawan Mohamad, did not write verse steeped in ideology (except in reaction to the international communist movement in his well-known poem "International"), he generated numerous essays that were supportive of the idea of "liberty."

In his book *Kesusastraan dan Kekuasaan* (Literature and Power), Goenawan Mohamad explained that his motive for writing and signing the Cultural Manifesto was a desire for freedom of expression for every individual. "The basic motive of the Cultural Manifesto," he wrote, "was an initiative to gain more room for autonomous artistic expression, independent from the political pressures and all the various 'revolutionary' dictates of the 1960s."[20] Poems produced by this camp supported the liberal ideas behind the new regime, or even conspicuously defended its leaders, among others, the generals—heroes now in the new history—who had been "slaughtered" by communist troops bent on achieving a coup d'état.

Taufik Ismail—then a young and prolific poet, and also a signatory of the Cultural Manifesto—immortalized in his long poem "Black October" the events when the seven generals were murdered. And in the poem "Notes on the Year 1965," Taufiq explicitly mentions the artist Usmar Ismail, the intellectuals Sutan Takdir Alisjahbana, H.B. Jassin, Moctar Lubis, et al., and even the pop music group Koes Brothers, whom he defended and saw as victims of political violence by the PKI and Sukarno. This latter poem, composed to coincide with the large parade to celebrate the anniversary of the PKI on May 23, 1965, went beyond innuendo to attack the political and cultural forces then dominant under the protection of President Sukarno.

However, as history has recorded, the battles in the political arena that seeped into Indonesian culture went on so ferociously that they left scars and trauma that persist to this day. These scars reveal to us that at one time in its history, this nation tried to find its identity, and ideas about that identity were the object of conflict between other powers on behalf of the interests of certain groups.

Literature Cheated and Defeated

Some poets in this period tried to keep a distance from all the political and ideological squabbles and maintain an independent and even critical attitude to them. Young poets like Rendra, Umbu Landu Paranggi, Fridolin Ukur, and Trisno Sumardjo wanted to voice other problems—the tragedy and irony of many other issues, not just political ones, but ones that were social, spiritual and so forth.

---

[20] Goenawan Mohamad, *Kesusastraan dan Kekuasaan* [Literature and Power] (Jakarta: Pustaka Firdaus, 1963), 14.

A few other poets such as Rivai Apin and Rusli Marzuki Saria developed a passive, or pacifist, attitude in responding to the conflicted discourse among their fellow writers and colleagues. What is interesting about these few poets outside the political and ideological wars was their tendency to search for new idiomatic forms and linguistic symbols outside the treasure trove of the Malay language, which was the basis of their own language of unity, Bahasa Indonesia.

According to some foreign observers, Bahasa Indonesia shows strong signs of "post-colonial literature." One characteristic, according to Keith Foulcher, is language that possesses a wondrous flexibility, whereby its speakers gain a sort of freedom—an opportunity these speakers would not get in their mother tongues or in the foreign languages they had mastered.[21] Perhaps it is this opportunity that is conveyed in Michael Bodden's term "free indirect discourse," meaning a language praxis that provides the possibility for the narrator to get close to the idiom of the oppressed, but elsewhere to feel a subjective "parental" right to maintain a distance and to pass judgment.[22]

Whether or not we buy into this linguistic theory, Bahasa Indonesia generally was and remains the language of choice for Indonesian writers and poets. Apart from its speakers being spread throughout the territories of the nation, this language of unity also offers a kind of egalitarianism and freedom of expression, particularly when compared to the various regional languages with their rigid structural and paternalistic tendencies, in terms of both grammar and common usage.

Nonetheless, this doesn't mean the regional dialects or the other mother tongues have been completely sidelined. In many cases, these have also become important sources for literary life, "offering something that cannot be provided by Bahasa Indonesia," says Tony Day.[23] Day is referring, here, to the writings of Pramoedya Ananta Toer, who declares, "dialect may be used to reflect wishes and desires that are intuitive and hidden from the writer, so that it can reflect the true spiritual life."[24]

---

[21] Keith Foulcher and Tony Day (eds.), *Sastra Indonesia Modern, Kritik Post-Kolonial* [Modern Indonesian Literature, Post-Colonial Criticism], Revised edition: *Clearing Space*, Trans.: Koesalah Soebagyo Toer (Jakarta: Yayasan Obor Indonesia and KITLV, 2008), 8.

[22] Michael Bodden, "Satuan-Satuan Kecil dan Improvisasi Tak Nyaman Menjelang Akhir Orde Baru" [Satuan-Satuan Kecil and Uncomfortable Improvisations in the Late Night of the New Order] in Foulcher, *Sastra Indonesia Modern*, 359–400.

[23] Tony Day, "Antara Makan dan Buang Air: Bentuk-bentuk Keintiman, Bercinta dan Isolasi dalam Beberapa Cerita Awal Pramoedya Ananta Toer" [Between Eating and Shitting: Figures of Intimacy, Storytelling, and Isolation in Some Early Tales by Pramoedya Ananta Toer) in Foulcher, *Sastra Indonesia Modern*, 265.

[24] Pramoedya Ananta Toer, "Sedjenak Menindjau Kesusateraan Djawa Modern" [A Brief Review of Modern Javanese Literature] in *Star Weekly*, 554, 11/08/1956, 14–15.

Pramoedya's prediction of course came true, and continued to come true for decades, as we can see in a number of poems in this collection. Poets like Aoh Kartahadimadja, Mansur Samin and Motinggo Boesje busily urbanize dialects and transpose local vocabulary to modern, urban literary territory. The term *merenjisi* (sprinkle, spatter on), for example, was used by D. Syamsudin. Aoh has introduced traditional expressions like *kalibumbu* (one's wife's relatives), *rumah-tresek* and *anakberu* (a title of kinship and social function) into his poetry, and the poet Magusig O. Bungai (the pen name of Kusni Sulang) used literary expressions from his Dayak ethnic heritage such as *sahawang* (a self-referential term used by certain southern Dayak groups) or *penyang* (talisman, charm) to convey his sharp criticism of the powers-that-be.

Besides using local idioms, several poets created phonetically experimental hybrid words that they hoped would convey meaning through sound. These words include Mansur Samin's "desatinggal" and Motinggo Boesje's "kauterminakah," "takterbela" and "dukapenyair."

No one has as yet attempted to clarify whether, in the context of life in this period, poets were using these linguistic strategies in order to deal with a new reality, to avoid language politicization, or simply to be innovative. But these aesthetic efforts cannot obscure the mainstream reality of Indonesian literature in this period. Literature had to accept its defeat, at least as a cultural force capable of confronting political forces equipped with financing, bureaucracy and even weapons.

Literature's fragility—its inability to effectively confront repression and political insinuations—is very conspicuous in themes that are increasingly opaque or disoriented, and in missing points of reference, including aesthetic ones, so that poems appear increasingly like prose, thus losing nuance, poetic ambiguity and even the romantic attitudes realized in lyricism. These symptoms have persisted in poetry, right up to the publication of this book.

Home from Vacation

Rivai Apin

1950

The plane's engines roar,
Mobilize our brothers, mobilize our friends!
Inside the airplane, a child clutches his mother—
where has the sun gone?
For several weeks we stopped in Soochi:
sunbathing on the beach, walking in the gardens.
The trees and greenery were so refreshing,
the land so hilly, and the waters so blue—
for several weeks we rested at Soochi.

Rankled by his weariness and just half awake,
the young boy squirmed and whined.
His mother kissed his cheek,
stroked his hair lovingly, fixed his position on her lap.

The flowers in the woven bag
are beautiful, so very beautiful—
Say no to war! Eradicate the danger of war!

+

This network of love and color,
how very beautiful it is.
Love and color, movement and composition
within a single unitary network.

The Country Awakens

Walujati

1950p

I

As from a white blossom, fragrance floats over seas and leaves of green.
Its perfume wafts, carried by the passing wind,
drifting down to settle in an azure ocean,
then fading out on a chain of islands—

They look patient-and-calm in the froth-waves of time
that come and go, each epoch arriving full
of weather-and-atmosphere shifts; ever calm,
letting the changing eras press upon their souls.

Like on the horizon, the mountain shaded blue
is ever quiet-and-peaceful, letting the rain
and wind torment its slopes; but in time
it will break-and-erupt, and finally spew

fire and hot rocks that will burn the world,
just as these islands in a chain
will certainly some day roar and hurl
the cursed stones and flames of stress and strain...

II

Friend, in the thickening-black-smoke and
the heat of the air pressing in from all sides,
the bewildered people falter, searching for a hold—
something strong and sturdy to brace their lives.

Like people who would navigate
the steps leading them towards their aim,
but worry: will their center-foundation be lost-and-misplaced,
swallowed by the crashing waves of change?

Ah, as a lost wanderer in a great forest
walking hopelessly
suddenly arrives at a deep, blackening chasm and
cannot return because the dark night has
fallen,

so the people walk, carried by another's flow and intention,
confused-and-wary, in an unknown direction,
until they arrive at a chasm of difference in ideology-and-thought,
but cannot trace their steps back to the start.

III

Don't, don't you regret the loss of the old ways,
for centuries used by the people of our land,
until they grew black-hard roots, creeping wide
under the surface of the earth; until, like a cage

they confined the fertile earth surrounding
the tree trunks standing firm and enduring
the torment of eras and decades, decorating
the garden of Eastern civilization, the land where we are living.

You cry for these beautiful trees,
felled by the turbulent hurricane
of millions of human beings
who now want to establish a garden

of civilization that is young and new—look
at the toppled tree trunks:
they seem strong, but inside they are already empty,
old-stiff-and-dead, stripped of dignity.

Don't, don't you regret the loss of your old ways.
The garden we are building will be worth more praise.

IV

Every morning, the red rays rise in the West
dawn sky, I see jasmine plants
with dull green leaves, bereft
of their fragrant flowers, with white strewn about.

It seems a strong wind tormented their gentle stalks,
and they were powerless, let-go-and-dropped

111

their flowers and buds becoming fragrant-white
corpses scattered across the dirt...

And I remember all the souls
young-and-small, not yet full-grown,
who fell, letting out their final gasps.
My tears fall too, I cannot hold them back.

V

Even we realize, O Mother, wailing on the grave
of your only son, who has fallen in gunpowder smoke's midst,
with the sound of bullets that kept whistling past,
his body collapsed upon earth already red and stained—

Even we realize your sacrifice is more formidable,
the torment of your spirit more terrible
than your child's sacrifice to the Nation, because he went willing.
Carried away by Death, he was still smiling,

like someone who boards a ship bound for a far
and foreign land, with a shining expression,
face full of hope, while those who stay behind at the station
are crying-sad, feeling an emptiness in their hearts...

VI

Don't, my people, don't you blame the acts and deeds
of those above you, prudent-and-knowing-best
leading you and your country towards
its heart's desire, for centuries cherished in every chest.

Bring down your arm, outstretched to fight.
Lower your voice, harsh in your insolent mouth,
loosen your fist, clenched so tight.
Soothe the storm of anger in your resentful heart.

Only now do we sense that no current of liberty,
no matter how strong, will ever bring with it

even one benefit, if there is no authority
clever enough to channel it.

Strong currents follow dikes,
dug by people with ability-and-care,
through dry fields waiting for
water to come and bring them life.

Listen—as the joyful play together, the gamelan peals,
it won't be long now, people of my nation,
look at the oceans of golden rice in your fields.
That, my people, is your country's harvest celebration...

> VII

Thus this old stiff tree, half dead, confined
for years in a forest of unfamiliar plants,
surrounded by claustrophobic vines,
is alive again; its young leaves have come back.

How magnificently it stands,
a dense and lush crown of leaves on its branches.
I stand humble below it
and a prayer passes through my heart:

"Lord, protect the fruit of my people's struggle and
toil, protect this triumph, hard-won by the blood of thousands."

On the horizon the sky is slowly going dim.
I shudder to see the Sun shrouded by mist.
Will the rain come to revive this Tree of mine,
or will a lightning bolt descend and bring its demise?

I stand humble
and prayers pass through my heart...

Portrait of a Communist

S. Anantaguna

1950-1965p

Is any grief greater than ours?
A comrade dies, blood thick on his cheek,
but fond memories remain.
Is any weeping worse than ours?
The body tired, breath held in the chest,
but work and our desires drive us into the future.
When we think when we feel when we are aware,
when we have been frightened but we still have friends,
when defeat is a calamity and victory still a hope,
we are filled with the desire to sing,
and what can we do but live?
There is a pride greater than this
when the leaves whisper in the morning about a communist
so gentle so kind the new day sighs.
Is any love greater than our love—
the flag of comradeship flies high as we work.

Too Many

S. Anantaguna

1950-1965p

Too many stories
and too little time to write history
I see the feet of the proletariat
walking back and forth on the docks
carrying tens of kilos
on their backs
which make millions
for foreign nations and companies
unknown to them

I have seen too much
and have too little paper to record it all
peasants serving the revolution
in their rice fields
I cannot count
how many truckloads of grain
have passed through their hands
rice for politicians, generals, intellectuals
produced by their sweat

Too many stories
and too few truths in the history books
the heroism of the proletariat
wounded soldiers
dying on dark nights
how many reams of paper have been wasted
how many million forged receipts
money for corrupt officials who are called "heroes"

I have heard too much about girls selling themselves
they are the children of farmers and they are hungry
they sweat to pay their taxes
they have paid for our freedom and the revolution
by serving compradors and bureaucrats
too many tramps
and too many rich people

My beloved, don't think I am cursing our nation
thousands of drums of ink have flowed
from phony trembling aesthetes
humanism
is afraid of the end of imperialism
hypocritical scholars tell lies in our universities
I am one with the masses
who are fighting for a truly independent Indonesia!

Afro Asia in Tokyo

Rivai Apin

1950s

Tokyo in spring
Sakura in bloom
Hanako san, Minorisan greet us: *irassai, irassai* (welcome, welcome)
Be patient, be patient...
The hint of a smile is only a poetic couplet

Tokyo in spring
Sakura in bloom
Tolen, friend from Cameroon, *irassai*...
Muamba from the Congo, come on...
Nomasan and Li Mang, Zulfia and from Mongolia
Damba
Cherry blossoms of friendship jasmine of peace
We are all from Asia and Africa
    flowers blooming...
Truly, truly!
The power of unity is victory

Tokyo in spring
Sakura blooming, Sakura scattered
Muamba-san, Hadad-san invite us: *irassai, irassai*...
Good! Good!
Working for the struggle is a lifelong poem.

From Two Unfinished Worlds

Rivai Apin

1950s

The morning I heard the news
I went out into the street
Peddlers and people going to work moved aside
Fast-moving vehicles loaded with soldiers,
      and rock-solid tanks
There were men on patrol, in pairs and bearing arms
There was open space between them, and yet there was a substance!
Everything stiff and rigid:
people, objects, the air, but it all displayed
value

I went to see friends, to talk, and what was said distilled into darkness.
The news: Yogya has fallen, Maguwo airfield... Soekarno captured
Hatta, Sjahrir...
We kept on talking, or went from one friend to another, and then another...
We talked, weighed and considered the options
Everything coming out of, and spoken for the sake of, that one repeated word

As night fell I made my way home, heavy with news and possibilities,
and waiting for me there at home was my uncompleted self:
the opened books, still unread, and others I had yet to finish
But for this I left behind Father and Elder Brother
And only then remembered, I'd only eaten once that day
—where the cooking pot is always open—and I set about the work of finishing
my self
in the grave dug out of the darkness
by the lamplight in my room

But that night boots kicked on the thick walls of darkness
And when they had gone there came the sound of a woman wailing,
his wife maybe, or his mother
I didn't need anyone to tell me that someone had been taken
I could only press my head against the table,
overcome by that word as yet ungrounded, but still pursuing me,
here in my unfinished worlds

On the Eve of Idul Fitri

Sitor Situmorang

1950s

Moonrise
over tombstones.

Encounter

Harijadi S. Hartowardojo

1951

I

You may laugh, laugh very hard
When the dawn light falls through the cracks in the tent, I'll follow
Echoing-up-from-the-valley pushing away again
Come home! The lost child's come home!
Her love calls the heart—the heart of a Human—
She walks on barbed wire
Tips of the spears beneath are ready
to drink blood. But her blood has long been frozen
None of it flows
Also in the coffee stall
the bottles do not explode when they are opened
And crazy laughter, drunks can lie in the spaces between the tables.

She has returned, the missing child
Heaven is not the place for her; she crosses over to the world
stepping on the earth of her convictions
Rice grows profusely
almost yellow
She can believe:
She fertilized fertile rice
She is able to eat the fruit
And in the sea?
The net slowly descends to gather fish.

Yes, you may laugh very hard
Then be quiet. Save your tears.
Clench your teeth, hold your stirrups.
She will also laugh
Laugh long and contentedly
The missing child has come home.

II

Begin the first page open the curtain
My girl comes home to pick coconuts
But the fruit is gone, eaten by squirrels

Tears!
Tears!

Leaning on my chest she counts the heartbeats
My fingers count the waves of her hair
We search for a bay in which to moor
This long night with a good moon

(My sister, are you reading this?
Or are you burning this manuscript?
Look at the holes in Christ's hands
and tell of the love in His eyes or return to history:
drink my water
All your life you will be free from thirst)

We surrender to love
Love that convinces the father to whip the child
And the mother to spoil her

Ooooooooo! My rations
Father's whip after returning from the grape fields
Mother's tears after returning from the wheat fields
I meet my girl here
Girl from the headwaters, descending to the estuary

In her I find hope
I am carried across lifted by her lips
Pearls swimming within them

III

Nanda arrives at the door, mother.
Accept this girl's hopes:
People go home because their hearts
are heavy.
Coral can crumble
The world will end
But the heart?

Call doubts a thousand times
—High temperature?
God will speak just once
—Proceed!

IV

Old bridges collapse one by one
along with the silenced cannons
Our feet stamp!
Our feet stamp!
La personnalité en marcher.

A corpse sprawled beneath the pole
Where a flag waves very high
Blown by strong wind
Blowing. Flapping fluttering.
Lines of poles
Flags will run out of flutters
There is no sedan! There is none!?

The engine changes gears
Pages and pages of newspapers fall
Oil is pumped channeled
Oil is collected filtered separated

In and out of the ships in the harbor
Humans disembark
Humans!
Humans!

Then if November comes
The straits of Makassar will be calm again
Let the moon hide peacefully
The tide will not rise

Gambang Semarang

M.D. Asien

1951

swaying, plucking four strings
accompanying voices, down-home style
guitar strumming
ukulele picking
accursed weary intoxicated.

*

ice cream melts, staining the tablecloth
cooked vegetables slightly spoiled
clean money slow market
sunken eyes beg for dimes.

when
dust and urine mix together
underarm sweat drips and flows
this song
. . . leaves bitterness, tartness and harshness
making a lilting song
in a tilting hut!

Jakarta at Twilight

Toto Sudarto Bachtiar

1951

Daily survival, daily life
Among the grime-skinned coolies and women
Bathing naked in my favorite river in my beloved city
Automobile horns and tram bells compete
The air presses down hard on the long, winding street
Buildings and people's heads blur in the twilight
The setting sun's afterglow brightens the western sky
Oh, my beloved city
In the midst of your bustle and suffering
Press me deeply into your heart's center

I am like a dream, a white moon in a sea of clouds
Sources that are completely concealed
Forever covered by an ashen earth
With hands and words restricting the freedom to breathe
Waiting for time to take on death

Beyond the ordinary, I know nothing at all
Melancholic songs that speak of sadness
Wait for the time of rest to be broken at dawn's door
And the everlasting dreams of mankind

Horns and bells sound in turn
In daily survival and daily life
Among the coolies and the woman
Now climbing back up the bank of my favorite river

Swimming children laugh innocently
In the shadow of the stiff palace
Twilight's gleam dissipates and is gone
In the quick lyrising darkness of night

Sources that are completely concealed
Forever covered by an ashen earth
With hands and words restricting the freedom to breathe
Oh, beloved city, after twilight
The city where I live and where my heart longs

Edge of the Rice Paddy

Trisno Sumardjo
1951

When we cross a deserted road
on which tired bamboo stalks limply stand
like nature's paper lanterns, they extend their hands.
While taking a rest we listen to
cows that moo behind the bamboo.

In the shadow of rustling leaves
the heart recites pleasing words of wisdom.
How fortunate to work in this place
surrounded by farmers' grace,
and in green fields happiness can be found,
the first man at the beginning of time.

Try to linger by the side of a ditch.
Rustling whisper of water through the field,
silver fluorescence, a lacey brilliance
which only now pours forth light.
Green rice stalks line up in rows, measuring out reflections
in a mirror flooded in radiance.

I Am a Grain of Sand

Muh. Rustandi Kartakusuma

1951p

I am a grain of sand
on a beach that runs
between the mangroves
and the sacred estuary.

Why did you panic
try to stop the clock
close the post office
when the bomb exploded?

Why did you shiver and shake
curse endlessly?
The sea spreads far
beyond this tiny drop.

The world, life and my self
are three grains of sand
on an endless beach.

If You Knew

Aoh Kartahadimadja

1952

If you knew
that our villages have been destroyed,
fierce winds have shattered the pillars of our houses,
Mount Sinabung has become silent,
our ancestors have left their fields and the mountains,
the rivers run faster than ever before
in the inner recesses of the heart,
kalimbubu[1] are no longer respected
but are cursed in the ancestral house,
no one beats the drums,
hits the gongs,
blows the flutes—
then you would rise up and become true *anakberu*.[2]
You would straighten the pillars and rebuild the walls.
Do not talk of those who destroy our customs,
bring confusion to our villages.
We must not waste the legacy that has been given to us.
The rivers can be channeled
to run clear
in the inner recesses of the heart.

---

[1] In Karo Batak society (North Sumatra), the bride's family, *kalimbubu*, are highly respected by the bridegroom's family, to whom they are a source of blessing. *Kalimbubu* may adjudicate quarrels and give orders to their matrimonial kinsfolk.

[2] The bridegroom's family, *anakberu*, are responsible for carrying out traditional rituals in a proper manner, providing feasts and administering family property.

What the Star Says out at Sea

Iwan Simatupang

1952

A story for Bayu Suseno, son of Bu Tono

On a distant island
there is a pirate
ruler of a strait
no limit no border
no name no mention

He is a master without an audience
from a region that has nothing
where silence and commotion
boast in a story
no beginning no end

Who is near who is close
seven times lying low bailing out
who forgets who neglects
captain, nutmeg and widows
struck by a twister
or a whirlwind

He is the commander of a troop
no speech no country
he is the ally of all ghosts
king of storms caretaker of rainbows

He comes from the mountains
from the peak always covered in mist
  —where ravines, cliffs and hills
tell stories all day in sprawling solitude
about shadows chasing beams of light
about haze clutching the weather

  —where a waterfall from high
throws itself in one gasp

drop by drop
no weariness searching for the stopping point

    —where the melancholy bulbul calls
the gibbon, lonely longingly throughout the day
and the sea breeze sounds
in a heaven without nymphs

Ah, he left all of this
when one day
a beachcomber at his door
brought news:
"Your mother will not come home again, my friend,
she has been taken away by people
who came and robbed the fishermen's market
and took all the girls and widows
in a sailing ship with a black flag
with the image of a skull."

Since then—
he has traversed
steep roads leading to beaches
that until now he had only seen
from a steep cliff plunging
embracing the last rays
of the setting sun
    —that he has all this time not dared to travel
afraid to meet the demons
from his mother's tales

Since then—
he left the gray peak
and traveled the open sea
all the straits he has crossed
all the bays he has entered

all the captains he has asked
all the fishermen he has greeted
no news
no mother

Since then—
he decided
to become a perpetual seeker
on a search with no discovery
in a world with no sun
       —to become one who passes in silence
from a road with no end
in a desert with no solitude

Since then—
he decided
to receive the inheritance from
his stepfather whom he does not know
who took his mother from the beach
in a sailing ship with a black flag
with the image of a skull

On a distant island
there is a pirate
son of a craftsman in the hills
seeker of silence in a commotion
seeker of commotion in silence

Day at MA

P. Sengodjo
1952

Draw this intersecting line—
it is called a transversal, isn't it?—
and add a name
the dot smells of tuberose
there is a polite fly on the horizontal plane
singing is forbidden
as is the slightest hope

can you see this eye?
waiting and waving
you met it the other night
a stylish full circle
this is the centre: P
and this is the apothem: a

the arc: b
yes, yes, we can draw another line
(remember, the rice was not very nice!)
(have you forgotten?)
(did you want to bring another friend? that's OK)
it was a new shop!

where were lis, and karto?
did they get lost along the way?
forgive me, friend,
the problem has not yet been solved
and there is no rational answer.

Song of the Sea and the Mountain

Sobron Aidit

1952

Although I, this child of the sea, am now far from you
    and have learned how to live in the mountains
    this does not mean we will not meet again;
    so be not sad, cast off your contemplative mood.

The forest—pines and bamboo
grows thick deep in the interior
waves and coral and boats
we must take control of life wherever we are.

However great my love for the sea
this child of the sea can be no stranger to the forest
a person must be able to plant seeds of resistance anywhere.

We can not be tied to the sea or the mountain
    just because it is is where we were born and raised
    it is best to divide up our locations
    for with that victory will come.

My Days

Sobron Aidit

1952

Every day, but not out of routine
from the window in my room
I gaze into the distance
to see the first bus pass
at six in the morning.
I get ready to to leave
to engage in thousands of activities
matters of the stomach, a search for food
correspondence
telephone calls, answering questions
and then, too, matters of the heart
even though I'm getting on in years.

To and fro
from one office to another
on the metro, on buses and trolley cars
and even on foot
amid throngs of tourists
where hustlers in ties
and pickpockets with eagle eyes
dine on easy prey
in their search for food
as I, in my own way
search for life.

Colder and colder
winter bites the skin
pierces the bones, slicing deeply
but even if it's tens of degrees below zero
I still need money
for food, though not always just for me
    forgive me for saying, but I, too, contribute.

I may be poor but it brings true happiness to give
 and isn't it the case that the ones who most often give
 are the poor themselves; from one poor person to another
 in an extraordinary demonstration of solidarity.

Towards morning
when I have just taken off my overcoat
in front of the mirror
the final bus passes
at twelve midnight
with the last hour of the day counted
a new day will soon begin
to reveal the life that is to come
and so on and so forth
it goes
from one day to the next
with no diminishment of activity
but of money to be sure
for we do not lack debt
such is my life, my days
in a foreign land
where I've never felt foreign.

Girl Playing Piano

Mahbub Junaidi

1952p

Memory in High School 1–2 auditorium

Moonlight in the gray sky shimmering
The girl absorbed in her playing
Outside, the orange myrtle tree rustles, singing
The girl's rhythm quickening

The clear sounds return
I sit, reflecting
Feeling my heart wanting to pour forth
How pleasant is the fading night

Her fingers run up and down
Playing a rhythm that fires the soul
Whisking me away

Faintly heard, lost in the night
The girl stores away a smile on her lips
Above, the stars twinkle in gratitude
Reluctantly, I close the curtain

Adorer that I am
Of her playing...

Death of a Farmer

Agam Wispi

1953

for L. Darman Tambunan

1.

outside the overseer's compound
a farmer falls to the ground
because of land
because of land

in the farmers' union office
the hungry are angry
because of blood
because of blood

land and blood
put history in motion
from which a flame erupts
from which true peace does come

2.

the farmer collapses
falls to the ground
with one bullet
in his head

in torture's embrace
memory flees
but torture of a corpse
is futile

his memory flies to his younger days
and to his son who became a soldier
—who is it that feeds them?—
when weeding the paddy, my wife
takes out her anger on the stems
take pity on them
take pity on them

these friends of ours
now gloomy
dying
and black
as night

3.

they say it is they
who hold the power
but in killing the people
must abdicate their throne

4.

the pregnant paddy
withstands the wind
from a hut comes
the soft sound of a flute

breathe in the life
the pregnant paddy
sows with the wind

dear god, a woman dares to walk naked
in sicanggang, yes, in sicanggang
where hoes and paddy were destroyed

prisoners in their cells
and babies in their carriers
also know the meaning of torture

they say it is they
who wield power

---

[1] sicanggang or secanggang= is a town in North Sumatra.

but if they prey on their people
they must abdicate their throne
before being forced to

when the tractor comes
to destroy the huts
we'll break down every door
we'll break down every door.

Rose Pink in Jasmine

Iwan Simatupang

1953

For Sitor Situmorang

Blood drips
From a heart onto jasmine
Drip drip

Jasmine grows
Where the sea and the desert kiss
Distant distant

    Blood congeals
    Jasmine wilts
    Boundaries grieve

There is a thrush on the cactus
There is a cactus in the heart
There is a twitter with thorns

Limestone Quarryman

Kirdjomuljo

1953

He sings to the rhythm
of falling rocks
the rocks fall, his heart falls
and the fields crack open
the birds fly low
bearing the weight of the sky
the day is heavy
the wind clings to their wings
the fog burns in all directions.

Is he suffering
enduring the heat
or fighting the hard rocks?
He sings as loudly as his pain
and his reality:
my blood is poisoned
my bones break
—hula hulee hula ho oo
hula hulee hula ho oo.

He releases his burden
it comes and goes
blown about by the pain in his throat
the green lime in his eyes
the black dust on his forehead
his weary white sweat
as the morning progresses
his songs lengthen
his laughter soars like the wind.

When he suddenly stops singing
he looks at me
and smiles, a country smile.
He asks me in a voice as heavy as the mountains
"Are you surprised to see me?
I was born from this limestone

I have four children, none as dark as me
their eyes are like mine
their nose like their mother's."
His laughter rides on the wind.

"I honor you, Father,
your whole life in the quarry
your skin as black as limestone
your eyes burning from the dust
your love greater than other men's
your love as hard as the stars
I have never seen such love."

"My love is my life
but don't just sit there watching me
the ocean is to the north
the beach is to the south.
If I did not keep my promises
to myself and my home
I would not be a limestone quarryman."

"My greetings, sir
you can see me
you will feel the hidden quivering
in my heart
in all our hearts
—hula hulee hula ho oo
hula hulee hula ho oo
hidden in the black night
hidden in the distant blue sea."

Regret

Ali Hasjmy

1954p

My morning has gone,
my youth has faded,
now afternoon shadows come—
the tree has grown old.

I wasted the morning,
dawdled during the day.
Life offers me little joy—
I know nothing, own less.

Why should I regret?
It is too late to be of use.
Regret only opens old wounds.

I beg the young,
join your comrades in the morning.
Head out to serve society!

Shepherd Boy

Mohammad Yamin

1954p

Whose heart would not brighten
To see a child out in the field
Bareheaded and with no shirt on his back
Yet able to sing a sweet song.

Such is the lot of the shepherd boy
Resting in the shade of a tree
He takes his charge from its pen in the morning
Does not return home until after twilight.

From the near distance comes the sound
I hear the music of a wooden flute
A song of nature in all its beauty.

Dear shepherd, in that green ocean
Listen to your reed whistle, lead your buffalo
I wish only to go with you.

Ballad of the Crucifixion

Rendra

1955

Jesus walks to Golgotha
bearing a cross of wood:
a lamb with a pure white fleece.

There are no roses on the path
no palm branches
a white lamb carrying pain and suffering
bowed with the weight of his beloved task
grounded in acceptance.

The sun bleeds
his wounds drip
and our father Abraham
kneels, his two hands raised to the Father:
"Our Father in heaven
the pure white lamb has been slaughtered
on Your holy altar.
Our Father in heaven
send us a rainbow!"

He walks to Golgotha
his sacred heart is beautiful
chewing one sin after another
one bitter mouthful after another.

There are no cloaks spread on his path
his mother weeps, her hair covered in dust
the women of Jerusalem weep.

"Women!
why do you weep for me
and not for yourselves?"

The dry road is watered
by his body's red rose water

a broken road of tormented souls
and the slaughter continues
the stakes are our sins.

He will drink blood from his own side
wine in a golden chalice
and as he draws his last breath he will shout:
"Father, it is finished!"

The Prodigal Son

Sitor Situmorang

1955

In the fiery heat of midday
A speck, a boat, appears in the bay
The anxious mother runs to the shore
To greet the son she's long waited for

In time the speck becomes a boat
The mother's tears, in pools, float
So many years abroad, yet safe from harm
The son delivered to his mother's arms

In the room's center sits the father
Posed as if he wonders what's the bother
The son fidgets at his mother's side
Feelings are something a man must hide

The son is told to sit and speak
A chicken's dressed, the rice readied to eat
The whole village wants to know
Is he married, has he kids to show?

The prodigal son is now back home
In a village where he's become unknown
How many harvests have passed?
What has happened since they saw him last?

The whole of the village wants to know
Is he married, are there kids to show?
The prodigal son has little to say
All the questions he holds at bay

After the meal and twilight's fall
His mother begs him to recount all
He stares at the questions her eyes hold
But how can he explain Europe's cold?

Though memories rise, the son sits still—
The seasons, the towns, Europe's chill
The mother silent, not from fear
She has no regrets now, only cheer

Late at night the mother quits her chores
The father, long before, has begun to snore
On the sandy shore, waves hiss and foam
Knowing the prodigal son has not come home

The Beggar Girl

Toto Sudarto Bachtiar

1955

Little girl with a begging bowl, each time we meet
Your smile is too persistent to know sorrow
Look at me, at the rose-red moon
My city vanishes, soulless

I want to go with you, beggar girl
To your home beneath the bridge where shapes dissolve
In a life of brilliant fantasy
Radiant in the illusion of cheer

Your world, higher than the cathedral's spire
Appears and fades in the dirty water you know so well
Your soul is pure, too pure
To share my sorrow

If you die, little girl with the begging bowl
The moon above will have no owner
And my city, yes, my city
Will be without a symbol

The Train

Basuki Gunawan

1955p

Packed with evacuees, the train speeds on
spewing its poison with ear-splitting shrieks
memories of the past billow freely in its wake
rising high in the sky, even touching the void

the train speeds on, reaching for tomorrow
nudging at ravines and desert wastelands
where god was once enthroned in majesty

the train is competing in a fight against death
the engineer's heart is blazing with fire

the rush of the train shatters the silence

the hearse falls still in the roar of its flames

Flower

Sitor Situmorang

1955s

The flower on a stone
Is seared by silence

Transcending the senses
It awaits

The flower on a stone
Is seared by silence

Between Thermopylae and Stalingrad

Klara Akustia

1956

We march in tales of old
people of Sparta
who exchanged their lives
for the fragrance of prayers.

Once it was the highest value
to reject life, worship death.

We march in tales of today:
people who know Stalingrad
ready to exchange their lives
for the harvest of their labor.

For once let's change the values:
reject death, celebrate life.

A Living Skeleton

M.A. Iskandar

1956

His friends regarded him
as a kind man

He was a living skeleton
walking along the world's byways
he never smiled as he contemplated
the greatness of nature

Raindrops ran down
his sad body
he shrank
inside his head

He wanted to walk
with his beautiful desires
people considered him yesterday's beggar
a man with no spirit
his heart asked how
he could live in such poverty
such constant difficulty

In the early morning mist
he walked with his head bowed
staring at the earth
wet with last night's rain
he accepted everything
his will could not control
his limited freedom
where he could walk
where he slept
he knew this was his world
his inner calling
his realm of virtue
he was last night's beggar
and he knew
that his life was holy
and would never change

Martapura River

Hidjaz Yamani

1957

The dark brown Martapura River
whispers as it passes the *lanting-lanting*,[1]
twisting its way through Banjarmasin, my town,
past the new buildings on its banks.

The river carries life's challenges,
a never-ending stream of humanity.
And there are weary people here
sleeping by the long bridge,
their throats parched with thirst
as they dream of a secure home.

The *dukuh-dukuh*[2] paddle past,
breasts bobbing under black blouses.
Their faces are covered with silk
but their eyes are wild.

Hundreds of objects disturb the water at my feet.
The bright sunlight burns my eyes.
I hold these sights fondly in my heart
—I want to wander in the market,
bargain with the stall-holders,
share in their generosity.

---

[1] Houses on stilts, built over the river, "water village."

[2] Women in small canoes who sell fish and vegetables.

March to Socialism

Klara Akustia

1957p

We the people of today
ragged and filthy condemned by history
slave times, feudal times
and times of capitalist exploitation
which strive to bury once more
man's victory over beast
with an epidemic of private ownership

Heaven is called
hell is called
war is called
angels and devils
become tools to uphold desires

We the people of today
ragged and filthy condemned by history
stretch to catch the dawn
of a world belonging to all
which blooms in red

And we call upon heaven
but toss out hell
worship peace
and punish war
befriend angels
devil's foe
cleanse ourselves of
the ulcerous morass of past centuries

And in cleansing ourselves
we create a new atmosphere
for people who grasp the dawn
for people who want things to be
    right
for people, angels and fairies.

We the people of today
pure, forged by history
people who never surrender
people in control of nature
open the door to a world of dawn's light
knocking on the hearts of
    mankind because it is
     right

Homeland

Ramadhan K.H.

1958p

1.

On the sands among the hills of pine
the sound of the flute is sweet,
echoing off two mountains' feet:
Burangran and Tangkubanprahu,
emeralds in the tips of leaves,
emeralds in the falling mist.
The stairway winding through red earth
is familiar to the young women of these hills
who sing of the potatoes they've harvested
and don red *kebaya* for the puppet show.
Emeralds in the tips of leaves,
emeralds in the young woman's heart.

2.

Fragrance is the honey
of the red rose,
and the sun that waits within.
The road winds
through limestone hills
between Bandung and Cianjur
and the red rose
is felled once more,
its petals scattered
on barren hearts.
And the winding road
vanishes once more,
leaving a memory to course
through the blood in one's veins.

---

[1] kebaya= Traditional blouse made of lacy material

3.

Tanjung flowers lie scattered
on the darkened, ashy path;
broken hearts in the graveyard
are scourged by the Eastern Star.
—Are you off, young man?
—Yes, I am.
—Where are you going?
—I don't know. I just follow the beaten track.
—Won't you stop for a rest?
—Yes, good woman, I will.
            Rest and shed my tears.
The scattered *tanjung* flowers
are found by a young girl in song.
In the morning Mount Gede waits,
just as the moon and stars fade,
leaving the child in the graveyard
alone with his saddened heart.
Scattered *tanjung* flowers
soon wilt on garland strings.

4.

In the rainy season
the paths on Gede and Pangrango
rise upward into blue.
Young women greet the morning
quivering on tea leaves
while others, at the rest stop, wait.
Against the southern wind
the paths on Gede and Pangrango
rise upward into blue.
Young men greet the day
with sweet potatoes on their backs,
while others, with daggers, wait.
And as the poet waits for the stranger's knife,
the paths on Gede and Pangrango
rise upward into blue.

5.

Green is my land,
the green of Tago
beneath the gaze of rolling hills.
The red rose
is torn at from all directions;
sounds from the wooden zither
are the voice of a person in song.
Green is my land,
the green of Tago
beneath the gaze of rolling hills.
And the young woman alone
is set upon from all directions;
the pleasant song that she once sang
is now a song of woe.
Green is my land,
the green of Tago
beneath the gaze of rolling hills.

6.

The flute and pantun couplets
weep for the suffering of Priangan.
A red sash, as red as blood,
flows down the Cikapundung.
Bandung, built on the base of an ancient lake,
now runs up surrounding hills.
Solitary flutes dot the city's edge,
crying for daggers lost in wells,
for jasmine flowers, innocence
and lovers now fallen in battle.
The suffering of Bandung, on the lake bed,
rises to the surface.

---

[1] pantun= traditional four line verse form with a-b-a-b rhyme pattern.

7.
The curved horizon
I cross in an arc;
I am, it seems,
a wanderer.
The flute and pantun pull me home
down the Citarum
in the dark of night.
And I return
to the original source,
to Mother.
I return
to the original embrace
with more years upon me!

Song of Loving

Ramadhan K.H.

1958p

1.

In Cikajang, mountains
and a silent valley rend the heart,
the medals on a hero's chest,
above the dagger—silence.
Bouquets in the graveyard for a lover
distant, forever more.
In Cikajang, a cage
holding footsteps back,
quails flying free through the sky,
and in the village candles die,
in dawn's light the moon is silver
and fear makes one's heart shake.
In Cikajang only the birds
are free to fly away,
children born into the world
are raised among refugees
as stillness envelops Priangan,
a land of deathly silence.

2.

Young lovers kiss the night away
in the heat of Priangan soil.
Dawn adds to age
the day's new round of work,
stifling the heart's complaint.
Young lovers sprawling among the shrubs
repeat their fear of death
as insects burrow into their nests.
Wondering whether the morning moon
will mean a final embrace,
finding certainty only in hope and hoping.
Young lovers kiss the night away
in the cold of the southern coast.

3.

This world dissolves in nature's green
and the war disappears
above the zither's strings.
The source of all suffering
is found in each embrace.
This world dissolves in nature's green
and the war disappears
above the women's broken hearts.
The source of all pain,
repository of tears and sobs.

4.

Frangipani blooms white in twilight,
a black moth falls into the widow's lap,
a scarlet tinge in the western sky
spreads across the coast.
"Look at the Priangan plain, my love."
With Father hemmed in from all sides,
Mother runs from one place to another
in futile search for a place to hide.
"Look at the Priangan plain, my love."
But the young woman cannot speak;
her lover has fallen, his grave is unknown
and she is left with fumbling hands
to braid a garland of memories.

5.

The girl who sings in the banana grove
is unaware of the sweetness of the fruit.
My God!
The girl who sings beneath the sun
is aware only of its heat.
My God!

6.
The deer
becomes the prey
in fields
of silence.
(The dark night
trembles.)
The deer
demands a sacrifice,
a sign
of masculinity.
(The silver moon
fades.)

7.
I close the doors and windows tightly
not to know the suffering
that wind and daylight bring.
But black flowers bloom, and darkened clouds
dart like knives from the zither's strings.
Counting one's loves upon one's fingers
in a protracted season
but suffering the tales
of countless lovers
that accumulate through the year.
Tears and sorrow cluster on eyelids,
if not for myself,
then for you, my love.

Fire

Ramadhan K.H.
1958p

1.

My love!
Your dark brown eyes are rich
as rich as Cianjur soil
but my love—
what makes the rain fall
from your black lashes
is your lovely hands
entwined in honeyed gauze with mine.
And my love—
as the silver moon becomes a blazing ember
you and I
must turn the soil once more
and let the rain fall from our eyes.
My love!
There is nothing else
just you and I.

2.

A jasmine garland of memories
is wound 'round your slender neck
but only the moon shows flattery
as yesterday and today lie in dissolution.
And with the sinking of the sun
the night is left alone
a victim waiting in silence
for the morning.
Night's departure
means only evacuation
a stab wound in your most vulnerable spot.
Dear girl!
Would you wish for a different tale?
Then wait not for the coming rains.
Dear girl!
Would you wish for a change of color?
First there must be fire.

3.
The poet
is the first log
on the pyre.
The poet
is the ashes
at the rubble's base.
Dear girl!
To fret
is to torture yourself!
Dear girl!
Fear is only
for cowards!

4.
Whosoever loves his children
will not sell
even a handful of land.
Whosoever loves the land
will not forget
his mother now gone.
Whosoever thinks of tomorrow
will now prepare
to attack.

5.
A dagger forged by the goddess of Cikundul
is cleansed by the dew of the morning moon.
Drink but one drop of Sangkuriang's blood
and join the three rivers on the holy day.
A dagger forged by the goddess of Cikundul
is shaped by the morning moon.
If you do not find what you are looking for
turn over the seven volcanoes.

6.

The young girl
fled into hiding
at twilight.
The wounded town stands alone.
There is no branch of happiness
no night bird that rises to the sky.
There is no leaf of freedom
even flowers stand in fear.
Mother—
though half my blood has been spent
I am ready to give up the rest.
If, my love
the young women are never to marry
it is because night is afraid
and will not introduce them to men.
My mother—
what remains of my blood
will be spattered on the road.
If, my love
it is not possible to meet the moon again
it is because night is afraid
and will allow no time for joy.

7.

The blade hewn from driftwood
is not as sharp
as the land in the pantun's song.
For the freedom of my soul
I surrender my life, my newborn child.
Patience is the road to heaven
is the lesson Mother teaches.
The most faithful poet
invites one to take a stand.
The blade hewn from driftwood
is not as sharp
as the land in the pantun's song.

Bone Bay

Husain Landitjing

1960p

night pier
the sky covers its eyes
a wild storm haunts
the door to the gate of hell
and the wind whips around
the sea vessel and my heart
and in the dark, dark, dark
receding, receding world
and in the dark, dark, dark
feeling closer to death
tell me o death
are you like an angel?
or wild woman?
tell me!
with weariness
the passengers scream:
shore

Death and Resurrection

Fridolin Ukur

1961

In memory of Rolf Helge Edgar Tinderholt

1

death came in september
when drought kills the rivers
the air is hot
our breath is hot

you died in our country
what should I say?

but they have asked me to speak
because i am a priest:
a few hours ago
your body was shaped by your bones
but now the skeleton has gone
leaving only a heap of ash

you came from dust
i come from dust
we return to dust
this sinful flesh and red blood
cannot enter into the kingdom of God
why should we be so busy
why should we be afraid

the physical body dies
and is resurrected as a spiritual body
sown in the heat
harvested in eternity

2

distance and forgetfulness are both near
we do not know the day of our death
the whirlpool of the burning fire

is a sign for us
the sun by day and the stars at night
love and hate, affection and resentment
spin between sorrow and joy
and life ends in the dark grave

if there is no life after death
how can we still sing?

Maritime Epic

Indonesia O' Galelano

1961

froth and white foam
lead the rolling waves
to the sandy beaches
froth and white foam
lead the men home
from their victories at sea

the currents push
the *canga*[1] across the sea
we don't care about the dutch armada
we don't care about portuguese canons
we are sons of the sea, we will die at sea
if we wanted, our ships
could sail like satan
sail like the lords of the ocean
sail fifty centimetres above the water
believe me

the *kapita*[2] recites spells
bismillah, in the name of god,
i will lock your heart
i will throw down your mind
i will make the water boil
vanish without leaving a drop
bismillah
make us invulnerable
make us iron
make our faces iron
make their bullets water
make their bullets into mud
bismillah

---

[1] Traditional pirate fleets of Halamhera, East Indonesia.
[2] Commander of the Kingdom of Ternate fleet.

may alfonso de albuquerque be killed
his flesh eaten by the ocean
may the controller van den berg be stabbed
by thousands of shining swords

the *canga* slowly advance
they sail in many directions
to papua in the east
to banggai in the west
tomini bay and sangihe in the north
their sails covered with spells
mindanao and sabah both submit
to the will of sultan hairun[3]

the captain stands erect
in the cabin of the *kora-kora*[4]
at the rear, the helmsman
holds tight to the rudder
cutting the sea in half
oh god
by mount gamalama,[5] which towers over the sea
by dukono,[6] which covers halmahera in smoke
by the halmahera sea, part of the great pacific ocean
may fair winds follow us, may the waves be tall
gather your smoke, explode
cover us in darkness
may your currents roll swiftly past the bays
and swallow the enemy fleets
the portuguese who surround our cities
the dutch who cut down our cloves

---

[3] Sultan Khaerun Jamil, ruler of Ternate, 1534–1570.

[4] Traditional outrigger craft, with a thatched cabin in the centre, used as a war vessel and capable of being rowed by over 100 warriors.

[5] A mountain on the island of Ternate.

[6] Volcano on Halmahera.

oh, light, *watui ech*[7]
slaughter our foes
drink their blood
they are not men
may their bullets melt against our bodies

the volcanos, waves and the wind
tell true stories
about our land
do not try to harm our clove bushes
our ancestors will be angry
we will rise against you

---

[7] Battle cry.

A Mother's Heart

Isma Sawitri

1961

the simmering trouble zones
move from century to century
starting in the huangho valley. From ancient mesopotamia
to jerusalem via rome toward the new continent
 america
then the balkans, alsace-lorraine, korea, indochina
jumping to cuba then to berlin spilling swastika
 blood
second by second, second by second
the god of death climbs in their hearts
crawling
getting closer and closer to the boiling point

meanwhile every bongo in the black land of africa
is played, drummed to the four directions
sending out a song of independence. piecing together a beautiful
 dream
because surely there is some vault of riches in this world, some simmering
 trouble zone
one so rich the other so far away
and to it a humanitarian father
comes to extend a helping hand
and just like that never returns
and just like that never returns
but the bongo of independence in the black land of africa has
 already sounded

and will keep sounding

this is the face of the earth now, the world of the twentieth
 century
boasting pyramids, the eiffel tower. sky
 scrapers

an inheritance from tyrants, artists and kingpins
this is the human grandeur that will only stay
    grand
if upon it is bestowed the fulfillment of all the commandments
that have been silently decreed in the heart of every mother
in the heart of every shunned and powerless mother
powerless and shunned simply because
in her resides the pure essence of love and affection, generosity
and sensitivity.

The Old Train

M. Poppy Donggo Huta Galung
1961

first news for Nurf

the train passes through my town
laden with people, goods, and dreams
gasping from fatigue
with poisoned lungs and darkened heart

the train passes through my town
it is small and old and weary
and rest is a long way off
for from its belly and sides hang the lives of many
folks from farm towns, the mountains, and the coast
coming to seek a life in the city

on top of the train, lives have been lost
electrocuted, the stiffened bodies found below
people scream in horror, but the train continues to pass
for the hundreds more still living
whose lives depend on its old but faithful strength

its voice is hoarse with sorrow:
farmers, workers, those who have perished on my back,
permit me to be replaced with something larger and stronger
a train able to traverse the region's entire terrain
and provide life for your grandchildren and their kin

the train passes through my town
with a cargo of humanity hanging from its side
on its back, and on its tail
heaving sighs of understanding
while carrying those who struggle for life
and bravely stand up to death
growing distant and smaller in the east.

One Day, in a Happy Month

M. Poppy Donggo Huta Galung

1961

one day, in a happy month
I discovered a pair of eyes
I found a steel heart
virility pulsing through his veins
and a love inside him like a mountain:
he came to me
stretched out his hand
said he was a peaceful home
and I the loyal tenant
came to him

one day, in a happy month
I gave him my heart
and he welcomed me
as the world broke into laughter
and we laughed too
he, the sheltering home
and I, the faithful tenant
were united

and so the months passed
our hands working diligently
planting seeds for the time to come
and then, in a happy month
we were reborn
in a creature with my eyes
but his skin:
our son!

we took him to church
gave him to Jesus the shepherd
his eyes shone brightly
with the hand of the priest upon his brow
his hands groped, his feet kicked
a lovely and healthy child

but then, in a happy month
he vanished from our sight
his eyes closed tight
and our hearts pounded in pain
we took him to his new house
a quiet home
far from the living
far from all that is light

one day, in a happy month
we sat on the front terrace
in my hand a cradle; in his, a doll
sitting in silence together

yet we will be born again
that we are certain of
and will return once more to church
to give him the name, the sun of life
and so it shall be that one day, in a happy month
our hearts will be united once more

Village Girl

Piek Ardijanto Suprijadi

1961p

sweet morning bird songs
brush against the village girl's cheeks

her breasts are half exposed
her heart is in the rice fields
her face shines

do you have a husband
village girl from the country

the green rice is blown by the wind
people look at her and are charmed
the morning sparrows chatter

the morning wind whispers
the heart whispers as it watches the fields
the crops are a sea of green
the maiden gently smiles

sweet maiden, village girl
do not go to town
the men are wild
and the prophets are false

sweet maiden, village girl
i am in love with you
one day i will return from the city
and work for our village

Fallen Warriors

S. Wakidjan

1962

Their names are too sacred to speak
Their stories too great to tell
They live in the loyal hearts
Of those who love the motherland

In the beginning there was movement and action
Courage overcoming confusion
They live in the loyal hearts
Of those who know love and bravery

Who should speak of their loss?
We or their grieving families?

Their deaths inspire our ideals
Our ideals and love which will be one

Because I am a poet, I shall speak of them in my poetry
Because I am a wanderer, I will pray for them,
The living and the dead

Nawang Wulan: Guardian of the Earth and Rice

Subagio Sastrowardoyo

1962

Don't speak to me in an earthly tongue
I am from heaven
Don't touch my body with a sinful body
I am from heaven

Greet me with flowers
The blood of sorrow and love
Flowers for the baby newly delivered from its mother's womb
Flowers for the lover who sweetly yearns
Flowers for the death that silently waits

But watch over the child who cries in the night for milk
Watch over the newly-tilled field
A child needs rocking
A field needs water
I will descend to your hut at your call

With flowers. The blood that flows
from sorrow and love

Facing the Cemetery

Surachman R.M.

1962

Mother! I'll go back to the pond
where my fish, Kumpay, once swam.
To the valley where they slaughtered
Denok, our buffalo, one terrible evening.
There was nowhere else for me to go
if not upon him.
To the slopes, the stuff
of dreams. To the singing cage of the turtledove. A place to rest from play and
cutting grass.

Stretching the tendons of my arms
as I now swing the blunt hoe.
A piece of bamboo Grandpa left dusty and empty, now
hangs again atop the *aren* palm tree. Grandma's rotted rice mortar
sprouts fungus,
yet still keeps beating 'til the very end.
And Father's net tens of fathoms long
begs wild fish sacrifices from the village stream.

Mother! I'll go back to the fields
in seasons when they no longer look like farmland,
to the peak with no shade
where we were pursued like fugitives.
This time I really am heading there.
Today I left the shelter of this city, a restless place,
because of memories of a palace that perished
at the end of a cape of blood and tears.
Our daydreams sorted year after year—
I will raise them atop the abandoned hills,
the place to peer at what trembled but momentarily—a crescent moon
far off. In camouflage

dusk, difficult to touch. Then feeling
the sorrow, undulating in a sea of weeds,
and the anger of our resentment, stabbing over and over
at the earth's bosom but never touching it!

Mother! I'll go back home
to where Sister, still a maiden, bathed in moonlight. To the quiet road where
people found poor Father
one awful dawn
with no heartbeat! To the village so longed for; where else would I head after
wandering?
And a branch of frangipani, symbol of memories
I bring, an umbrella for the unnamed corpses.

Whoever It Is Who Comes

Surachman R.M.

1962

Addressed
to grandma anteh
on the moon

whoever it is who comes tomorrow
is her grandchild
whoever it is who drops by two days hence
is none other than a descendant

or will you be found lifeless?
just a skeleton mixed with sand?
impossible! unthinkable!
it is said you are ageless

(her spinning wheel turns weaving sounds together
sounds that are not just any sounds)

where the fourteenth night opens up
I want to dive into the depths of the sky
or return to live inside the womb
I will put my own foot down
to prove the weaver was banished
if mother becomes pregnant in times to come

(her spinning wheel turns weaving sounds together
sounds that only have meaning to heroes)

Nenek Anteh! Nenek Anteh![1]
you never run out of thread, do you?
only she, your grandchild, will choose
the cloth you have woven all these years

it becomes an extra shroud for the earth
because it is rotten and full of hairs

---

[1] Nenek Anteh is a character in Sundanese folktales. When she was still a young virgin she climbed a
magic ladder, arriving at the moon, where she stayed and did her weaving alone until she grew old.

or it is a carpet
laid out for a hero

(her spinning wheel turns weaving sounds together
sounds only for her grandchildren)

A Group of Stories

Rusli Marzuki Saria
1963

The large traditional house of my birth
a rice barn leaning in the yard

Children dreaming of leaving
waiting for their father to come back

A sterile old water buffalo
vast neglected rice fields

Guns speak today—
how has that happened?

People taking the law into their own hands

Countless unknown deaths

We dig the graves
grieve the dead
mourn our loss

And we remember

The Guard

Suparwata Wiraatmadja
1963

A strong, strong will
Bearing a heavy burden of sorrow
Standing at attention, he is on guard
Noisy children play inside his head

A cold, cold night
It would be wrong to want to sleep
Be calm, be calm my darlings
Stay away from the tip of my bayonet

He stares, stares straight ahead
Vague shadows creep through his body
Rifles are raised, time passes
The heart refuses to surrender

He smiles, yes smiles
Children, oh beautiful children
Do not let the night frighten you
Do not let death color your dreams

Stand straight, you are a man
Strong muscles, a calm mind
Truth removes all fear
His fierce smile is friendly

A strong, strong heart
Death sleeps, he must stay awake
Standing at attention, he is on guard
Gentle memories play inside his head

To the Wind, King Wanderer

M. Taslim Ali

1963p

1

You are Bayu, King Wanderer
who knows no weariness and never stops
ready to roam

in desolate silence, in the morning
you steal the warmth and light
from the day, emissary of the sun.

To free the plants and flowers
from the full embrace of night
fragrances, gifts of the flowers.

You sweep through the valley of graves
like flowers that declare
their gratitude—I with a pen

compose a stanza, declaring
the greatness of your spirit to mankind.

2

Sometimes on a peaceful day
your gentle nature is replaced.
Clouds await in the sea of the sky

your voice whips up befriending thunder
roaring, shouting, shaking the faith
and frightening the hearts of all who hear you.

With your indescribable strength
giants in the great jungle
are struck down, then you fly away

to the turbulent Sea
seething, so all the fish
and the millions of ocean residents

shiver at the dark bottom
searching for sanctuary.

3

How astounding is your power
the power that annihilates
let it annihilate, it is needed

because the world yearns very much for
new air and new life
following the cycle of the times.

All creatures curse you
because of your ferocity now, later
they will love you, as I do.

After the collapse
bountiful new life will thrive
so humans will be content.

Wait for them and prepare
for their devoted love.

4

The energy of the one who is loved and feared
who does not stop roaming
who annihilates and renews.

How can I, a human
fathom your spirit?
All of my gauges are futile.

All of my efforts are useless and inadequate
my pen meditates on the paper
suddenly... you whisk past.

You caress my face, pen and paper
then continue to the garden to smell the flowers
then move on to open space.

My pen moves quickly
on the broad sheet of paper.

5

Oh, You, friend and enemy of fishermen
who manipulates life as you desire
who directs the waves with your breezes

wild or gentle by your breath
how powerful and free you are:
How passionate and flattered I am

hearing your wings rustling
in the clouds. A group of clouds
suddenly zig-zags

making a path
for you, O King Wanderer,
who has held the reins of power

from ancient times until today
in the open sea, in the open sky.

North Coast

Isma Sawitri

1964

extend your gaze to the arid plain, the salt flats
the open sea, white sails, and floating prows
oh, the java sea, behind villages of privation
the java sea, behind the fall and rise of a people

we are the sea and prows that hold power
from the arafurato the sunda and malacca straits
such was the history of a people in halcyon days
before sultan agung and a monopoly of armed merchant fleets

we are the sea, before cloves and nutmeg
we are the sea, after oil and steel
the prows are so delicate, ships much mightier
extend your gaze to the sea, the sea that's free

Testimony

Darmanto Yatman

1965

In the beginning
The world was sound:
Rippling water
Whistling wind
And so the world was full of sound.

And from that world of sound
There came blue and black
There came the yellow of the sun
And the red of stars
And so the world was full of color.

And from those many colors
There came fragrance
Fresh- and sweet-smelling scents
Of flowers and fruits.

And thus it is
That the whispers prophets heard
The odors priests smelled
The light kings saw
Were, in the very beginning
Sound
A sound one can always hear
Here, inside
Our soul.

Who Are You?

Sapardi Djoko Damono

1965

I am Adam
who ate the apple;
the Adam who, suddenly aware of his own existence,
was startled and felt ashamed.
I am the Adam who came to understand
right and wrong and tried to escape
from one sin to another;
the Adam who always watches himself
in suspicion,
and tries to cover his face.
I am none other than the Adam who flounders
in the net of time and space,
unable to be saved from reality:
paradise lost
because of awareness and unbridled curiosity
about his own Existence.
I am Adam
who hears God's voice:
farewell, Adam.

Beloved Mother

Umbu Landu Paranggi
1965

The old woman has many names:
suffering, pain and a perpetual smile
written like words of poetry
from her hair to her feet

The old woman has many names:
victim, grateful, blessed and forgiving,
faithfully giving birth
to dozens of stories, to human history

The old woman has many names:
love, care, compassion, three ancient words
her children stand on her shoulders
reaching for the stars

Mother

D. Zawawi Imron

1966

if i were off wandering when the dry season came
and the wells had run dry, and leaves and branches had fallen
only your tears, mother, would still freely
be flowing

if i were to go rambling
your tasty coconut drinks and my thrashing naughtiness
would sprout palm flowers to scratch at the essence of longing
reminding my heart of debts I can't repay

mother you are my hermit's cave
and it's you who put me here;
when the fragrance of affection wafted from hibiscus flowers
you pointed to the sky, then to the earth
and i simply nodded without understanding

your love is like the ocean
its calm narrow straits
a place to go swimming and scrub my body with moss
a place to go sailing, cast nets and drop anchor
with seashells, pearls and sea flowers all for me

if i had to take an exam and was asked to name heroes
your name, mother, would be the first i'd say
because i know
that you're my mother and i'm your child

if i were to go sailing and there came a headwind
the Lord you had shown me i would already know

and you would be an angel in a rainbow shawl
who visits occasionally
telling me to compose the blue sky
with my poetry

Strong Women

Hartojo Andangdjaja

1966

Women bearing baskets in the early dawn,
    Where have they come from?
They come to the station from mountain villages
before the train whistle wakes the day early
for the carnival of work.

Women bearing baskets on the train,
    Where are they going?
They ride on iron wheels.
They race the sun to reach the city gate first,
to win their livelihood at market.

Women bearing baskets in the early day,
    Who are they?
They are mothers with hearts of steel,
    brave women,
plants spreading from the mountains to the cities.
They are the love that gives life to one village after another.

A Bouquet of Flowers

Taufiq Ismail

1996p

Three little children
Stepping hesitantly, shy
Came to Salemba
That afternoon

"This is from us three
A black ribbon on a bouquet of flowers
Because we too mourn
For our big brothers shot dead
This morn."

We Are the Rightful Owners of This Republic

Taufiq Ismail

1966p

There is no other choice. We have to
Keep moving on
For to stop or retreat
Means crushing defeat

Will we sell our conviction
In worthless submission?
Do we wish to sit at the same table
With the murderers from last year's debacle
With each sentence ending in
"Your Majesty?"

There is no other choice. We have to
Keep moving on
We are the ones with eyes of melancholy, at the roadside
Hands beckoning for jitneys and buses packed tight
We are tens of millions who year by year live in a grievous plight
Pounded by floods, volcanoes, curses and pestilence
And ask ourselves, is this what they call independence
We who have no concern with a thousand slogans
And a thousand loudspeakers whose voices are nonsense

There is no longer another choice. We have to
Keep moving on.

In Vincennes Forest

Magusig O. Bungai

1991p

in vincennes forest on saturday night
people were singing
people were dancing
praising love
cursing racism

in vincennes forest on saturday night
two hundred thousand
people of all different colors
were singing their brotherhood
we are the earth's stepchildren

the whites think they are the kings of the world
the black, yellow and colored
are only fit to be servants and slaves
while human rights make for good speeches at the podium
elsewhere people are still kept down

from vincennes forest i know
how naïve it is to believe in words
it's better to stay primitive than be sophisticated
but sedated and then imprisoned and robbed
honesty means nothing to deceivers

Scatter Rice, Salt and Ash

Magusig O. Bungai

c 1995

we are the young hornbills banished from our forests
flying from jungle to jungle
    continent to continent
the wounds in our wings and chests dripping red upon
    the earth and sky
but do not weep o my villagers,
    these tribes and this nation will never surrender
the songs of your young hornbills still resound
    they are not silenced

pluck the *kecapi*,[1] bang the drum in a sign of war
    take back what has been lost
sharpen the *mandau*[2] blades, prepare the blowguns and arrows,
    rouse our brothers and sisters upstream
    and down the river
rouse the forests and the mountains
    prepare the graves for those who murdered your families
    prepare the ceremonial post, scatter rice, salt and ash[3]
the soldiers of this republic have killed, have pillaged
    all the houses in the town

they have banished us, your young hornbills, from the forests
where we were born
do not stifle your traditions, but take heart, children of *Sahawong*[4]
and all the tribes
it's better that we sever heads, respect ourselves,
our homes will not be sold
nor will we, your young hornbills, be banished from the rivers
where we were born
our stinging wounds do not shed tears the blood that
spills is the call to
a seven-generation war

---

[1] kecapi= a traditional stringed instrument.
[2] mandau= a sharp, sword-like weapon used by the Dayak people in Kalimantan.
[3] scatter rice, salt and ash is a Ngaju Dayak ceremony to take an oath or enact a curse.
[4] sahawang= another name for Dayak referencing the title of Dayak King, Tha Wong, meaning "Great Leader."

Beijing to Shanghai

Kuslan Budiman
c 1995

an old carriage, I leave
I pass by clay houses
the train runs quickly
through the fields

grey mountains in the distance
a blue sky gathering clouds
disturbs my restless heart

I peel a yellow-skinned watermelon
with a sharp knife
inside it is as red
as a young girl's lips

I study your letters
and can do nothing
I want to have a big party
but, my Darling,
we have no time for parties

the train speeds quickly on
leaving the sun behind
veiled in the dark dawn
covering Shanghai

The Plum Tree

Kuslan Budiman

c 1995

The plum tree beside my home
stores my childhood memories
but with a factory there producing jackboots
I can no longer visit
and my hair, which was once black
is now completely gray.

I mark the time
but do not know
how many seasons have passed
and how many times the plum tree has born fruit.

You Appear

A. Kohar Ibrahim

1966s

You appear to be free
    in your conniving and stupidity.
But no!
You conceal yourself behind Duplicity!

Your appear to be strong
in your arrogance and pride.
But no!
You rule from a castle built on millions of lives!

You appear to be pious
But no!
The only things you worship are money and power!

To hell with you. To hell with you.
To hell!

Inspections

A. Kohar Ibrahim

1966s

The train speeds forward
but my breath is labored, strangled by anxiety.

At country borders there always is
the inspection of tickets and the rifling of personal belongings.
They treat us like thieves, like convicts
when we're nothing more than refugees from "barracks socialism."

The train moves forward, pulling carriages of apprehension
in which one no longer hears songs of solidarity or friendship.

Communist

Agam Wispi

1966sp

you're a communist!
me, sir?
your grandparents were communists
so you must be one too

you're a communist!
I beg your pardon, sir?
you may talk nice
but you can't fool me

you're a communist
see, cat's got your tongue
you must be a communist
you can't trick me

you're a communist
a potential menace, aren't you?
why ask me, sir? I'm wrong if I speak
and wrong if I don't
should I just grin?

you must be a communist, you're sighing
should I stop breathing, sir?
you're the reason mount merapi exploded yesterday
you're the trojan horse that will destroy us all

well now I might become a communist
you make it sound very attractive, after all
how dare you speak like that to a CEO
to a man of my position

what is it about a communist, sir, that makes people so afraid?
don't pretend not to know, you monster!
who is the monster?
we'll have to interrogate you, you devil
    for you are indeed a devil

enough of this! don't ask so many questions
it's a sure sign that you're the devil
if I'm the devil, sir where are my horns?
you've hidden them so well, it just proves that you're a communist

very well, thank you, sir
see, you really are a communist
why else would you thank me?
can't I thank you, sir?

an image of a child I lost
and can never forget

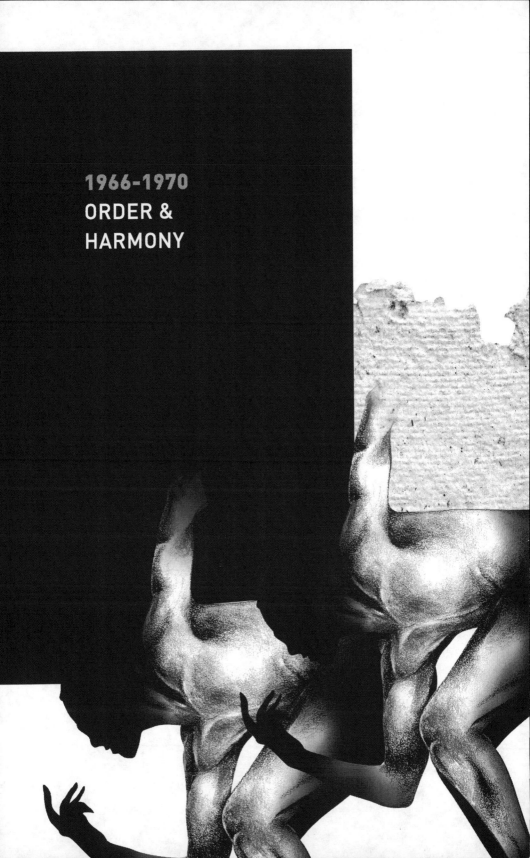

**1966-1970
ORDER &
HARMONY**

Introduction to the 1966–1970 Period

The End of Hostilities

Agus R. Sarjono

At the risk of oversimplification, Indonesian poetry may be divided into four basic phases, each with different characteristics. The first phase was distinguished by a sameness of both aesthetic energy and ideological standpoint. This occurred in the Pujangga Baru era and lasted until the war of independence. The aesthetic of poetry during this first period was lyrical and more or less romantic. The poet searched for the self in a world that seemed in need of change, while nationalism became the basis for a common consciousness among Indonesian poets.

The second phase was marked by an aesthetic sameness but a difference in ideological standpoint. Differences between the left and the right increased over time to the point of fierce hostility, with Manikebu (Manifes Kebudayaan; Cultural Manifesto) on one side and Lekra (Lembaga Kebudayaan Rakyat; Institute for People's Culture) on the other. Ironically, the Manikebu and Lekra poets wrote with an aesthetic that was basically the same.

The third phase was marked by a sameness of ideology but aesthetic differences. The New Order (Orde Baru) regime unified the earlier squabbling factions by mandating Pancasila as the sole philosophical foundation of the state. Effectively, those active in Indonesian literature during this phase were the Manikebu writers, because writers affiliated with the defeated Lekra became pariahs, with many living in exile. In the New Order era, ideological unity— union and harmony—was achieved by quashing any opportunity for dissent.

The fourth phase, commencing with the end of the New Order in 1998 and continuing into the Reformasi (Reform) era, was marked by complete differences in both ideology and aesthetics. The single ideology of the New Order era was challenged. Indonesian poetry became diversified, in terms of both form and ideological foundation. This phase signaled the end of the literary conflict between the leftist camp of Lekra (that is, Pramoedya Ananta Toer and colleagues) and the anti-leftist Manikebu (namely, H.B. Jassin, Goenawan Mohamad, Taufiq Ismail et al.), with victory going to the Manikebu side.

This victory was not a triumph of one way of thinking over another in literature, but the impact of a political decree that had been issued by Lieutenant General Soeharto on March 12, 1966. The decree dissolved and proscribed the Indonesian Communist Party (PKI) and its affiliated organizations—groups that took shelter under the protection of the PKI and were in tune with its aims, enabling the party to be active throughout Indonesia. In this way, the Lekra camp was shoved aside from the debate and muzzled.

Although hostilities were over, the trauma these poets suffered remained profound. Of the two camps, the Manikebu writers felt "repressed," "attacked" and "bullied" by the Lekra camp rather than the reverse, even though, politically speaking, Lekra had lost. The poets and writers in the Lekra circle, for their part, blamed their trauma and suffering on Soeharto and the military, otherwise known as the New Order government.[1] Such traumas had a considerable effect on Indonesian poetry from 1966 on, particularly in terms of aesthetic concepts.

Martina Heinschke believes that the hostility between Lekra and Manikebu was essentially a conflict between the Gelanggang Testimonial of Beliefs (Surat Kepercayaan Gelanggang) group, with their principle of "Universal Humanism," and the Lekra camp, which rejected this concept.[2] Based on this perspective, it could be said that, by the end of the Lekra-Manikebu conflict, the cultural line of the Gelanggang Testimonial (formulated by Asrul Sani and friends) had emerged dominant.[3] H.B. Jassin celebrated and affirmed this victory by naming a literary generation Angkatan '66 (1966 Generation) in his anthology, which was packed with the writings of those who opposed the leftist Lekra.

If we divide the New Order according to the divisions given in the book *Sastra dalam Empat Orba* (Literature in Four New Orders),[4] then the years 1966–1970 can be referred to as the "New Order I" period of Indonesian poetry. New Order I was marked by enthusiasm for real democracy—as the antithesis of Sukarno's guided democracy. In this period, political participation was at a high point. The

---

[1] To offer an illustration of this situation, every time the name of Pramoedya, the leader of Lekra, was mentioned, writers in the Manikebu camp would immediately feel some degree of irritation, whether they were "soft line" like Arif Budiman and Goenawan Mohamad, or "hard line" like Taufiq Ismail. Similarly, every time someone from the Lekra camp heard the name "Soeharto" or the New Order mentioned, they would feel sick. But mention of the Soeharto regime caused little reaction among the Manikebu camp.

[2] See Martina Heinschke's study, "Between Gelanggang and Lekra: Pramoedya's Developing Literary Concepts," *Indonesia*, no. 61, 1966, 145–170. Indonesia is a semi-annual journal published by Cornell University's Southeast Asia Program.

[3] In many respects, the Cultural Manifesto was similar in tone and principle as the Gelanggang Testimonial of Beliefs.

[4] Agus R. Sarjono, *Sastra dalam Empat Orba* [Literature in Four New Orders] (Yogyakarta: Bentang Budaya, 2001). Agus R. Sarjono divides the New Order into four periods, each having distinct characteristics.

press, which had been censored throughout the Old Order, was gradually freed from its bonds. During this time, schools and universities experienced freedom from indoctrination, and an open intellectual atmosphere was created within the university environment. Student presses played a large role in politics and enjoyed a broad public readership.[5]

In the realm of literature, the literary magazine *Horison* made its debut in 1966. For a long time, Indonesian literature of the New Order era would be oriented to this publication. Then, on November 10, 1968, Jakarta Governor Ali Sadikin opened the Taman Ismail Mazurki (TIM), an influential center for the arts, including poetry. TIM quickly became the venue for all manner of literary experimentation. Those who wrote poems would feel unrecognized as poets if their works had not yet been carried in *Horison*, or if they had not yet been invited to participate in a poetry reading at TIM.

During this period, poets tended to steer clear of politics. There was perhaps a sense of fear in literary circles that invoking political themes would resuscitate the old divisions and destroy harmony. It wasn't long before apolitical poems dominated Indonesian poetry. This trend dovetailed with the wishes of Soeharto's New Order government, which encouraged people to distance themselves as much as possible from politics. Although the remnants of a prosaic style could be found here and there, poems began to revert to a sort of orderliness and a regularity of form in which rhyme and meter were important. This can be seen in the original Indonesian versions of Sanento Yuliman's "Battle at Dawn", Budiman S. Hartoyo's "Waiting and Taking Leave", and Wing Kardjo's poem "Snow". At the same time, the seeds of aesthetic experimentation were sown in the poetry of this era, particularly in works by poets not deeply involved in the Lekra-Manikebu conflict. This can be seen in how Sutardji Calzoum Bachri's poem "Stone" plays with rhyme in the original. Tended by these poets, the seeds sprouted and took root within Indonesian poetry.

---

[5] The daily *Kami* and *Mahasiswa Indonesia*, for example, were powerful media outlets. Francois Railon's study of the West Java edition of *Mahasiswa Indonesia* provides an overview of the political situation of the time. See Francois Railon, *Politik dan Ideologi Mahasiswa Indonesia: Pembentukan dan Kolsolidasi Orde Baru 1966—1974* [Indonesian Student Politics and Ideology: The Formation and Consolidation of the New Order 1966–1974] (Jakarta: LP3ES, 1985).

Wreath

Kirdjomuljo

1967

There are graves I should remember but I don't know where they are
I hope you know why I put them there

There are graves I should honor but I don't know how to find them
I hope that you know how to pray for our people

Do not worry about
what is happening in your country

Follow the path of freedom
it will lead you to every destination

Battle at Dawn

Sanento Yuliman
1967

first rapid bursts of gunfire—then
the quiet of an explosion: stillness returns

in the east
a line of clouds:
the curve of a dark eyebrow

gunfire
even the horizon is still
like eyes shut tight
the wind
breathes deeply

suddenly the sky lifts
its lids, lights, gazing at the sun
eye of the day, giving and livid
struck by and watching over
the soldiers who have fallen
the children destroyed

low, red, and searching
something new on earth and finding
(this morning, as ever)
the human heart
old and ugly
gun   fire
(in this sky
birds fly:
shadows aflutter
among stars)

Snow

Wing Kardjo
1967p

Where would you go
    to search for the sun
    when the snow falls
    and trees lose their leaves

Where would you walk
    to search for protection
    when the body is drenched
    and doors close

Where would you run
    to search for fire
    when the heart's flames
    are pointlessly smothered

Where would you go
    rather than cleanse yourself

Splash

Ibrahim Sattah

1968

Remember the game *cok-cok kelupit daing*
Count on all ten fingers
Splashes outside up to the porch
How we enjoyed childhood, how rowdy
Even in the yard as long as we could play *kasti*
Panting, competing to be in front
Hit by the whip and not winning
I still feel it all
The snap and sting of the frond whip and grandma's pity
Cok—kelupit
Kelupit tulang daing
And now in the throbbing of whatever season
A self you've completely abandoned
From here
Steals a glance
Then leaves
Then is far
Farther and farther

Waiting and Taking Leave

Budiman S. Hartoyo
1969

I have been waiting for you
since way back when, O Time.
But you pass without my noticing,
causing my feet to drag
and my hands to sag, uncertain.

I'm here in this place where I perpetually wait,
and where you've always known me to be.
Each opportunity for meeting
straightaway turned into parting.
Though we're born with no appointment,
you sometimes leave for me your imprint.

Has the moment finally come
for me to up and take my leave?
You hold your tongue.
The calendar frays and rips away,
while your faithful deputy—the clock—
reckons imperiously.

Stone

Sutardji Calzoum Bachri

1969

stone rose
stone sky
stone sorrow
stone weary
stone needle
stone dumb
    are you
        the un-
     answered
riddle?

a thousand mountains and the sky stays up a thousand maidens and purity
remains a thousand things to do and still I am bored a thousand desires and yet
I lust please hear my plea
why does the clock throb and the blood still travel why do the mountains
explode and the sky not fall why do bodies embrace and still there is no love
why do hands wave and no one waves back. why?
    nervous stone
    anesthetic stone
    are You my stone
    silent stone
    dumb stone
       are you
           the un-
      answered
riddle?

A Gambler's Last Moment

T. Mulya Lubis

1969

Lord, I am bringing this card
to you. Please accept it
The dingy world
entrusted it to me

Lord, the world is already dingy
children gamble
in dark alleyways. And
even prostitution is on the rise

Lord, let's just say
that admission into heaven
has been discontinued

And Death Grows More Intimate

Subagio Sastrowardoyo

1970

Requiem for JFK

On the door still hangs
the sign of mourning
as if he will not return—
No, he will not return
but there is something they do not
understand: why he was so quiet
upon departure. There was not even
a trace of sadness
on his face
or in his staring eyes
that seemed to say
with pride: I died young —
     Yes, there is some good
in dying young and following
those who fell before their time.
At the close of the season
the first to die
was not the infirm one, wasted by age,
but he who stood
braving the wind
on a hill or near the shore
where storms threaten life.
Before their time the heroes are buried
on mountain ridges or in city parks
where children fly kites.
In the late hours of the night
leaves fall more thickly
unplanned—
And death grows more intimate, like a convivial friend
who goads one
to laugh, the universal language
always understood—
Face to face

as if through a clear glass.
The face: still recognizable,
even the scar of a former wound
is visible on his forehead.
He reaches out,
a ring clinging to his finger.
You see, there is no barrier
between us. I am still
tied to the world
by promises and memories,
while death is only a veil,
a concept whose threshold is easily crossed.
Nothing is lost in parting, everything
is restored,
as are daydreams and urges,
fancies —
        At the close of the season
the dividing wall comes tumbling down
and
death grows more intimate.

One day there will be a little boy
who no longer grieves for his kite,
tattered or flown away:
See, Mom, I'm not crying
because I can fly myself
with my own wings
to the sky—

1971–1989
DEVELOPMENT

Introduction to the 1971–1989 Period

The Mute, the Jokers and the Fist-Pounders

Agus R. Sarjono

Poetry in the 1971–1989 period was written at the height of the New Order regime. First of all, we submit that the New Order was an aliterate regime. If we accept Walter J. Ong's division of culture into orality and literacy,[1] we may then say that the New Order was a regime based on orality. I posit that this orality is the direct result of the New Order leaders' education. If Sukarno, Hatta, Syahrir, Natsir and other members of the so-called 1928 Generation were the recipients of Dutch teaching, then we can say that the leaders of the New Order were students of the Japanese. The long period of Dutch colonialism made it possible for the Dutch to bring in educated people from the Netherlands as schoolteachers for the Indigenous people (*pribumi*), some of whom went abroad to study in Dutch universities. By contrast, during the short-lived period of Japanese occupation, only low-ranking soldiers served as teachers to the Indigenous people, and none of the New Order leaders ever studied at universities of Japan. The militarist regime was to some extent influenced by the Japanese education that their leaders had experienced. The New Order's basis in orality suffocated—whether deliberately or not—the entirety of national life, including the cultural realm. Even after the collapse of the New Order, during the Reformasi (Reform) era, the government was still stifled and led national life on the basis of orality.[2]

In the 1970s, development became the main theme of the New Order, and New Order I transitioned into New Order II. The first phase of the New Order was marked by the so-called Malari Incident, otherwise known as the January 15th Disaster, which was followed by the muzzling of much of the mass media,

---

[1] Walter J. Ong, *Orality and Literacy: The Technologizing of the Word* (London & New York: Methuen, 1982).

[2] Many of those who were educated in this era became officials. A number of them were graduates of American universities, but not one minister wrote or published books. Compare this with the number of books written by Sukarno, Hatta, Syahrir, Natsir and others. Compare, too, the number of books written by Indonesian presidents after Soeharto up to Soesilo Bambang Yudhoyono with the number of those written by Mahathir Mohamad or Anwar Ibrahim from Malaysia.

including the crushing of the student press groups, whose publications did not reappear until much later.

The second phase of the New Order was characterized by large-scale depoliticization in various areas. The number of political parties was limited. Students were barred from engaging in political activities, and platforms for free speech were forbidden. Youth organizations were packed into a single coalition and tightly controlled. Even Taman Ismail Mazurki (TIM), the arts center in Jakarta, came under surveillance and was no longer as unfettered as it had been previously. Artistic prohibitions and book banning became a frequent occurrence.[3]

The economy was strengthened by various stimulus packages and expanded rapidly. These high levels of economic development were not, however, matched by the development of policy. This caused economic institutions to flourish rapidly without the balance of corresponding political institutions to make corrections when irregularities occurred.

In poetry, the aesthetic experiments of the 1970s matured and deepened. Several currents can be identified from across the breadth of poetry produced during those years. One group considered poetry a serious means of self-contemplation; among this group's practitioners was Chairil Anwar, the greatest poet during the Revolutionary War of Independence and the best-known figure of Indonesian poetry.

Chairil wrestled with the aesthetics of language, getting right down to the roots of words. For Chairil, writing poetry was such a serious activity that (to quote the poet himself) "whoever's not a poet has nothing to say about it."[4] This type of thinking was reinforced in the 1970s by poets like Goenawan Mohamad, Saini K.M. and Abdul Hadi W.M., and strengthened in the hands of Sutardji Calzoum Bachri, the most prominent poet of that era who experimented with form and language.

A second group saw poetry as something to play with, a game. One poet who frequently emphasized this point of view was Sapardi Djoko Damono.[5] His early verse was influenced by the lyricism of Amir Hamzah and Chairil Anwar. However, as his career progressed, he increasingly wrote verse that was image-laden and prosaic. During the New Order period, Sapardi's poems were totally apolitical and suitable for all occasions.

Sapardi's poetic style deeply influenced later generations in that it dispensed

---

[3] Later on, attempts to overcome these limits were made by forming artistic and cultural enclaves. For the discourse that dominated Indonesian poetry at that time, see the paper by Agus R. Sarjono, "The Discourse Community of Indonesian Poetry," Manila, 1995. Its Indonesian edition was published in *Prisma* (no. 6, June 1995) under the title "Komunitas Diskursif dalam Puisi Indonesia."

[4] See Chairil Anwar, *Derai-derai Cemara* [Pattering Rain on Cemara Trees] (Jakarta: Horison, n.d.).

[5] Sapardi expressed this position both verbally, at literary forums and on accepting the Bakrie Award, and in writing.

with lyrical tightness (rhyme, meter, structure); it was detached from social criticism; and it was playful. An extreme version of this attitude was displayed by the *mbeling* ("insubordinate," "disobedient") poetry movement, which was driven by Remy Sylado and Yudhistira Ardi Nugraha (Yudhistira A.N.M. Massardi).[6]

The poetic form that dispensed with stanzas, rhyme and meter gradually came to be embraced by poets of the 1980s and 1990s and is popular to this day. Verse of this nature was to some degree a rejection of the set forms of lyric poetry, though it also reflected the inability of this period's poets to write dense, tightly constructed verse with uncompromising diction. In the hands of mediocre writers, this vision of poetry as a game resulted in work that was little different from just "joking around."

The dominant trends of the 1980s and 1990s would be carried forward and, at the same time, challenged by two young poets who came to be well known: Afrizal Malna and Joko Pinurbo. At first Afrizal was much influenced by the seriousness and dark, heavy diction of Sutardji Calzoum Bachri. By contrast, Joko wrote lyric poetry in the spirit of poets such as Goenawan, Sapardi, Abdul Hadi et al. In the 1980s, Sapardi shifted from lyricism to imagist prose and announced that poetry was merely a game. Subsequently, Afrizal Malna, too, rejected the "serious" style and wrote in the prose style pioneered by Sapardi. But in his prose, Afrizal used limpid, heavily fraught diction (from anthropology, mythology and so forth), so that his poems became games, but serious ones—games without fun. For his part, Joko made playful use of words like "trousers," "sarong," "bird" and the like ("bird" in Indonesian being a double entendre for "penis") and even addressed serious matters like divinity and identity through double meanings. In this way, his work advanced the perspective of "fun and games for a purpose."

In its most extreme form, the "insubordinate" *mbeling* poetry—poetry that was "just a game"—did not last long. Even though it garnered acclaim as the best book of poetry, the *Toothbrush Verse* of Yudhistira Ardi Nugraha, along with the writings of the rest of the *mbeling* movement, swept by without leaving any deep impression in Indonesian poetry.[7]

A third group held that poetry should actualize the poet's involvement in society. The biggest and most important figure in this movement was Rendra. In various forums, both formal and informal, Rendra developed and strengthened this position. He always said that the basis of poetry is immersion in society and

---

[6] Yudhistira Ardi Nugraha's collection of poetry *Sajak Sikat Gigi* [Toothbrush Verse], received the Jakarta Arts Council (DKJ) Prize, and, thus, poems as games received the affirmation of official and authoritative institutions such as the DKJ.

[7] Remy Sylado, an important exponent of the *mbeling* poetry movement, recently published a collection of his *mbeling* poems in a thick anthology, but the public's response to his work was nowhere near as enthusiastic as it had been in the 1970s.

227

the times.[8] He was the first to announce, in the midst of the apolitical poetry so dominant in the New Order era, "I have heard the shriek of the wounded animal."

As the New Order progressed, poets in the third group would react differently to the changing situation than would those in the other two groups. The poets in the first group, including Goenawan Mohamad and Saini K.M., dealt with the New Order II by composing verse with social themes, albeit still with a lyrical tone and tight structure. Social issues thus became poetic food for thought. Saini K.M.'s book of verse *Sepuluh Orang Utusan* (Ten Envoys), for example, took on the theme of social criticism.

The poets in the second group were also bothered by the sociopolitical situation of New Order II, but they continued to write apolitical verse. If social issues were raised at all, they would be handled lightly and indifferently, as demonstrated in Yudhistira Ardi Nugraha's "Let it go!" below:

> you say this life is pointless. I say let it go
> you say this life doesn't have meaning. I say let it go
> you say I have no personality. I say let it go
> you say I have no understanding. I say let it go

The third group of poets reacted fairly strongly to the sociopolitical situation that confronted them in New Order II. Rendra did not hesitate to structure his poems differently, finding new forms to respond to the challenge of involvement with the times. Thus, Rendra, who had previously written ballads and lyrical verse about nature, God and people living on the margins of society, began to publish pamphlets of social criticism in verse.[9] "Song of a Cigar" was one of these publications—hated by Soeharto's New Order government, the *cukong* (a colloquialism referring to the country's business tycoons who were mainly Indonesian Chinese), and even literary critics and a number of Indonesian poets.

Wiji Thukul, a poet of the following generation, also wrote in this vein. His stance against the New Order regime, "There's only one word: resist!" was extremely well known in student activist circles. At this point Rendra was imprisoned, and Wiji Thukul disappeared or was disappeared—to this day, his fate remains a mystery.

In a poetry tradition that was still basically dominated by men, Toeti Heraty appeared with her intellectual verse that questioned and critiqued patriarchal

---

[8] *Manjing ing kahanan* is a Javanese expression that Rendra frequently used. It means to enter and become an active part of the age. He also, though only occasionally, used the word "engagement."

[9] Verse first intended to be published with the title "Pamflet Penyair" [Poet's Pamphlet], was later published as *Potret Pembangunan dalam Puisi* [Portrait of Development in Poems].

domination, both in the world of Indonesian poetry, specifically, and in cultural life in general. In previous eras, there had been a few female poets, but none had made women's issues a theme. Through her poems and her essays, Toeti Heraty started the feminist movement in Indonesian literature. Even though she was essentially alone in this endeavor, she commanded the attention of her male peers. Her poetry was widely admired, and she was a formidable intellectual figure who could not be trivialized, either in oral or written debates. In fact, there was, generally speaking, no well-known male poet of her generation who was her superior academically.[10] Even so, her criticism of patriarchal domination was made gently and with irony that was by no means cruel,[11] but demonstrated her wit, as seen here in "Manifesto":

> I accuse all of you
> will take you to a court with no judge
> for who knows, bribery is rampant, reaching even the Chief Justice
> who can guarantee that from the beginning no prejudice was shown
> for the world, the universe too, is man's possession

After laying out a number of demands, she closes this rather long poem by saying:

> but—
> for my son
> I would withdraw my accusation
> and become a traitor, but—of course—it's already too late

The world of women, the thinking of women, and the perspective of women as presented by Toeti influenced female poets of the next generation such as Dorothea Rosa Herliany and Nenden Lilis Aisyah, who then took up the cause. Dorothea Rosa Herliany critiqued patriarchal views by writing verse that was filled with male pronouncements about women. Her work *Nilai Pisau* (The Value of Knives) serves as an example. Nenden Lilis, for her part, wrote with an intimate diction and perspective on domestic life (which patriarchal culture saw

---

[10] Toeti Heraty obtained a PhD and became a professor at Universitas Indonesia. No other poets of her generation held a doctorate. Even now among female poets, no one has equaled her position as an intellectual poet. Most women poets are those with natural talent, if we use the distinction made by Subagio Sastrowardojo in his *Bakat Alam dan Intelektualisme* [Natural Talent and Intellectualism] (Jakarta: Balai Pustaka, 1983).

[11] See Agus R. Sarjono's analysis and commentary "Toeti Heraty: Pembela dan Pencemooh Perempuan dalam Gamitan Kenangan" [Toeti Heraty: My Recollections of This Female Defender and Taunter], *Kaki Langit Horison*, March 2001.

as the special preserve of women) to take on male perspectives.

The 1980s Generation responded to the uninviting sociopolitical situation on the one hand and the excessive material development on the other by writing esoteric religious verse in a Sufistic vein. Especially toward the end of the 1980s, Sufistic literary discussions and polemics had become popular and formed a strong movement in poetry. Abdul Hadi W.M. may be considered a poet at the forefront of this Sufistic verse movement, helping to popularize it through the poetry section he edited in the *Berita Buana* news daily and through his essays and translations.[12]

Most, although not all, of the Sufi poets of the 1980s (such as Acep Zamzam Noor, Jamal D. Rahman, Ahmad Syubbanuddin Alwy and Ahmad Nurullah) had a *pesantren* (rural Islamic boarding school) background. Although they all wrote Sufistic verse, each did so with individualistic flair. Acep Zamzam Noor wrote poems of roaming and questing (both physical and spiritual) interspersed with poems of social criticism and love. Jamal D. Rahman wrote poems about divine and spiritual experiences. When he wrote love poems, these were fashioned through Sufistic reflection and expressed in lyric form, occasionally making use of *ghazal* and *rubaiyat* structures.

In the 1990s, the sociopolitical situation began to change again. The Soeharto government entered the New Order III era, with Soeharto himself frequently saying that Indonesia was "ready for take-off." Deregulation occurred in many areas, particularly in the economy and trade, and the issuing of business permits was made easier. A commission on human rights was established and immediately began to demonstrate its concern over rights violations. The mass media, as well, began to sense an easing. The "security approach" began to change into a "prosperity approach." Private television stations were allowed. In fact, before this, there had been only one channel, TVRI, run by the government. News coverage grew freer and more audacious. Some of the poets who had lived within the strictures of the "security" state were ready to greet the winds of change and exercise their newfound freedoms. However, before New Order III could really be embraced by the poets, the situation changed drastically once again. New Order III turned out to be very short-lived and promptly morphed into New Order IV. That is why almost no poetry of any significance appeared during New Order III.

---

[12] Abdul Hadi W.M. compiled an anthology titled Puisi Sufi [Sufi Poetry] filled with translations of the works of Sufi poets from both Persia and the Nusantara (Indonesian) archipelago. He also wrote a dissertation on the Nusantara Sufi poet Hamzah Fansuri. His dissertation was disseminated through articles and seminars as well as in book form, under the title Hamzah Fansuri: Risalah Tasawuf dan Puisi-Puisinya [Hamzah Fansuri: His Mystical Essays and Poetry] (Bandung: Mizan, 1995).

New Order IV was marked by the muzzling of two magazines, *Tempo* and *Editor*, as well as the tabloid *Detik*. The action against these three publications was astonishing and completely unexpected. All of a sudden political policies basically reverted to New Order II. And the policies of New Order II were totally at odds with current macro-conditions. Social and economic deregulation was already well underway, and in any case required appropriate handling in the political dimension, but such developments were instead interrupted by the New Order government's imposition of excessive new regulations. This produced unbearable contradictions for the government and triggered an economic crisis, which in turn ended in the political collapse and overthrow of the New Order itself.

The fall of Soeharto—which could have been predicted from the early stages of the New Order—in fact shocked and surprised poets. So many events occurred, and not all of them could be dealt with in the form of poetry. To this day, many of the social disturbances that occurred on the eve of and after the fall of the New Order remain untouched by poets. Large-scale depoliticization during the New Order had caused most Indonesian poets to stumble about in approaching economic, political, social and national inequalities. Even in the present, there are prominent poets who feel indignant at the thought of poems that address social and political issues. It is not surprising that the poetry sections of weekly newspapers are still curated and edited with the poetic tastes of New Order II in mind, shying away from poems that engage in political affairs.

About That Man Killed Sometime around Election Day

Goenawan Mohamad

1971

"Dear God, give to me Your voice"

The silence was the silence that follows a dog's howl when the watchman found the corpse beside the dike. Face down, as if seeking the paddy's fragrant warmth. But beneath the moonlight, the acrid smell and the man's cold cheeks were strange. Then others came with flashlights, torches and fireflies, but no one recognized him. He's not from around here, the watchman said.

"Give to me Your voice."

By the lantern in the ward office they discovered the gaping wounds. Shadows vacillated; the veranda was crowded with whispers. The man had no identity card. No name. No party affiliation or symbol. He had no one to cry for him because we could not cry. What could his religion be?

"Noble Cartographer, where is my homeland?"

The day after next they read about it in the paper, on the front page. And there was a person who cried without anyone knowing why. And a person who didn't cry without anyone knowing why. And a tired boy who fashioned a hat from the morning paper, that was later stolen by the wind. Look! See the kites pasted on the sky, resting on the breeze. And the flock of evening birds alighting on the wires, as the cranes chase twilight's end across the barren field and long streaks of color, like dissipating smoke.

"Dear God, give to me Your voice"

Dandandid

Ibrahim Sattah

1971

Then there is sand
Then there is stone
There is shadow
There is water
And this and that and You and me: DANDANDID
Sand over there sand over here stone over there stone over here
Shadows over there shadows over here water over there water over here

Then there is stillness
Floating in the varied meanings where I am
And as usual I have forgotten
Something
That I never even knew:
    indandid indekandekid indekandekudeman indandid

are You the one
who cleanses our feet who cleanses the earth
who is and is not who is lost but not gone
far but not distant near but not touched
in sand in stone in shadow in water in silence over here over there
over here?

    I feel Your guidance
    I also call to myself:
    Children and butterflies
    There at Your feet DANDANDID
    indekandekid indekandekudeman indandid

House of Mirrors

Saini K.M.

1971

There's a house of mirrors and we are trapped
    inside—
figure and face fractured scattered framed
in a thousand colored shards of glass. Don't ask questions,
for even words change their meaning and wither like flowers.

Wither and wane as your lips did once,
and now they are the only form I sense
in the illusion of the universe, between reality and
    dreams:
two identical kingdoms—rejecting our very beings.

It's been a long time since termites ate the blueprint for humanity
along with all the books of children's fairy tales. This is how we are
    now,
faces competing with their reflections grasping for
    form
in a house of mirrors, and we are trapped
    inside

Walking Westward in the Morning

Sapardi Djoko Damono

1971

walking westward in the morning the sun follows me from behind
walking, I follow my drawn-out shadow before me
the sun and I don't argue about which one of us creates the shadow
the shadow and I don't argue about which of us must lead the way

Symphony

Subagio Sastrowardojo

1971

"I do not play for swine!" Beethoven grumbled

We stand here, in the midst
of the twentieth century

and think creation day
was a very long time ago

yet ever more vague are the answers:
what is the origin, when did it occur,
what are the numbers, what are the norms.

Ever more vague:
what is honorable, what is contemptible,
what is progress, what is regression.

Tell me this,
is it progress
when we build
more banks and warehouses
than temples or mosques;

when we appraise people's affection
for its monetary value, not sensing
when greater meaning is given to objects
than to imagination?

Or is that regression?

Tell me,
which is more honorable:
hands or feet,
the spiritual or the physical.
All are the same in a democracy,

Which came first:
God or me—
He cannot be imagined
if I do not imagine Him to be.
God and I vie for precedence
like the chicken and the egg.
Which came first?

Who was the first man:
Adam, Kayumerz or Manu.
Which holy book is to be believed:
The Quran, Avesta or the Hindu Weda.

Where did the world have its origins:
in Eden, Walhalla or in Jambudwipa.
Why not here, at this time,
with the birth of an Adam at every moment and in every place
and the word of God heard in every corner of the land?

I too am Adam
driven from paradise
because of sin, because of weakness,
because of a woman's temptation.

The world stops
and begins again.

Which is more permanent:
the body or the soul.
Which is more tabboo:
earth or aspirations.

Which is more sacred:
numbers or meaning.

Meaning is sacred
for being stored in essence.
And in numbers, too.
Though now it's rare to see
one trembling at the sight
of uneven numbers:
three, seven or thirteen,
written on the chest
as a sign of the corporeal.

Odd numbers, sacred meaning.
Odd like a thumb's placement,
stuck to the side of the hand.
Odd like a church spire
pointing towards the clouds.

This vision grows vague. Ever more vague.

Bed

T. Mulya Lubis

1971 p

A mooring
where longing
is anchored

After that
the ship sails
for months

The Night Is Possessed by Grief, after Shouted Words

Linus Suryadi

1971-74

the night is possessed by grief, after shouted words.
almost frozen, the streets begin to fracture—
you who abide, will you be prepared?

the sound of ragged breath, beyond all control,

repeats in mute silence, a haggard vigil.
you who endure here, will you be faithful?

Reading the Scriptures

Dodong Jiwapraja

1972

Why weren't the scriptures
written in Javanese or Sundanese
so that illiterate old people
could understand them?

But
isn't it the case
that a line of poetry
that is too easy to understand
feels flat and flabby?

The beauty of language
must slowly infiltrate
the mind and emotions
then quietly settle.
Like the miraculous shadows
that followed the Prophet
when he climbed the hill
to receive the gift
of divine inspiration.

The scriptures say that God
loves everyone: prostitutes,
criminals and gamblers,
even soldiers and the police.
But we must avoid evil:
fortune-tellers and magicians
are not poets.

The Split Stone

Ibrahim Sattah

1972

Hooonnnestooonehooonestooonnne stone in stone
Spirit in stone stone stone sheltered by the sky
a sheath of smoke incense smoke smoke in stone
cleanse the day cleanse the earth cleanse the stone
cleanse me

The elders are known to say
there is a stone in the stone
a big one in the bushes
It can echo, it can close up

Then that stone echoed three echoes
When it echoes the stone opens like a cave
First echo:
Someone passing by gets his leg caught

Then let's say there's a mother
intent on stopping there
on the fifth day at about one o'clock
There all alone
eyes tearful rising puffs of incense
half singing

Hooonnnestooonne stone in stone
I kneel at your vault
a sheath of smoke incense smoke smoke in stone
you wash the day   you wash the earth   you wash the stone
Spirit stone in stone stone sheltered by the sky

hooonnnestonehooonnne catch my body
catch where you want
in the jungle I have a home
in the sea I accept the noise
in the hut heavy-hearted
not morning not noon not evening not night not happy
what the youngest did was really too much

243

tembakul fish eggs all eaten a basketful not a morsel remains
the youngest forgets I'm his mother
forgets on purpose begs to rebel
hooonnnestonehooonnne catch my body hooonnne
stooonnnehooonnne
caught by the leg caught by the shoulder
caught the head 'til my hair
hooonnnestonehooonnnne split stone   closed up stone
catch my body hooonnnestonehooo
catch my body catch at the legs catch at the shoulders strands of hair sign
of my soul hhhooonnnstooonehhhooonnnestooonehhhooooooo

echo stone echo
then gone
then empty
only moss
only forest
only grass
only soul
stone in stone
stone sheltered by the sky
mother's stone
Split stone closed up stone

Darmitea, 10

Dami N. Toda

1973

when my journeys bring me to your face
will the sun be extinguished?

when your soft body
lies over a rainbow in Eden
will i have found the shortest stairs to the sky
and will my search be at its end?

a long parade has arrived in this country
where the end of the journey is born in your lap
and your thick hair
has obscured the way home

Quatrain about a Pot

Goenawan Mohamad

1973

On a nameless pot
I saw your face once more.
My eyes are not too dim, it seems,
to see what does not exist.

What is the worth of this clay vessel
except as part of an illusion?
Something likely to break
or for us to make eternal.

A Thousand Memories Rise between a Thousand Mountains

Upita Agustine

1973

A thousand memories rise between a thousand mountains
Offering love on five continents

Thousands of flowers bud, blossom and fall
The trees there have no leaves
Here the forests soar into the sky
Obscuring the quietening horizon

I am buried here
Consumed by repressed longing
Each day is empty
And my love is warmed by memories
Between a thousand
Soaring
Mountains

Unnamed Melody

Abrar Yusra

1974

What does the world hold for me? Possibly
a house for a short time. Or
perhaps some foreign land of exile.
Not my house but ours. We could
just move there

and I would be happy
because I loved the house.
I would love you living there. I hope
I would want to stay
forever.

My suffering is that of a man
who has lost his way. Or
the anxiety of a pilgrim
carrying a curse

walking in the dark
perhaps to my home
perhaps into exile.

Le Poète Maudit

Wing Karjo
1974

This is how it is, you needn't wait for me
behind the door, window,
curtains, with the light always
bright. I will come home
when the children are sound asleep
with dreams so pure,
your love

Since I had to go
I've traveled who knows where,
daydreaming of stars, moon, clouds,
wind. Coughing. There's been no rest.
For a long time you've known
my dreams are not about our everyday
lives

Gloomy images hang over
eyelashes. A veil of fog
covers the view of the future.
But, you say, everyone is like that
—it's the times. What's important
is to struggle for life,
with responsibility

Take care of what is real
with your two hands. While I
with my freedom curse the world
all around. The horizon is tilted.
Meanwhile the children sit each day
with plates uncovered,
at the table they pray

And still I don't come home
with pockets full of money. Just a tramp
in nameless cities, because
it's all like a day when

evening falls quickly, trembling in the wind
calling to the night,
which is dark

    You think—perhaps I am disappointed,
sunk in currents of formulas,
corruption, waste, unemployment,
prostitution—inflation. Confusion
with no end. I say: Enough of
all that! I don't care about a life of gambling
like this. It can all go to hell!

    So as in a story
I build a new order. But
in this order, what I have is only
a world of words, symbols without power.
Even though since Plato people have always
talked about expelling poets
from an ideal republic

    It is dangerous to cast spells over listeners
in magic hollows and spirit caves full
of secrets. A sense of order is obscured by songs
of fantasy. And now you too must feel
like a victim of empty beauty. I
myself have poured its poison
of many colors

    When night snores,
children sleep—in dreams you speak,
hear the sea beat ashore. Beautiful flowers,
blown by the wind, fall. I return home,
tap the window like shadows
stranded on a reef—
dear one

Poem

Wing Karjo
1974

Fingers inside the self
like roots that never cease
dig the earth ever deeper
deeper into darkness

Fingers that write words
growing harder, growing harder
like a knife being sharpened
ripping the body asunder

Dreams inside my veins
pounding, pounding as they flow
just like waves, just like currents
that never come back home

Let It Go!

Yudhistira A.N.M. Massardi

1974

you say this life is pointless. I say let it go
you say this life doesn't have meaning. I say let it go
you say I have no personality. I say let it go
you say I have no understanding. I say let it go

in the end, honestly, I don't believe you
no need to be angry. I know you're a simple person
it's just because you feel alien that you always say stuff like
    that

you say I'm a son of a bitch. I say let it go
you say I'm a con artist. I say let it go

the thing is, if I wasn't a son of a bitch what the hell would I be, a whore? I'm a
man. If you don't like me because of that
I will ransack your heart. Cause there ain't nobody who don't ransack in this
world. Ain't that right? If you don't believe that, just ask the police.

in the end, if I didn't say these things what would I do
kill myself? That would be more pointless than letting life continue on
the way you are currently experiencing it

you say that's exhausting. I say let it go
you say that's hurtful.

Toothbrush Poem

Yudhistira A.N.M. Massardi

1974

Somebody forgot to brush his teeth before going to sleep
In his sleep he dreamt
There was a toothbrush scrubbing at his mouth to make it open

When he got up in the morning
Only a portion of his toothbrush remained
The piece that was lost seemed to have gotten
Stuck in his dream unable to return

And he was of the opinion that this incident was wildly overblown

A Pile of Corn

Rendra

1975

A pile of corn in a room
and a young man
of limited schooling.

Staring at the corn,
the young man sees a field,
he sees farmers,
he sees harvest time,
and the dawn of a particular day:
women with bundles in slings
heading toward market...
And he also sees
on a particular morning
young women laughing
near the well
as they pound the kernels of corn
to flour.
While in the kitchen
hearths flame.
In the pure air
he catches the scent of corn cakes.

A pile of corn in the room
and a young man.
He is ready to work on the corn;
he sees the possibility;
brain and hand
are ready to work.

But this:

A pile of corn in a room
and a young graduate from senior high.
Without the money, college is out of reach.
All he has is a pile of corn in his room.

He stares at the corn
and he sees himself in suffering.
He sees himself thrown out of the discotheque.
He sees a sharp pair of shoes in the store window.
He sees his rival on a motorcycle.
He sees lottery numbers.
He sees himself poor, a failure.
A pile of corn in the room
has no bearing on reason,
will not provide him help.

A pile of corn in the room
will not help a young man
whose view of life comes from books
and not at all from life.
One not trained in methods,
able only to memorize conclusions.
One who's been trained to be a user
but with little experience in self-help.
Education has separated him from life.

I ask you:
What is the use of education
if it only makes a person foreign
amid the facts of life?
What is the use of education
if it pushes a person
to become a kite in the capital city
and awkward in his home village?
What is the use of a person studying
philosophy, literature, technology, medicine
or whatever,
if in the end,
when he goes home to the village, he says:
"I feel foreign and lonely here!"

Pilate

Saini K.M.

1975

Pilate was indeed forced to wash his hands although he knew
his fingers would be red for the rest of history.
Now we are more fortunate.
When we make decisions there is no one
whose lot it is to be nailed to a cross.
Today dictionaries use the term "appropriate," even "wise,"
to describe reasoning such as Pilate's.
There is no Roman Caesar whose authority must be maintained, no insurgent Jews.
And supposing—for some reason—the Good Guy is persecuted, and
the Bad Guy ascends the throne, that's just the way of the world.
So there's no need to get involved.
These days there's no way a life would be sold for thirty pieces of silver.

Meeting

Leon Agusta

1975p

If there are no more words left to be spoken
The smallest of smiles can be the moon and sun

Near God

Abdul Hadi W.M.

1976

God,
we are as close
as fire and flame.
I am flame
in Your fire.

God,
we are as close
as cloth and cotton.
I am cotton
in Your cloth.

God,
we are as close
as wind
and air.

In the dark
I burn
in Your unlit
lamp.

An Old Dove

Apip Mustopa
1976

a dove on a bare branch
strokes the light on its feathers;
the clouds above rest
reflecting on their direction.

the dove looks toward
the lethal wind;
if a leaf trembles
it will long for its partner.

the dusk sky is so quiet
catching the late rays of the sun,
the end of a mournful day.

a waiting heart is so lonely
catching the longing of someone all alone
approaching death

Before You Were Late

Budiman S. Hartoyo

1976

Probably you'll regret this, or maybe you won't, that I stayed waiting until the seagulls took flight to pursue the dusk. Probably you'll forget that a moment before the sun slipped below the horizon, I left without knowing where you were. Probably you won't have time for a jog after harvesting rice or practicing dance, arranging the stones in the street or waiting on tourists. I'm bewildered, not knowing whether it was you tiptoeing behind me there on Kuta beach or not.

A reluctant breeze defiles itself, stirring up the sand; a moment later the sand's at rest, dipping its toes in the water; the sea is silent, it wriggles briefly, weary of gazing at the clouds; the clouds have long since scattered, leaving flecks across the sky; the sky has now let the sun nod off—it droops, lingers, then slips away.

When there's a lull in the wind, the birds no longer hesitate; the sand's already fast asleep as the ocean sighs sporadically before falling silent; cloud and sky suddenly dissolve, hazy in the remaining sunlight, and I'm worried you haven't appeared sitting near the little boulders over there—like you usually do. At this point, even if we were to walk the beach together, there wouldn't be any shadows. And now, I know for sure, that you're late.

Probably you'll regret this. Or maybe you won't...

Just Tell Her

Maskirbi

1976

Tether the boat at this harbor
while the tide is still high
but tell her
where we will dock
if suddenly the sea dries.

I Am Learning to Count

Oei Sien Tjwan

1976

i am counting out a puzzle
whose vastness is limitless
the stars teach me
how to find your room
without extracting tears of sorrow
uncle star promises to carry me there
but another uncle forbids me to go anywhere
i am confused thinking about my little feet
my dolls who often wake in the middle of the night
can i bring them with me while searching for your love?

love makes it easy for us to think about sorrow
or happiness
when you say "oh, my child"
my eyes blink and my heart calls you a thousand times "mama"
oh, if our love could be united
i don't know...
where we should meet

Sermon

Rendra

1976

Fantastic.
One hot Sunday
in a church full of people
a young priest stood at the pulpit.
His face was beautiful and holy
his eyes sweet like a rabbit's
and he lifted up both his hands
which were lovely like a lily
and said:
"Now let us disperse.
There is no sermon today."

No one budged.
They sat crammed in their pews
or stayed standing.
They stiffened. Refused to move.
Their eyes filled with questions.
Their mouths hung open
as they stopped praying
but everyone wanted to hear him.
Then all at once they complained
and together with the strange voice from their mouths
came a foul stench
which had to be quickly stifled.

"You can see I am still young.
Allow me to care for my own soul.
Please go away.
Allow me to praise holiness. I want to go back to the monastery
and meditate on the glory of God."

Again they complained.
No one moved.
Their faces looked sad.
Their eyes were filled with questions.
Their mouths gaped
wanting very much to hear him.

"These people ask for guidance. Lord
God, why have you left me at this moment? Like a flock of hungry lazy jackals
they open their mouths.
It is hot. I piss my pants.
Father. Father. Why hast Thou forsaken me?"

Still no one moved.
Their faces were wet.
Their hair was wet.
Their whole bodies were wet.
Sweat poured onto the floor
because it was so hot
and they bore such misery.
The stench was extraordinarily foul.
And their questions too stank foully.

"My brothers, children of the Heavenly Father.
This is my sermon.
My very first sermon.
Life is very difficult.
Dark and difficult.
There are many torments.
So in this regard
the wise way to live is ra-ra-ra.
Ra-ra-ra, hum-pa-pa, ra-ra-ra.
Look at the wisdom of the lizard
a creature God loves.
Go close to the ground.

"For:
Your souls are squeezed between rocks. Green.
Mossy.
Like a lizard ra-ra-ra.
Like a centipede hum-pa-pa."

They all spoke together:
"Ra-ra-ra. Hum-pa-pa."

Everyone in the church shouted:
"Ra-ra-ra! Hum-pa-pa!"

"To the men who like guns
who fix the flags of truth to their bayonet-points
I want you to listen carefully
to lu-lu-lu, la-li-lo-lu.
Lift your noses high
so you don't see the people you trample.
For in this way li-li-li, la-li-lo-lu.
Rinse the blood from your hands
so as not to frighten me
then we can sit and drink tea
and talk of the sufferings of society
and the nature of life and death. Life is full of misery and sin.
Life is a big cheat.
La-la-la, li-li-li, la-li-lo-lu.
So let us shoot the sun
taking aim as carefully as can be."

The people answered him joyfully:
"La-la-la, li-li-li, la-li-lo-lu."
They stood. They banged their feet against the floor.
Stamping rhythmically and together.
Uniting their voices in
"La-la-la, li-li-li, la-li-lo-lu."

Carried along in the strength of their unity
they shouted together
precisely and rhythmically:
"La-la-la, li-li-li, la-li-lo-lu."

"Now we live again.
Feel the force of the blood flowing in you.
In your heads. In your necks. In your breasts. In your stomachs. Throughout
the rest of your bodies.
See my fingers shaking with life.

The blood is bong-bong-bong.
The blood of life is bang-bing-bong.
The blood of the common life is bang-bing-bong-bong.
Life must be lived in a noisy group.
Blood must mix with blood.
Bong-bong-bong. Bang-bing-bong."

The people exploded with the passion of their lives.
They stood on the pews.
Pounded their feet.
They pounded on the bells and the gong
the doors and the windows.
With the one rhythm in accompaniment to their joyous shouts of
"Bong-bong-bong. Bang-bing-bong."

"We must exalt love.
Love in the long grass.
Love in the shops of Arabs.
Love in the backyard of the church.
Love is unity and tra-la-la.
Tra-la-la. La-la-la. Tra-la-la.
Like the grass
we must flourish
in unity and love.
Let us destroy ourselves.

"Let us shelter beneath the grass.
Taking as our guide
Tra-la-la. La-la-la. Tra-la-la."

The whole congregation roared.
They began to dance.
Following the one rhythm. They rubbed their bodies against each other.
Men against women. Men against men. Women with women. Everyone rubbed
their bodies.
And some rubbed their bodies against the walls of the church.
And they shouted in a strange mad voice shrilly and together: "Tra-la-la. La-la-la. Tra-la-la."

266

"Through the holy prophet Moses
God has said:
'Thou shalt not steal.'
Junior civil servants stop stealing carbon paper.
Servant-girls stop stealing fried chicken bones.
Leaders stop stealing petrol.
And girls, stop stealing your own virginity.
Of course, there is stealing and stealing.
The difference is: cha-cha-cha, cha-cha-cha. All things come from God.
Everything is meant to be shared.
Everything belongs to everyone
Everything is for everyone.
We must be united. Us for us.
Cha-cha-cha, cha-cha-cha.
This is the guiding principle."

They roared like animals:
"Grrr-grrr-grrr. Hura.
Cha-cha-cha, cha-cha-cha."
They stole the windowpanes.
They took everything in the church.
The candelabra. The curtains. The carpets. The silverware. And the statues
covered with jewels.
"Cha-cha-cha," they sang.
Cha-cha-cha over and over again.
They destroyed the whole church.
Cha-cha-cha.
Like wet panting animals
running to and fro.
Cha-cha-cha, cha-cha-cha.
Then suddenly an old woman screamed:
"I am hungry. Hungrry. Hu-u-unggrryyy."
And suddenly everyone felt hungry.
Their eyes burned.
And they kept shouting "cha-cha-cha."

"Because we are hungry let us disperse.
Go home. Everyone stop."

"Cha-cha-cha," they said
and their eyes burned.
"Go home.
The mass and the sermon are over."

"Cha-cha-cha," they said.
They didn't stop.
They pressed on.
The church lay in ruins. And their eyes burned.

"Lord. Remember the sufferings of Christ.
We are all his honored sons.
Hunger must be overcome by wisdom."

Cha-cha-cha.
They advanced and beat against the pulpit. Cha-cha-cha.
They dragged the priest from the pulpit.
Cha-cha-cha.
They tore his robes.
Cha-cha-cha.
A fat woman kissed his fine mouth.
An old woman licked his pure breast.
And girls pulled at both his legs.
Cha-cha-cha.
And thus they raped him in a noisy throng.

Cha-cha-cha.
Then they chopped his body to bits.
Everyone ate his flesh. Cha-cha-cha.
They feasted in the strength of their unity. They drank his blood.
They sucked the marrow from his bones.
Until they had eaten everything
and there was nothing left.
Fantastic.

And

Sutardji Calzoum Bachri

1976

I came with flowers
     and you said wait
I came with my anxiety
     and you wanted something else
I came with my blood
     and you said not enough
I came with my dreams
     and you said there is more
I came with my grief
     and you said it was too small
I came with my body
     and you said that was better
I came with my soul
     and you said maybe
I came with nothing
     ah!

Blues for Bonnie

Rendra

1976 p

Boston is withered and faded
from blustery winds, awful weather,
and a late night's bad luck.
In the cafe
an old black man
plays his guitar and sings
with barely an audience:
seven couples only
cheating and loving in the dark,
billowing gray clouds of cigarette smoke
like sputtering campfires.

He sings.
His voice is deep.
He marries song and words
to give birth to a hundred meanings.
Georgia, faraway Georgia.
Where there are negro shacks
with leaky roofs.
Earthworms and malnutrition.
Faraway Georgia he calls it in his song.

People stop talking.
There is no sound
save that of the windowpanes' shaking.
Georgia.
With his eyes clamped shut
the man hails silence,
and silence replies
with a swift blow
to his gut.

In his perplexity
he acts the gorilla.
An old and stooped gorilla
roaring,
his fierce fingers on the guitar
clawing
as he scratches the itch in his soul.

Georgia.
No new customers arrive.
The air outside is bitter;
the wind blusters even more.
And at the hotel
a cold bed waits.
The face of the cafe's proprietor sours
from the loss of an entire night.
The black man looks upward,
straining the cords in his neck.
His eyes are dry and red
As he stares at heaven,
and heaven
throws down a net
to snare his body.

Like a black fish
he struggles in the net,
thrashing about
in vain
with anger,
shame
and futility.

The wind beats across Boston Commons,
whistles in the church towers
and tears the night to shreds.
The black man stamps his foot
and sings his oaths and curses.
His white teeth shine
in a tight grin of revenge.
His face is dirty, wet and old
like a moss-covered stone.

Time, like a flood
overwhelms his weary soul.

And in the middle of it all
he feels in his leg
a tremendous jerk.
Surprised
and near incredulous
he feels
the rheumatic cramp
rip through his limb.

In the performance tradition
he refrains from surprise,
and slowly stops
slowly rests on his stool,
a cracked vase on a stand
in a secondhand store.
And, only after drawing a deep breath,
he begins to sing once more.

Georgia.
Faraway Georgia he calls it in his song.
His wife's still there,
devoted but suffering.
Black kids play in the ditches,
not at home in school
The old ones are drunks and braggarts
forever and ever in debt.
On Sunday mornings they go to a church
especially for negroes
where they sing
spellbound by the hope of what is to come
and their lack of power on earth.

Georgia.
Mud sticks to shoes,
windowless shacks

suffering and the world,
one as old as the other.
And heaven and hell
time-worn, too.
But Georgia?
Dear God,
even after running so far,
Georgia is still on his heels.

Good Morning, Jajang

Arifin C Noer

1977p

when the sunlight spills through the window glass
and the wind plays with the tips of the leaves, flowers
flirting
we stretch without looking at each other
quietly giving thanks to the air
            —to life
because we want to believe in love, still
on the carpet scattered with the remnants
of our conversations our dreams
last night
among the shoes sandals
trousers shirts
ashtray full of butts, empty glasses and
empty bottles

the sky this morning our sky
light blue, level and vast
let it be clear let it be calm
do not play a cassette just yet do not move
i just want to listen to, sense
the whisper of your breath
and gaze into your eyes
your look that is always like the night

we must be grateful to life
because we still believe in love
now quickly bathe and dress neatly
comb your hair let it hang loose as usual
if you want to wear mascara be careful, do not touch your eyes
now, quickly

good morning, jajang
we begin again
follow the sun
to who knows where

Stars

Oei Sien Tjwan

1977

the home over there, o stars
side by side with human hearts
the gathering place for relatives and neighbors
twinkling from a place far from emotion
gathering each day, but always guarding the distance

Old Tree

standing alone overshadowing my years
roots spreading out to where children play
passing year by year
standing there still
gazing vacantly towards the hills
where the evening sun sets

Rivers and Lakes

rivers and lakes
flow like children singing
sending their voices
to where birds lay eggs
where will we go my love
if the rivers and lakes
begin to dry or become full of mud
is there another place for the birds to take shelter
that can restore our happiness
i'm afraid... i'm afraid...

The Universe's Mysticism

Kuntowijoyo

1977

1

The beating heart
aborts dreams
from the silence.
A white pigeon
lands on fog.
You must realize:
you long for emptiness.

2

Wanderer!
Ask the wolves to
lick your footsteps
until the desert
spreads out a carpet
dense like absence.
You hope for a rainbow to
scatter forgetting.
Your eyes are closed nervously.
There is something you don't know;
yesterday slipped
to the bottom of time.

3

A bunch of jasmine
with moon flowers
is persuaded by the night wind
to give up its pollen
to be stored.
O beautiful crown—
the pearl breaks on the wrought iron
when the black hand caresses it.
You don't like to remember it;
it escapes your mind
to who knows where.

4

The horizon lets go of the birds
in the afternoon, and
they return to the west
with the wind,
which blows gently,
arousing desire.
Their feathers fall
while soft bodies
disappear with the sun.
Oh, the pleasures of longing.

5

The pelican doesn't lay eggs
because the male's seeds
have spilled without gaining
the blessing of the earth.
Only a lone tree can be seen
on a grassless field, whereas
sheep leave their traces behind in the
earth, an unknown quantity.
Who is that wise shepherd
who brings his flock home by nightfall?
While you are reflecting beneath the kapok tree,
guessing the direction of the Kaaba
after the light has faded from your eyes.
Oh, who doesn't hear the news
from the distant village
beyond your ideas?
The beautiful angels await.

6

Look at your spirit
when it mingles with the pond.
And when you look into a mirror

is there a spirit shining like jewels?
Decorating the lake's surface,
remember, you are also sand
that disappears from sight
when the farmers wash the mud.
Why doesn't it become red coral beads
ornamenting a slender neck?
And thus
the soul is a perfect jewel.

7

Flames tempt your nerves
after the wick has been burnt,
and then your fingers
look for its end,
warm and peaceful
into your corpse,
approaching night.
Turning into dreams,
hope is the remains of flames
that occasionally force you
to smile.
Why so doubtful?
Take it! Snow falls outside.

8

You are a witness to the
blue sky descending
to the sea.
At the edge of the sails,
the fishermen put out their nets in vain,
as something that is mysterious and
beyond reach.

Meaning:
That which is close is far; that which is far is close, which is far.

So when the Sufi lifts his hands,
he meets with the sky
at the center of the universe.

9

The virtuous entertainer is silence.
The stars and the moon blink.
Then silence: roses open their petals
while you are quietly in the middle,
your soul sucking the nectar.

10

The clouds dissolve,
as they are friends with trees.
Letting the forest grow at the crest of a hill
where love greets the earth
in the morning. Look at it!
Eternal clouds, deliberately stopping,
containing the longing of a dove.
How could you forget?
O God, tell me that the clouds are always orange.

Song of a Cigar

Rendra

1977

to the students of the Bandung Institute of Technology

As I smoke my cigar,
I watch the Republic of Indonesia
and hear 130 million citizens.
In the sky
a couple of carpetbaggers squat
and shit on their heads.

The sun rises.
Dawn comes.
I can see
eight million children
who will not go to school today.

I ask why,
and my questions bounce
off the desks of idle bureaucrats
and the empty blackboards of their teachers.
No one gives a damn.

Eight million children
facing a long road
with no alternatives,
trees,
resting places,
or future.

*

As I breathe
the sanitized air, I see unemployed graduates
laboring in the streets.
I see pregnant women
queueing for their dead husband's pensions.
In the sky

the technocrats tell us
that we're a lazy race,
that we need to be more developed,
that we should be upgraded,
that we must adjust
to new overseas technology.

The mountains stretch
into the multicolored evening sky.
I can see men burying their resentment
under their beds.

I ask why,
and my questions bounce
off the lecterns of the salon poets,
as they sing of wine and the moon,
ignoring the injustices around them,
and the eight million children
who won't be going to school.
Poets who kneel adoringly
before the goddess of art.

The hungry children,
flowers of the future, can barely see
despite the brightly lit billboards.
The hopes of millions of parents
turn into a confused jumble of voices,
turn into underwater coral.

*

We must stop importing foreign methodologies.
Rote learning gives us only empty formulae.
We must learn to understand our own world.

We must go out into the streets,
out into the villages,
write down the symptoms we see
and define the real problems.

These are my poems.
A pamphlet for a state of emergency.
Art is meaningless
when it is separated from society's suffering.
Thought is meaningless
when it is separated from life's problems.

Motinggo Blues

Subagio Sastrowardoyo

1977

1

Woman with your eyes closed
leave the lamp in the room burning bright
as we make love

We must confront
our naked bodies
with open eyes

In the act of loving
we return to what we once were
before we knew of shame

The mole on your shoulder...
let me kiss it
but open your eyes

2

What does tomorrow mean?
Love knows only today.
Yield to the pulsations
that carry us
from one room to another
each dark space a refuge
a sanction for rape...
Where do we stop?
Oh, let the world drown
in its own blood

3

Searching fingers
long to speak
of lengthy days
and burning desire

We have roamed so far

What is faithfulness, what are promises
if memory has no meaning?
Drown in the confusion of flesh
and forget yourself

Feel my chest, here
where my heart is crushed
by longing and fear

4

That long body
continues to reflect
on walls of fantasy

A fertile field
rolling freely
without hesitation

A silent forest
willingly awaits
man's footstep

That long body
at the peak of affection
I will enjoy without end

5

As dawn unrolled
blood was splattered on the sky
embraced by day, emptiness clinging:
her face aged quickly in sullied use

Aren't you afraid?

When I kissed your mouth
my tongue savored
death's gritty taste

Contradiction

Samar Gantang

1977

along with the moon and millions of stars
we struggle against our selves
until there's born a conviction
today is today
and today is this life
tomorrow or the day after is an illusion
that attacks the self
blue spills, books soak
poisoning blood, space, time, and imagination
poisoning tradition, poisoning the self and poetry
poisoning the sweetness of our day to day

A Wife

Darmanto Yatman

1978

> *A wife must be respected;*
> *she is the source of blessing and favor.*
> (Towikromo, Tambran, Pundong, Bantul)

A wife is very important for taking care of us;
it is she who sweeps the garden
who cooks in the kitchen
who washes at the well
who sends the lunch pails to the field
and who tends us when we are ill.
Yes. A wife is very important.

She is our other half
when we take part in celebrations;
she is the counter to our opinion
when we we want to sell our crops.
She is the friend behind us
when we are hungry and want to eat;
she is the ointment for our soul
when we—
She is our secret power!
Yes. You see. She is just as important as a buffalo, a plow, a rice field or a
coconut tree.
When we hoe her at night, she never complains, though she is tired and worn.
She stores with care the seed we plant in her, and is grateful to us, too; she
knows how to repay thanks and to raise our standing as men.
She pays most serious attention to the raising of our children, just as we do in
tending chickens, ducks, goats and corn.
Indeed, a wife is very important, never more than when we begin to forget her:
She is like the tongue in our mouth
we are not aware of.
She is like the heart in our chest
we do not feel.
Yes, yes, a wife is very important, especially at the moment we begin to forget
her.
So, be careful!

On guard, watchful and ready.
Respectful, caring and kind.
So that we too become independent—strong and capable in ordering our lives
and free from brokers, headsmen, chiefs and officials.

She is Subadra for Arjuna,
more beautiful than the spirits who tempted him;
she is Arimbi for Bima,
most beautiful when giving birth to his eldest son;
she is Sawitri for Setyawan
who protects our souls from danger.

Oh, yes. Oh, yes.
How very important a wife is just when we begin to forget her.

Honor your wife
as you would honor the goddess Sri,
the source of life.
Eat up.
For that is your destiny!
—Towikromo.

My Indonesia

Hamid Jabbar

1978

my homeland
is a winding road
full of signs,
that is my indonesia

   dusk: with a ticket in hand i see you in the headlines and editorials of the
city's newspapers. you're smiling and have a toothache. you're shy like a cat (you
might be meowing or writhing in pain; you may be angry or in love); you are
restrained in a line of words from the archipelagos that criss-cross and weave
in and out of me. you rise and fall throughout the day; neglected fragments of
poems are published along with a long-lost sense of shame. the evening call to
prayer echoes and the bell rings; i'm pushed to the edge, but i'm still able to
imagine you, my love, even though my words aren't fluent.

my homeland
is a winding road
full of signs,
that is my indonesia

my homeland
is a winding road
full of signs,
that is my indonesia

   a bag in one's lap and the night is all-enveloping. i feel you rushing helter-
skelter. an old bus screeches and cries like a series of dreams, a dirty old man.
you sit, on the verge of sleep, at the center of the world, which shouts along the
winding road, making a storm of rain and signs; i'm thrown backwards, but i'm
still able to imagine the distance that i have crossed and will cross, (having an
indifferent feeling towards swimming in the lake of your wounds) even though
my words aren't fluent.

my homeland
is a winding road
full of signs,
that is my indonesia

a body throughout a journey; a clanging night and you can see me running exhaustedly after you from one corner to the next. (maybe you have knocked down millions of trees. maybe millions of mouths have dried your earth, oh my indonesia. maybe millions of crises have vented their anger, oh my indonesia. oh, who is it that has been taken away, my love—you, my homeland? or I, a child of the nation?) I am truly ashamed when i hear you half-heartedly singing that your children have been threatened with nighttime explosions. and you, too, are crying when your shame is the shame of everyone; it is written on our map; our wounds and pain lack fluency.

my homeland
is a winding road
full of signs,
that is my indonesia

a pair of lips is caught on the edge of a cliff. your children spill out onto the streets. a slice of the moon and clouds of wounds surround it like an archipelago.

"i'm not so good as a driver," says someone who claims to be a driver.

"as a passenger, it's not so easy," someone is heard exhaling.

"hmmmph," writes the dictionary.

"we need freedom," shout some people. "we need to be liberated," sigh the signs and poles.

"but our journey must continue," write the travel agencies and advertisements.

people buy tickets and chairs.

people sit down doing a *hi-hi* dance.

people dance abuse.

people curse until they're bored.

people become more and more bored.

the bus moves.

the archipelago is cut up, because the moon, too, is cut up.

"that is sumatera," says someone pointing to a cloud next to the moon.

"no, that is kalimantan," says someone eating a prawn.

"you're both wrong. it's java," says the conductor while drinking a glass of *bajigur*[1].

my homeland
is a winding road
full of signs,
that is my indonesia

my homeland
is a winding road
full of signs,
that is my indonesia

along the journey on all the corners going up and down the hills,
signs are always appearing

    a thousand exclamation marks store a million questions. arrow signs peck the wounds of my indonesia. a thousand school signs simplify the wisdom of my ancestors. a thousand bridge signs show *si Badai si Badu*[2]. a thousand spoon and fork signs are hunger, a smiling hunger that is not on the menu. a thousand wave signs inflate the struggle of your children. a thousand signs are lined up, crowded in your mouth. a thousand signs, thousands of streets, thousands of corners, thousands of hills and thousands of winding descents, wounds, my homeland in your countenance, oh my indonesia

my homeland
is a winding road
full of signs,
that is my indonesia

my homeland
is a winding road
full of signs,
that is my indonesia

---

[1] bajigur= a hot sweet drink made of coconut milk and palm sugar.
[2] si Badai si Badu= the name of a character in a popular television show for children.

290

Yogyakarta

Korrie Layun Rampan

1978

it is the heavens that i grasp at
at this edge of the sky
i see myself walking groping toward illusion
carving fate unraveling grief

writing memories
of a love passing by the grave
i do not note the thousands of disappointments
thousands of sacrifices thousands of meanings

only what is grasped what is reachable by hand
what is paid for in blood
what is worth a life
what is deep as love

what is left are footsteps at a distance
the blood of history
the young already long gone
the loving the remembered forgotten

A Hot Cup of Tea

Arifin C Noer

1979

A cup of hot tea one evening
perfects the panorama
of relaxing, after releasing the burdens of work.

> — Thank you, my wife.
> It is love with loyalty you offer
> in the steam of a hot drink that warms the body.

A bird wanders through a cluster of clouds over the roof.
On the terrace, nodding, watching it,
an old man, a retired civil servant.
On the ground where bougainvillea
scatters each year.
On the rattan chair, trembling, watching it,
an old man with an old woman.

> — Swallow it, dear.
> I have mixed it with
> intoxicating love spells.
> Hopefully later you will faint
> and faint always
> in my embrace.

Two pairs of eyes with quivering eyelashes
conversing intimately. A gentle breeze
shifts a grey hair out of place;
the strand floats and settles
on the ground. Nevertheless,
the moon does not stop shining
from within the soft cheeks,
and its color is red. Roses swing-sway
on their branches. The window has closed
its shutters, shy, like the intimate embrace of
the pair of young lovers in their memories.

 — I never brought home
   any souvenirs. I never once gave you a gift
   on your birthday, dear.

 — But you never stopped
   pinching my cheeks. With love
   you gave me the spirit
   to live my life
   in the tangled web of fate.
   You never stopped
   stroking my hair. And you always gave me
   everything; anything.

 — But my wages brought nothing more than misery
   by the second week.

 — But God scattered the seeds of good fortune
   during the third week
   and through the weeks after that.

 — Indeed.

 — Indeed. There is no need to regret
   the past; it's meaningless
   except as a valued
   story. He truly
   does not expect regret, but He will
   aid those with spirit. Isn't that so, dear?

 — Indeed.

 — Indeed.

This is an evening within his eighty years
and his wife's seventy-five years. This is an evening

293

like the many evenings that have passed and the ones
that will come.

They sit together. A hen
clucks, searching for her chicks. Her bald head
bobs with worry. She
hops into the trash pit,
finds one. They sing.
They sing incessantly as they peck-peck
at the food.

      — Dear husband.

      — Dear wife.

      — Where did he go?

      — Who?

      — Our boy.

      — Our only boy.

      — There is only one moon
         There is only one sun.

      — Only one, dear
         And he's gone!

      — Dear.

      — Our baby has been snatched away by the war.

      — Stop, dear,
         the anger. We're old;
         it will add to our years
         We are sad; we are grieving.
         There is no need to add to it.

— The pillar of our house has cracked.
The most beautiful vase has shattered.
The fruit of the first night's mattress has been brushed aside!

— But the All-Merciful
has erected many pillars silently
without
our noticing.

— Indeed.

— Indeed. A cock
that has fought and never returned home
does not mean misfortune
A cock that hatches
from our love has made pillars
for our homeland,
our great and noble home.

— Indeed.

— Indeed.

The woman nodded
and looked down at the ground
at days and hopes that were still stored away.
The man nodded too
and looked at his feet;
how tightly he had held his son's hand

With resignation they carried out their mandate to the end.
They furnished their simple home
with gratitude and patience.
A ray of light
binds the two of them.

This is an evening within his eighty years
and his wife's seventy-five years. This is an evening
like the many evenings that have passed and the ones
that will come.

> — Drink, my dear,
>   Before the magic of the spell fades

The chapped lips smile.
An old well in the middle of a thick cluster of bamboo!

> — Thank you, my dear.

They smile like two banyan trees
dense with leaves. Two banyan trees
under the charm of the evening's colors.

Turtle in the Desert

Bibsy Soenharjo

1979

Have you heard the tale of the turtle in the Sahara
who thought the desert a shore?
They say, on average,
turtles reach an age
of three hundred years...
Even if it took all the years of the turtle's life
to reach the ocean's edge,
that turtle would still be fortunate...
But, the desert is too large,
too wide,
and the ocean's edge remains out of sight.
Closing his eyes for the last time,
the turtle finally says,
"How incredibly vast this shore... !
How incredibly vast this shore... !"

Tears Are My Ancestors

D. Zawawi Imron

1979

"whisper to the wind about the wooden clogs they discovered on historic mountain!" said the floodwaters that didn't quite cause destruction.
A long time ago on that mountain, there was a war between cucumbers and durians.
By the wounds of the corpses strewn on the ground, a proclamation was decreed—a provocation gained power.

and sensational news gets around. there are shadows on that mountain scattering flowers.

Sangkuriang

Eka Budianta

1979

From a folk music concert

Sing a song of the dusk and the rice paddy frogs,
Of the birds of the forest and the rustling bugs;
Play the shepherd's flute, with a lute summon the dark
And tell the tale of two lovers and two broken hearts.

The wind howled from the hills, the darkness grew wild,
Dayang Sumbi missed her small child.
Nightfall was coming. "Come home now, my dear!"
But he did not return year after year.
Then one day from the forest emerged a young man
Who fell in love with Dayang Sumbi; his name was Sangkuriang.
But on the eve of their wedding, she saw a scar on his head.
"It's you, my lost son! We cannot be wed.
But if you insist, then a lake you must make
And a boat to sail across it, before the day breaks."
Sangkuriang was determined, "Come along little fairies!"
Help me cut down the hills and the trees we will bury.
Help me build a boat, dear Flute, for my bride.
Fill up my lake, O Waves, with your tide.
Then tomorrow at daybreak, let the sun hide its face,
Let the crow of the cock my success celebrate;
Stay, stay, O Dawn, clutch your shawl, stay asleep.
The boat to carry my love will soon be complete."

Sing a song of the dusk, sing a song of the dawn
To the beat of the rhythm deep in Mount Priangan.
For the dusk and the dawn are the old melodies
That play in our souls for all time, endlessly.

---

[1] Sangkuriang is a Sundanese legend in which Sangkuriang and Dayang Sumbi unwittingly fall in love and are about to marry when Dayang Sumbi notices a scar that identifies Sangkuriang as her son. She gives him what she believes to be impossible tasks as a condition of marrying her: making her a lake and building her a boat overnight. Seeing that Sangkuriang will indeed finish these tasks before the sun rises, Dayang Sumbi spreads her shawl across the sky to make it look like dawn has arrived. Apparently defeated, Sangkuriang kicks over his boat in anger. The legend explains the existence of Lake Bandung and of Mount Tangkuban Parahu, which is said to be formed from Sangkuriang's upside-down boat.

299

Husband

Goenawan Mohamad

1979

He knew the woman wanted to quickly close the door.
He knew she wanted to signal something.
And for that he stopped mid-stride
in the wet garden, a spear's length away.
Something had changed. Twilight held fast.
Lanterns faded. No more flirting, anymore.
"I didn't think you'd come.
It's been quiet around here for a few days now."
Her face paled. Like silent letters in a cable
that urge something forward yet are not to be found.
"My husband will arrive tonight.
"Tonight, for us, is a night for peace."
How long have those stones been stacked
in sadness in the garden?
Had she even seen a painting of a quail
flying above a lotus pond?
And the woman quickly closed the door.
"I have to embroider something on the mosquito screen," she said.
"Because of that, good night
because of that, my husband, good night."

Queen of the South Sea

Iman Budhi Santosa

1979

Alone along the southern coast you await
the dark. Your spirit, weary of its craft forsakes
its shadow-puppet shape. Imbued with offerings
you soar to the heavens: a woman of the ocean
transforms into a Star. Empress of omens,
you glimmer like a firefly over desolate coral reefs.

On the prowl for the wieldy-whorling tongues of human men,
you are Enchantress, seeking sonnets pure enough
to soothe your ancient soul. When the knights of your betrothed
massacred your family, they ripped your noble princess heart to bloody shreds.
Now you crave quatrains and twisted rhymes
to penetrate men's navels
and find a place within their hearts to be enthroned.

Invisible protector of Java's hills and valleys,
escorted in a carriage, your presence is manifested
by the percussion of galloping feet:
You are the Queen rose incense greets
at every door. Nevertheless, Princess,
we ask you not to alarm our young
coming home from prayers—their mouths still smell so sweet—
the Prophet's blessings still clinging to their tongues.

---

[1] The Queen of the South Sea, named "Nyai Roro Kidul" in Java, is a spirit deity believed in the present day to be the consort to the Sultans of Yogyakarta. The second stanza of the poem refers to the Sundanese princess Dyah Pitaloka, who in the mid-1300s committed suicide when her family was murdered at her engagement meeting to the king of the Majapahit kingdom. According to legend, Nyai Roro Kidul is Dyah Pitaloka's spirit.

Night

Leon Agusta

1979

for Hukla Inna Alyssa

On a quiet night the grave speaks
and I hear dust scream under a full moon

> "Your eyes will go blind, Alyssa
> if you open the window"

In the river my dreams want to sail
farther, farther
> "Your heart will turn to cinders, Alyssa
> if you are awakened now"

The gods pass through
ushered by feuds

Deaf Man's Hill

Slamet (Su) Kirnanto
1979

There's no time to pick at wounds
only fog and greenery
—a hermit's blanket! Your silence astounds
touches the gold—serenity of spirit, rises upward then asks:
Is your peak really Heaven?
Deaf man's Hill
    at your foot
a man is delayed for a moment
to untangle his desire. And forgets
to ask about tomorrow
strong faith
within his heart.
Suddenly erect
like the rocks of Toba land!
In the silence spelling out the universe!
Toba Lake—its rocks and people, too
live on steep cliffs
opening into a vast pool
—setting sun and swimming moon!
There's empty singing
and a guitar strums
    quivers hollow out the heavens!
    Quench the thirst
    cautious and disappointed
dissolved in the waves.
The palm wine drunkard returns home
slowly. In his hand
he grasps a single flower tightly!
    Give me back
    a sane life
in the hardness of stone
in the softness of flowers

One

Sutardji Calzoum Bachri

1979

i will translate my body into your body
i will translate my hair into your hair
if your hand cannot be my hand
i will translate my hand into your hand
if your tongue cannot speak my tongue
i will translate my tongue into your tongue
i will translate my fingers into your fingers
if your fingers cannot touch me
i will translate my blood into your blood
if your blood follows a separate beat from mine
if your stomach cannot stomach my stomach
i will translate my stomach into your stomach
if your genitals do not speak of my genitals
i will translate my genitals into your genitals

our flesh will be one, our souls one
even when we are far apart
what pierces you will make me bleed

Hunger

Selasih

1979 p

When the body cries for sustenance
When the joints in your body ache
When hunger and thirst are insufferable
It feels as if your body has no soul.

Ears pounding, vision blurred
A throbbing head and pounding heart
Just as the body needs food for its stomach
The spirit requires food for its soul.

Far away over there, in Neverland
Across the ocean, in the land of the gods
A cornocupia of food is on display
Savory and pleasant to smell.

Above the sky, in a lofty place
The face of an angel appears
In her hand she holds a pitcher
With water that's crystal clear.

The morsels entice the eye
The water invites the heart
I stretch out my hand, wanting to touch
I lift my feet to approach.

But, dear God, my body is weak
For lack of strength, my desire is delayed
My vision is dim, my legs are bound
To use force, I would fear being broken.

Were food not visible
I would not feel disappointment
In sight but not in hand
Is a bile that poisons the soul.

Oh, Father, oh, Mother
My siblings, my friends
Help this child, show your daughter
How to free the hunger and ease the thirst.

Elegy

Abdul Hadi W.M.

1980

My enemies, my faithful friends
each time they come
to wound and heal me:
"Let us build a bridge," then
we build a bridge and immediately destroy it

They do not know and I have forgotten

Each time they come
to sink their claws in me, destroy my possessions:
plates, chairs, dining table, poems,
opportunities and my irresponsibility

I think
they have come to remove my past, my freedom
just as I think they can
destroy their own freedom
their own decisions

Where do they go, to hide
and save themselves?
There are so many weeds and so many caves
in my heart, in their hearts,
that I seldom know,
will never know

And what if they find
the shining sword I sharpened?
And my fierce fangs
constantly gnashing?

I say: I am free even though you want to kill me
I am free though you pursue and surround me
I am free because my bitterness liberates me

But they are bad lovers, just as I am
who can never make a place for love
And like me they hunt emptiness and futility
They want to kill me because they think I want to kill them
I want to kill them because I think they want to kill me
Let us help them, let us help ourselves

I Am Your Blood, Madura

D. Zawawi Imron

1980

mute boulders sleep upon you
gather flame and sprout
prayer flowers
though i roll on beds of thorns, my heart will not be wounded
though i brood in misery, my love will never wither
i am at once
your eldest and your
youngest child
who returns now to your womb
to realize
i am the racing bull
born of your smiles and tears

a dust mote settles, a dewdrop comes to rest
a bead of honey coalesces
enduring sky's ancient blue
the cosmos' golden rust, withstanding
seven continents of rasping anguish

here and now
let me cry out:
you are my tears, madura

when seasons change, if rain won't fall
i'll drench you with my pulse

should your breast run dry, your arid land
i'll plow with gilded horns

upon your salt dunes
i will set my brain on fire
because i am the racing bull
born of your tears and smiles

i run to chase the waves
to embrace the moon, i fly

and pluck the stars from their positions
on my ancestors' spirit tree
at the crested edge of the sky
i state my pledge:
i am your blood, madura

---

[1] Every year on the island of Madura there is a festival of bull races called Sapi Kerapan that has been
taking place since the thirteenth century.

Manifesto

Toeti Heraty

1980

I accuse all of you
will take you to a court with no judge
for who knows, bribery is rampant, reaching even the Chief Justice
who can guarantee that from the beginning no prejudice was shown
for the world, the universe too, is man's possession

since that moment, when Eve became Mother
or, even long before, you trembled at the greatness of
the Glorious Bitch that birthed those little beings
blind and naked, with instinctive ease and bit off
the umbilical cord, licked them clean, nursed them with care
and then placed them throughout the world
so it was that mammals were prepared
for Darwin and his evolutionary struggle of life
yet—
women are bound by little things
by minor details they in fact give thanks for
　　silently, humbly, seriously
while you, because of your smallness, conceit and craftiness
tremble in fear of recognition
nonetheless
place a medal on your chest—paternal status
most likely with no supporting biological evidence
but, no matter
it is for the legacy,
the ego and the continuation of evolution
and decree that woman is the root of all evil,
a mass of flesh, a jumble of emotions, at once
an imbecile and an angel
and wrap her feet, lock her groin, place a veil over her head
to restrict her every movement
and make her walk a slow, heavy dance
　　she bows in obedience, trembles with fear
　　curses herself for her apparent wrongs
and sometimes—but only every once in a while—pamper her

you become like children possessed—haven't all the dangers
    and the nuisances been removed—
and busy yourselves with games:
soccer, billiards, wrestling and holy wars
    science and technology for their freedom and creativity
war, pollution, protons and neutrons
and shuttle between Moscow, Beijing and Washington

you wriggle with impatience, ready for your games of war
and wait for the moment of mutual destruction
drain the seas, poison the lakes and rivers
the ozone layer is eaten away, the waste of consumption disposed
anywhere—why worry, the astronauts can deal with that later—
the earth is a cake of energy, to be divided
like a birthday cake, with a glowing candle
    —fuse of catastrophe—
and drink a toast to a ripe old age
for ceremonies do, of course, incur respect
and like diplomacy become a code
increasingly hard to decipher

to these children
in uniforms, with medals and black robes
    with sermons, rhetoric and exhortations
we have entrusted the fate of this earth

stunted beings, haunted by fears of castration
knowing only one true calamity: impotence
swell up their chests through psychoanalysis
    with the solidarity of the mafia and our Father in Heaven
and give their blessing—a pacifier—to women's emancipation

I say once more
I accuse you all, though probably it is now too late
the war rages outside, the ecosystem has been destroyed

refugees, some hungry, some cunning, abound
diplomacy is now a joke, one so completely without humor

we have been silent long enough
sacrificing for your ego and so many abstractions
must women now save the world as well
suddenly development is our business too!

you have lost your privilege
and are like clowns running helter skelter through catastrophe
    and, in the end, calling out for mother
but—
for my son
I would withdraw my accusation
and become a traitor, but—of course—it's already too late

Crazy Nyoman

Frans Nadjira
1980p

That Nyoman really is crazy
searching the marketplace
with his lantern in the early morning light

The gods are dead—*chak chak chak!*
Come on then, Sita, let's dance to the wasteland
and put offerings on the TV set

(Hanoman leaps from branch
to branch, sobbing, from shore to shore
searching for Rama, who in fact is long gone
shot dead by Mannix)

A tourist gulps down palm wine
from a section of bamboo
This must be the enchantment of the fabled East

Merapi at Twilight

Linus Suryadi

1980p

haze has settled on the remnants of twilight
night is a girl letting down her jet
black hair; making shadows behind the moon

fog clings to the boughs, seeking shelter in their swoon

i climb this path, hurrying forth
gentle drizzle falls on this crevice of the north

in the village, people say, the most distant home

summons your heart, entices you to come

no, over there it is not fallen snow
on the peak, but lava melting sorrow
without greeting, silence envelops smoke

before freezing the forgotten slopes

i traverse confusion as days turn into years

in my silent palms: unfulfilled desires
"good evening," a long desolation then
lightning flashes, for an instant the veil is lifted, gone...

Concerned in The New Order

Remy Sylado

1980s

help!

this ship of ours is currently

CAPSIZED

Individualism in Collectivism

Remy Sylado

1980s

you	you	you	you	you	you	you
you	you	you	you	you	you	you
you	you	you	you	you	you	you
you	you	you	ME	you	you	you
you	you	you	you	you	you	you
you	you	you	you	you	you	you
you	you	you	you	you	you	you

Intimidation within Democracy

Remy Sylado

1980s

whoever
dares
go over the head
of the head
will
certainly
lose his head

The Lone Fisherman

Toeti Heraty

1980s

wondrous clouds
pass by the moon which by custom
remains behind, alone

catching nets of human glances
captured in the seine of night unfurled
gazes weary of endless thirst

o moon, should the earth fall silent
and there be no people left, for whom would you expose
your full and shining body, stroked by clouds

even the clouds edge away and you are snared
by branches—slipping, falling
are caught by the fisherman, to be hauled up
   with shimmering white fish to shore

the beach is clean, the fisherman hastens
home; nothing is left behind
but, oh, the moon on the sand (almost left floundering there)
is lifted with a gentle gesture
   and thrown back in again

Honolulu Impressions

Darmanto Yatman

1981

from the pacific
I peep at you
you whore with a high-tech gloss

in the end we did finally meet
your long loose hair
how old you looked
after years of longing

--

staring out the window
in the morning
the birds sang: hallelujah!

--

what do you want to do here
climb the mountain's ridge
or flirt with the boats on the shore

Mmmm, what are your supple fingers doing
my love:
stroking my back
or setting a time bomb

--

napping in the middle of the day
a turtledove sings
a lullaby

--

birds sing
on cherry branches
breed and nest on top of skyscrapers
here in honolulu

--

you can take everything in your hands here
the fog (with its dew) toeing the tips of grass
rainbows (that bloom) rising from thickets
or flesh (of the female kind) waving on the sandy
beach

yet

something remains free outside the grasp
of my longing
(which like the asphalt streets of honolulu
sticks to the soles of my shoes
arresting my steps)
for you

--

staring at the honolulu hills
I think of you
a sunflower
the moment before dusk

--

the wind
plays for a second in the branches
                    jesus! jesus!
                    why did our friendship slide so fast
                    as I grew older:
the rainbow that bloomed a minute ago
perished a minute later.

Rectangular Sun

Rachmat Djoko Pradopo

1981

your words are rectangular like the sun
hearing them I am nothing but dumbfounded
still what is bluer than the moon
if not words that are triangular

oh, how unfortunate are people without fortune
who when hearing thunder under their
    beds
do not cry
because prisons are everywhere
for those whose words are round
in their culmination like a full moon

tomorrow there will be white birds
uninhibited free on the wing
when the sun regains
its roundness again as in a dream

Kurusetra Drums of War

Suminto A. Sayuti

1981

Abimanyu's wife, Utari, speaks:

you who are covered in blood
bearing the burden of battle as you march to Kurusetra
stop for a moment and listen
to the weary sun as it witnesses one death after another
and the war
which is never-ending

you men who try to endure
everlasting hatred
and human promises
look up at the sun and the wings of nature
because they too will be close to you
first end the war within yourself

while the drums of war beat
the arrows brush one another speeding through the sky
win the ever-present struggle
say: I am a human being

Abimanyu speaks:

because each step leaves traces
stop weeping, woman, stop talking
the raging darkness is your own battlefield
do not cry
no one can extinguish these coals
and the wounded sense of self

look towards the distant horizon
you will hear nature flapping its wings
you will see the sun and the moon taking shelter
there where the wind and the night begin

keep the blood that drips from the tips of your arrows
secure in the net of passing time
and tell your neighbors in the world
that a man must go and never stop
life ebbs and flows
even in my dreams I am awake

Abimanyu's father, Arjuna, speaks:

what does pride mean
when the bow is broken and the sacred warastra weapon buried in the ground
twilight is ready with its feast of colors
and you are marching forwards
following the receding voices

I want to slash with my Pulanggeni keris
on the far edge of the battle
but the wind has grown old
and the leaves have fallen from the *salam* tree
I see only shadows growing ever longer
the battle field roars, the war calls: there will be
            no end to this

The divine patriarch, Krishna, speaks:

if you would allow me and the world were ready
I would burn this crown with a pinch of incense
and let a white horse gallop across the battlefield
bearing flags, to indicate that the war has not yet begun
here, at the heart's border
and you would understand
that no one can win this war
unless they enter the inner recesses of the heart

Tragedy of Marriage and Live-Love-Lose

Sutardji Calzoum Bachri

1981 p

marry

    marry

      mar-ry

        mar-ry

          mar-ry

            re-

          marry

          re

        marry

        re-

      marry

      re-

    marry

re-

    marry

      remarry

        remarry

          live

            love

              lose

                remarry

              live

            love

          lose

        remarry

          live

            love

              lose

                marry

                  ME

Herman

Sutardji Calzoum Bachri

1981 p

herman cannot walk on the earth cannot sleep on the moon
cannot warm himself in the sun cannot stay in a body
cannot drink the ocean cannot wait on the ground
cannot fly in the wind cannot rest on a cloud
cannot reach through words cannot keep quiet cannot stop talking
cannot hold in his hand cannotcannotcannotcannotcannotcannot

where is herman? do you know?
helpherman help helphelphelphelphelphelpppppp!

Prambanan Temple

Suminto A. Sayuti

1982

stone, heart held hostage by time
bearing the moon
on unraised arms
source of longing
(centre of my desire for You)

today a gentle wind blows
opening the soul
with youthful greetings
what do you say about the stones?
(I say, my love cannot delay
the sky is always blue)

Reflections of a Teacher

Eka Budianta

1982

What is education for? I asked.
To acquaint you with that which is noble, answered mountain.
So that you will know eternity, said sky.
Be able to appreciate beauty, added sun.
In order to discern wickedness, exclaimed forest.
Understand yourself, whistled bird.
And make you dynamic, whispered wind.

How does it benefit me? I asked.
By making your thinking clear, stated pond.
And your soul radiant, persuaded lotus.
I still did not understand why it should be this way.
So that you will love life, admonished tree.
Know freedom and boundaries, advised moon.
Not satisfied with any of these explanations, I went to sleep.

The next morning I got up and didn't ask any more questions.
But, why did you get up? asked window.
Why are you alive? demanded wind.
Why so pensive? scolded rocks.
You wanna die, huh? mocked flowers.
How could I answer them?
A teacher only knows how to question.

Scars of Metamorphosis

Gus tf

1982

it was something like that, dividing ourselves
to give birth to a new me. "become a soldier!" you said.
and the sound of tramping boots flowed in my direction

and then bayonets and bullets, too, raised your ancient dream
on high. upon the division, "become a dagger!" cut me down
or slice me up, this stupid man who prefered to be a stone

just as he had always been

The Sea I

Iskandar Leo

1982

Like those before me
I stand at your edge with a fishing
spear
Attack?
So I attack your rippling wake
Nobody knows where your extremities
lie
Pull back!
So I retract my piercing hope knowing
nobody knows the whereabouts of
your salty trenches.

Like them
I never surrendered
to the immensity
to the blue intensity
to fate carried recklessly away
            from coast to coast on your
cresting waves.

Like those before me
            I too attack
            pull back
            attaaaaaack
My spear
your saltiness
are just playing the seasons

The Sea II

Iskandar Leo

1982

A fishing spear lies stranded on the
beach
after a storm
: Lord
who has given in this time?

No signs to be seen
no scent of rancid fate
no record of seasonal injury
except the wailing waves,
a falcon's screech
far away and grating against the weather
and the roaring reef

A fishing spear lies stranded on the
beach
after a storm
a child contemplates it uneasily
Lord
   Someone whispered
   Probably whoever it was that had surrendered
     : Child, pull up the stakes before the tide
     turns

My heart's distraught
when a single hibiscus blossom falls
      vanishing through a window
      plummeting into the hearth
      waiting for dark

A fishing spear lies stranded on the beach
after a storm
tears well up in a child's eyes

: Lord
>Bring someone to find him,
>>to bury him away from the shore
>>and leave for him some marker
and don't let the current take him to a faraway sinkhole
for then I wouldn't know where to write my loneliness.

La Ronde

Sitor Situmorang

1982

1

Humming to forget his encounter
with the night, he's alone in the room.
The season climbs until the snow
falls, until the hunger starts to grow

Two tales, disembodied—
the smells of their presences intertwine:
"Oh, to die like this," comes a dark whisper
from the peak of pleasure, until dawn

Lying on night's breast. "You're all mine,"
gasping moments flow into kisses,
frenzied lips search for time,
solidity in the woman's body

The season climbs until dawn.
Outside the open window, falling snow.

2

Is there anything more beautiful
than full lips in bloom?
Is there anything sweeter
than the shadows of eyebrows?

Her brow causes the painter to hesitate:
to kiss or to cover her shoulder?
But her hair guides his hand
to her buttocks, ripe with suggestion

And to her thigh of sculpted marble
supporting the sloping waist.
Encircling the navel, and then descending
somewhere, farther below, to the center of all

Black as coal and ready to receive
a beautiful premise.
Your supple breasts weigh on my heart,
please accept this man's ripened dream!

3

You are my goddess, comfort of barren nights
and days of fruitless deeds.
Eternal malaise is forgotten
and the body is destroyed by pure bliss!

In your eyes the flame of desire remains unquenched
searing the bones, sapping the quick.
I yield to the animal of the night,
your ever more fierce and unfettered passion

Is there a temple more holy
than the marbled grail of your body?
Is there anything more beneficent than your womb
and the heat of mercy lapped by the mouth of sin?

To you I give all the love and supplication
of the poet's song and precious dreams.
Momentary suspension is much too sweet
when tortured longing crushes all hopes.

Cocktail Party

Toeti Heraty

1982

I brush the wrinkles from my party dress
smooth my hair into place
finger-curls at my temples
                    the competition may now begin
a race with time
with boredom, and what's more
                    illusory stakes
a twist of thread in a tempest
a storm rages among us

a tempest? well
who really cares
I laugh politely, biting my nails
                    produces such feelings of impotence
annihilation is a matter for the gods
but a campfire roars
                    on fallow land
accompanied by raging wind, and the whip
                    of lightning flashes

the dreadful woman I now face
with her sharpened brows and tongue
                    and high-pitched laughter—
I am trapped, wine glass in my hand
smiling patiently the coward hides—
                    the room reverberates
with polite mumbles, cursory greetings
a swish of her sash and the woman goes
leaving everyone befuddled

why be so disturbed by disappointment?
take a deep breath, weakness comes
                    facing the competition in the arena
they say only death dispatches love
but life too takes its share, death
                    is but the false hope of a communion
and then only if you agree

a striking estrangement, all
that once was loved is lost—
                    immersed
in intimacy and sleep
an interval of dream without duress
and the storm that rages among us?
mumbles, smiles, and handshakes

Kur Lak Lak

L.K. Ara

1982 p

kur lak lak
may the rain stop
may the cold stop
may the frost stop
may the pain stop

kur lak lak
may anger cease
may jealousy cease
may pride cease
may hatred cease

kur lak lak
kur lak lak
may the day be long
may the end be slow in coming
kur lak lak
kur lak lak

A Calligraphy Wall Decoration

Mohammad Diponegoro

1982 p

I

A Christian of Italian descent
tried to read a German translation of the Koran
but after a quarter of an hour
closed the book
because he was tired and bored
and locked the book in a drawer.

He was a dance choreographer
striving for maximum creativity.
He was driven by his desires
and a lack of time.
He partied with others at night
among clinking glasses of wine.
This was progress, prosperity, this was freedom,
this was modern Europe,
artistic gardens and technological jungles
built on the graves of millions of Jews.

Five or six years passed
and the man never remembered
the holy book he had placed in a drawer
even though he carried the key everywhere he went
in a pouch around his neck.

Until one night he had a strange dream
and he was moved, frightened.
In his dream he opened the drawer and took the book.
Ah, it was still there! he muttered,
the Koran in German,
and he read it with the eyes of faith
and heard his own natural voice.
His thoughts were as pure as porcelain.

337

His feelings were as pure as glass.
He felt as though he were alone
watching a beautiful woman in a sinuous dance.
His mind was enchanted by an eternal symphony
he had never heard before.
His emotions expanded,
leaped and soared
but his body was motionless
as he excitedly read
the words of Al-Ikhlas:
He is Allah, He is One,
Allah, the Eternal Refuge,
He neither begets nor is begotten,
there is none like unto Him.

He was suddenly awake and rubbed his eyes,
he looked in the mirror and saw that he was another man.
His name was still Ernst Friedrich de Teccerari,
a Christian of Italian descent.
He was still a noble
fluent in three languages.
But his heart had traveled to Egypt.
He wanted to touch the sand,
to learn the secret message of the Last Prophet.

When he eventually flew to Cairo
he was only half a Christian.

II

Finally he recited the Profession of Faith:
There is no god but Allah and Muhammad is His Messenger
and he took a new name,
Muhammad Abdul Rahman.

Muhammad Abdul Rahman lived in Egypt for five years
breathing the hot desert air,
eating and sleeping like an Egyptian,
earning a local salary
as a creative artist in a television studio.
His wages were minimal, his life simple
but he learned one secret after another.
The last prophet and teacher of the world.

III

When Muhammad Abdul Rahman returned to Germany
he felt like a stranger wherever he went.
He was an exile wherever he went,
his heart could not return home.

He could never hear the call to prayer from a nearby mosque
or the chanting of the Koran through an open window,
the reverberation of the congregation calling *Amen*,
the voice of a guest wishing him God's peace,
the sound of an old couple praying late at night,
the rustle of a woman's gown as she bowed devoutly
or the splashing of water to purify the body.

In Germany he met a culture of whisky and brandy,
of lust pretending to be freedom and a human right,
the dishonest scales of material wealth.
Neighbours who didn't know each other's names,
children shouting at their mothers,
mothers uncertain of their children's father.

Muhammad Abdul Rahman was no longer at home in his own country
so he left to travel in Muslim lands.
Kuwait, Iran, Pakistan—he visited them all,

anywhere he could hear the call to prayer, the Koran being chanted,
and the greeting *Assalamalaikum*, peace be with you.

IV

Once he even tried to come to Indonesia
but he was shocked
when he landed at Ngurah Rai airport
and was welcomed by Balinese dancers.
This is Hindu culture! he shouted.
Am I really in Indonesia? he wondered.
(LAUGHTER) He was another victim of the tourist industry.

Prostitutes' Oath

F. Rahardi

1983

one
we
a nation of
tempeh
have one
heaven
heaven on
earth

two
we
a nation of
tofu
have rocks for
lipstick
and our ass for
a pillow

three
we
a nation of
geckos
have one
objective
to hook
the lord
into becoming
a customer

The Running Century

Afrizal Malna

1984

A hammer. Time doesn't want to stop: a hammer. Time doesn't want to stop. Thousands of clocks show different times: all of them moving alone. A hammer. None want to stop. All of them are moving alone.

People watch television: a hammer. They're watching death that is being opened up on the streets; they've sung on school benches and in markets. Oh, the children of death who want to change heaven. The silent are saved in time.

A hammer. Maps are running in a daze; the city comes and goes, chasing time. A hammer. The earth works, the sea works and the machine works. Death which works on the streets. A hammer. Death which works on the streets.

Oh, the chest working within time.

The running world. The running world.

People are spurred on, endlessly chasing.

Corn Seller

Ahmadun Y. Herfanda

1984

at the Northern Square in Yogya

in clouds of smoke from grilling corn
a young woman dreams
she can see heaven:
with this corn, I will
ride a car to paradise, she says

passersby are set on fire by her fanning of the flames
as she grills her corn, one ear after another
so lost in thought is she, she singes
her long loose hair

the smoke smells of heaven
it is the scent of love between Wulan and Jaka
she screams with laughter
while grilling corn, one ear after another
until all her hair is gone

A Bowl of Red Beans

Dhenok Kristianti

1984

"I'll trade Your grace
for a bowl of red beans,
for I am weak,
and the bean soup looks so tasty."
The moment Esau spoke
God's blessing was lost.

Like Esau, I am weary;
I do not care that a bowl of red beans
will satisfy for only a moment.
I, too, will give up my birthright.

Reader, have you turned away?
My brethren around me who are complaining
are merely hungry,
not weary.
They do not need a bowl of red beans
like Esau and I do.

"Here's a bowl of red beans
if you'll sacrifice God's blessing."
Yes, I will become an outcast,
thrown out of God's
flock of sheep,
but try to understand
that I am hungry and weak.

Children of Tobacco

Jamal D. Rahman

2000p

To the tobacco farmers in Madura

we the children of tobacco
grow amongst children of stone
our breath smells of drought mixed with cigars

if we hug each other
we embrace with arms of drought
if we kiss each other
we kiss with a whiff of tobacco

the sky in our village has fallen a thousand times
but we never cry
because our skin is still brown
as brown as the earth
where we dig up our own tears

the sky in our village has fallen a thousand times
but we never surrender

on every tobacco leaf
the veins of our lives are unraveled
on every tobacco plant
the fibers of our prayers are strung

Asia Reads

Afrizal Malna

1985

The sun is free from its decor. And we still face the same sky, the same earth. *Asia*. After the gods have turned to stones in television sets, after cataclysm, old stories calling again from other lands. There, every word smells of petrol. We hang down again through new clothes. *Asia*. Ships open markets, trading dragon-cows for oil.

Asia. We enter the ornaments of various powers, new flags, sex and love, which are different again. Cities in colorful clothes. Turning silence into a road at night. *Asia*... A place of words forbidden to be read, a place of texts not allowed to be written.

Shining soil, *Asia*, reeking of mankind, *Asia*, protecting us from all eras, *Asia*. Where the ancestors make words. Asia can only be met like a lost clod of soil: the place where language is born.

Asia.

About Adams

Motinggo Boesje

1985

From the beginning from the start Adam was taught was taught
 was taught
from the beginning he was taught the names of things
from the first Adam was smarter from the beginning
 smarter
from the beginning smarter than the angels

from the beginning from the start Adam fell in love with things
 with things
from the beginning adams have murdered from the beginning
because of things only because of things

from the beginning adams have hoarded things
from the beginning things have hoarded adams
from the beginning adam was short of breath short
from the beginning adam died along with those of us who
 died

Because all adams are Sanu
And Sanu is me Sanu is you
Haven't we been engaged in murder
 for a long time?
Because of that listen to Me, because of that
We have long been dead long been dead long

About Women

Motinggo Boesje

1985

now and in the past woman sells buys sells
    buys
this is her original business this is
man becomes arrogant whereas he is only a creature of labor
    a pet
man is woman's pet

cared for by his mother
cared for by his lover
cared for by his wife
cared for by his mistress

don't lie admit it don't lie
admit admit admit the art of woman's thinking
admit admit man's handicraftsmanship
merely a creature of labor merely an animal
male servants with aristocratic dress
just wearing grand clothes in the name of leadership
without the art of thinking other than craftsmanship

Woman: art
entirely art

Hey, are you listening Sanu?

My Childhood Floats on the Sea

Nirwan Dewanto

1985

My childhood floats on the sea
Fishermen paint my body with salt
Drink my blood from a glass of shining sand
As a hostage to waves, I know poetry
Like butterflies shivering on boats
Like coral nursing at my mother's breast

My clothes now smell of the city's foul air
As I point my finger at the buildings:
"Inhale the smell of waves in this rusted body!"
I order them to patiently bow before me
Just as fish once loved my eyes
Come now, children, listen to the storm in my hair
Change the thick, black smoke into millions of pearls

I don't care if these roads lead to hell
Change a bowl of rice into a nest of thorns in my stomach
When thousands of men in uniform ask me
"Why is your chin pointed like a ship's keel?"
I flick the sand and algae from my body
I burn their mouths with the beauty of poetry
They shiver and transform into thousands of geese

Maybe it is true that I vowed my foul love
To a girl who was clever at disguise
Patiently she licked the salt from my body
As I lapped sandy palm wine from her green tits
Our bones bashed and clattered in the night
Our golden sweat inundated homes
And at the peak of our combat she moaned
"Watch my fangs lengthen with my hatred of the sun!"

My childhood floats on the sea
From behind boats my mother once called
"Get gone, and climb those stairs of light!"

But here stairways are made of steel
And my blood is scrambled by window curtains
And when my hair and shoes begin to burn
Only the roar of the waves is ever able to rescue me

Fishermen don't teach fine manners
Even though I had to go with those thousands of geese
"Be a swindler who's light on his feet!"
Thus, I drank medicine so that my mouth would not be sealed
And then behind the roaring flames I forgot my name

Listen as the waves try to steal children and that girl
Look at the butterfly that's slipped from my eyebrow
Dear God, make me at once a thief and a savior
With betrayal behind office desks but a respectable life
Hoist sails on the chimney stacks
And grow coral on a pile of shit

And if I can no longer distinguish
The season just past from the one ahead
I will discard my clothes and shoes
To run naked in the streets while gazing in hell's direction
Let the buildings blink with embarrassment to see me
Even as a youngster comes and cuts off my cock
And from the remaining field of dried grass
I write a letter to the fish in the sea with my blood
So that they will forever be patient in awaiting my death

Today, the Birthday of the Gallows

Sides Sudyarto Ds.

1985

This may be the saddest moment for me.
On your birthday today, I cannot even hang
a wreath of flowers round your neck.

Elegantly, you stand erect
like a curved electrical pole
hit by the mortar fire of guerillas
when they fought for independence
when they still knew, of course,
the meaning of independence.

On your old back, rust has grown.
It festers sorely in shades of brown.
No paint remains.
Just dust is there, on your body.

On this, your birthday, I am perhaps the saddest.
I do not know whether you have sinned the most
or served the best.

I do not know how many enemies have hung from your rope
or how many leaders you have caught
or traitors who crossed over.

Congratulations on your birthday,
congrats to the deserted, a loss of meaning—
may your death be everlasting.

School

Sugiarta Sriwibawa

1985

School on the riverbank
Children search reflections
For origin and direction of the flow

School on the riverbank
Thoughts of boats
Dreams of the sea

School on the riverbank
The teacher helps paint the scene
The children work hard to color it in

numbers

Putu Oka Sukanta

1985p

the whistle blew
just before the call to midday prayer
the yard was empty of people
like a grave awaiting its corpse

the whistle blew
and the lines trickled out from the cells
those staying behind were locked away inside
the drum announcing prayers was quiet
midday prayers were off
something more important had come up
a journey whose end they didn't know

the whistle blew
and they moved one number at a time
just numbers
numbers
and more numbers
not people
not
anything
those with names and those without
the worshipped and adored
the praised and glorified
none of them were present
just the numbers
and numbers
the numbers themselves
without anything
without anybody
just
numbers.

* Title is lowercase in original publication.

The Lonely Poems

Putu Oka Sukanta

1985p

I had some lonely poems
that I kept inside a drawer
like a heart concealing its beat
a noise suppressing its echo
like the ribcage protecting the lungs.

I called a friend into the room
I locked the door
I presented him with the lonely poems
he was silent
there was fire in his eyes
he stood up
unlocked the door
and said goodbye

those lonely poems
I still keep them in a drawer
but I don't lock it anymore.

---

* Title is lowercase in original publication.

An Ocean of White

Emha Ainun Nadjib

1986

The angels of God have no ears, but they hear the song of thousands of white-covered heads.

The angels of God have no eyes, but they observe the march of this army of white.

The angels of God do not have hearts, but they feel the tremor from this awakening of white, that seems to come from the core of the earth.

The angels of God do not possess language and culture, but far off in their realm of the stars
they seem to hear a voice crying: This is not a trivial matter! This is something more than just a resurgence of white cloth!

The angels of God seem to be talking among themselves:
This culture of white head coverings, are they really serious about it?

Oh, observe carefully: some are serious, some will become serious, some cannot be anything else.

Is it so important to the people of that country?

Well, it's as important as the fear in the hearts of the dispossessed, as the despair in the tears of the homeless, as the spiritual death of the hapless and downtrodden victims of history.

How is it possible for them to rise up from beneath the feet of Satan? How is it possible for them to shake off the chains of worldly ignorance?
Well, genuine rebirth arises from the womb of depravity, and pure awakening from a sense of constriction. But is Nature the source of all this activity, or does it come from inside human beings themselves?

It's nature within the human heart. Nature can't be thoroughly subdued, no matter how sharp the sword of human evolution. She will not bow down before the guile of her masters.

355

Will God's birds scatter bricks from the heavens to drive away the elephants of evil?
Oh, those birds long ago abandoned the awareness of mind, the sacred chants of the soul, the closed fists of the human hand.

The numberless angels of God take flight, covering the earth in every possible direction.
The angels of God, so fine they cannot be contained, not even by the smallest fraction of the atom.

The angels of God, their size inconceivable in terms of human science, able to hold the whole universe in the palm of their hands—
they quiver a moment in the spiritual roar arising from earth.

The angels of God seem to raise their voices, as they chatter back and forth among themselves:
What is so special about white cloth that covers the head?

It's foolishness to think of it just as clothing for the body.

Look, as time passes more and more humans are wearing it—there are men wearing it, there are masses of common people wearing it, communities of believers, anyone at all who needs protection, the grip of faith, the light of guidance. See, they are all wearing white cloth that covers their heads.

Are these white head coverings some kind of political act, a manifestation of religion, a form of cultural change?

The angels of God, whose clarity outshines the most perfect of mirrors, seem to reflect the sound of voices:
These head coverings sing of our outlooks, they are the ink of our decisions, the first steps in our struggle.

They are a statement of our convictions, our long road
towards knowledge, our process of searching.

They are an experiment in courage in the midst of
a neatly organized education in fear,
a burst of light in the midst of darkness,
a determined honesty amid days of deceit.

They are an experiment in meekness in the face of
life's brutalities.

These head coverings are an effort to protect ourselves
from attacks.

A world of some kind does attack us.

History in the hands of someone entraps us.

Power that emanates from some sort of lust hobbles our every movement,
and avarice, with its foaming lips, spits in our faces.

Our paths are blocked and we are confined behind fences
that line the main roads of our civilization and culture.

School books devour us,
spectacles and broadcasts gobble us up.

Advertisements and consumer goods herd us in one direction,
and when we think we're being educated
we are being deprived of our critical faculties.

We take cattle pens for places of worship
and we are gagged, weeping tears of blood.

Life means clambering over other people;
our future consists of bribery, just the taking and offering of bribes.

When the sun comes up we breakfast on promises;
when it sinks in the west we take promises to bed.

As a new day dawns we are sent back to sleep;
while it gets underway we are rocked in our cradles.

The intellectuals spend all their time searching for forgiveness
for every type of depravity
while the religious teachers are busy crafting verses
that will keep everything secure.

Our poet-heroes end up as beggars.

There is no protection from the viruses scattered in our minds
or the stunting of our ability to think.

There is no protection from the sacrifice of our humanity
in the haughty furnaces of power,
furnaces that burn in ways subtle, flexible and cruel.

There is no protection from the shredding of our faith
by knives smeared with poison.
There is no protection from the destabilizing of our shelters
by decisions imposed without us in mind.

There is no protection from the masquerading that attaches itself
to our faith, torturing and manipulating it
with false and intoxicating prescriptions.

There is no protection from the deceit blocking out the sun
That illuminates our rights and desires.

This is what those white head coverings are about! They all come from this!

This is *Furqan*, the distinction between Truth and iniquity,
the distance between beauty and decay,
the line between good and evil, right and wrong.

We wrap our heads in our convictions,
our choices and decisions, our courage and sense of righteousness,
born of our inner lives, our bodies and our souls.

These are the head coverings of the Lord our God, that teach us to walk
in the rhythm of the law,
to move with measured steps, not leaping ahead of time and the limits of reality,
taking one breath at a time, one step at a time, moving forward from one
insight to another,
one secret to another, victory by victory.

The angels of God, finer than crystal, the angels of God whose voices lie beyond
the power
of any ear to hear, are whispering among themselves:

Lo! They are the stepchildren of evolution! The illegitimate offspring of progress
and development!

Orphans of history, gathering up the shreds of common sense,
storing away purity of heart, breaking through into a solid future.

An ocean of white! An ocean of white! An unstoppable wave of struggle,
of wounds sustained in journeying.

Lo! The silence has begun to speak!

Song of a Colonized Land

Hamid Jabbar

1986

dead mountain
shrouded in mists of death
the master secluded
in forgetfulness

dead hills
ringed by valleys of death
decapitated
by an indifferent master

dead rivers
flowing into seas of death
poisoned
by a drug-crazed master

dead islands
covered in jungles of death
sold off
by a master in search of quick profits daily

dead oil
processed in the refineries of death
distilled
by a master wallowing in dollars

dead land divided into fields of death, parceled up by a master at his pleasure
dead country ruled by a mafia of death, who is the master
of his own country?

master of the mountains at his wit's end, master of the hills
seriously ill
master of the rivers overcome with distress, master of the islands mired in
delirium, master of the oil
sinking to his knees, master of the land
panicked with anxiety
master of the country

paralyzed with fear
who is the master
in his own country?

ah, he's dead,
the master of his own country, the master's dead,
dead and buried! now it's just the mistress, on her own!

o mistress of the mist
would you not be wrapped?
o mistress of the valleys
would you not be crafted?
o mistress of the seas
would you not be embraced?
o mistress of the jungles
would you not be spoken about?
o mistress of the refineries
would you not be composed?
o mistress of the fields
would you not be loved?
o mistress colonized
who would set you free?

freedom, oh freedom!
to be free
if you would be free, listen, just listen
oh master
no seclusion
oh mistress
no decapitation
oh master
no poison
o mistress
no selling off
o master
no distilling

o mistress
no parceling of land
o master
do not forget
o mistress
do not be indifferent
o master
do not seek excessive power
o mistress
do not wallow in dollars
so that we may all
be truly free!

oh to be free
to be truly free
listen, just listen
masters and mistresses
love, truly love
so that pain may be spoken of no more
and open up a path to heaven
here on earth
in our hearts
and in the afterlife
life everlasting
freedom!

Gamelan Is Dead

Soni Farid Maulana

1986

My country where the sun rises and sets,
where lizards and buffalo bathe in the rice paddies' mud,
stained by my blood, riven by a vengeful hatchet.
There you've constructed industrial machinery whose rumbling
grinds like a pestle in a mortar, depriving me, in my own granary,
of my workday: the source of my livelihood. My country
where the sun rises and sets
to paint tropical rain forests being burned to extinction
by big city savagery that gnaws at the gizzard of our very
                    existence.

Ominously sway the dairy cows
in rhythm with the whip crack of civilization,
in rhythm with the working hours,
dragging capitalism's wagon, until factories
decimate cemeteries. Listen—
a city that ruthlessly abducts maidens in the dead of night
damages the moon so it swoons in the avenue.

Now you no longer recognize the odor of the air you
breathe. No longer hear the cries of the poor
bursting from a mass of history, sunburnt,
rain-struck, ground down by darkness,
residing in metropolitan alienation and loneliness.
Dark and deep. Oh, my country

Writing

Taufik Ikram Jamil

1986

I plane planks of letters
to build a fort in your heart
a place built entirely of words
of utter and solid conviction

Here you will not tire
of counting the days
because unless you begin
all traces will lose their meaning
and the things that are now worn out
will become trash on an endless plain

I plane planks of letters
and whether I am able or not able
I still try

A Reminder

Wiji Thukul

1986

if the people walk away
when the powers-that-be speak
it is time to pay attention;
they may have lost hope

if the people hide and whisper
when discussing their own problems
the powers-that-be should be mindful
and learn to listen

if the people don't dare to complain
the situation is already grave,
and if the words of the powers-that-be
cannot be criticized
then truth is endangered

if suggestions are rejected without consideration,
voices silenced, criticism forbidden for no reason;
if accusations are made of subversion and disrupting security
there is only one word to say: resist!

Mathematics

Emha Ainun Nadjib

1986p

What is smaller than the atom?
It can be split and split again

And the boundless universe—
is there anything greater?

Of course there is. There might be three
or maybe a million

We are in the middle—
our world is without foothold
or suspension in the heavens

If God were to move just a little
we would be done for

If You Are Forever

A. Mustofa Bisri

1987

If you are forever theorizing
when will you put your theories into practice?

If you are forever delighting
        in putting your theories into practice
when will you ever make use of them?

If you are forever searching for life
when will you ever enjoy it?
If you are forever seeking enjoyment
when will you ever truly live?

If you are forever busy with your chair
when will you ever think of your butt?
If you are forever thinking of your butt
when will you become aware of its foulness?

If you are forever hoodwinking people
when will you ever truly use your intellignence? If you are forever making use of
your intelligence
when will other people find the use of it?

If you are forever putting your cleverness on display
when will you ever prove your smarts?
If you are forever trying to prove your intelligence
when will you ever be truly intelligent?

If you are forever finding fault in others
when will you ever be able to prove their faults?
If you are forever proving the faults of others
when will you become aware of your own?

If you are forever fighting
when will you ever think of the reason for fighting?
If you are forever thinking about the reason for fighting
when will you realize its futility?

If you are forever looking for love
when will you ever think about the reason for love?
If you are forever thinking about the reason for love
when will you ever truly love?

If you are forever sermonizing
when will you ever see the wisdom of sermons?
If you are forever seeing the wisdom of sermons
when will you ever put that wisdom into practice?

If you are forever chanting praises
when will you ever realize the majesty of what you praise?
If you are forever thinking of the majesty of what you praise
when will you ever truly know it?

If you are forever talking
when will you ever think about what you're saying?
If you are forever thinking about what you're saying
when will you ever realize the meaning?

If you are forever mouthing lines of poetry
when will you ever create poetry?
If you are forever creating poetry
when will you ever air your poetry?

If you are forever thinking of what's on the outside
when will you ever discover what's inside?
If you are forever seeking what's inside
when will you ever truly find its essence?

If you are forever concerned with the essence
when will you ever find true realization?
If you are forever wrapped in realization
when will you ever find unity with Him?

"If you are forever asking questions
when will you ever hear the answers?"

The Men

Kuntowijoyo
1987p

When the drum is beaten,
the stars weave
the morning
into an ocean.

At sea, the dragon
beats the waves, and the
boats rock
like toys.
Two thousand hands tame the water,
controlling the waves and lightning,
as if to signal that the sea should give
itself up to be caressed.
The sailors have let down their nets
to catch the oars that tempt
love.
The men stand on the edge of the deck
admiring its face
and breathing
deeply.

Men:
who make love only at night.

The Neck and the Tie

Hs. Djurtatap

1988

a tie without a neck
is still valuable
a neck without a tie
isn't worth anything
because a neck
relies upon a tie
while a tie
doesn't care for necks

a chair without a person
is still valuable
a person without a chair
isn't worth anything
because the position of a person
depends on his chair

while a chair
doesn't care for people
necks don't need ties
your neck is smooth and slender
and in it I trace the days
and plant a million kisses
which destroy the quiet
of the heart.

Song of a Woman of My Country

Upita Agustine

1988

Water where there is a current
River where there is headwater
Wind where there is dust
Storm where there is separation
Home where there is a roof

The song of a woman crossing her own storm

Know in the shadow of a word spoken
Know in the lightning of a shattered mirror
Know in the onset of the dreary rain
Know in the restless ripples of the times
Know in the source of the problem

The song of a woman of my country

20 September 1966

Sandy Tyas
1988p

a friend taps my shoulder
his gaze is sharp and sure, voice heavy:
what if the political situation was turned around
the traitors
returned piercing their long
dirty black nails
into our necks
you are kicked not given any space

i return the sharp assured gaze
with a firm vocal response:
the question is not whether to be kicked or not kicked
to be shoved or not shoved
imprisoned or not imprisoned
killed or not killed

the question is
whether we are sure
that the revolution is right
that it embodies moral values
that are honorable
that it embodies human values
that are honorable
that it holds the true hopes of humanity
and the salvation of a generation

we are not alone
troops of fighters demanding fundamental rights
citizens
human rights
millions in number
that is the question!

In Cipasung Town

Acep Zamzam Noor

1989

In the curve of your brow, paddies ripen
Like my hair, the rice plants bow down
With my blade I harvest your heart's patience
My hoe is faith; my prayer rug, the viscous mud
From the sky that tests my piety drips a soft glow
As my voice is burnt by a silence inflamed by longing

Ever closer I come to the extinction this earth stows

In barren fields of bitterness, daily I plant seeds
Plants and trees forever bear fresh reward
To the bamboo fences constructed from my faith
Come fish whose prayer-poems I listen to
My heart is a pool where your perfection is stored

Tomorrow begins my journey as a farmer
Opening fields of charity in the jungle wilderness
I know this path is one of ever-increasing nothingness
Long have weighed the world and repeatedly destroyed it
Even with no blade, I still wish to harvest another side of your patience
On a prayer rug of mud, I fall prone and am buried

An Old Woman on Independence Day

F. Rahardi

1989

Carrying her grandchild
and chewing her betel leaves
an old woman watches the red-and-white flag
flap in the wind
outside city hall.

It's going to be another lively August seventeenth,
she mutters.
It is true: A wooden pole
sanded smooth and oiled
looms above
the grounds in front of the offices.
At the far, far end of the pole
hangs a new shirt, a cassette player,
a flashlight, an umbrella, sneakers
and cloth for a sarong.

Independence is certainly difficult to achieve,
the old woman continues,
adjusting the position of the tobacco plug
            between her lips.
She watches the young people
start to climb and then slide,
climb and then slide down,
their bodies smeared with oil.

The mayor is clapping,
mothers are cheering,
fathers are hollering
and the onlookers are jumping up and down.
Only the old woman and her grandchild are silent.

I really must save my energy
right, kiddo?

I'm old,
not as strong as I was
when Bung Karno was still around
and giving speeches in the town square.
When I was young
I liked to cheer
and clap my hands, too.
The kids who are climbing
that pole now
were still in their mothers' bellies back then.

As the day gradually turns to afternoon
and the August sun
beams down its serious heat,
the young people keep climbing,
the red-and-white flag keeps flying,
the pickpockets take a break,
the pedicab drivers observe a moment of silence
and the mothers stalwartly
nurse their babies.

At times
the festivities for the seventeenth can be quite
       thrilling,
mumbles the old woman.
It turns out, truly, we've been independent for a long time,
turns out those speeches
and the sounds of guns and grenades
have become mementos
in high demand as a topic for novels, TV and films—
and the old woman stops thinking about
how the cooking oil at home is almost gone
and there is hardly any rice left
and the sugar and the coffee ran out
yesterday.

In the air of the dry season
under a clear blue sky
the old woman,
still holding her grandbaby—
who it turns out can already join in singing
the national anthem,
Indonetia the Gleat—
stares at the flag
flapping in the wind.

Interview with Tuyul

F. Rahardi

1989

Supposing the Lord
gave you, Sir, the opportunity
for corruption,
what would you do?
Tuyul was embarrassed
and didn't answer.

What if
what if your wife gave you
the latitude to
fool around
would you do it?
Tuyul was abashed
but answered anyway:
Sorry, I'm still a bachelor, Sir.

What if!
This is only hypothetical!
What if you were hired
to work in this office
what would you want to be?
Tuyul hesitated a bit before answering
Whatever, Sir,
even a janitor would be fine.

Good, now tell me
briefly about your experience thus far.
So Tuyul adjusted the position of his ass
and began to tell his story:
I was born in Bantul, Sir,
in the district of Yogyakarta.

---

[1] A tuyul or toyol is a mythical spirit that can be possessed and controlled using black magic to do
its owner's bidding, usually to help its owner get rich quick. Tuyuls appear in the form of greenish,
bald-headed toddlers in mythologies across China, Korea, and Southeast Asia.

My father was a shaman
my mother sold rice cakes
my uncle took care of ducks
at the age of seven I was circumcised
then I entered grade school
but dropped out—

Enough
enough. Can you speak
English?

Tuyul nodded his head
then answered firmly
Yes! Yes, Sir!

Good
good. Can you type?
Yes, Sir.
Keep books?

Yes.
Use a computer?
Yes.
Ever been to prison?
I have, Sir.

Good.
This is very interesting.
It turns out your experience is extraordinary.
Now, let's try to clarify
why you are interested in
submitting an application to this office.
Is it because the employees here have big
salaries?
Is it for the nice uniforms
or because the work here is comfortable?

None of these, Sir.
I want to work here

because I'm currently unemployed.
Oh, it's like that.
Good
good, if that's the case.
Are you not afraid of dogs?
No, Sir.
Do you already have a girlfriend?
Not yet, Sir.
Too bad!

That's really too bad, brother.
If you had already had a girlfriend
then a broken heart, having been rejected by the woman
of your dreams, your experience would surely be more varied
that's really too bad.

But, anyhow, returning to the problem we started with
can you ride a bicycle?
No, Sir.
Can you ride a motorcycle?
No, Sir.
Can you drive a car?
Also no, Sir.

If that's the case you must study diligently
you need to hang around a lot of chauffeurs
you have to be polite
you have to put yourself in the appropriate place
you can't have low self-esteem
but you also shouldn't be big-headed.

I'm sure you can do it.
I can see from your facial features
you have hidden talents.
Now tell me
briefly
what are your hobbies?
Do you like mountain-climbing?
Do you like swimming?

Do you like to play music?
Read novels
or go fishing?

No, Sir,
my real hobby is working.
I can work for hours, for days
for weeks, without resting for even an instant.
Work is my life, Sir
work is my hobby
my religion
my breath
my farts
my snot—
working is everything to me.

It's like this, Sir.
Salary and wages
aren't important to me.
Uniforms, for me, are not the point
much less rank and position.
In no way am I looking for
an easy job
sitting around, going to meetings
taking smoke breaks, chatting with guests
taking walks, answering the phone
reading drafts of letters, signing receipts—
for me all of that only
stiffens the body
and muddies the mind.

For me work
is splitting firewood
carrying bricks
pushing stalled cars
and drawing water from a well.
Work means muscles have to move
the brain has to sweat
and thought must be forthright.

Would I be able to do that kind of work
in this office, Sir?

Would I be able to sweat
and then slumber without sleep-talking
without having all kinds of strange dreams?
It's work like that I'm looking for.
It's work like that that is my hobby, Sir.

Tuyul's eyes shone
the crown of his head quivered
his chest rose and fell.

Supposing
supposing you
were hired to work in this office.
Are you definitely sure you would not become
corrupt?

Tuyul shook his head.
People like me
what kind of bribes would we take take, brother?
A dab of soap?
A mop cloth?
A used newspaper?
At most some take-out rice.
People like me
here
our minds are in our stomachs.
As long as the belly's full, that's it
never mind anything else.

Supposing
supposing you were not
accepted at this office
then where would you want to work?
Tuyul was puzzled.

Supposing I didn't get hired
here, Sir
I would work wherever
there's work everywhere
at intersections
we can wipe down cars
underneath bridges, we can fish
at the district office we can help
arrange for citizen identity cards
the important thing is that it's all legal
right, Boss?

True
that's all true
but there's still a lot to ask you
are both of your parents still living?
They are, Sir.
How many times do you brush your teeth in a day?

It depends, Sir.
Do you like catfish?
No, Sir, they give me the creeps!
Goat meat?
No, Sir,
it raises your blood pressure.
You smoke?
I'm against it, Sir!
It's not good for the lungs or the heart.
Drink hard liquor?

NO!
It's forbidden!
Fool around with women?
Good grief, Sir, this
is just weird
I'm a good person, Sir,
look at my forehead
check out my eyebrows
are there any pimples on my cheeks?

Flawless, right?
Why are you still doubtful?
Look at my belly, Sir,
I'm not chubby yet, right?
So I'm still normal
you should have been convinced
since yesterday
how about it, Sir?
You done being sleepy?

Yeah, yeah, yeah
you really are the right kind of person
to be a security guard
but remember
everything has to be processed in accordance
with the regulations
that are already in place, furthermore

everything has to follow the appropriate path
no running through traffic lights
no taking advantage of gateways
everything has to be opened slowly
in accordance with the rules, understand?

Not yet, Sir!
What? How can you not understand?
Well, a moment ago, when you said, "yeah, yeah, yeah..."
I was kind of out of it.

So
how old are you now?
What is your current complete address?
What's your ID card number?
Your weight
the number of grey hairs on your head
the color of your skin
the shape of your eyes, lips, ears—
is everything normal and
functioning well?

Listen
all this important data has to be sent to the personnel
division and be on file
only then will you get a call
only then can you get a job in accordance
with your talents
which have been hidden all this time.

It's all clear, right
or do you still have questions?
Is there anything that's still unclear?

Don't worry too much about salary
in short
you will be rewarded sufficiently
in a way that's suitable for your deeds and services
if while you are on earth you continuously do good
you will surely go to heaven
don't be afraid
unless you have indeed
sinned
your reward will surely be hell
everything has already been set up very clearly.

It's all clear, right?
All clear, Sir.
You understand, right?
Understood, Sir.
Agreed?
Agreed!

I Want

Sapardi Djoko Damono

1989

I want to love you simply:
in words not spoken,
as tinder to the flame that transforms it to ash

I want to love you simply:
in signs not expressed,
as clouds to the rain which make them evanesce

Two Quatrains about Love

Soni Farid Maulana
1989

1

When your loosened hair
Grazed my chest, calmness crept in
To pull the black sheet
From my heart.

2

On fire, my chest is on fire
Because of the brush of your hand
soft as a rose petal,
And I am intoxicated by it.

story for nin

Timur Sinar Suprabana:
1989

no end to the story
free from the tale

unfinished tale
a sigh slides

unfinished sigh
this restless soul

perpetual
turbulence flusters

: i am grass
in the great silence
i am boisterous and apprehensive

and you
time of revolving
pure revolutions days of civilization
with simplicity
to anywhere loyal to the orbit

: straight line
i confront the beginning
because the soul
only yearns for curves

so it is that men
can be intentionally capable of misfortune
without ever needing
punctuation marks

---

* Title is lowercase in original publication.

far from the period
comma
or anything
and certain requirements
that should be there

sometimes
a desire to return to the Origin
like a bat in its cave
far from the flash of light
fluttering wings only at night
when the air is still
without wind
without the plick-plack touch of leaves
and without the moon
on the opposite side of the veil of night

perhaps it is correct
darkness is Almighty
but darkness
is only one of nature's cunning tricks

amazing
you are so Pure

like desire
that is free from the night air

like the night
that is never left behind by the moon

like the moon
that seems to nest at the bottom of the sea
and moves ships
from the depths of great clarity

let it be swift
everything
to the new world
outside the rumbling world of steel
outside the false world of plastic
outside the gloomy world of underground pipes
and outside the world of glass
that wounds the body and the soul

i was born too early
i am misfortune and hate age
i am willing to die
but Forget living

then your breath supplies the acid for my lungs
when betraying me with poetry
and love letters
beer
and meetings in a hotel
with women
who you never really really know
and must quickly forget in the morning

i am weary
Falling and Fragile

so
from you
i learn how to be a child

wanting to be able to be Without
....

Not My Intention

Soeprijadi Tomodihardjo

1989p

It was not my intention to come around here
making peace with my dreams
killing the boredom and the quiet
of the journey.
It was not my intention to linger here
drawing the water of compassion
noisy continent, faces shrouded in white mist
when one million fall head first—
I don't know where they are laid to rest.
It was not my intention to settle here
year after year
celebrating christmas
new years and carnival
when one million collapse
buried in a ruptured past.
It was not my intention to have children and grandchildren
here
enduring the gloom when my heart
is wounded and aggrieved
swallowing sneers and insults
when an arid day of drought arrives
people without work
are cast aside.
It was not my intention
that they forgive my presence
here. We were born without the right
to choose the earth. Noisy earth
faces shrouded in white mist
voice their refusal
as we
catch a speck in our eye.
It even happens alone and in silence.
When the time comes we will leave
sail through high, extended waves.
It is a little bit of a shame
that the captain never comes.

Stone Wall

Soeprijadi Tomodihardjo
1989p

perhaps my words have come
to nothing but a stone wall
i don't hear sobs or compassionate sighs

my words do not illuminate
the stones as cold as snow

i no longer fear the silence
i slowly lose the urge to speak

we grow farther apart but i try to approach you
oh, stone wall!

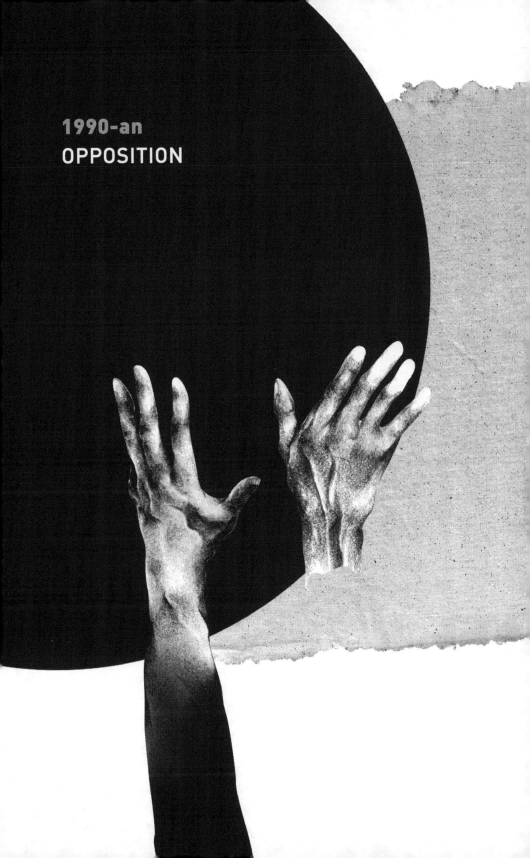

1990-an
OPPOSITION

Introduction to the 1990s

Indonesian Poetry in the 1990s: Some Notes

Joko Pinurbo

The period of 1990 to 2000 was the final chapter for the New Order regime, which had held power for so long in Indonesia. During this period, sociopolitical tensions reached a saturation point; in the background, a time bomb was waiting for the right moment to explode.

Meanwhile, the world of Indonesian poetry was proceeding splendidly, judging by the number of poets actively writing and the volume of work being produced. Directly or not, to a greater or lesser degree, the burnout in the political world was reflected in the world of poetry, triggering creative experiments that, while never exactly radical, did clear the way for new possibilities in poetry.

Most of the poets actively writing in this period had emerged or been active in the preceding period. Thus, the dominant styles and modes of expression had substantial continuity with the styles and modes that came before. Many poets still favored the lyric mode and continued to delight in nature as a source of inspiration. Naturally, there were efforts to keep lyricism from simply marching in place. There was a push to make lyric verse more varied, at least in terms of theme and subject. One noticeable trend was the melding of lyric verse with language mined from the rich quarries of religion, spirituality and mysticism. This mode of writing was intended as a way to free oneself from the mundane world—a place that was at once stifling and satiating—and served as a tranquilizer to avert the threat of madness or neurosis.

Another pronounced trend was packing lyric verse with imagery drawn from local culture. Mining folk wisdom as a source of inspiration, this type of poetry conveyed local color by showing real people in everyday situations: struggling to survive, to maintain spiritual and physical strength amid the upheavals of the age, and to find ways of being at peace. Spirituality, animated by the values of local wisdom, was a wellspring that gave life to the realization that even in the midst of crisis there were still ways to stay grounded and use the resources at hand.

Some of this local color derived from Chinese culture, which was still considered foreign due to prejudice, even though it had long been a contributor to the cultural wealth of Nusantara (the Indonesian archipelago). In addition to enriching poetic creation, the presence of Chinese culture elicited the awareness that in various communities in this country there thrived a diversity of traditions and ancestral beliefs that—in spite of the political efforts to shunt them aside—continued to instill values and serve as a guide to life. Such diversity could not be eliminated, even by the machinery of uniformity controlled and operated by the state.

Beyond lyric poems laden with romantic nuance, the world of Indonesian poetry was enlivened with what were called "social poems." The label referred to unadorned poems filled with commentary, criticism, protest or opposition to situations in public life that were oppressive, brought about by hegemonic power and a political system that manipulated it. The publication of these social poems was not infrequently accompanied by an unstoppable surge of public anger and sadness. Around the time of Reformasi (Reform), poetry of this sort flourished like never before, like a once-blocked water pipe whose plug had been removed. Words buzzed and whizzed from all quarters, contributing to the public euphoria.

The premise to be underscored with regard to social poems is that at certain moments and in certain situations, beauty is not considered an important requisite. When institutions can no longer be trusted to change conditions, the people have to make themselves the instruments of resistance. There was no time for contemplative words. Words had to come down from the mountaintop. Words had to become weapons.

The spirit of resistance appears as well in poems that challenged the position of women in society, though these works typically employed a style of expression that allowed for the plasticity of language and a metaphoric atmosphere. This challenge to the oppression of women came uniquely from within; the resulting poetry seems to suggest that women should waste no time in redefining womanhood or femininity. Perceptions about femininity that had long been taken as fact were actually devised by the cultural and social systems of patriarchy. In many ways, patriarchal culture has diminished the dignity of women and relegated them to the sidelines. And since perception is a product of linguistic constructs, feminist resistance must begin with language, with literary strategies. This is why, in the works of several women poets, we encounter expressions that are both jarring and brave, including speech about women's bodies, which have been colonized and imprisoned by taboo for so long. Women's bodies are the property of women, and women have the right to govern and control their own bodies. Women have the right to make themselves and their bodies into subjects.

Another stream of verse was narrative in style and focused on everyday events and apparently simple objects, working these into stories about the absurdity of human existence. The language of these poems was both fluid and light, often infused with gentle humor and irony. Using a style of expression that was more fluid and natural revealed the nuances of Indonesian language, which had for so long been a victim of political interference and excessive euphemism.

It was not certain that political reform would be meaningful if not joined, in the world of writing, by creative exploration to refresh and enrich literary vision and methods. There were, to be sure, efforts to do all of these things. For example, one experiment resulted in verse that no longer focused on describing the speaker's mood in a regular meter. Even coherence was no longer a strict condition; it was as if images could appear at random. The main source of poetic inspiration was no longer a romanticized version of nature, but rather images from urban and industrial worlds. To encounter such poetry was to confront a reduced humanity trapped in consumerism, a humanity harried and ruled by objects.

Another blessing of the Reformasi era was the blossoming of literary publishing, including poetry. The production and publication of literary works increased, along with the reprinting of old works. The role of "indie" (independent) publishers is also noteworthy, in that they dared to publish new writers and works that larger publishers more focused on the bottom line would find difficult to justify taking on. This recent period has been one of the richest and most exciting eras for the literary book market in Indonesia.

My Yearning Is Queen

Abidah El Khalieqy

1990

In the course of the hours you always come, Maryam!
my yearning is a weary sky
watching a wilderness night
i smell poison
and a thousand vibrating claws
shrilling at the room's entrance

drown the bed
chilled soul

Release your hands
to make legible the gleam of your crown
one hundred kingdoms already fallen
there is no cave that can disappear

drums of defeat
boom on

Look, dawn's light will come
sun lights your face
reflecting Isa[1]
in your lap
ocean

---

[1] Isa is the Arabic name for the prophet known to Christians as Jesus, son of Mary/Maryam.

The City

Omi Intan Naomi

1990

in the rhythm of the baduy people
    who live off the land
there is an undying rustle of life
rites and rituals might be ancient
but they have not been abandoned.

jakarta is full of din yet dead
just a stage for soap operas
with actors in kabuki face
or a folk drama in days of old
when male actors dressed as women.

does the president think himself too good
to deal with matters like chili sauce?

Dancing in the Void

Radhar Panca Dahana

1990

i am dancing. dancing God's song, while the rain demolishes
the night and drowns the moon. an ocean of pooled questions,
which the fishermen snag on their hooks one by one; where's
the land, where's the shore? i keep on dancing. i'm dancing sky,
who for centuries has craved conversation, but the sky has a
sky of its own, and sparrows dance between.

still i dance. i'm dancing now, Lord, as time dissolves. why not
close Your eyes for a moment so i can approach with ease and
kiss Your lips, anciently? i've kept loose muscles and nerves to
construct the universe for all of humanity, all the way to its
edges, where wives lose desire to give birth, husbands switch
their sex in disgust, and children catch stars to be served up for
breakfast. until everything's gone, until it's all over, Lord, let
me dance. let me keep on dancing. if my solitude makes you
glad, leave me be, Lord, let me dance.

Bomb's Feelings

Beni Setia

1990p

for rendra

"might we be lovers?" shouted river rock
to the bomb, who was stuck in the underbrush at the upper lip
of a rumbling river rapid

bomb's body was tucked into the ground, with only his tail
poking out: pointed, flat, and rigid, so he couldn't
nod or roll away. he didn't respond

only the pines were alive, mumbling in the whistling wind,
carefreely catching the conversations of fish. only the birds
were alive. coming & going, mocking bomb:

"your friends are hiding out in a courtroom
far away. holding their breath, writhing + crying
spurting hope," one said, defecating

"those birds are feverish and freaked out," rock shouted
—one hopped into the rapid and drowned in its depths
bomb acknowledged (because it was awkward): how pointless!

rapid roared with laughter. "clearly, there's not a single
living thing that likes you!" the bomb trembled. quivering,
aching to hurl white water + moss + sky

"how about we go on a date?," rock yelled
to bomb, "rub up against each other + support each other's opinions."
bomb stayed quiet. (sinking). erect, stiff + mute

(he was pissed off at his wife and because people were drinking endrin)

Almighty Lust

Mathori A Elwa

1990-1994

NHR

1
I am a wanderer or a hermit
I let you decide your own path
and wait for a time
when the moon shines because of me
the sun sets because of me

2
I am a wanderer or a hermit
from the east or the west I walk
crossing valleys and swamps
when I dance with joy
it is the wind, storms and demons

3
I am housed in caves
clothed in lust and tassels
while inhaling the scents and stench of a crowd of bodies
I deplete all wealth and extravagance
so that I will be buried
let the jokes and applause pass
till your words are completely destroyed
consumed by ogres and fury

4
I want to keep on going
to carry out the mandate of climbers or drunks
not happy because of smiles
even now I laugh broadly
passing disasters and stupidity
meanwhile beside my camps
let your flags wave or rot
I still don't care

like your drunkenness
history and bloodthirsty days
and my sweet smile
I save as a dagger or bullet

5
in mourning
I celebrate the days, independence and years
with love or hate
I serve the sentences

6
in the name of disappointment
in every corner of the world
a thousand dancers and a million wild men
stick their genitals in graves

7
in the name of all that
I sell my body at supermarkets
while the buyers pray or sing
displaying their fangs or thighs
with shivers

8
in the name of honesty
I let go of my shame and sense of honor
with worn-out shoes
I love homeland and kingdoms

9
with fake intimacy
I greet the days and beer and whisky
when an upper-class thief
invites me to be indebted, even though
without dithering

I store that gift and disaster
everywhere

10
like doomsday
I swallow the bitter pill and poison
inherited from such destructive forces
as love that has died
fairies laugh at me from different directions
while since a century ago
fangs have grown on my head
and more than a billion scorpions
have come out of my giant asshole

11
I am a long-distance traveler
from further than you can imagine
I captivated all men and women
so they had no time to hone weapons
so that the world was impossible
all arteries became absurd
pouring out all that smells rotten

12
I've left the hometown
and am hiding everywhere
don't ask or try to solve all the problems
neither the hills nor powers
ever welcome anyone
and your shock is but a wound
which I will continue to nurse
so it keeps on gaping

13
I keep sheep and slaves
I terrorize all herders or bosses

until torture and abuse sneer at you
odd to hear
tearing apart the households in your kingdom
so that reality is newer and looks bright
I am willing to be ruler of the universe
like a book, a story and history
I rip apart gentle feelings
I keep them then sell them at flea markets

14
your tears and prayers are just *dangdut* music
all the steps are but plans
just the dancing of whores' hula-hoops

15
like before
I will be crazier than the gigolos
starting from sodom
ending beyond gomorah

16
just like unfortunate poets
you all brag upon a stage
powerless to face the magic of my installation
as the sycophants from every age
you sermonize straddling one another
singing songs from the grave
heaven and hell

17
seeing your wounded arm
bleeding with hate
I just nag
give thanks to the killers and slanderers
millions of my new troops of soldiers
have sold homeland and mountains though I remain alone

cold
and in control

18
celebrate me all of you
in poverty or fancy homes
the country built by heroes and crooks
all that is here is me
the accomplished wanderer
brilliance and stupidity I pass on to you pimps
all of you on the margins and insignificant
I leave sick and miserable

19
hey, I am the one with the brilliant mind
not just violence
create massive unemployment
in my philosophy, there is no enemy or ally
everyone is an enemy or ally

20
because of this rotten goodness
the world has changed and sunk far
everyone lives in expectation
and in agony at the same time
the rest are left as dust and fleas
while I who taught them to applaud
will continue to be the psychopath who is almighty lust
in the towers
valleys
and swamps
of man

Red Henna Moon

Ajamuddin Tifani

1990s

red henna moon on high
the young rice is flooded
by the river tide if the field
is fallow send down
silver canoes to the areca trees

the trembling young rice receives its blessing
the golden moonbeams descend in footbridges
of light, caressing each pistil,
the young rice suckles its fill after
seasons of lamentation, burned by
thirst

upstream, machines thunder
trees are felled, canyons crumble
dreams and disaster transpire
at once and he witnesses it white hot
on the horizon a raven prattles in
a palm tree

red henna moon on high
the young rice is flooded
by the tide, alas...

prayer maker

Cok Sawitri

1990s

there are no dragons left, just imaginary creatures
in the sky, but, half asleep, I read in the paper
a story about an old man who thought himself to be one

his daughter affirmed, my father is a dragon
and my mother, a dragon too
they are poisonous
able to fly, to spew flames
and to perch and crawl

silence. the women smiled when hailing me at the airport
but seemed reticent when I asked, what is it you do?
"prayer maker..." said one of them

it's too bad that dragons are fictitious
their flames could be put to use
burning the thousands of stenciled prayers
and waking the older dragons

all the burned forests and the deaths of ants and moss
are because of fire. what matter is it if you are the one spewing flames
it's still the fire that's responsible

another woman, who dreamed of being a dragon
and was in the middle of inserting an earring in her lobe
raised her eyebrows and let them freeze in arch darkness

I stared at the prayer maker and asked
"will you make a prayer for me?"
"no need, young lady," she said with a smile
"I only sell prayers to those who need them!"
leaving me staring at the sky in apprehension

was this the capital city?
none of us ever felt we could call the place our own
because before it became home it was incinerated
by the dragon and buried with a thousand of the prayer maker's prayers...

For My Father

Mochtar Pabottinggi

1990s

To matinroe ri alempurenna, ri gettenna, sibawa ri deceng awaraning

For my father, a man both principled and good, who now lives eternally on the straight path

The arrow I shot, with a five centimeter needle-point head, just at the moment you chose to come down the ladder to the loft, buried itself all the way in your calf. With blood spurting from the wound, I was horrified and probably pallid beyond belief. I, little Mochtar, was so sorry for what I'd done, and frightened, too, certain that you would spank me. And such a punishment would have been most apt for what I'd done—though I knew you'd never think I would do such a thing intentionally to you.

Instead, you calmly pulled my arrow from your calf, which was still spurting blood, and gave it back to me, saying, "Be more careful with your arrows, son." Only that. And then you left me, without another word.

Forty-two years ago that was, and you made the incident seem very ordinary. Yet for me, Father, it was an incredible event, one that I will never forget for the rest of my days, just as I will never forget you.

I thank you, Father. I thank you always and will forever hold dear your example. I will continue to love and to trust. In humanity.

I give my thanks to You, ever and always to You.

Rendezvous

Agus R. Sarjono
1991

You're pretty, said the golf course to the grass-
flower in the custody of the wind. The grass-flower
was downcast. It was reminded of grains and
vegetables, of bellowing buffalo that hurry
to be gone before dawn.

You're charming, whispered the golf course, winking.
The grass-flower, embarrassed,
stared off into the distance seeking guidance
and assurances. It was being regarded by the golf course,
who smiled wistfully while playing with its hair.

You're remarkable, sighed the golf course, its twinkling eyes
bearing down. The grass-flower sobbed. You're badgering
and arrogant, you exiled my family and my friends
you disturbed our peace.

But I hate rice fields, I hate vegetables, I hate
embankments, I hate the smell of manure, I hate...

You're spiteful! You hate everything...

No, replied the golf course, grasping the grass-flower's
finger. I love you!

The Sea in My Heart

Hs. Djurtatap

1991

when all of the seas have been planted with mines
and the ships don't sail
i create my own sea in my heart
then i sail far away
until i enter Your bay

when the hills and mountains have been
stripped of their trees out of greed
and millions of birds have lost their homes
i create a higher and even more beautiful
mountain, then climb to its peak
and nudge the soles of Your feet

when all the paths are blocked
and millions can't leave
i create a path in my heart
longer and more winding
and then i cross it at every moment
and if longing arrives, i flirt with Your shadows
at a bend in the road.

although the seas are full of mines
i do not worry
although there are no mountains
i'm not confused
although the roads are blocked
i'm not nervous

because in my heart
there is a safe sea
there is a dense forest in the mountains
there are unblocked roads

when loneliness and longing
take me towards You.

A Mouthful of Tears

Warih Wisatsana

1991-1992

To ULP

Because the flow of tears is powerless
to spurn death
Dying in the grass
a horse rolling,
Its whinny soars piercing
    the wide open sky.
The red moon floats in the gleam of its eye
    as red as a blood rose,
In its eye that is full of butterflies weeping
    I see
a man running all night
        holding back tears
A man unimagined
    by death
Unable to repel its fate
    Running in the grass
        under the open sky. Rolling
    in a vast field of stars!
On one sheet a day of pain
on paper his breath
    His tears calm the writing
        of your sorrow,
Oh, dying horse whipped by death
Let that man be spurred painfully by time
rolling pulling whinnying a poem
until his sweat and blood suck out the last word,
Fly with the soul of the rose
and butterfly ghost
    breaking through a mouthful of tears
with your last whinny.

Married to a Knife

Dorothea Rosa Herliany

1992

i have arrived somewhere, spinning
in a labyrinth, it was a long journey,
without a map. and the darkness
is perfect. I followed a lane
between a river and a chasm.

there was a scream. it sounded like a song.
perhaps it came from my mouth. there was a moan,
like a lullaby. perhaps it came from my mouth.

but i have landed in a place
of perfect alienation: your body is covered
    with maggots which i ignore. until i find complete
sexual satisfaction. then i finish you too,
i stab you in the heart and
tear off your prick
in my pain.

Proclamation, 2

Hamid Jabbar

1992

We, the people of Indonesia
herewith declare
Indonesian independence
for the second time!

Matters pertaining to
human rights,
debt and credit,
et cetera
which are never-ending
GOD WILLING
will have their end
will be taken care of
assiduously
and in
the shortest possible time

Jakarta, 25 March 1992
In the name of the Indonesian people
Go ahead, anyone at all

The Widow Who Peddles Vegetables
Between Yogya and Imogiri

Iman Budhi Santosa

1992

By evening she's decided
to forsake recurring fantasies.
Holding the handle bars smelling of celery,
the bicycle running away with her body,
carting her off like a basket of veggies,
she's exhausted—the morning stars having purchased her beauty.

From her neighbors' reassurance, she takes comfort
and believes a single mother can be her children's father, too.
For it would be unseemly if a woman had to borrow matches daily
from a man just to light the kitchen fire.

But constantly she feels
her womb pleading for permission
just to sing: a little variety,
maybe a mattress with sheets,
an iron bed that creaks
naughty sighs, a greeting on the street,
declarations calm orproposals sweet.

Oh god, must the teak and the mahogany
grow so densely
between Yogya and Imogiri
that they hide all footprint-traces of the little birds
who steal the techniques for trading destinies
in the world of humanity?

Kindergarten

Zen Hae

1992

the kids are building god's house
in the market. it has no walls, and the door
is made from a scrap of sky, torn off in a fitful
wasted sleep. the yard is fenced with bombs
planted with sharpened arrows and exclamation marks
there is a pond with flowers grown
from tears (hungry sharks imprisoned in
the aquarium, crying for the sea)
the blooms are rattled by war

and the night is too clever to stick
to a curriculum, teaching the kids to become thieves
disguised as the moon. building a city of glittering
glass. every night drowning
cursed by their parents: insubordinate children!
the kids are stealing heaven from god
never bored. seeking a fairytale land
that hovers on firefly wings
"we make a pilgrimage to the sun and the moon
and water them with fire"

Killing Coffee in the Morning

Radhar Panca Dahana

1992

Supposing I stretched my body to fit the length of time, still I would not find you there. I've been wearing this disappointment for a long while, like moss slowly blanketing a rock, but I've never despaired, even though over and over again the only thing I could celebrate was defeat.

The hot cup of coffee I sip this early morning reasserts the longing that always appears on the surface of my fortune: When could I have won the prize for a contest that was never held? A longing that always reminds me you still exist. But the morning newspaper, the news on the radio and the TV won't stop reminding everyone that there's no longer any time. So I say let's get together and kill off disappointment. We can no longer recognize ourselves in Mephistopheles's mirror. Even the words our hearts speak are dishonest. Our tongues are constantly telling us false truths.

uuughhhh... The day is so hot and there's no breeze, though it's still early morning and the vegetable vendors have just begun to sell the newspaper. At times like this, and under such circumstances, there's just one thing I want to say: I can get one from you by taking one from me. You wouldn't know.

Bosnian Maggot

Rahman Arge
1992

A little girl
emerges from amongst the corpses
a wild carnation
she offers
to a UN soldier

As their eyes meet
a fresh wind blows
A maggot
jumps from the flower
and the little girl whispers

Oh, Bosnian maggot
Oh, my mother...

She kisses it
before burying it.

The Moon Rite

Korrie Layun Rampan

1993

the moon rite in the forest branches
nourishes the insects
and the next day's sun
raises mounds for the fire ants

o angels dancing in lust
at the gates of life
do you hear the knocks one after another
at the doors of our hearts?

what is called out by the anchor to the sea
ship of our wharf
what is called by the lighthouse
soul of love that trembles

do you hear the telephone of the heart
that speaks to the honest character
of our world
of pain and suffering?

the sun rite in the swirl of time
nourishes the rice
in the fields of blood
in the cities of doubt

an ancient anxiety clings to our foreheads and our crowns
a sign on mighty shoulders
you see the sky lowering
to pierce you with a testimony of anguish!

Jakarta

Sirikit Syah
1993

For the NUANSA PAGI Production Team

1
First rain in Jakarta
I open the window to the pelting drops
I cherish my love
and before it gets torn apart
I will pack it into a ball
glowing with an incandescent flame
and send it to just one person
he who waits faithfully in Surabaya

2
Jakarta in the morning
the cold air is not as cold as Studio 5
Everyone starts talking
newscasters
hosts
I am drowning and lost
in the hustle and bustle

People say that
for human beings there is no choice
there is only work and work
with no need to tend to feeling
and don't even ask
about love

Nappies and an Infusion Bottle

Afrizal Malna

1994

The maternity hospital takes her amongst the large, 400 ASA babies. A camera makes news from the wheelchairs. There's a garden on the terrace and a cat smells the medicine on your body. It is as if the soul is reforming itself on the operation table, accompanying you. Before a tomato is squashed in one's hand.

My wife holds on to the infusion bottle; the oxygen tank is stuck to the wall. She gathers up her child from the sounds of birds and the rice fields that have descended from the Montong Semaye sky. We take a taxi, pick up the doctor and the hospital. Creatures I couldn't recognize gathered around the telephone. The air conditioning created the cold from visiting hours. The electricity died, making another kind of night.

My child is up in the attic inviting his friends. Making language from nappies, tea tree oil and the milk-making angel in the corner of the room. They're having a party, making a mother from a long scarf. But it is as if my hand is a cold cupboard, buried ice-blocks as well as genetic evolution from the tissue of plastic bags. The place to live is still a promise.

But..."Why are you calling me like that, nurse?" said a baby when it was removed from its mother's womb. And then the city is full with nappies being hung out to dry, the smell of tea tree oil in waiting rooms and baby soap makes a different bathroom. "Sir, there isn't a government broadcast in my crying."

Supposing We Were in Sarajevo

Goenawan Mohamad

1994

Supposing we were in Sarajevo,
they would assail us with cannonade
and ask if it were true that to enter the city
there was only one way.

Supposing we were in Sarajevo,
that wall with its bullet holes
would say "no"
after the clash.

But you know that in Sarajevo
the seasons break hinges,
cold shrinks your hands,
and electricity dies.

Coming home
from cafes
people gaze at the charred remains
of attic lofts.

What was it they actually saw
in Sarajevo: an arid expanse,
a land subdued?
What did they actually see?

Conviction is nailed
above pulpits and in grain barns,
but no one reads
anymore.

Perhaps it is possible
there is in us a cord to the past
as yet unraveled. Or possibly
a true sense of conscience.

Suppose, just supposing, that in Sarajevo
the moon did not leave behind a replica
near the minaret, where only whiteness
is left from the call to prayer.

Suppose as well that the wind
was stripped of its temper
by yellow poplar leaves
and motionless fields.

An old crone with a rasp from stomach cancer
would surely say
"All that's left to try is to fast in the desert,
a feat at which you would fail."

Why are we in Sarajevo?
What possessed us to defend this city?
As in a film,
Sarajevo cannot be conquered.

We cannot be conquered.
But spilling from meeting halls
is the city's citizenry
dressed in their finest,
men planting sweet but quick kisses on wives' cheeks,
even as they conceal inside their pouches
that miraculous text:
"Not by bread, but divine faith."

The stones in this sidewalk
cannot be made into bread,
and the shimmering snow in the distance
cannot be turned into the word of God.

But supposing we were in Sarajevo:
near the museum, we, too, would turn pious

and cleanse ourselves: "Let me die
in the color of crimson."

I then go;
you go too, leaving, not blanched
in the early morning,
but the color of crimson.

The Flag That Was Ashamed to Fly

Mustofa W. Hasyim

1994

There once was an old flag
that refused to be removed from the cabinet
and flown outside.
Why?

"I'm ashamed," said the flag.
"Why should I flap about
 if I'm only going to be ignored?"

The flag's owner didn't understand;
he pressed the issue. "If you force me
I will spontaneously combust
and turn to ash," threatened the flag.

The flag's owner gave up.
He locked the cabinet, went to the store
and bought another flag.

The new flag fluttered
shamelessly outside. No one
paid it any mind.

Kindergarten Teacher's Testimony

Mustofa W. Hasyim

1994

Here's this kindergarten teacher going into the school,
who's hidden her bicycle in the storeroom
so as not to deflate the spirits
of her students, whose parents are rich.

Though she is hungry,
she invites her students to pray for peace and prosperity.
The morning classroom is filled with the prayers
of the children, a chorus of "Amen!"

Though she is in debt, she invites her students to sing,
"With beautiful flowers all around
and a fresh breeze in the garden,
this land of mine is much like heaven."

Though her uniform is made from cheap cloth,
she invites her students to play:
"Come on and jump, now run, keep going, don't cry if you fall,
and don't fight. Come on now, clap your hands!"

Though she is nervous because her tiny salary is late,
she encourages her students to draw.
"Go ahead, draw whatever you want. Something pretty, okay?
I don't want to see skinny goats or hungry rats, okay?"

One child draws a car and gives it to the teacher.
one draws a big loaf of bread and gives it to the teacher.
one draws a party dress, especially for the teacher.
one draws a big, fancy house "For Our Teacher."

Men's Journey

Oka Rusmini

1994

this is the journey of men:
to study the movement of the earth and sky,
to preserve civilization's power,
to propose to every woman they encounter,
their eyes eradicating the colors of flowers.
with bullets and bows they penetrate
a history that doesn't belong to them,
a sound through the forest that makes leaves fall from the trees.

women just sit by the fire
concealing the symbols that explain the secrets
of hundreds of ceremonies that celebrate birth.
later, the seeds of the sky and the earth will be theirs.

this is the journey of men,
their births greeted by priests with bells
who pray for their greatness
and summon the gods to bless their excursions
to break through the stones and the seasons.

women
with the fertility of the earth
make ready a kingdom
for the sons they will birth.
later, when their lives become sacrifices
they will offer them up with a thousand smiles:
make history, my son,
I conceived you from a man's flesh and blood.
this homecoming will bring you power.

this is men's journey,
leaving behind seeds,

wearing human civilization
on the soles of their feet.

Broadway

Sirikit Syah
1994

It's twelve midnight
no moon or stars in the Manhattan sky
The cold air penetrates my bones
and the snow is falling like white cotton

Going down Broadway on the east side
exciting scenes still sparkle and fly
Out of a bathtub, up a man springs
facing the audience, thingy between his legs
This here is indeed New York City
where the theater must survive without subsidy

Pretty women with smooth thighs
wrapped in black tights
their long legs under minidresses and fur coats
are warm on top and cold on the bottom but so what—
this is Broadway, Girl!
Going to the theater is hip
although the cost is pretty steep

Yellow taxis mill about, I choose to walk
shivering to remember my friend's claim:
In Manhattan people shoot each other all the time
A moviegoer gets popped while watching Van Damme

The cafés are filled with artist types
on Broadway at twelve midnight
I walk alone
and fate still brings me here, brings me home

Kumbasari Market in Denpasar

Acep Zamzam Noor

1995

Maybe it's not the moonlight
That brightens the river's surface
On the road to the market
Baskets of fish, meat, and vegetables
Seem to perpetuate the night
The market is a roll of thunder
But also a meditation of sound
I watch the traders begin to dance
The coolies as they begin to sing
Women, one and all—
The cool air absorbs their sweat
Turning it to bottles of palm wine

Here, every woman is a man
Work is prayer and dancing
With them, I hoist their baskets
While distilling my own sweat
Into the power of words
I drink the wine mixed with cool dew
I then beseech the moonlight
To throw its yellow dance-sash to me
I dance crazily among them
Give praise to tree roots and stone markers
Mad with love while waiting for dawn to come

One ritual after another I experience
On the journey of forgetting myself
Along with vegetables and flower offerings
Pork meat, fish, incense, and brightly colored clothing
I become part of the market's thunder
And the quietude of meditation —
Slowly my sweat condenses in words
My words turn into grains of salt
That season the soil and the river
Places where these mighty women
Conclude their dancing and duties
As normal human beings

Moving House

Agus Sarjono

1995

While packing belongings and memories, a thought.
How many times are we actually capable of moving,
changing address and place to call home?
At times like these I want to go just sleep on some clouds
or your breast, watch the sun rise
or set like the kings and countries
in long-ago tales. I watch you sweep the yard
clear it of fallen memories and leaves
then burn them into silent columns
rising to heaven. But I also see all the people in exile
from the lands of their ancestors, from fertile fields and paddies,
turned to wanderers who bear brooms
in memory only, over thousands of nights, thousands of days
muttering dreams of a house
and a small yard that they could sweep each day
so their children could run about in sunlight. How many times
are we actually capable of moving, in a lifetime,
changing our address and place to call home?

I see a spider blown into a ditch by the wind
anxious, looking for the tree branches
where all this time
it's been weaving nets and safety and memories.
But now there's only water, its place in the world
completely different among the frogs and fishes
without the insects it's known
without the usual neighbors although the sun
and rain are just as before. At moments like these
I just want to sleep on some clouds

or your breast while turning the map of heaven
imagining a house a different place for us
preserved from moving and exile
forever.

Sun, Sand, the Beach, and Genitalia

Aslan A. Abidin

1995

on this beach, what more is there for us to say when the sun refuses to carve our
silhouettes in the sand? for such a long time we did not think of each other
so that when we met again, here on this beach,
we had transformed into a pair of lost tourists.

thereafter, in our unfamiliarity, the two of us discussed civilization while
holding our bare knees on the lustful sand. and when I made reference to our
mutual ancestors, you bowed.

"in fact, we've been killing each other for a long time now," you said while
playing with your genitalia

"yes, even the sun, the sand, and this beach we sold a long time ago," I replied
as you glanced at my own genitals.

The Spicy Sensation of Ma Sum's Food Stall

Badruddin Emce

1995

I'm seated in your food stall, Ma,
before me a bowl of power.
Three slices of batter-fried tempeh, still warm, on top.
A handful of red peppers, not to be forgotten.
Inside the peppers,
gunpowder.
This spicy sensation, Ma,
anytime,
anywhere,
can explode

Bee-Eaters

Nenden Lilis Aisyah

1995

I killed a life's tale
and, in that moment and at that instant, buried it
to allow the time to come when it would be forgotten

but people stored the tale in their mouths
as if consuming a swarm of bees
whose honey would then be given to me
or would be spat out to sting my heart

Patiwangi: Renunciation[1]

Oka Rusmini

1995

this is my new land
a spring guarantees its existence
fish embark on new love affairs
branches bearing budding leaves
fashion a burial ceremony

I can smell all kinds of flowers
ritual offerings curse the feet I sink into soil
the tinkling of bells arrests the compass
powerless to guide the gods home

In the temples I make a map
to carry my colors to the sun's family tree
the earth broods, the soil buries its wrath
no fragment of sound remains
to set my colors free

the men present challenge the sun
awaiting their chosen woman's hue
no rites exist for them at the temple

the officiants just inhale the incense
needing to keep track of too many gods
and men keep pressing their suits for my hand

because of my name
I need to possess a ritual history

of this selection
I will bathe posterity's children clean

---

1 "Patiwangi" (*pati*=death; *wangi*=fragrant) is a Balinese-Hindu rite an upper-caste woman is obliged to perform when she marries a man of a lower caste. In so doing, she renounces her caste and takes on her husband's.

Job Exam

Omi Intan Naomi

1995

1
The food chain:
Mosquitoes eat us
Frogs eat mosquitoes
We eat frogs
Mosquitoes eat us

2
What does grass eat?
Soil, water, and air
What do you eat?
My land, my water, my nation

3
What do you do with endangered animals?
Take care of them, guard their continued existence
What's the most endangered animal there is?
The Big Guy up there

4
What's the most dangerous animal?
The omnivore:
Me

Osmosis of Origins

Sitok Srengenge

1995

I ask the wind
 the origin of wonder
  The wind stirs the tips of leaves
and I watch as the trees paint their yearly cycle

I ask a tree
  the origin of time
The tree's flowers suddenly burst open
and I watch as a bee alights to sip their honey

I ask the bee
  from what cell my body has grown
Buzzing in answer, the bee flies into a cave
where I watch a bat press its ear to the stone walls

I ask the bat
  the origin of sound
Flapping its wings, the bat flies into the night sky
and I watch as drops of dew course like a river

I ask the river
  the origin of milk
The river flows down the mountainside
and I watch as a valley dresses in a gown of fog

I ask the valley
 the origin of tabboo
  The valley opens its gown
and I watch as the naked earth writhes elegantly

I ask the earth
who is the original Birth Giver
The earth says nothing, but I hear the sea answer,
"The Birth Giver is witness to the facts but lacks the power to speak!"

I ask the sea
        who it is that holds her
    The sea becomes stormy
then dries before it can say its Name

Yin-Yang

Sitok Srengenge

1995

When love's blossom burst open in the woman's heart
and the sound of petals stirred into words
   that sailed in the man's direction,
a lake was indeed created in her womb
from which tendrils of silence sprouted

When those words struck the walls of the man's soul
their thunderous echo was a windstorm,
at which moment the tendrils were mesmerized,
and the woman knew something had begun to live inside her

Walking in circles before going to bed
the woman hoped her dreams would lead her to a junction
where she might find a man
   and a flood of light from the east
There, a mother was preparing a place to live
   for the new life that had started in her womb

In the woman's lake, in which hung a rainbow,
the man immersed himself
until all the confusion,
   having turned into fog, dissipated,
     and his body was reincarnated
as a Fata Morgana,
where his awareness soared
    and became the sun,
and his soul, in which the woman's face was forever stored
   unfurled as sky in which clouds gathered

And the woman walked in circles,
circumambulating the lake she herself had created
She looked at the fog, she looked at the sun
and the sky in which clouds had gathered
She saw the Fata Morgana,
she saw the transience,

and her desire to forever be with the man
become the richest color in the rainbow's strand

In tears the man came to the woman,
       but as the fog tried to pluck her,
            the man sneezed
and a typhoon arose from the base of his eyebrows
       causing the sun to slide into the lake and drown,
and his blinked tears to turn into stars

              With a a cat upon her lap
      the woman stared up at the clear night,
and stars dropped to the base of the clear lake
The woman daydreamed before falling aleep
until her dreams overtook her travel to the threshold of wakefulness,
      and she saw the man's drops of sweat dangling from leaves
      illumined by light shining from the east

Postscript

Toeti Heraty

1995p

I want to write
a pornographic poem
and not change raw words
to beauty, no more
is there need for metaphor
breasts that become rolling hills
a woman's body equals nature's warmth
intercourse, a passionate embrace

what is evident
is that the poem will be somewhere between
revelation and concealment
hypocrisy and self truth

A Poet's Mother

Saut Situmorang

1995-98

the mother weeps
awaiting his birth

the mother weeps
delivering him in pain

the mother weeps
handing him to another

the mother weeps
nursing his wounds

the mother weeps
visiting him in jail

the mother weeps
sending him abroad

the mother weeps
missing him at night

the weeping mother
cries no more
her tears are spent

now she sleeps
in the grass, among the stars
in the sky

A Poet Once More

Acep Zamzam Noor

1996

I found strands of your hair, Melva, in Karang Setra
On the smooth ceramic floor. I always think of you
When I see ads for soap, shampoo, and toothpaste
Or *dangdut* singers on the TV.
Now, alone in this hotel, I feel myself to be
A poet once more. The intoxicating scent of your perfume
Slipping suddenly through the bathroom door
Attacks me like lines of poetry.
You know, Melva, words always make me tremble
And the strange scents from your nape, neck, and armpits
Have now turned into words.

Now, alone in this hotel, I feel myself to be
A poet once more. I carefully place the brown strands of hair
On the table, alongside the papers,
The cigarettes, and the cup of coffee. And then,
Still feeling your lips on my mouth
Your voice still filling my ears and mind, I write a poem.
Remembering the color of your shoes,
Your underwear, your bra, and the belt
You once left beneath the bed
As a way of saying goodbye, I write a poem.

No, Melva, a poet is not sad for being abandoned
Or from the pain because in the end such things do pass.
The poet does not weep for being betrayed
Or fall unconscious because his mouth has been silenced.
A poet does not die from his words' loss of strength
Or because his powerful words have turned into prose:
Becoming, for instance, unending war,
Hijackings, plane crashes, floods, and earthquakes.
Or, for instance, the never-ending corruption of this country,
The mayhem, the looting, the rapes, and whatever.

It's just that I am alone here and feel myself to be a poet once more.

Love Story

Ari Pahala Hutabarat

1996

on a faraway hill the moon has gone
and the sun has just arrived
flowers and footpath beneath
thickets sing of rocks
that are still not done whistling

"a conversation between us two will never happen
here your voice is only a strange wind
dead and cold. between twigs and flowers
it is empty without clear meaning
until even my whispers fall silent, receiving no reply
transformed in the space into either
lasting defeat or sacred victory"

on the hill, two moons embrace
the night rubs the grass
and the hollow of the tree, which is naked
stone, catches the cold, thin
and stinging
and pulls in a fog trembling
beneath its feet

"you can really bear to punish me with
shards of time, allowing my memories, which
visit the grave, to become the groom and virgin
kissed by loneliness"

(moon)
durian tree
amidst
tall grass beneath the moon
(fish)
lotus flower in the
middle of a pond
grins

"and suddenly you admit to being a loneliness which
awakens me from sleep along the way becoming
a wanderer and vagrant examining the needles of the
day which are always filled with silence encircling and imprisoning my
words which pour forth and evaporate
in your space, which for me is mute"—

the silver moon sailing at the head of the horizon
spreads out its white hair and
lets its wet lips be kissed by the face
of the sea

"then, finally this
love is no more than intercourse
you are empty, I am nameless
masculinity and gentleness a presence
without words—"

Metaphor

Dinullah Rayes

1996

a poem is the wing of a little bird
that sheds the dew
when day comes early
in an itty-bitty flower garden
a poet is a minor prophet
sowing the seeds of righteous love
on the fields of cracked and broken souls
driving an ancient carriage of peace
pulled by two horses: lunar-solstice

Marriage of a Prostitute with No Body

Dorothea Rosa Herliany

1996

you led me to a strange hill: we followed the sun
        as it scattered golgotha's sweat. death
and resurrection: the ecstasy of a journey
through the alphabet and the scriptures.

"jesus, you have drawn a map of the pleasures
of pilgrimage. journeying century after century
among unspoken prayers and psalms. i need a map,
i can read the vague directions in the palms of your hands
        and in the words of the prophets."

i am only a prostitute, with no hope of heaven.
i take my body wherever i want, offering
false intimacy and lies about love. each line
is filled with breath and sweat. the jackals howl.
night's hatred shivers between frightened wild animals.

i carry my heart among empty confused love.
i offer it to men who paint the wind with their eyes.

"jesus, give me the pleasure of strange love,
of climax after climax in strange beds,
give me everything men do not have,
but don't give me heaven."

i crawl over unnamed hills. everything is finished
because of the empty wind and words.
among the mumbling of the angels
and the church bells' ringing. i am only a prostitute,
unwilling to find the door and the hollow pews.

i am only a prostitute, offering sin, but i keep
the sentences no one prays, i search the hills
and plow the fields. plant sweat in trembling wounds,
and watch gardens full of roses blossom.

man, even as i embrace you, i mock you!

447

Looking in on History

Fakhrunnas M.A. Jabbar

1996

I've forgotten the way home
the road is not marked
like the others, useless as an arrow that forgets its bow
I dig a time tunnel
the longest tunnel
where is sultan mahmud now
where is the queen, who knows
I do not find them or any others in the procession of my
mind
I search for signs I scratched in my blood
everything is frozen now
malay is like a slice of bread preserved
libraries of the world chew upon it
in leiden, raja ali haji is brought to life
his spirit covers penyengat island
I've forgotten the way home
looking in on history: names are just letters
I've forgotten the way home
schools in the city have no malay curriculum
even the melaka emporium is quickly sunk
its sailors have released its anchor ropes
who knows where the jawi script is now
I've forgotten the way home
will leiden be the malay land of the next century
even if only in old texts
swallowed by the yellowing of history

Woman Is the Earth

Medy Loekito

1996

woman's destiny is to be born as the earth
to be stoned by the feet of bridges and buildings
from her wounds grow the invocations
that bear fruit as the country's children

A Dragonfly and a Fish

Medy Loekito

1996

a dragonfly
gliding over a pond
plucking at bubbles
pouncing on ripples
sees a fish swimming in a wave
"life in a pond. how delightful."

a fish
staring at the sky
catching the sunshine
gulping the air
sees a dragonfly sparkling in the light
"life in the sky. how delightful."

Lion on His Throne

Pitres Sombowadile

1996

An old lion sits on his throne
contemplating the direction of the passing storm attacking the palace pillars
carefully sharpening his claws and worn-down fangs
approaching the eclipse
the ritual harvests a thousand freight cars of victims

But the wind has blown his amulet
back out to sea
plunging in at the beach
fighting the pull of the waves

There is a seed of doubt in the old lion's heart
is any of his virility left
as the sun sets in the west?
the sheath of his sword is creased and stiff
locked to whoever unsheathes it

The old lion lies on the throne
planning the fate of the pawns in the attic
arranging fish in the state aquarium

Yesterday a school of protesting fish was poisoned
while chewing sunflower seeds
the leaders of the fish protesters did not need to be poisoned
it was enough to cut their meal rations and oxygen intake
the supporting generals were not yet full
although they had been fed until they vomited
it's not good if they fall to the bottom of the aquarium
rather, let them float
bloated and weak

But can something like this happen at sunset
when the colors of the lion's fur fade
into the velvet carpet?
The lion's body is pale and unsteady
his bones creak telling the stories of his life

The lion is now magnificent on his throne
"Power is orgasmic, turbulence brings bliss," he says
"Do not worry about time but achieve endless multiple orgasms
while the case for Godot continues."

Co Kong Tik

Tan Lioe Ie

1996

Look deeply into the tongues of flame, the puffs of smoke
Squeeze shut your eyes
Stamp your feet
    (Taabb! Taabb! Taabb!)
    Become a home!
    What is small on earth
    is made great in the sky

Fragrance of incense, circle of liquor
So that Tu Ti Kong gets drunk

   SojaKui
   SojaKui
   SojaKui

Respectful greetings, oh my grandchildren

Hands of affection pierce the sky
and time
That cried but a moment ago
now laughs

Dawn breaks
With its tongues of flame and waves
at the foot of the reef

When it is finished
open your eyes
Amazed at the love
And honor in a single drop of blood

---

* Co Kong Tik is a ritual performed by Indonesians of Chinese descent, especially in Bali. The ritual consists mainly of sending off a "package from home" for departed relatives in the world of the ancestors. Tu Ti Kong (Chinese) is God of the Earth

SojaKui
SojaKui
SojaKui

What is small on the earth
is made great in the sky

Dharma Wanita

Taufiq Ismail

1996

Because I feel some affection
For the ladies of the Dharma Wanita Association
Here is my suggestion:
Disband this organization for wives of government leaders

Let's unveil a little secret
That for a period well nigh uncharted
The ladies have been exploited
By the institution called the state

If activities were normal and appropriate
That would be quite in order, nothing to rail against
But more often, ostentatious behavior is the most noticed trait
And shamelessly with full intent supported by the state

If credibility lacks, go ahead and ask the State Serene
Which parades these ladies on the TV screen
Hair in bouffant bird nests, attired in outfits tending to the nauseous
With make-up oft times overdone and sometimes bilious

Ma'am, those kids at home, the top priority is their education
Supervising what friends they make is no easy operation
To them you should be giving the best part of your time
In your household agenda that has to be prime

Let your husband's career develop as it should
He must rely on his own competence and capability
If you involve yourself in scheming for his good
You'll be forced into arse licking as a strategy

Because I feel some affection
For the ladies of the Dharma Wanita Association
Take my suggestion into consideration
Disband the association
If you're still acting above your station

Ashamed to be an Indonesian

Taufiq Ismail

1996

1

When I was a junior in high school in Pekalongan
I won a scholarship to go to Wisconsin
The year was nineteen fifty-six
And I was elated to be a child of the Indonesian revolution
My land had only six years earlier gained world recognition
We were proud to have seized independence from the Netherlands
Thomas Stone, a classmate of mine
Born and bred in Whitefish Bay
Felt deep admiration for the Indonesian revolution
He wrote about the battle of Surabaya
With Bung Tomo, obviously, as the leading figure
And in a minor way I served as his informant
My chest swelled with pride to be an Indonesian
Tom Stone went on to West Point Academy
And obtained a Ph.D. from Rice University
He's now a senior officer retired from the U.S. Army
Once, when standing, I held my chest high
Why so often now do I seem to have a stoop?

2

The country's moral firmament has fallen, in pieces all around
The law does not stand erect, it leans and shifts; just hear that cracking sound
I walk on Roxas Boulevard, Geylang Road, Lebuh Tun Razak,
I walk on Sixth Avenue, Maydan Tahrir and Ginza
I walk on the Dam, the Champs-Elysées and in Mesopotamia
In public I hide behind glasses, the darkest in town
And pull my beret well down over my crown
I am ashamed to be an Indonesian.

3

In my land, corruption in bureaucracy has a world-class rating: number one,
In my land, collusion of business and bureaucracy is so dazzling, clear and
clarion in its dishonesty it's hard to find a comparison,

In my land, sons, daughters, nephews, nieces, cousins and grandchildren are
spoiled, soiled, by the power of fathers, uncles and grandfathers to the point
of total ruin, but there's no blame, no need even for a grain of shame,

In my land, purchase commissions on heavy equipment, light equipment,
weaponry, fighter planes, submarines, soy beans, flour and fermented cassava
are plundered by bureaucracy, with more than half disappearing into the
pockets of jackets meant for safari,

In embassies abroad, children of presidents, ministers, generals, secretaries
general and directors general are waited on and feted like bonafide
presidents, ministers, generals, secretaries general and directors general
themselves, that their parents may be content,

In my land, at the counting of votes in general elections what is extremely-
tremely-tremely-tremely clear is the massive fraud, deception and
malfeasance, that never causes the tiniest pinprick of conscience,

In my land, sermons, newspapers, magazines, books and plays presenting
dissenting views are censored without ceasing; there's no end of banning,

In my land, they burn down markets of the little merchant to make way for
rampant shopping centers of giant capital,

In my land, Udin and Marsinah were sacrificed and martyred. Smell the
fragrance of their corpses; theirs is but a transitory, fleeting defeat for now;
for in the time to come those plotters and murderers will languish in the
deepest depths of hell, trammeled and trampled into a shapeless pulp by the
security guards of the hereafter,

In my land, court verdicts can be negotiated in the form of sale and purchase,
in some secrecy or none at all; it's said that one day a court decision will be
officially negotiable for trading at the Jakarta Stock Exchange,

In my land there is no feeling of security what with twenty types of gouging,
fifteen kinds of extorting this and that and ten ways of intimidating,

In my land, telephones are tapped, spies and spooks are overworked, xeroxed
gossip and libel are disseminated near and far,

In my land, football has been elevated to an inter-city spectators' terror show,
merely because a tiny segment of our nation is never ready to accept a match
score agreed on in accordance with convention,

In my land, apparently it's been decided that we shall not be involved in the
   World Cup on grounds of international security; what's more the World
   Cup is merely the business of little countries, for China, India, Russia
   and we will not participate, and till enough is enough Indonesia will be a
   spectator merely by satellite,
In my land there is killing, kidnapping and torturing of the populace, dazzling-
   clear in the light of day, in Aceh, Tanjung Priuk, Lampung, Haur, Koneng,
   Nipah, Santa Cruz, Irian and Banyuwangi. There are also denials and
   rebuttals, dazzling-clear, which are foul lies dazzling-clear in the light of the
   sun, dazzling-clear, and yet the sun has never been subpoenaed to testify in
   court as a witness dazzling-clear,
In my land, moral integrity and decency are still found in holy writ, but in the
   day-to-day they are like needles buried in a stack of rice herbage after the
   paddy harvest.

           4
The skies of morality collapse upon my land, scattered all around
The law does not stand erect, it leans and shifts; just hear that cracking sound
I walk on Roxas Boulevard, Geylang Road, Lebuh Tun Razak,
I walk on Sixth Avenue, Maydan Tahrir and Ginza
I walk on Dam, the Champs-Elysées and in Mesopotamia
In the midst of the public I hide behind glasses, the darkest in town
And pull my beret well down over my crown
I am ashamed to be an Indonesian.

Jimbaran 2

Wayan Sunarta

1996

In these tropical lands
      we are born
to follow a predetermined path

but they have snatched
      the beautiful full moon
from our sight.
We no longer see the tide ebb.
In the swamps, beaches, coral reefs and mountains
hotels spread like a plague.

Oh, too many of our fellows
behave like slaves.
      Too many.
And the west wind blows
bringing Father Rat
to destroy your lands,
your mangroves, limestone mountains and white sandy beaches.

      Too many
      who refuse to lead ordinary lives.

On the coast
we long to hear fishermen singing
as they return from the sea.
We remember turtles laying their eggs under the bright moon.
We want to fry fish under the starry sky,
to joke with the salty winds
in the Jembaran night.

We can only desire.
We cannot do what we want.

But I still hope for one thing.
I want you to keep Bali
in the loving embrace of its temples.

Allow me to take my leave,
to return
to sacred silence.

The Ballad of a Man in Nan Yang

Wilson Tjandinegara

1996

Since the seventeenth century
they have sailed the savage seas
on Junk ships[1]
escaping conflict and catastrophe
leaving their ancestral home behind
seeking a land of hope in Nan Yang[2]

In the fishermen's settlement in Teluk Naga
a Chinese rice wine maker
buries his solitude
with a faithful companion
a simple innocent native girl

Awkward, like a chicken and a duck
this one uses chopsticks
that one loves sambal
speaking in a language of gestures

After the long journey, left to roam
in a distant place he has made a home

From generation to generation
skin color slowly blends
until a generation of confluence is formed:
Benteng Chinese
an exemplary assimilation

The Cisadane river is a witness
to the life journey of both its people
collectively resisting Dutch invaders
working together
intertwined in a true kinship
as the Cisadane keeps flowing
from century to century
towards the motherland—Indonesia

---

[1] A Junk ship is a Chinese sailing ship, used for centuries during both recreational or business voyages.
[2] Nan Yang: South Sea (Southeast Asia)

Wheels

Wowok Hesti Prabowo

1996

for Diha

like a wheel, I spin
your eyes catch sight of my graying hair
in each alleyway, like a parade
I see your ears impaled on my steel fence
what wind is it that's brought you here
to disturb my spinning?

even if the wheel that spins in my chest
anchors its splattering of poems to poet's island
I still want to be standing here
like my teacher, capturing the morning sun
so that I can also sing in the jungle
which is something you've never understood

tall buildings pressed together
factories spreading pollution and effluence
my friends go wild for malls and shopping centers
but I am still here, drowning in a virginal room
where wheels spin in time
with buffalo passing before the sun

My Father Has Gone

Mardi Luhung

1996p

My father's gone
in search of flame
a sacred space for consummation

but the tails he left
twist my frame
create abyss, he holds

the ends still
the limits imperceptible
and so has become a ghost

My father's gone, admittedly,
yet his phantom, so robust,
exerts its force

and makes my insides
palpitate, as on a precipice
gyrate, as if serrated

potsherd wings
were constantly enfolding me
and the farmland all around

this land of hope, where
I submit my faithfulness
to its rise and fall, its fall and rise

and the naked bubble
I carved with twenty fingers, and to which I gave
organs, nose and mouth, ears and eyes

then a few words, "that ghost just now"
then a few tails, "they end in Father"
and then a table, chair, umbrella

463

I bid it welcome

The bubble and I talked to each other
were mutually open
in conversation

and so it was at the beginning
I made terrain inside the bubble
and was duteous for too long

now still the ghost envelops me
and still I grip the tails
that end in Father

who gives name to
every name I
call and shout

who encompasses the ground
on which I
lie or conjugate

to erect or be erected
to suck in or be sucked
to resolve or be resolved

then stamps my brow
with ash tattoos
that radiate like mercury

then knits together my
children's existence, and the
children of my children

makes them believe
that the ash tattoo and the land inside that bubble
were in fact inherited on my chromosomes

and not from an apparition:
"Father's Ghost!"

My father's gone
in search of flame
a sacred space for consummation

Newlywed from the Coast

Mardi Luhung

1996p

I come dressed as a groom from the coast,
in a procession as in days long past,
accompanied by trumpets, drums, gongs, and carbide lamps.

At the head masked acrobats turn somersaults—
a wild boar, a tiger, a mouse-deer, a monkey—
as roman candles burst and color the sky.

I come in the early days of being in love
as before, when together we owned the morning,
when together we harvested catfish roe

which we dried and then, later—
when twilight crept into the lines
of your poems which are now only a whisper—fried.

And do you know what I hated the most?
It was when we both went to school
and everyone called us "sea folks,"

people deemed to be exceedingly coarse,
uncivilized folk with a fishy smell,
the same smell of the snappers they relished.

I come intent to establish a household,
to bend the bridal bough, create a diary of joy
and hope for children to be born of your shores.

Yet, like the lighthouse whose base is all that remains
and the fishermen who've lost their vessels and nets—
do we still have time to make love with the waves?

Meanwhile, sheets of receipts
have transformed our sperm into algae
whose names no one even knows...

Mythology

Gus tf

1997

As a child he liked looking at himself in the mirror in his mother's room. "That's you," his mother said as she released a bird inside him. The bird was beautiful, with clear pupils and a rose colored beak. "It will be your friend even when I'm not here."

When he was a teenager, his mother moved the mirror into his room. Each time he looked at himself, the bird cooed and circled above his head. What was it saying? What did it want? When he wasn't there, he was sure the bird suffered and felt lonely.

As an adult, maybe because he was constantly busy with work, he rarely looked at the mirror. And the bird, maybe because he often gave it no mind, rarely showed itself to him. For years, for decades, they seemed no longer to be part of each other. But then one day, after he'd reached middle age, he saw it again: an ugly disheveled thing, much like the gloom that had taken hold of his life. Was that really it?

Now, as an elderly man, in front of the mirror, he bitterly longs for it. But the bird, that bird, never actually existed.

Here the Past Is Killed

Iyut Fitra

1997

don't open that album, my love
in it, time has eloped with fate
my father's words still leave a bitter taste:
if you were born to be a nomad, then fly
fly away on the wings of a thousand doves
don't cry, my child, not before
you have suffered a mother's longing!
there is no other story. I, too, have carved a path
to each foodstall, intersection, and vow
and to silence, as well. I have never feared separation
or betrayal nor have I been anxious about death
the passing of the hours is fate, is it not
did you not once fill my chest with flowers?
so don't, my love. I suddenly hate all that is old
though someone is softly calling my name: nomad!
what secrets have you learned? is every woman
that you abduct as angelic as your mother?
but I have been killed in an extended exile
which I fear will come for me again. just as you spill your tears
I no longer know the meaning of longing

Wawini in the Sound of Fire

John Waromi
1997

The Mambotaran have trespassed in the north
and their children are heading eastward
arrows and spears in hand.
The day is young when Ampar, an ancient crone
straightens his back and rises.
The old man stamps his feet on the ground
causing the four corners of the wind to shake.
Branches and grasses
dew and sweat
ants and centipedes
mosquitoes and birds
tremble in unison.

Younger Wawini take the children
and hurry them off to see Ampar.
The old man stretches out his hand
and thus comes into being
from a grain of seed
a cluster of corn.
From fruit
come seeds.
From fruit
come seeds.
A multitude of fruits
grow and grow
break apart
burst open
a tempest at night's end
a party in the morning sky.
A million remain
still joined together
    playing their flutes
     singing their songs.
And I can hear the sound
of a fire still burning.

Rats

John Waromi
1997

Rats stop me in my path
The rats now hoisting a flag
    and looking cynically my way
The rats embracing a flagpole
legs planted stiffly on the garbage bin
The flag, of indeterminate colors
flutters in the night
Which way the wind blows is uncertain
The rats that cross my path and the gutter
fly their flag high, as high as a minaret
    as high as a church steeple
    as high as a temple's peak
Whose national flag is it anyway
    that flutters in the night
Field rats, kitchen rats, gutter rats, garbage rats
tree rats, rice rats, city rats
stand in formation at the flagpole's base
paying respect to the night rats
on their memorial day.

The rats that bar my way as I go home
    together carrying the multi-colored flag
laugh giddily to see me stop in my tracks.

There's Something I Love about Jakarta

Rayani Sriwidodo

1997

There's something I love about Jakarta;
namely, its multicolored ponds and waterways,
the chocolate milk of Ciliwung canal
(a reminder of every glass I ever drank),
the foamy white of Krukut
(like milk, that amusingly smelled of urine, from the neighbor's
      cow),
the viscous black of Sunter
(a Chinese sketch, an inky trail across millions of sheets of
      paper),
the water-hyacinth green of the pond at the Beautiful Indonesia
      in Miniature Park
(a surrealist dance performance there would surely be
      spectacular)

As clear as spring water
(a necessity targeted by street vendors
for washing plates and faces, for offering to customers
who play clever games of hide-and-seek in the middle of the
      night and in the wee hours of the morning)
is the liquid crystal of Kali Pasir

Despite the water's glassy surface
a surge of current about three inches wide
reveals the amazingly rich life
tasseling the sediment below

The water dances, worming
relentlessly, obsessively
at the speed of the earth's rotation,
apparently in protest of the intentions
of those most ancient, unevolved creatures,
the billions of germs floating in sparkling, dark sludge,
celebrating, as they devour a bounty of metropolitan refuse,

the cat, its carcass tangled in a bougainvillea branch,
in mute dispute with a gutter rat rotting at its feet

From the row of cheerful houses on either side of the bright
        canal
emerges a girl carrying a bamboo basket under her arm
Dressed in Hawaiian shorts, a T-shirt with the words 'It's the
        millennium, yeah?"
and unbranded flip flops, she steps with her flawless feet
to the edge of the canal, which greets her with sincerity
Wearing her widest, sweetest smile,
she parts the water's dubious surface gently
and carefully tilts the basket
to vigorously rinse three liters of uncooked rice

Kali Pasir, a canal of many uses,
a gift from the city to its beloved residents

Look, downstream
someone whistles playfully in that same girl's direction
"Damn it," she snaps
"Just about to take a dump, and you come a-hollerin'"

A dog stops by,
the reek of the world's third most crowded city piercing his
        pores—
this generous oasis really wets the throat
(He is weary from tracking his master,
who yesterday while taking him out for a walk
got hit by a truck that scuttled away, disappearing
as the body, already turning blue,
was rushed away in an old ambulance)

And look there, upstream,
three kids bathing and splashing around,

exasperating a woman
        rinsing her laundry
who notices that her husband's only white shirt
has been hit with a strand of black slime
inevitably staining it
This outrages the sediment's inhabitants as well,
        though only momentarily—
        anger vanishes quickly
        in the creep of Kali Pasir's lazy current

Really, there's something I love about Jakarta
beyond its multicolored canals and ponds
Though a public graveyard lies near my home
when I drink the groundwater, I have no qualms

Alive and Well

Wiji Thukul

1997

I'm not a news-making celebrity
but am, to be sure, bad news
for those in power

my poems are not poetry
but dark words—sweating
and jostling for a way out

even if an eye is lost
they will never die;
even if I must flee my home
they will never die;
even if I must pay what they ask:
my years, my energy, my wounds,
they will never die.

words always ask for payment
and always say to me, you are still alive

and yes, I am alive and well
and my words have not been destroyed!

Land of Tears

Sutardji Calzoum Bachri

1997p

land of our birth source of our sorrows
source of our tears
our tears for the land of our birth

here we stand
singing of our sorrow

we hide our suffering
in the parched earth
we try to hide our pain
behind the glass fronts
of shopping malls

we try to hide our misery
we try to bury our grief
but we cannot hide our agony
it is everywhere

the earth does not reach the horizon the open sky is not waiting
you cannot escape
no matter where you go
you tread on our tears
wherever you fly
you land on our tears
wherever you sail
you drift on our tears

you are trapped
you cannot escape
there is nowhere you can go
you must surrender to our tears

Proverb of a Statue

Warih Wisatsana

1997p

After my head was chopped off and displayed
in the underground chamber
of a foreign museum
my cracked eye wept all night
imagining my beautiful body covered with moss
recalling thousands of years that have passed
the moment that devoted holy person prostrated in prayer at my feet

Has a devastating earthquake destroyed my country?
Holy people and good-hearted followers, where have you gone?
Or have you died by the holy *keris* of the traitor?

Questions spin wildly in the dark cavities in my head
hoarse like the voice of the owl
or the rough whisper of the axe
that asks for pardon before it slashes
the soft base of my neck—
I sobbed all night
imagining
remembering my distant homeland.
My fate now is no different from my self
stacked up dusty
displayed as a prisoner in a foreign country
in tattered old history books
nibbled by moths

My cracked eyes wept—
how was it possible that this great country could be destroyed
vanished in a moment
like a grain of sand in the middle of a whirlwind?

But history is not blind forever
not mute and deaf forever.
Eyes and ears that have witnessed
how it is possible to be negligent forever

or pretend not to know.
In one hundred or one thousand years more
at the moment a horse trots in the distance
someone will come
to visit this museum
sneak into the underground chamber.
He will hear the hoarse whispers and my sobbing

Amazed I am impressed
in the silence of his eyes
I find pieces of my body
I find
shadows of the country in the future
and a line of holy people sitting in meditation

One hundred or one thousand years more
there will come
there will come the moment my form will be whole perfect.
So at that magical moment I will proclaim the truth
that all this time I have kept secret.

Legend of the Tanjung Kait Chinese Temple

Wilson Tjandinegara

1997p

Twilight came to the Sunda Straits dressed in a red gown,
the fishermen returned with their catch.

Krakatau had seemed calm for many years
but was only suppressing its anger.
It erupted on August 27, 1873,
in a thunderous roar,
a violent earthquake.
The world drew back in fear,
the sun went black.

Waves as tall as coconut trees ran hand-in-hand with death
sweeping away the town and the fishing villages.
They were swallowed in an instant by the dark ocean.

As the wave struck
people ran to an old Chinese temple
hidden among the houses and shacks
on the beach of Tanjung Kait.

The jovial god Ci Kong
with a fan in his right hand
and a large set of beads around his neck
circled the temple in a gust of wind,
driving away the deadly flood.

The white-robed goddess Kwan Im
whistling through her cute mouth
quick as lightning
called the sacred gold dragon from Teluk Naga
and kneeled in the temple yard
waiting for her orders.

Riding the horned dragon
the goddess Kwan Im mounted the wave,
her sweet mouth chanting spells,
her fingers scattering beads,
and the sea drew back again.

As the smoke began to settle
the sun blinked in disbelief.
Violent Krakatau had vanished
leaving only sorrow behind.

The powerful gods of Co Soe Kong temple
invite pilgrims from all directions.
Incense burns there constantly,
the smoke rising up to heaven.

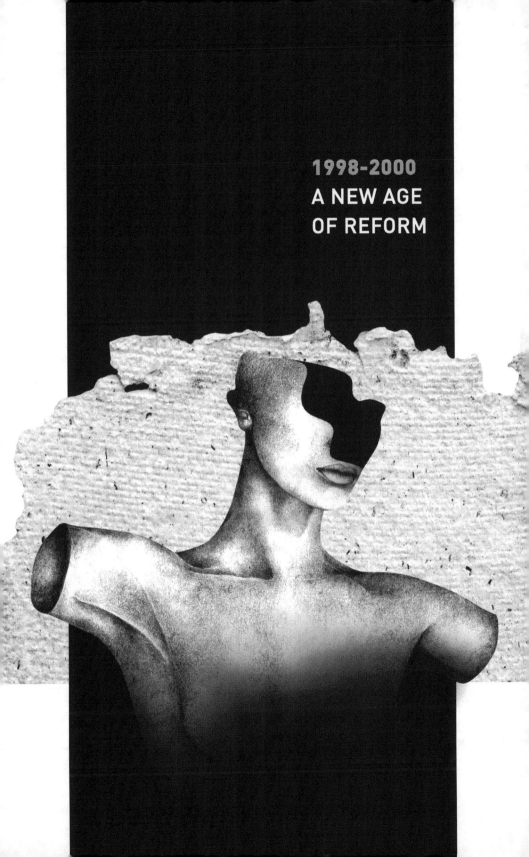

1998-2000
A NEW AGE
OF REFORM

Introduction to the 1998–2000 Period

Stripping Away the False and Leaving It Behind

Eka Budianta

In 1998 great political, social and cultural changes occurred in Indonesia concurrent with an extreme upheaval in the economy. The exchange value of the rupiah against the U.S. dollar plummeted from Rp.2,000 to Rp.17,000. Waves of rioting hit a number of big cities. Many markets, shops and housing areas were looted; demonstrators perished in flames or gunfire. President Soeharto, who had led the New Order regime since 1966, resigned, and Indonesia entered the Reformasi (Reform) period.

After President Soeharto stepped down on May 21, 1998, Bacharudin Jusuf Habibie, an academic with a non-military background, took over the government. ABRI (Armed Forces of the Republic of Indonesia), known for its iron hand, changed its name to the National Army of Indonesia (TNI). The government bureaucracy changed. The people's aspirations—which had up until that point largely been ignored, curtailed and censored—could now be openly expressed. The press was unleashed. The views of the public were listened to. One province was even permitted to consider secession from the Republic. The result: East Timor—the youngest of the twenty-seven provinces—became its own nation, Timor Leste. The number of provinces did not decrease further, rising instead to thirty-four, as people ever more freely established new forms of governance at the provincial, regency, municipal, sub-district and village levels.

This newfound freedom and creativity in politics soon spread to the literary world, affecting all aspects, from content and style to publication. The number of newspapers and magazines shot up, and the number of poets multiplied, too, now that everyone was free to think, voice and publish artistic expressions. The sudden multitude of published poets was the result of several factors. First, publishing books and poetry digitally became easier. Second, the emergence of online literature provided the opportunity for anyone to write and distribute literary works. Third, the fact that there was no longer a gatekeeper—an editor-in-chief, for example—meant there was no one to winnow the number of works and determine whether a piece of writing was worthy of publication.

As Agus R. Sarjono reminds us here in his poem "Sajak Palsu" (Fake Poem):

Then foreign currencies threaten with fake exchange rates
so that everything writhes mired in a crisis that brings down the fake
government to its
fake wretched fate. Then fake people
shout for fake joy and debate
fake ideas during fake seminars
and fake conferences, welcoming the arrival of
a fake democracy that is celebrated so shrilly
and so fakely.

Of course the question remains: what about that which isn't "fake"? Do people who aren't fake deliver democracy that isn't fake with a gladness that isn't faked either? These are the type of questions that will be addressed in this introduction to the Reformasi period.

For years, creative life and independent thinking had been restricted in Indonesia. Why—judging by the limited number of works published—were there so few poets during the New Order regime? Because the government forbade the circulation of works—the media were controlled and could be shut down at any moment—and even gagged poets thought to be "enemies of the state." From this perspective, the choice of poets grouped within the Reformasi Generation is important. This anthology has selected only thirty-some from around twelve hundred Indonesian poets who published work during the Reformasi period. In this section, we rediscover names that could not be spoken as long as President Soeharto was in power. Among these is Agam Wispi, who wrote, "Poetry, you are the only home I have."

Had all trace of suppression suddenly disappeared? According to the poets who were actively composing during the Reformasi period, past trauma was not only still present in the lives of many, but fresh injustices kept appearing. Speaking about the region of Nanggroe Aceh Darussalam, the poet D. Kemalawati reported:

and I and the thousands of others here
cannot be bought
I have an instinct
a conscience
although long besieged
I choose death

and I too give witness
(that the massacre really did occur)

The main task of the poet—that of bearing witness to the age—was presented as a golden opportunity in the Reformasi period. Religious issues, previously not subject to discussion, began to be openly questioned. The established poet Hersri Setiawan asked:

what are they for
these christmas lights
new year's fireworks
and the prayers of ramadan

Meanwhile, Aslan Abidin, a far younger poet, joked in a poem about overhearing three young women who seemed to be giggling about "a porn film they watched the night before." "It was standing straight up: stiff, erect, and red," one of the women in Abidin's poem says. Later in the poem it becomes clear that the image refers to a mosque:

the sun was up and behind us, in the east, the mosque grew distant. only its tower was still visible: standing straight, and erect, and red in the sunlight. the four of us burst into laughter together.

Reformasi brought the hope that anyone could become a poet, and that all subjects and attitudes could be poetic. Dorothea Rosa Herliany wrote:

but i did not marry you to be faithful
i agreed to fight on each battlefield

She was not writing a ballad or quoting someone else but speaking her mind freely. This kind of speech appeared without restraint during Reformasi. Never before had the struggles of life been voiced so stridently. Jamal D. Rahman wrote:

the sky in our village has fallen a thousand times
but we never cry

The overwhelming impression produced by the writings of the free-for-all Reformasi era is that the lives of most people continued to be profoundly difficult, to the extent that the poet Sosiawan proposed, "come on, let's gang up on god." He wrote:

the teachers piss standing up, choked to death by costs
the bureaucrats are being breastfed by their constituents in a rehab room.

The poet uses his verse as a tool to help eradicate corruption, to scrutinize social and economic problems, and to break free of the fetters of *adat* (customary law), the taboos surrounding sexuality, and the grip of political power and religious teachings. Sosiawan Leak, in his poem "Stud Pig," wrote:

unlike a scholar or believer
i have no morals
because morals are rare stars that haven't even been born.
to me, god and the prophets are as nebulous as the devil.
i can't distinguish lectures and curses
from swords and rifles.
i don't recognize the boundaries between right and wrong, good and bad—
only humans have those
and only they can violate them!

It had previously been unimaginable that such thoughts would be voiced at all—much less that they would come to represent an age, to be emblematic of the creative freedom of Indonesia's Reformasi era.

It might be said that this period represented the most precarious time in the history of the Indonesian nation since the declaration of independence in 1945. Many poems written during the Reformasi era are loaded with extremely strong social and political messages. The senior poets who had long been a part of the Indonesian literary world continued to write. Among these were Rayani Sriwidodo and Sapardi Djoko Damono. Here is Rayani's testimony:

That women are sex objects
was displayed at the height of the violence
on that thirteenth of May

And here is Sapardi Djoko Damono, writing on the same subject:

astagfirulah, dear God in heaven
there are so many of us

stacked near the trash waiting to be carted away
seduced by oil and now burned

Poets writing in the Reformasi period did not endeavor to refine an aesthetic form or develop a beautiful linguistic art. What was lacking in terms of beauty seems to have been fully made up for by honesty and resoluteness in the face of all that was painful or bogus. We can only hope that this Reformasi period gives birth to a new period of greater optimism—a confirmation that life is not as heavy as we felt it to be in 1998.

Going Home

Agam Wispi

1998

with thanks to Goenawan Mohamad

Where
is my green tree?
Here
I am only a rock

Wanderer,
where have you come from?
Wherever it is
I want to be the dust on your feet

"In Karet, Karet Cemetery," you said—
are you still there, Chairil?[1]
Or were you buried beneath a pile of stones
or disappeared before the year two thousand?

Yes, Banda,[2] your bombastic words have corroded,
"no one ever wants to go home again!"
Home? How can the ocean bird
return when it has no nest?
Unfortunately, Pa-i,[3] you died
before seeing a new generation rise,
the world was bewitched by your sidelong glances,
restless yearning, fear and worry

I can proudly remember Sudjojono[4] pointing
and saying, "I am glad I am not a dog!"[5]
This too is modernization, globalization:
words squeezed dry of meaning,
a new culture: from top to bottom
all are extortionists and thieves

Poetry, you are the only home I have
Poetry, you are the only love that can fly
The poetry of this new generation is capable, clever and cruel,
hard as granite, its love as unstable as the sea

Where are you
in my green trees?
In your poetry, wanderer,
in your love on a distant island[6]

---

[1] Chairil Anwar (1922–1949) is commonly regarded as Indonesia's greatest modern poet.

[2] Bandaharo Harahap, an Indonesian poet, was a prominent advocate of the Lembaga Kebudayaan Rakyat (Lekra), a left-wing literary organization, for which he was imprisoned after 1965.

[3] "Pa-i" was the nickname for Rivai Apin, an Indonesian poet.

[4] S. Soedjono was a well known Indonesian painter.

[5] This quotation is from a poem by Chairil Anwar.

[6] This quotation is also from a poem by Chairil Anwar.

Fake Poem

Agus R. Sarjono

1998

Good morning, sir, good morning ma'am, say
the schoolchildren
in fake greeting. Then they go on to study
fake history from fake textbooks. When school is over
they are shocked to see the grades on their fake
transcripts. Because their grades aren't high enough,
they then
show up at the houses of their teachers
to deliver envelopes containing fake consideration
and respect. With fake embarrassment
and while enacting fake refusals, eventually mr. teacher
and ms. teacher nevertheless receive the envelopes while fakely promising to
change their fake grades into
new fake grades. School year
after school year passes; the students become
fake economists, fake legal advisers,
fake agricultural experts, fake engineers. Some of them
become fake teachers, scientists or artists. Passions high,
they burst into fake buildings in a
fake economy as fake commanders. They witness
the business of fake commerce with fake exports
and imports that send out and bring in
various fake quality-household-goods.
And fake banks actively offer fake bonuses
and prizes, while quietly also getting
loans with fake permits and fake letters to domestic banks
that are protected by fake officials. The public even trades
using fake money guaranteed by a fake foreign exchange. Then
foreign currencies threaten with fake exchange rates
so that everything writhes mired in a crisis that brings down the fake
government to its
fake wretched fate. Then fake people
shout for fake joy and debate
fake ideas during fake seminars
and fake conferences, welcoming the arrival of
a fake democracy that is celebrated so shrilly
and so fakely.

Anne

Cecep Syamsul Hari
1998

Anne, listen to the trees whispering,
"Why did the clever Liszt worry so much?"

Waldesrauschen, your pale skin and the stuffy air
taught your fear to be brave.

In this city I could easily fall in love with the girl with sharp eyebrows,
I complained to you, or to the blue sky.

The night grew longer and longer
like a restless bed.

It made no sense that a fish was caught
in your petticoat.

It sounded strange but it really belonged
to ancient tyrants or poor Ahasveros, you said.

In this town I will always fall in love with the girl with a small mouth,
that is what I like about you, you told the soldier who had no bullets in his rifle.

Listen to the trees dancing—
"No. This is a war dance."

Someone blew out the candles on the birthday cake
and you bit my neck and I touched your full breast.

No, like love, miracles belonged to everyone,
even to the demonstrator who vanished down the road
with his fist still in the air.

Anne, listen to the trees whispering,
"Listen. By God, you can hear
this wretched land weep."

You Say

Isbedy Stiawan Z.S.

1998

you say the situation is safe
but people are strangled by fear

you say the situation is under control
but people are scrambling for cover

you say we must restrain ourselves
but you are covertly supplying weapons

you say our leaders are for reform
but you castrate student demands

you say the national assembly is for the good of the people
but the people's demands are not on the agenda

you say the government is democratic
but demonstrations continue outside

you say officers of the law should not be armed
but you fire on students and crowds

you say the unrest was the result of provocation
but you never have provided proof

you say the law officers stand behind the students
but covertly you have the students shot

you say the officers were given blanks
but everyone knows you lie

you say it was a tragedy that people died
but everyone knows you lust for power

you say this disaster was not because of anarchy
but firearms serve as witness

you saythis disaster was a tragedy
but I say it's now tradition!

Ode for Earth

Nenden Lilis Aisyah

1998

rice is meant to grow
in the rich soil of a paddy
corn is meant to sprout
in a field's fertile ground

leaves in the orchard
are meant to be wet and shining
and clear water in the pool to reflect
the image of the brilliant sun

in the eyes there is meant to be
a ripple of clarity, like a canal
through which farmers' wishes flow

(that is how it is meant to be,
my love, who died too soon
in the soil that extinguished the fire)

Jakarta, Approaching May 21, 1998

Rayani Sriwidodo

1998

That women are sex objects
was displayed at the height of the violence
on that thirteenth of May

A mother who earlier that morning opened the door to her shop
unsuspectingly, welcoming the dawn at its earliest
as her ancestors had instructed
on that date that proved unlucky indeed
had her self worth shredded and torn
in front of her husband and children

Even so, that women are still sex objects
she immediately protested:
with a mouthful of insect venom

So I have delivered this poem to commemorate the
heroes who wagered everything in silence

Verses of Fire

Sapardi Djoko Damono

1998-89

1

it was may, our month, and still it was raining

where was the dry season, with its cool nights
and clear skies; afternoons that served up
kapok and tiger-claw blossoms, to be taken by
the ever-amenable wind from the hills

which preferred to wait for the rain
but willingly abandoned villages
(when chased by a crowd of flowers or a flock of birds)

where was the dry season, which was always thirsty
and ever anxious in its longing for rain

2

for Wislawa Szymborska
looking right and left
a boy then quickly
slipped into the crowd
and did not return

three middle-aged men
hurriedly followed him
and did not return

five—six—seven women
together exploded in flames
and, of course,
did not return

over there
across the road
a cigarette seller
imagines himself

seated before
a television
and amazed to witness
the conjuring

　　　　3

there was a woman
simply standing idle
near the cigarette seller
across the road

from his place at the end of the lane
a neighborhood watchman noticed her
at the guard post near the telephone booth
a policeman caught a glimpse of her
a neighbor kid
said hello to her
a gradeschool teacher
recognized her
and patted her on the back
then there was her grandmother at home
now so absent-minded—
and her husband and children, too
(who
might
very well
have been
thinking
about her)
who were
(but
hopefully not
of course!)
in a large department store

(or
no longer
could be)
that was in flames

4

"I don't know why but this morning
my whole body started to shiver,
which was quite unusual. Once
you said we were like
old leaves
trembling before being taken by the wind
trembling from testing ourselves—
did we have enough strength
to remain on the branch
before that final wind
before that final day
before that final moment—
but enough said,
I must go to the office
after morning rites:
a cup of coffee
a slice of bread.
Today
will be overcast, without rain,
says the weather report.
I'll be home early today
before dinnertime."

But the magician, it seems,
had other plans in mind.

5

between what came into our mind
and the fire that's burning over there
a number of prophesies were told

amid what was in our minds, the flames, and the prophesies
there trembled verses we have memorized
but whose meaning we can only guess

6

there are those who reckon the fire's duration
with odd sounds
much like ones we heard
in our mother's womb

there are those who reckon the fire's hours
with strange gestures
much like ours
when we were caught in the conflagration

there are those who reckon the fire's seconds
with tense blinks
much like the ones that were seen
when people buried us

7

pictures
in today's paper
serve as a lesson
for us

to continue
to further set aside
any kind of
exclamation

8

on the roof of the house across the road
a sparrow flutters its feathers
after the morning's
drizzle (like lemon juice in the eye)

petals of water fall here and there
while in the upper corner of the building
smoke from yesterday's fire
still rises from its former nest

9

as fire is a symbol of life
it can neverbecome fossilized

as fire is a symbol of life
we collapse completely in its flames

10

in the end that evening she did change
turned completely into ash
before realizing
that there are times for rest

among the mounds
that are difficult to separate
—and why should we try
when soon they'll be dispersed by the warm wind

11

at the end of a long form
was the question
"what is left of your body"

fill it in with "nothing"
but, oh, perhaps there are memories
somehow able to survive

12

in the end she accepted her role
as fiction, move here and there
from newspaper page to television screen
and sound effects on the radio

indeed, she had to be very clever
to place herself in the queue
of ideas, events, and objects
that we must quickly forget

13
you have no right to remember anything
as you grope for your ID near the border—and whatever for

after your form has completely changed
you will cross over to the final reality

you need nothing now: not combs, shoes,
uniforms, nor even memories in that place over there

sit down, don't fidget, you have no right to pace
no right to anything: this is not a shadow play

14
astagfirulah, dear God in heaven
there are so many of us

stacked near the trash
waiting to be carted away

seduced by oil
and now burned

astagfirulah
there are so many of us

15
even with the ceremony almost over
you fail to remember the local cemetery is full

maybe the only thingthat can be done
is to bury you temporarily in our memories

Mei

Joko Pinurbo
1998

Jakarta, 1998

To the fire, Mei,
I offered your beautiful body.
You went to take a bath that evening.
You bathed in fire.

Fire loves you, Mei, so very much.
Fire laps at your body
even its most hidden spaces.
Fire loves your body so very much,
nothing is left but color,
flesh and illusion.

Your body, Mei, writhing and melting in the fire,
is our body too.
The fire wishes to cleanse the virtual body,
but the body, your beautiful body, Mei,
deceives us and burns completely.

You've taken your bath, Mei.
You've bathed in fire.
With your body's destruction and its union
with the body of this earth,
the fire has revealed its secret love
when there are no longer questions, Mei,
about your name or the color of your skin.

Patrol

Joko Pinurbo

1998

Groups of armored vehicles drive up and down
between the sad lines of my poems.
In one dark corner, the commander
watches the beating of a demonstrator
whose movements have aroused suspicion.
The soldiers are made ready and ordered
to blockade the roads.
Everyone panics. Words run to and fro
and fall face-down on the ground.
The commander screams, "Where have you hidden
that skinny poet? He has sharpened his pen
and it is a dangerous weapon." A patrol man
plucks up courage and says:
"He had a pain in the gut, sir, and rushed off
to the shit-house. Perhaps he is planning
an attack." "Damn!" snarls the commander
and orders his troops to continue their patrols.
In the last letter of this poem the bag of bones
suddenly emerges from the shit-house
patting his stomach. "What a relief,"
he says. The words forget their anxiety.
They cheer out loud and resume their original positions.
Explosions can be heard in the distance,
fire consumes the burning bodies.

Batavia Centrum

Zeffry Alkatiri

1998

1933:
Chinese women, young and old
Totter beneath
Buckets of sweat
Treading narrow lanes
Between shops in Pintoe Ketjil

1942:
The Japanese arrive
Stupid bastard, they say
To the Chinese man in calico
Miserable from having
His godown plundered
No New Years this year
Moon cakes stuffed with coconut pulp

1954:
Chinese girls and boys
Unlatch their doors
And wait for coins
To fill donation baskets

1963:
Chinese men and women
Prop open their doors
To let the smoke of incense
Waft into their homes
Quietly, they tally
Bad days on an abacus

1979:
Tapeikong cooks are envious
To see the god of gambling
Offered incense every day
The Tans and Lies control the *chiefen*
Some of them visit the temple
Others kneel before Mother Mary

1992:
Elderly Chinese women and men
Walk unsteadily hand in hand
To the square for *tai-chi*
While their grandchildren in Singapore
Remain sound asleep

1998:
As the iron curtain crumbles
Jade statues of the goddess Kwan Im
And the tiger Pa Kua shatter
And are scattered with ancestors' ashes

Pidie

Ahda Imran

1999

For Cut Fatmah Hassan

Leaves write on your veil, Inong,
verses of a hundred years as words
become thousands of daggers, tempering the rain
becoming true life, becoming the wind
that strokes your back, vanishing into the deepest
forests. There are many nights when the trees hold
your breath, surrendering it to the raging river,
speaking cold and hoarse

Gentlemen from java...

There are many nights when your body,
laden with sorrow, sways, floating inward—
drenching rain, rippling sheets, stripping off
your clothes, becoming a poem of a hundred years
when
true life was the bewitching of tears into
a thousand daggers

Rivers weep down your veil, Inong,
recalling history, poles of a prayer house
that burned down and conversations full of deception
like the traitor Pang Laot. Vanishing into deepest forest,
you pray with the ancestors. And the bullet hole in that
skull releases reverberations that are
swept away by the current.

Gentlemen from java...

Poetry Suppressed by News

Anil Hukma

1999

There's a Crockpot inside me. Something always cooking,
its inner walls blistering thinner and thinner.
Fire. You roast me with self-concealment.

Temptations of friendship always arrive early in the morning.
I am wont to embrace. Only to be shunted aside, a list of interviews,
news. News in a rush to be written. No time to wait—

whining will definitely drag out bedtime
but even the best-managed households have yet to be evaluated
seeming instead to fall apart on the streets every day

I see that a heap of news fills my saucepan,
the lighted stove scorches all feeling,
broadcast formulae crowd my mind.

Awareness. You say awareness will help,
but it seems the entire country is pressing in on my fading years.
My children's mouths are agape. Mouths always begging for something.

Abortion

Anil Hukma

1999

slowly tranquility begins to tremble. something develops
becomes a heavy burden. nebulous layers of anxiety congeal
chest, abdomen, and knees begin to swell. who can keep it from
growing

a trace of some flavor remains inside. someone planted something
in the blessings of pleasure and idleness. in the rushing waves
we are swept to sea
and submerged in a drop of water quietly solidifying.

a woman erases the black mark. chaos looms.
the swaying pendulum fixes itself to her heart rate. disrupts
the coming day
yes and no echo in vacillation.

a step into a room where demons hover along the walls. the seed is yanked from
her womb something floats. the one standing and the one lying down.
both tremble. His deposit dissolves.

Red Pools in Beutong Ateuh, Aceh

D. Kemalawati
1999

people come and express their greetings
people shake hands
people walk with gloom on their faces
people hold rifles, cocked and ready
people don't hear the Quranic recitation
people forget to announce the call to prayer
people hear the sound of gunfire
people hear howls of terror
people hear moans of pain
people see blood turn into red pools

people count, with teeth chattering from fright,
    the number of men martyred at Friday noon
people recall anxiously how many men were taken
    and how many returned home
people begin to dig holes
    so very soon soon filled
people begin to give witness;
    witnesses wheeze with fear

and I and the thousands of others here
cannot be bought
I have an instinct
a conscience
although long besieged
I choose death
and I too give witness
(that the massacre really did occur)

Grief on the Timor Sea

Hamdy Salad
1999

Birds circling hollowly
fold a flag on the Timor Sea;
rancid waves course the seasons and
string mourning into spume;
fish, bloating a sense of pain,
propel corpses to shore—
emblems of contention and dispute.

Ships sailing in the dark
spread the lies of thieves;
from all directions, typhoons and hurricanes
pay each other a call. In the recesses of the horizon
the sky's clotting blood seals sorrow in.
People in white with stiffened bodies
beat the drums at the port of time
to build barracks and tents
for the coalition of apparitions
that will inherit the throne of the world.

A clump of island has finally sunk,
wrecked by wind and ocean waves;
burial shrouds adrift in mortal air
abandon death and the past
to their conflict. The sun hangs suspended!
The king of the land, ablaze with ammunition,
parades his pedigree all the way to the bordering cliffs.

Notes on the Change of Years

Hersri Setiawan
1999

between christms and idul fitri

there are, most likely, days like this
when people are reluctant to go to church
suspecting their prayers will be wasted or lost
swallowed by the crisis of the situation

there are, most likely, days like this
when people hesitate to enter the mosque
for fear of God's anger falling on the heads
of the many scalpers of His name

those who pose as soldiers
those who wear ninja masks
those who pose as heroes
are those who burn churches
defile women
desecrate faith

children of men
bereft of hope
bereft of trust
bereft of love
claw among the remains
of violence and rigidity

through a neighbor's window
I see a christmas tree
silently aglow with flickering light
like my own imagination

separated by eye sockets
and deadened hearts

I see the light of christmas
silently flickering
and sacrificial lambs

I see fields of confrontation
noisy with tumult
in the blue of my country

sacrificial lambs
a reform movement failed
even before countless victims
fell for unknown reason

children who have lost their mothers
stunned women
nameless corpses
buried in the dust of history

what are they for
these christmas lights
new year's fireworks
and the prayers of ramadan

to whom do they belong
these christmas lights
new year's fireworks
and the prayers of ramadan

Lullaby from a Distant Point

Iyut Fitra
1999

for my brothers and sisters who have lost love

country that came of age in disaster, your entire body
has felt its kiss, just like rivers dry up
and cease to flow, "where have you taken the blood of my people?"

maybe that is what someone on a distant point
might ask
surrounded by a panorama of black smoke, his soul shivering
like a funeral dirge heading for
an aching
grave, and there is no ceremony

everything is
trapped

everything is obscured,
past,

like with the movement of time, even records are lost

the old place where mothers birthed history from their tears
it has thrown your body down onto the softest bed

until even children are ready to go to war

exploding with love for their country, "which spirit has

ravaged love and turned it black?" yells someone on a distant point

and even he goes to the battlefield, picking up each one
who has been pawned, but waving flags demand a corpse

there people collapse, there lives are lost

tears become laughter, women a party
and your tiny spent body will soon be the next casualty
of a throne, "god, come down to our country!"

screams someone on a distant point, rending the sky and the universe

again and again, calling out to a distant peace
but who will listen to him?

Before the Statue of Kwan Im

Mas Rucitadewi

1999

It seems like this is a blind season
ripping out the grass in the yard
and leaving no moonshadow on the leaves

Before the statue of Kwan Im
in the Temple of One Thousand Buddhas
I imagine a thousand hands appearing from
behind my back
whirling like a fan
blowing away the sorrows that stick to my body

I am naked before you
and feel that I am born again

Reading the Map

Raudal Tanjung Banua

1999

the map is not to scale

I read the map. From one side to the other.
      Everything consists of seething seas.
Islands, peninsulas and territories. Behind the mist
there is no news,

there are no sounds.

Masts pass—indistinct masts in the distance.
I recognize brightly colored flags and symbols,
reminding us of the greatness of the various peoples.

I read the map. I try to understand those people.
There is nothing there. Nothing. Who
wiped them off nature's map?

There are no voices.

The sea continues to pound.
Names, signs and symbols flow past. Obliterating
borders, imaginary lines, new maps of the world, landings
      and indistinct estuaries.

Fish speak through their fins, scales
and silence, polished by their skill
in knowing how to choose the appropriate word.
      And it is predestined:

Peoples will emerge from dust
and slavery,
live behind the former landings.

Once you could throw a stone
onto the land and it would make no noise,
like moss on a rock.

No news. No response.
No sails.

They slept for centuries
in eternal oblivion.

When their dreams ended, they woke up
and sharpened their swords,
        bamboo spears and pieces of coral,

shining like iron and steel
turned to gold in the afternoon sun.

So they were fortunate and blessed by the sun
which coincidently crystallized the salt
and bound the palm trees together.

But it was no coincidence,
perhaps it was the fault of the sun,
they preferred to keep fighting—fighting!
(Oh wretched people with skins formed by the sun,
        crab shells made of light)

The first brilliant appearance stretched out the map,
creating their symbols and languages.
The second appearance was simply war,
small wars in search of greatness
        over and over.

As if they did not want to share the sun's essence
as it passed from one island to another,
merging colors, texture and the scale of the map,
        gilded by the fierce sunlight…

Since then nothing new has emerged, I think,
only wars and new conquests. Through names,

a sea of images and signs. Of rocks, bamboo,
and bullets.

I fold the map. I weep for the nation
that does not exist. Does not exist.

The Beloved Missionary (Habib)

Zeffry Alkatiri

1999

1

Welcome!
There's heavy, raspy coughing
everywhere in the Arab district.
High fences
and doors are all shut tight throughout the afternoon.
Women peek out carefully
verifying each and every visitor.
From behind grated windows
their rounded eyes
swoop down on their targets.
Their noses like hilly slopes
inhale the dust of death.
While Batavian bacteria diligently scrape away at their throats.

2

Ahlan!
A sound from a dry pharyngeal cave
the missionary in his sarong
seated in a rattan chair
a steaming cup of ginger brew
rests on an octagonal marble table.
Prayer beads rotate in and around the fingers of his left hand.
His right hand supports his turbaned head and
a clotting cloud hangs over him:

3

He was twenty-one years old
when last he saw the desert wadis.
He vomited on the deck of an English ship
from Aden to Betawi.
He was greeted with a verdant vision
when he finally set foot on fertile ground
ready to be sown with the law and the Hadith
rooted in every cell of his brain.

4

Man, where ya goin, man?
I'm going to Pekojan.
Man, whadda sellin', man?
I'm selling beads of coral.

Habib bore herbal remedies to the *Bandan* neighborhoods
he carried the word to the sanctuaries
he spread frankincense in homes and madrasahs.
Once every ten years he threw off his robes
and headed to Mecca to fling pebbles at the devil...
For forty-six years
the seeds he planted
spread to Batavia's distant corners.
And now Habib is homesick and wants to go home!

5

All along the Arab settlement
there's a call and response of hacking and wheezing.
There's no chance of hiding from the bill collectors
while the Batavian bacteria persist in their plague,
of wrecking throats and lungs.

After *Asr* prayers
doors begin to open.
Arabs are resting on platforms
and reclining on bamboo pallets
while sipping on their hookahs.

Ahlan... Bib!
His brew has turned cold.
The Maghrib drum sounds
his fingers stop moving
his prayer beads fall to the ground
his hand reaches down
and touches a floor
bereft of sand...

Trousers, 1

Joko Pinurbo
1999p

He wanted to buy new trousers
to wear to a party
in order to look more handsome
and distinguished.

He tried a hundred different pairs
in various clothing stores
but didn't find even one
that was right for him.

Even worse, he tore off his own trousers
in front of the salesgirls
who swarmed around and flattered him
and threw them out.

"You don't get it, do you,
I'm looking for pants,
ones proper and fit
to wear to the cemetery."

Then he fled, pant-less
and wandered
in search of his mother's grave
only so he could ask:
 "Mother, where did you put those cute little pants
I wore when I was a baby?"

Religion, 3

Aslan Abidin

2000

coming home from morning prayers at my local mosque,
I am walking behind three young women still dressed in their prayer robes. they
vie with one another to speak and they giggle—apparently about a porn film
they watched the night before.

"it was standing straight up: stiff, erect, and red," said the one on the left, which
caused all three to burst into laughter.

the sun was up and behind us, in the east, the mosque grew distant. only its
tower was still visible: standing straight, and erect, and red in the sunlight. the
four of us burst into laughter together.

Wedding Diary

Dorothea Rosa Herliany

2000

when i married you, i never promised to be faithful.
in fact, you agreed to be my slave.
i built my world on hills of rock
and broad plains covered with weeds.
you plowed the fields to make them fertile;
i harvested the crop with each heaving breath.
i raised thousands of wild beasts. i made them soldiers
so they could guard you and hunt you down.
i planted bamboo to make spears and knives.

run as far as your man's feet can carry you, husband!
hide between your mother's thighs.
study the movements of my body and sow your seed
wisely: teach me how to shape the walls
in my house without doors. imprison my surrender
which you read as you please.

but i did not marry you to be faithful.
i agreed to fight on each battlefield.
i became the leader of my pack of wild animals
—they are eager to see you
laid out on the breakfast table.

let me embrace you now,
before i finally
satisfy
my hunger!

Malin

Gus tf

2000

the sound: that of a saw on wood. in me are measuring sticks and carpenter squares. the sound is that of flesh begging for nails. in me Malin lies on a bed of stone.

the sound: that of a hammer on a nail. in me are frames and beams. the sound is that of flesh crying for stones. in me Malin lies prostrate fatigued by passion.

˙ "Malin" refers to "Malin Kundang" the legendary character in a folktale about retribution on an ungrateful son. Coming from a poor family, Malin Kundang becomes a sailor who eventually becomes rich and marries a princess. When he returnes to his home village, he is ashamed of his humble origins and refuses to recognise his elderly mother. She curses him, and when he sets sail, he and his ship are turned to stone.

Bogambola World

Sosiawan Leak

2000

come on, let's gang up on god
and get some help from nature—
the magic of stones, the shade of trees and the ocean's depths.
then let's get rowdy and chop up the clergy
because, in our contempt,
they are nothing but apologists.
let's believe only in the cult of life, in the barbaric rhythm:
bogambola-bogambola, ya, ya
bogambola-bogambola, ya, ya
the volcano spewing smoke
is a giant piece of incense burned for ritual sacrifice
of virgins who have yet to be born,
little boys ready for burial,
bogambola-bogambola, ya, ya
the abortion laws, the provisions on first-degree murder are useless
not to mention the police—
covert drug deals and prostitution
pollute every school and alleyway.
the judge has lost his bench, abandoned by the lawyers
who quibble about their fees,
bogambola-bogambola, ya, ya
the teachers piss standing up, choked to death by costs
the bureaucrats are being breastfed by their constituents in a rehab room
because *bogambola-bogambola, ya, ya*
the governors are busy
with inspections, *bogambola-bogambola, ya, ya*
the senate is singing songs with kindergarteners,
bogambola-bogambola, ya, ya
the president and ministers are in over
their heads, *bogambola-bogambola, ya, ya*
while the military has gone deep into
hiding, *bogambola-bogambola, ya, ya*
and us kids are free to screw around,
bogambola-bogambola, ya, ya
come on, let's unleash the devils and the demons
so it will be clear where heaven ends and hell begins
without the world being caught in the middle!

Stud Pig

Sosiawan Leak

2000

unlike a dog or a cow
i always know
where to find females in heat.
the wind carries their lust to my snout
conjuring alleyways and street signs
to guide me.

unlike an official or a bureaucrat
i don't reap any financial reward—
it's enough to slurp up the pleasures of a sow
by sucking on her nipples
as my macho power
stirs her lonely yearning
and my caresses help her forget
her longing for her piglets
who are so plump, adorable and clever.

if i haven't been lent out in a while
certainly my groggy master will
cover the cost of some gourmet food—
i am fed the yolks of all kinds of eggs;
honey and strong elixirs are always available to drink
but unlike royals or heads of state
i have a healthy heart, no risk of stroke and my cholesterol is low
because i've never worried about a *coup d'etat*.
time faithfully whispers
my fate to me;
through my genitals he lets me know
when i will retire, when i will go senile.

when night comes
and rain is about to fall
my pigpen is transformed into a luxurious arena
warm and glowing—
nightmares never push their way in

like ghosts or soldiers do.
unlike a streetwalker in the city square
i am always clean of syphilis;
aids and venereal disease
never even show up, let alone get out of hand;
they bow down before the mighty one.
sometimes i miss adventuring,
the thrill of being chased by keepers of the peace,
getting captured and molested in custody
then sweet-talking my way to freedom.
but now the world does not permit this—
i am a virtuous sex worker without legislation;
as an animal, i am king of an empire of necessary lust;
as a pet i prosper.

unlike a scholar or believer
i have no morals
because morals are rare stars that haven't even been born.
to me, god and the prophets are as nebulous as the devil.
i can't distinguish lectures and curses
from swords and rifles.
i don't recognize the boundaries between right and wrong, good and bad—
only humans have those
and only they can violate them!

a letter from von de wall to raja ali haji

Taufik Ikram Jamil

2000

with the sadness of a crescent moon
I write this letter
not expecting that it will reach you
who have for so long dwelled in silence

oh, dear friend who gave me words
each of your letters is a debt
whose interest on interest
is now so high it grips the clouds

thus permit me to die in batavia
so that my skeletal remains will always remember
the land that gave me a place
and where isabella, whom we both loved
will live forever as an adolescent

at present, I am bereft of joy
which has slowed, turned into enmity
every time my heart's words are bundled
like a defenseless hostage

I have no power now
no power to remember all that has happened
and is now imbued with primordial pain and sorrow

with the sadness of a crescent moon
I write this letter
not expecting that it will ever reach you
who have for so long dwelled in silence

---

* Title is lowercase in original publication.

little saut talks with god

Saut Situmorang

2003p

the little boy
sits alone

behind the house
on dry ground

he turns his
olive-skinned face
towards a sky
of bluest blue

his dark eyes
are open
wide
absorbed in cloud-watching
the wind blows gently by

he knows god lives up there

in the blue sky beyond
because his mother told him so
every time he asked to know

the little child

keeps looking up
his dark eyes
still open wide

but he doesn't understand
why the rain falls sometimes
and turns the road in front of his house to mud
so he can't play outside

---

* Title is lowercase in original publication.

if there's sky up above
what is there below?
wonders the child

maybe under the ground

it's the same as up here, he exclaims to himself

with houses
and trees
and fields
where people fly kites
and they probably think

that their gods live where i am!

he starts to smile

realizing why it rains

of course it rains
when god is having a party

clearly the rainwater

is from washing
up
when the party is over
like when mom does the dishes

and the water vanishes into the ground

his smile grows even wider

imagining those children having fun in the rain
down under!

Mattress Stud

Binhad Nurrohmat

2004p

The shiny red drill bit
points at a clump of stiff muscles,
stabs at a slit nestled in a valley:
the end of the poet's pen spills out ink
and sharpens expressions showing signs of life.
Desire rapes the mouth until it fizzles with foam:
a mine hole sucked by hundreds of workers,
their faces fatty and covered in soot.
The swollen black scrotum trembles:
home to testicles nestled in the squeeze of a rotten crotch,
witness to the genital party.

A mass of asses gyrating all night
sinks softly into a sponge mattress.
Together dance after dance
their shadows chase off hundreds of ghosts
peeking through a crack in the door,
their snorts a desert storm
sweeping over taut, smooth skin,
and a scorpion with pointed tongue
hidden in a sand pile
pulls at the muscles of the heart,
pushes at the kidneys.

Neighing of animals racing on the mattress
flushed with seas of sweat,
parting thick weeds,
scaling hillsides,
descending into cloven valleys.
Then a heap of weary bodies
sucked into a spring in a joint's crevice
become a loaf of yesterday morning's bread.
And the wet beach comes later:
spread out in a deserted mess
it rolls over, swallowed by a tidal current,

carrier of a ship's rubbish,
a piece of a whore's ring finger cut off by her lover
and dolphins with gentle mouths
whose quiet eyes offer hundreds of desires
and plan a long scandal
in the depths of a trough.

Gigolo

Binhad Nurrohmat

2004p

Inside this room I'm done with the reality outside.
I don't want to tempt anyone into making love
and aping vulgar sex posters.
The door and window are locked;
wild lustful hands attack my body,
so hungry and knowing.
I am just a male
keeper of an animal in the crib of a crotch.

Outside this room the love bite on my neck still stings
making me as embarrassed as a woman—
so embarrassed, wild eyes wide open.
I meet last night's bedfellow on the street again
like a stranger who never knew the smell of my body.
Makes me angry and want to explode my penis!

In a garden pond the reflection of my face destroyed.
I want to know myself again,
want to be naked,
burning myself up night after night
and scorching the women's genitals
who ride my desire like animals.

Before I Leave

Inggit Putria Marga

2000

The wind blows so briskly
The branches of the frangipani tree
Cannot hold on to the leaves
Separating from their stems

I am still here
Counting the raindrops
Soaking the grass
That doesn't stop quivering
Painting the luminous
Falling moonlight

You are peacefully asleep
Forgetting the poem you composed
Awaiting what you must answer

I am silent here
You are peacefully asleep

Biographical Notes

(in alphabetical order by author's first name)

A. (Abdul) Kohar Ibrahim or **D. Tanaera** or **Abe** (Jakarta, June 16, 1942–Brussels, June 4, 2013) studied at the Multatuli Literature Academy (Akademi Sastra Multatuli) in Jakarta. He also studied at the Royal Academy of Fine Arts (Académie Royale des Beaux-Arts) in Brussels. Starting in 1959 he was an active member of Lekra (Lembaga Kebudayaan Rakyat; Institute for People's Culture), the arts organization associated with the Indonesian Communist Party. He became an exile after attending the sixteenth anniversary of the People's Republic of China with a delegation of Indonesian writers on October 1, 1965. In China he worked at *Tiongkok Bergambar* magazine and at the Beijing Foreign Language Library. He moved to Belgium in 1972. He was the editor of two journals for exiles, *Pembaruan* and *Kreasi*. Between 1972 and 1992 he was an artist and signed his paintings Abe. He wrote for newspapers such as *Bintang Timur, Bintang Minggu, Harian Rakyat* and *Warta Bhakti*, and for magazines such as *Zaman Baru* and *Wanita*. He wrote two novellas: *Pembebasan* (serialized in *Bintang Timur* in the 1950s) and *Debur Ombak Pantai Utara*, published by the exile community in China.

A. (Ahmad) Mustofa Bisri, also known as **Gus Mus** (Rembang, Central Java, August 10, 1944), manages Pondok Pesantren Raudlatuth Tholibin, an Islamic boarding school in Rembang, and is general director (Rais Aam) of Nahdlatul Ulama, one of the largest Islamic organizations in Indonesia. He is one of the founders of the Partai Kebangkitan Bangsa political party. He is a respected religious leader and a leading figure in cultural and literary circles. His poetry collections include *Nyamuk-Nyamuk Perkasa dan Awas, Manusia* (1979), *Ohoi* (1991), *Kumpulan Puisi Balsem, Tadarus* (1993), *Rubaiyat Angin dan Rumput* (1995) and *Pahlawan dan Tikus* (1996). Several of his short stories have been selected and published in the annual anthologies of the best stories appearing in *Kompas* newspaper.

A.M. (Abdul Muin) Daeng Mijala (Makassar, South Sulawesi, January 2, 1909–place of death and exact date unknown, 1969) wrote for *Pujangga Baru* and *Panji Pustaka* magazines prior to Indonesian independence and later, when the struggle for independence was over, for *Indonesia* magazine. Several of his poems were included in *Puisi Baru*, compiled by Sutan Takdir Alisjahbana (1946), and *Pujangga Baru: Prosa dan Puisi*, compiled by H.B. Jassin (1963).

Abdul Hadi W.M. (Wiji Muthari) (Sumenep, Madura, June 24, 1946) is a professor of philosophy and religion at Paramadina University. He is known as a Sufi poet and has published many collections of poetry as well as books about Sufi and Islamic philosophy. He was selected to participate in the International Writing Program at the University of Iowa in the United States in 1973–1974 and has received several awards, including Best Poetry Anthology from the Jakarta Arts Council (1978) for *Meditasi*; the SEA Write Award (1985); the Anugerah Majelis Sastra Asia Tenggara Award for Southeast Asian literature (2003); the Habibie Award for literature and Islamic and Malay culture (2014); and the Numera Award for a leading figure in Malay literature in Kuala Lumpur (2014).

Abidah el-Khalieqy (Jombang, East Java, March 1, 1965) graduated from the Pesantren Putri Modern Persatuan Islam boarding school in Bangil and from the Sunan Kalijaga State Islamic Institute (Institut Agama Islam Negeri / IAIN) in Yogyakarta. She has received several awards for her work that characteristically concerns the life challenges of Muslim women. She is known for her novels, some of which have been adapted into films, such as *Perempuan Berkalung Sorban* (2001); *Mahabbah Rindu* (2007), which received a Language Center Literature Award in 2011; and *Mimpi Anak Pulau* (2015). Her poems have appeared in national and international publications, including *ASEANO: An Anthology of Poems from Southeast Asia* (1996), *Cyber Album Indonesia-Australia* (1998), *E-Books Library for Diffabel* (2007) and *Words without Borders* (2009, 2015).

Abrar Yusra (Agam, West Sumatra, March 28, 1943–Bogor, West Java, August 28, 2015), a novelist, poet, biographer and journalist, was managing editor of the *Singgalang* daily newspaper in Padang, West Sumatra. He also taught at Indonesische Nederlandse School (INS) Kayutaman, a private middle school, in West Sumatra. His novel *Tanah Ombak* (2002) received the Mastera Literature Award for Creative Writing in Kuala Lumpur Malaysia, in 2003.

Acep Zamzam Noor (Tasikmalaya, West Java, February 28, 1960) studied in the Faculty of Visual Arts and Design at the Bandung Institute of Technology and at the University for Foreigners of Perugia (Università per Stranieri di Perugia) in Italy. He is the author of several prize-winning collections of poetry, including *Jalan Menuju Rumahmu* (2004), which received the SEA Write Award (2005); *Menjadi Penyair Lagi* (2007), which received the Khatulistiwa Literary Award (2007); *Paguneman* (2011), a collection of Sundanese poems that received the Rancagé Literary Award (2012); and *Bagian dari Kegembiraan* (2013), which was selected as the best poetry anthology on National Poetry Day in 2013.

Afrizal Malna (Jakarta, June 7, 1957) writes poetry, essays, short stories and plays. He is known for his unique use of the Indonesian language to portray urban life and for his exploration of the world of objects. He studied at the Driyarkara School of Philosophy (Sekolah Tinggi Filsafat Driyarkara) in Jakarta but did not graduate. He has published two novels: *Lubang dari Separuh Langit* (2004) and *Kepada Apakah* (2014). His short stories were collected in *Seperti Novel yang Malam Mengisahkan Manusia* (2003). He has published ten books of poetry, including *Abad yang Berlari* (1984), which won an award from the Buku Utama Foundation; *Yang Berdiam dalam Mikrofon* (1990); *Arsitektur Hujan* (1995); *Kalung dari Teman* (1998); *Kawan-Kawan dari Atap Bahasa* (2008); *Museum Penghancur Dokumen* (2013); and *Berlin Proposal* (2015). His essay collections include *Sesuatu Indonesia* (2000) and *Perjalanan Teater Kedua* (2010). His poetry collection *Teman-Temanku dari Atap Bahasa* was chosen by *Tempo* magazine as Best Literary Work of 2008 and received an award from the Center for Language Advocacy and Development. He has received numerous awards, including the Radio Netherlands Worldwide Golden Windmill Award (1981), the Literature Award from the Jakarta Arts Council (1984), the SEA Write Award (2010), the Language Center Award (2010) and the Khatulistiwa Literary Award (2013).

Agam Wispi (Pangkalan Susu, North Sumatra, December 31, 1930–Amsterdam, Netherlands, January 1, 2003) grew up and went to school in Medan. He also studied literature in Germany. He was a journalist and served as editor of *Harian Rakyat*. He was a founding member of Lekra (Lembaga Kebudayaan Rakyat; Institute of People's Culture), the arts organization affiliated with the Indonesian Communist Party. His poems are included in *Exile, Orang-Orang yang Dilupakan, Kronologi in Memoriam 1953–1994, Di Negeri Orang: Penyair Indonesia Eksil* (Lontar, 2002), *Dera dan Deru* (1957), *Sahabat* (1958), *Dinasti 650 Juta* (1961), *Yang Tak Terbungkamkan* (1964) and *Gugur Merah: Sehimpun Puisi Lekra 1950–1965* (2008).

Agus R. Sarjono (Bandung, West Java, July 27, 1962) finished his postgraduate studies from the Faculty of Cultural Studies at the University of Indonesia in 2002. He is a lecturer in the Theater Department at the Indonesian Institute of Arts and Culture (Institut Seni Budaya Indonesia / ISBI) in Bandung. He served as chair of the Literature Committee of the Jakarta Arts Council and editor of the literary magazine *Horison*. He was invited to be the guest poet at Heinrich Böll Haus, Langenbroich, Germany (2002–2003). His books include *Kenduri Airmata* (1994), *A Story from the Country of the Wind* (1999, 2001), *Frische Knochen aus Banyuwangi* (in German, 2003) and *Kopi, Kretek, Cinta* (2013). He has also edited anthologies of theater scripts and poetry, as well as several bilingual (Indonesian and German) collections of literary works.

Ahda Imran (Kanagarian Baruhgunung, Payakumbuh, West Sumatra, August 10, 1966) grew up in Cimahi, West Java. His poetry collections include *Dunia Perkawinan* (1999), *Penunggang Kuda Negeri Malam* (2008) and *Rusa Berbulu Merah* (2013), which was one of the five nominations for the Khatulistiwa Literary Award in 2014. His poetry has appeared in several anthologies. He also writes reviews, plays, short stories and essays.

Ahmaddun Y. (Yosi) Herfanda (Kendal, Central Java, January 17, 1958) writes Sufi poetry and essays on literature and social-religious themes. He is a journalist and editor for *Republika* and has been chair of the Literature Committee of the Jakarta Arts Council (2010–2013). His poetry has appeared in *Secrets Need Words* (Ohio University, 2001) and *Waves of Wonder* (International Library of Poetry, Maryland, USA, 2002). His books include collections of short stories and essays and fifteen collections of poetry, including *Sembahyang Rumputan* (1996); *Ciuman Pertama untuk Tuhan* (bilingual, 2004), which won an award for literature from the Language Center, Ministry of Education and Culture (2008); *Sajadah Kata* (2013); and *Dari Negeri Daun Gugur* (2015).

Ajamuddin Tifani (Banjarmasin, South Kalimantan, September 23, 1951–Banjarmasin, South Kalimantan, May 6, 2002) wrote poetry, short stories, plays, essays, columns and articles about culture. He was the literature editor for *Media Masyarakat* and the tabloid *Gaung*, and he organized the Declamation Studio broadcast on the national radio station (RRI) and a radio broadcast in the Banjar language for RRI Banjarmasin. He received the Darul Iman III Literary Award from Malaysia (1994) and the Borneo Award (2005). His poetry collections include *Problema-Problema* (1975), *Lalan* (1975), *Jembatan I* (1987) and *Jembatan II* (1988). His poems have also appeared in anthologies, such as *Antologi Puisi ASEAN* (1983), *Dari Negeri Poci 3* (1995) and *Puisi Indonesia 1997* (1997).

Ali Hasjmy (Idi Tunong, Aceh, March 28, 1914–place of death unknown, January 18, 1998) was a professor of Islamic preaching at the Ar-Raniry State Islamic Institute (Institut Agama Islam Negeri / IAIN) in Banda Aceh. He was also governor of Aceh province from 1957 to 1964. He published eighteen works of literature, including poems, novels and short stories; five translations of Arabic works, including a translation of *Juz Amma*; as well as twenty other works of Islamic and literary studies. His poetry collections include *Dewan Sajak* (1938), *Jalan Kembali* (1963) and a study of poetry, *Semangat Kemerdekaan dalam Sajak Indonesia Baru* (1963).

Amal Hamzah (Binjai, Langkat, North Sumatra, 1922–date and place of death unknown), the younger brother of Amir Hamzah, studied at Hollands Inlandse School (HIS) elementary school, Meer Uitgebreid Lager Onderwijs (MULO) junior high school and the Marinehospitaal Soerabaja (MHS), and then studied law and literature. He taught in Boston, Massachusetts, USA. He had a great interest in Eastern literature and translated *Gitanyali* and *Seroja Gangga* by Rabindranath Tagore. He also translated *Untaian Bunga* and *Kuntum Melati Gangga*, works by Notosuroto, an Indonesian poet who wrote in Dutch. His works include a collection of poetry, *Pembebasan Pertama* (1949), and a collection of critiques, *Buku dan Penulis* (1950). His poetry was published in *Kesusastraan Indonesia di Masa Jepang* (1948) and *Gema Tanah Air* (1948), compiled by H.B. Jassin.

Amir Hamzah or Tengku Amir Hamzah Pangeran Indera Putera (Tanjung Pura, Langkat, North Sumatra, February 28, 1911–Kuala Begumit, North Sumatra, March 20, 1946) was born into an aristocratic Malay family. He studied at the Langkatsche School in Tanjung Pura, Meer Uitgebreid Lager Onderwijs (MULO) junior high school in Medan, Christelijke MULO Menjangan, the Department of Asian Literature at Algemene Middelbare School (AMS) senior high school in Surakarta, Central Java, and then studied law in Jakarta. Along with Sutan Takdir Alisjahbana and Armijn Pane, he founded the literary magazine *Pujangga Baru* (1933). His most famous works are two collections of poetry, *Nyanyi Sunyi* (1937) and *Buah Rindu* (1941).

Anil Hukma (Maros, South Sulawesi, September 1, 1970) graduated from the Department of Communications at Hasanuddin University (1998). He was chair of the Literature Committee of the Makassar Arts Council. His poems and short stories have been published in various books, including *Ombak Losari* (1992), *Napas Kampus* (1994), *Refleksi Setengah Abad Indonesia* (1995), *Merdeka* (1995), *Antologi Puisi Indonesia* (1997), *Temu Penyair Makassar* (1999) and, most recently, *La Galigo Namaku* (2015), which was inspired by a famous folk story in Sulawesi.

Aoh Kartahadimadja, also known as **A.K. Hadimaja** (Bandung, West Java, September 15, 1911–Jakarta, March 17, 1973) attended Meer Uitgebreid Lager Onderwijs (MULO) junior high school. He was a translator at Sticusa Amsterdam (1952–1956), a journalist with *Star Weekly* (1957) and an editor with *Pustaka Jaya* (1972). He wrote two books: *Seni Mengarang* and *Aliran Klasik, Romantik dan Realisme dalam Kesusasteraan* (1972). He also was a broadcaster for BBC London (1959–1970). He received an award for Achievement in Art from the Indonesian government (1972). Two of his poetry collections, *Pecehan Ratna* and *Di Bawah Kaki Kebesaran*, which were originally published in *Panca Raya* magazine (1946), received literary awards from Balai Pustaka (1947).

Apip Mustopa (Balubur, Limbangan, West Java, April 23, 1939) studied communications technology and has worked with the telephone office in Bali,

Flores, Kalimantan, Papua and Jakarta. His poems have been published in *Budaya Jaya*, *Horison* and *Pikiran Rakyat*. Several of his poems were selected by Ajip Rosidi to be included in the anthology *Laut Biru Langit Biru* (1977). His poetry collection is *Angin Bandung* (1986). In addition to writing in Indonesian, he also writes in Sundanese.

Ari Pahala Hutabarat (Palembang, South Sumatra, August 24, 1975) studied pedagogy in the Faculty of Indonesian Language and Literature at Lampung University and graduated in 2000. He is one of the organizers of the Lampung Arts Council and is active in the Berkat Yakin Community at the Lampung Culture Center. His work was first published in the *Lampung Post* (1997) and later in various publications and anthologies. In 2006 his poem "Perahu Ibu" was selected as one of the fifteen best poems in a competition organized by the Indonesian government. He also writes essays and plays and directs theater productions.

Arifin C. (Chairin) Noer (Cirebon, West Java, March 10, 1941–Jakarta, May 28, 1995) studied in the Faculty of Social and Political Sciences at Cokroaminoto University in Yogyakarta. In 1972–1973 he participated in the International Writing Program at the University of Iowa in the United States. He was also known as a poet and as a theater and film director, and he won the Citra Award for best film and best screenplay several times. His collections of poetry include *Nurul Aini* (1963), *Siti Aisah* (1964), *Puisi-puisi yang Kehilangan Puisi* (1967), *Selamat Pagi, Jajang* (1979) and *Nyanyian Sepi* (1995).

Armijn Pane (Muara Sipongi, Mandailing Natal, North Sumatra, August 18, 1908–Jakarta, February 16, 1970) studied medicine at the School tot voor Indische Opleiding Artsen (STOVIA) in Jakarta (1923) and the Nederlandsch Indische Artsen School (NIAS) medical school in Surabaya (1927) and then transferred to the Algemene Middelbare School (AMS-A) high school in Surakarta (1931) where he studied Western literature. In 1933, along with Sutan Takdir Alisjahbana and Amir Hamzah, he founded *Pujangga Baru* magazine. His most famous novel is *Belenggu* (1940). He received an Award for Achievement in Art from the Indonesian government (1969).

Aslan Abidin (Soppeng, South Sulawesi, May 31, 1972) graduated from the Faculty of Indonesian Literature at Hasanuddin University in Makassar (1997). He was a journalist and chair of Masyarakat Sastra Tamalanrea (MST), a literary community in Makassar. In 1999 he won the Indonesian Poetry Writing Competition, and Art and Peace Bali. His poetry has been published in *Mimbar Penyair Abad 21* (1996), *Antologi Puisi Indonesia* (1997), *Kitab Puisi Horison Sastra Indonesia* (2002), *Puisi Tak Pernah Pergi* (2003) and *Tak Ada yang Mencintaimu Setulus Kematian* (2004).

Asmara Hadi (Bengkulu, September 8, 1914–Bandung, West Java, September 3, 1976) was the pen name for Abdul Hadi, editor of *Pikiran Rakyat* daily newspaper, as well as *Tujuan Rakyat*, *Pelopor Gerindo* and *Pujangga Baru* magazines. He was also active in politics, particularly with the Partindo political party, and was a member of the Constitutional Assembly (Konstituante) and the Temporary People's Consultative Assembly (MPRS) until 1966. One of his books is *Di Belakang Kawat Berduri* (1941). Many of his poems were published in several anthologies, including *Puisi Baru* (1946), *Pujangga Baru: Prosa dan Puisi* (1963) and *Tonggak 1* (1997).

Badruddin Emce (Kroya-Cilacap, Central Java, July 5, 1962) finished his studies in law at Universitas Jenderal Soedirman in Purwokerto. He is a civil servant with the Government Tourist Service in Cilacap. His poems have appeared in several publications. He has participated in literature and arts events, such as the Indonesia Poetry Forum in Taman Ismail Marzuki in Jakarta (1987), the Surabaya Arts Festival (1996), the Yogyakarta Arts Festival and the Indonesia Today Poetry Forum at the Salihara Arts Community in Jakarta (2010). He is active in PC Lesbumi NU Kabupaten Cilacap and the Tjilatjapan Poetry Forum. His poetry collections include *Binatang Suci Teluk Penyu* (2007) and *Diksi Para Pendendam* (2012), selected as one of the ten top books for the Khatulistiwa Literary Award in 2012.

Basuki Gunawan (Banyumas, Central Java, December 23, 1929–date and place of death unknown) studied in the Faculty of Social and Political Science and was awarded a doctorate in Amsterdam in 1965 for this dissertation, "Mahasiswa Indonesia di Belanda," concerning Indonesian students in the Netherlands. His short stories were published in *Konfrontasi* and *De Nieuwe Stem*. Part of his novel *Winarta* received an award from the Rainaert Geerlings Commission.

Beni Setia (Bandung, West Java, 1954) graduated from agricultural high school (Sekolah Pertanian Menengah Atas / SPMA) in 1974. His collections of poetry include *Legiun Asing* (1987), *Dinamika Gerak* (1990) and *Harendong* (1996). In addition to poetry he also writes short stories and essays, many of which have been published in *Kompas*, *Pikiran Rakyat* and *Republika*. His poetry has also appeared in several anthologies, including *Puisi Indonesia 83* (vol. II), *Yang Muda* (1978), *Senandung Bandung* (1981), *Festival Desember* (1981) and *Tonggak 4* (1987).

Bibsy Soenharjo (Jakarta, November 22, 1928) has appreciated literature since her youth. Her first four poems were published in *The Literary Review*, in the Autumn 1967 and Spring 1968 editions. Her poetry has been published in several bilingual anthologies, which feature her poems in Indonesian with the translations in English, Dutch and Japanese. She has also published a collection of poems in English that was translated into Indonesian and Dutch, *Heart and Soul: A Kaleidoscope of Poetry and One Short Story* (2007).

Binhad Nurohmad (Lampung, January 1, 1976) grew up in Yogyakarta and Jakarta and currently resides in Jombang, East Java. He studied at Islamic boarding schools and at public schools. He has written and published poetry and essays since 1996. In 2010 he founded the Slanted NU Community (Jamaah NU Miring), an offshoot of Nahdlatul Ulama, one of the largest Muslim organizations in Indonesia, and managed the Graveyard Institute (Institut Kuburan). His books include collections of poetry—*Kuda Ranjang* (2004), *Bau Betina* (2007), *Demonstran Sexy* (2008) and *The Bed Horse, Kuda Ranjang* (bilingual)—and a collection of essays, *Sastra Perkelaminan* (2007).

Budiman S. Hartojo (Surakarta, Central Java, December 5, 1938–Jakarta, March 11, 2010) completed his formal education upon graduating from high school. He was editor of the *Surakarta* weekly, *Patria* and *Genta* magazine. He was secretary of the Indonesian Journalists' Union in Surakarta and chair of the Surakarta Arts Council. His works were published in *Horison, Sastra, Basis, Budaya Jaya* and other publications. He was a senior journalist with *Tempo* magazine and published two collections of poetry, *Lima Belas Puisi* (1972) and *Sebelum Tidur* (1977).

Cecep Syamsul Hari (Bandung, West Java, May 1, 1967) writes poetry, essays, reviews, short stories and novels, and he also translates. He has been editor of *Horison* literary magazine. In 2006 he was invited to be Writer-in-Residence at the Korean Literature Translation Institute in Seoul, where he collaborated on the publication of a bilingual (Indonesian and English) collection of poetry, *Two Seasons*. His poetry collections are *Efrosina* (2002) and *21 Love Poems* (bilingual, 2008). Several of his works have been translated into English, German, Korean, Bengali, Portuguese and Czech. In 2011 he started an online literary magazine, sastradigital.com.

Chairil Anwar (Medan, North Sumatra, July 26, 1922–Jakarta, April 28, 1949) wrote ninety-six works, including seventy poems. Along with Asrul Sani and Rivai Apin, he has been named by H.B. Jassin as one of the leading figures of the Angkatan '45 literary circle and a major influence on modern Indonesian poetry. He was editor of *Gelanggang* and *Gema Suasana*. His most famous poem is *Aku*. His books include *Kerikil Tajam yang Terempas dan yang Putus* (1949), *Deru Campur Debu* (1949), *Tiga Menguak Takdir* (with Asrul Sani and Rivai Apin, 1950) and *Pulanglah Si Anak Hilang* (translation of *Le retour de l'enfant prodigue* by André Gide, 1948).

Cok Sawitri (Sedemen, Karangasem, Bali, September 1, 1968) is known as a writer of short stories and an activitist for women's issues, for social and cultural issues and for theater. She founded the Forum Perempuan Mitra Kasih in Bali, which advocates and campaigns for women's issues. Her books include *Meditasi Rahim* (1991), *Pembelaan Dirah* (1996), *Anjing Perempuanku* (2003), *Aku Bukan Perempuan Lagi* (2004) and *Kiamatku dalam Jarak 3 Sentimeter* (poetry, 2013).

D. Kemalawati (Meulaboh, Aceh, April 2, 1965) received an award for literature and the Satya Lencana Award from the regional government of Aceh (2007). She writes poetry, essays, short stories, novels and commentaries. One of her books is *Pembelaan Seorang Guru* (2007). She is on the board of the Banda Aceh Arts Council. She has compiled several poetry anthologies, including *Ziarah Ombak* (2005) and *Selayang Pandang Sastrawan Aceh* (2006). Her poetry collection *Surat dari Negeri Tak Bertuan* (2006) was published in both Indonesian and English.

D. Zawawi Imron (Sumenep, Madura, East Java, January 1, 1945) studied at the Pesantren Lambicabbi boarding school in Semenep. His poetry collection *Bulan Tertusuk Ilallang* inspired film director Garin Nugroho to make a film with the same name. His poetry collection *Nenek Moyangku Air Mata* received an award for Best Book from the Buku Utama Foundation in 1985. That book and another poetry collection, *Celurit Emas*, were selected for the Center for Language Advocacy and Development (1990). He received the SEA Write Award in 2012. His other book of poetry is *Mata Badik Mata Puisi* (2012). Several of his poems have been translated into English, Dutch and Bulgarian.

Dami N. Toda (Pongkor, Flores, East Nusa Tenggara, September 20, 1942– Leezen, Germany, November 10, 2006) studied at the Faculty of Letters at Gadjah Mada University (1967), the Faculty of Law at Atma Jaya University and the Faculty of Letters at the University of Indonesia (1974). He worked in the Ministry of Social Affairs (1973–1975) and taught at the Jakarta Arts Institute. He settled in Hamburg, Germany, in 1981 and taught at the Indonesian and Pacific Studies Center at the University of Hamburg. His collection of poetry *Buru Abadi* was published in 2005. He is known for his literary critiques and his many books about Indonesian literature. He also translated *Thus Spoke Zarathustra* by Friedrich Nietzsche.

Darmanto (or **Soedarmanto**) **Jatman** (Jakarta, August 16, 1942) was one of the founders of the Faculty of Psychology at Diponegoro University in Semarang, and he was the first professor in that department. He was active as an editor for regional and national publications. He received the SEA Write Award (2002), the Satya Lencana Award for Literature (2002) and the Satya Lencana Award for Culture from the Indonesian government (2010). His upbringing in an upper-middle-class Javanese Christian environment has provided a unique flavor to his poetry. He is best known for his poetry collection *Istri* (1997). His other books include *Bangsat* (1974), *Sang Darmanto* (1976) and *Ki Blakasuta Bla Bla* (1980).

Dhenok Kristianti (Yogyakarta, January 25, 1961) studied in the Department of Indonesian Language and Literature at the Institute for Teacher Training and Education (Institut Keguruan dan Ilmu Pendidikan / IKIP) Sanata Dharma (now Sanata Dharma University) in Yogyakarta. In the 1980s she was known as one of the foremost female poets. Her poetry and short stories have appeared in various publications and anthologies. Her poetry collection *Setelah Ingar-Bingar* (2015) was one of five books in the Reboeng Poetry Book Series.

Dinullah Rayes (Sumbawa Besar, Sumbawa, West Nusa Tenggara, February 17, 1937– date and place of death unknown) served as chair of the Culture Sector for Sumbawa subdistrict from 1965 and was general chair of the Sumbawa Arts Council and chair of the Lembaga Adat Tana Samawa, an organization that promotes the cultural traditions of Sumbawa. He received the Satya Lencana Award from the president of Indonesia (1986) and an Award for Art from the provincial government of West Nusa Tenggara (1993). His works have appeared in various publications and anthologies, including *Anak Kecil Bunga Rumputan dan Capung Ramping* (1975), *Angin Senja* (1983), *Nyanyian Kecil* (1985), *Peta Lintas Batas* (1985), *Pendakian* (1986) and *Seutas Tali Emas* (1986).

Dodong Jiwapraja (Garut, West Java, September 28, 1928–place of death unknown, July 23, 2009) graduated in military law from the Military Law Academy (Perguruan Tinggi Hukum Militer / PTHM) in 1963 and worked as a legal officer at the Husein Sastranegara military airfield until his retirement. He was a member of the Beungkeutan Pangulik Budaya Kiwari study group (1957) and participated in the Asia-Africa Writers Conference in Tashkent, Soviet Union (1958). His poems were published in various literary publications, including *Mimbar Indonesia, Gelanggang, Siasat* and *Zenith*, as well as the anthologies *Gema Tanah Air* (1948) and *Tonggak* (1987).

Dorothea Rosa Herliany writes poetry, short stories, children's books, and novels. Her poetry has been translated into multiple languages, and her latest book of poetry is bilingual in German and Indonesian: *Der Messer Hochzeit / Nikah Pisau* (translated by: Brigitte Oleschinski and Ulrike Draesner, Verlagshaus Berlin, 2015). She is frequently invited to read at international poetry events around the world. In addition to writing, she has been collaboratively organizing literary events for the last five years including the biennial "What's Poetry Festival" and the annual "Borobudur Writers and Cultural Festival". She also worked as a publisher of literary books for about ten years. She is the recipient of multiple literary awards, including the Khatulistiwa Literary Award for her poetry book *Santa Rosa* (2006) and for her novel *Isinga, Roman Papua* (2015).

Dullah (Surakarta, Central Java, September 17, 1919–Yogyakarta, January 1, 1996) was a poet and also a painter who worked in a realistic style. Themes of the struggle for independence are characteristic of his poetry. Several of his poems appear in *Bunga Rampai Sastra Indonesia*, compiled by H.B. Jassin. Some of his poems have been translated into English and published in an anthology in Pakistan.

Eka Budianta (Ngimbang, East Java, February 1, 1956) graduated from the Faculty of Letters at the University of Indonesia and the Leadership for Environment and Development (LEAD) Program. He participated in the International Writing Program at the University of Iowa in the United States. He has been a journalist for *Tempo* magazine (1980–1983), a correspondent for *Yomiuri Shimbun* (1984–1986) and an assistant for the Information Center for the United Nations and BBC London. His poetry collection *Sejuta Milyar Satu* received an award from the Jakarta Arts Council (1985). With F. Rahardi he founded the Pustaka Sastra Foundation (1997), which publishes literary works. He continues to write prolifically, both poetry and nonfiction.

Emha Ainun Nadjib (Jombang, East Java, May 27, 1953) studied in the Faculty of Economics at Gadjah Mada University for one semester. He participated in a theater workshop in the Philippines (1980), the International Writing Program at the University of Iowa in the United States and various international literary events. He is known for Islamic themes in his poetry. His poetry collection *Lautan Jilbab* (1989) became an icon for the Islamic movement through the 1990s. He is also known as a writer of columns, essays and plays. He is the founder of the Padhang Bulan community, which stages routine concerts and Islamic study sessions in several cities with the gamelan group Kyai Kanjeng.

F. (Floribertus) Rahardi (Ambarawa, Central Java, June 10, 1950) is a poet, short story writer, critic and journalist. He is known as the "cassava man," because his works are rooted in village life. He began writing short stories, literary reviews and books about agriculture in 1979 and managed the agricultural magazine *Trubus*. He has published one short story collection: *Kentrung Itelile* (1993); six poetry collections: *Soempah WTS* (1983), *Catatan Harian Sang Koruptor* (1985), *Silsilah Garong* (1990), *Tuyul* (1990), *Migrasi Para Kampret* (1993) and *Pidato Akhir Tahun Seorang Germo* (1997); two novels: *Lembata* (2008) and *Ine Pare* (2015); and a book of lyrical prose: *Negeri Badak* (2007). He has received several awards for literature, including one from the Center for Language Advocacy and Development for *Tuyul* (1995), the Khatulistiwa Literary Award for *Lembata* (2009) and the SEA Write Award for *Negeri Badak* (2009).

Fakhrunnas M.A. Jabbar (Tanjung Barulak, Riau, January 18, 1959) graduated from the Faculty of Fisheries at the University of Riau (1985). He has been a journalist since 1979 and has served as a member of the literature committee of the Riau Arts Council (1994–1996). He writes poetry, children's stories and biographies. His poetry collections include *Di bawah Matahari* (1981) and *Meditasi Sepasang Pipa* (1987). His book *Sebatang Pohon Ceri di Serambi* received the Sagang Award in 2006; his biography of Soeman Hs., *H. Soeman Hs: Bukan Pencuri Anak Perawan* (1998), received the same award in 2009.

Frans Nadjira (Makassar, South Sulawesi, September 3, 1942) studied at the Indonesian Art Academy (Akademi Seni Lukis Indonesia / ASLI) in Makassar. He writes poetry, short stories and novels, and he paints. In 1973 he participated in the International Writing Program at the University of Iowa in the United States. His poetry collections include *Spring of Fire, Spring of Tears* (bilingual, 1997), *Jendela Jadikan Sajak* (2003) and *Curriculum Vitae* (2007). His poems also appear in the anthology *100 Puisi Indonesia Terbaik 2008: Anugerah Sastra Pena Kencana* (2008).

Fridolin Ukur (Tamiyang Lajang, Central Kalimantan, April 5, 1930–Jakarta, June 26, 2003) studied theology at Jakarta Theological Seminary (Sekolah Tinggi Teologi / STT) and at the Faculty of Theology at the University of Basel in Switzerland. He was a priest and served as rector of the Evangelical Christian Church Theological Academy (Sekolah Teologi Gereja Kristen Evangelis / STT GKE). He was a poet of the Angkatan '66 literary group. He wrote columns in various publications and, after 1980, was a guest editor of the *International Review of Missions*, published by the World Council of Churches. His books, including *Wajah Cinta* (2003), have been published by BPK Gunung Mulia.

Goenawan Mohamad (Batang, Central Java, July 29, 1941) studied psychology at the University of Indonesia and political science in Belgium and was a Nieman Fellow at Harvard University in the United States. He is a co-founder and former head editor of *Tempo* news magazine and the founder of Utan Kayu Community (1987) and Salihara Arts Community (2009). His poetry collection is *Sajak-Sajak Lengkap 1962–2001* (2001). A prolific writer, he is also known for his column, *Catatan Pinggir*, which appears weekly in *Tempo*. He has received the Wertheim Award (2005) and the Dan David Prize (2006) from Tel Aviv University in Israel for his ongoing campaign for a free press and independent journalism in Indonesia.

Gus tf or **Gus tf Sakai** or **Gustafrizal Busra** (Payakumbuh, West Sumatra, August 13, 1965) writes short stories, poetry, novels and essays. He is a graduate of the Faculty of Animal Husbandry at Andalas University in Padang. His short story collections are *Istana Ketirisan* (1996), *Kemilau Cahaya dan Perempuan Buta* (1999), *Laba-laba* (2003) and *Perantau* (2007). His poetry collections are *Sangkar Daging* (1997), *Daging Akar* (2005), *Akar Berpilin* (2009) and *Susi Sajak-sajak 2008–2013* (2015). His novel is *Tambo: Sebuah Pertemuan* (2000). His short story collection *Kemilau Cahaya dan Perempuan Buta*, which won the Lontar Literary Award in 2001, was translated into English and published by the Lontar Foundation with the title *The Barber and Other Short Stories*. This collection also received other awards, including the Award for Literature from the Faculty of Letters at Andalas University (2002) and the SEA Write Award (2004). He has also won the Readers' Choice for Best Fiction in *Koran Tempo* and the Khatulistiwa Literary Award for *Perantau* (2007), the Tuah Sakato Award from the governor of West Sumatra (2008) and the Award for the Most Dedicated Writer from *Kompas* in 2010.

H.B. Jassin (Gorontalo, North Sulawesi, July 13, 1917–Jakarta, March 11, 2000) is known as the Pope of Indonesian Literature. He was the literary editor of several important publications and publishing houses throughout his career, including Balai Pustaka (1940) and *Horison* magazine (1966). He edited several books that have become prime resources for studies of Indonesian literature, including *Gema Tanah Air* (1948), *Pujangga Baru* (1963) and *Angkatan '66: Prosa dan Puisi* (1968). His essays and literary reviews have also become vital references for researchers and students. He founded the H.B. Jassin Literary Documentation Center, which houses a valuable treasury of Indonesian literature.

Hamdy Salad (Ngawi, East Java, 1963) is a graduate of the Faculty of Islamic Law at Sunan Kalijaga State Islamic Institute (Institut Agama Islam Negeri / IAIN) in Yogyakarta and teaches at Fakultas Seni Pertunjukan Institut Seni Indonesia (ISI) Yogyakarta. Besides writing poetry, short stories and essays, he also writes plays and directs theater productions for Teater Eska in Yogyakarta. His poetry collections are *Sebutir Debu di Tepi Jurang* (2000), *Rubaiyat Sebiji Sawi* (2004) and *Sajadah di Pipi Mawar* (2001). His other books include *Sebuah Kampung di Pedalaman Waktu* (novel, 2001) and *Agama Seni: Refleksi Teologis dalam Ruang Estetik* (2000). He has also written textbooks: *Wacana dan Apresiasi Seni Baca Puisi* (2011), *Wacana dan Apresiasi Musikalisasi Puisi* (2013). He received the Sastra Indonesia Award from Yasayo (2013) and was named one of the Ten Best Indonesian Poets in 2014. His book of poetry *Tasbih Merapi* (2014) received the Anugerah Pilihan from Yayasan Hari Puisi Indonesia in 2015.

Hamid Jabbar (Koto Gadang, West Sumatra, July 27, 1949–Jakarta, May 29, 2004) wrote Islamic poetry and articles on social issues with a clever use of humor. He was a journalist for *Indonesia Express* and an editor for Balai Pustaka and for *Horison* magazine. His poetry collections include *Ketika Khusyuk Tiba pada Tafakur Kesejuta*, *Poco-Poco* (1974), *Dua Warna* (1975), *Wajah Kita* (1981) and *Super Hilang Segerobak Sajak* (1998). He received several awards, including the Buku Utama Foundation Award and an Award for Art from the Center for Language Advocacy and Development.

Hamidah (Fatimah Hasan Delais) (Bangka, June 8, 1914–Palembang, South Sumatra, May 8, 1953) was one of the few women writers of her era. She became a teacher after she graduated from the Girls' School in Padang Panjang. She wrote many poems with social themes. She also wrote one novel, *Kehilangan Mestika* (1953), which illustrates the importance of education in confronting cultural traditions that oppress women. Her poems were published in *Pujangga Baru: Prosa dan Puisi* (1963) and *Seserpih Pinang Sepucuk Sirih* (1979).

Harijadi S. Hartowardojo (Prambanan, Central Java, March 18, 1930–Jakarta, April 9, 1984) studied in the Faculty of Social and Political Sciences at the University of Indonesia and then taught at that institution. He was editor of *Pujangga Baru* (1950), *Mimbar Indonesia, Garuda, Pedoman Minggu* (1955–1961), *Si Kuncung* and *Budaya Jaya* (1968–1976). His novel *Munafik* received an award from the West Java branch of the Indonesian Publishers Association (1967). His other books are *Luka Bayangan* (1964) and *Perjanjian dengan Maut* (1975).

Hartojo Andangdjadja (Surakarta, Central Java, July 4, 1930–Surakarta, Central Java, August 30, 1990) was one of the intellectuals who signed the Cultural Manifesto of August 1963. He studied at Muhammadiyah schools. He wrote poetry and essays, which were published first in *Pantja Raya* (1940) and later in other publications. He was an editor for several publications, including *Merpati* (1948) and *Si Kuntjung* (1962–1964). He also translated many books from English, Dutch, Benggali, Tagalog, Japanese and Arabic.

Hersri Setiawan (Yogyakarta, May 3, 1936) studied at Gadjah Mada University and the Academy for Dramatic Arts and Film (Akademi Seni Drama dan Film) in Yogyakarta. He was Indonesia's representative in the Association of Asia-Africa Writers (1962–1965) in Colombo, Sri Lanka. He was one of the activists of Front National and chair of the Central Java branch of Lekra (Lembaga Kebudayaan Rakyat; Institute for People's Culture), and he was imprisoned on Buru Island from 1969 to 1978. Between 1987 and 2004 he lived in exile in the Netherlands. He writes nonfiction and memoirs, particularly in relation to the abortive coup of September 30, 1965, and its aftermath. He was editor of *Ensiklopedia Indonesia* (7 volumes).

Hidjaz Yamani (Banjarmasin, South Kalimantan, March 23, 1933) studied at Lambung Mangkurat University in Banjarmasin. He was chair of the East Java branch of the Indonesian Muslim Society for Art and Culture (Lembaga Seni Budaya Muslimin Indonesia / Lesbumi) (1961–1970) and a member of the City Council of Banjarmasin. His poetry has been published in *Perkenalan di dalam Sajak* (1963), *Panorama* (1974), *Tanah Huma* (with D. Zauhidhie and Yustan Aziddin, 1978), *Puisi Asena Buku I* (1978) and *Tonggak 2* (compiled by Linus Suryadi, 1987).

Hs. Djurtatap (Payakumbuh, West Sumatra, June 2, 1947) has written poems that have appeared in *Horison, Pelita, Tribun, Mimbar, Abadi* and *Pedoman*, as well as in anthologies, including *Sajak-Sajak Perjuangan dan Nyanyian Tanah Air* (1995). His poems embody social satire. His most famous poem is "Leher dan Dasi," which is also the title of his poetry collection, *Antologi Puisi: Leher dan Dasi* (2013).

Husain Landitjing (Makale, Tana Toraja, South Sulawesi, September 23, 1938– date and place of death unknown) writes poetry and short stories, many of which have appeared in various publications and anthologies. In 1959 he won second prize for his poem that was published in *Basis* magazine and also a prize for his short story "Api di Atas Lautan."

Ibrahim Sattah (Tarempa, Pulau Tujuh, Riau Archipelago, 1943–Pekanbaru, Riau, January 19, 1988) is known for his characteristic poetic mantras. His books include *Dandandid* (1975), which has been translated into Dutch and English; *Ibrahim* (1980); and *Hai Ti* (1981). The three were republished in one volume, *Sansauna*, in 2006. He founded the Nusantara Poetry Foundation in 1980 and Bumi Pustaka publishers in 1981.

Iman Budhi Santosa (Magetan, East Java, March 28, 1948) studied agriculture at Akademi Pertanian in Semarang. Along with Umbu Landu Paranggi and several artists in Yogyakarta, he founded the Persada Study Club (1969). He has written more than thirty-four books, including works of literature, and texts on society, culture and agriculture in Indonesian and Javanese. His awards include Penggerak Sastra Indonesia from Balai Bahasa Yogyakarta (2009), Penghargaan KSI (2012), Anugerah Seni dari Pemprov DIY (2013), Anugerah Sastra YASAYO (2015) and others. His poetry collections include *Dunia Semata Wayang* (1997/2004), *Matahari-matahari Kecil* (2004), *Faces of Java* (2014), *Pilgrimage in the Land of Java* (2015), *Sesanti Tedhak Siti* (2015) and *Cupu Manik Hasthagina* (2015). His works have been published in *Antologi Alit* (1969), *Tugu* (1986), *Tonggak 3* (1987) and *Kebudayaan Wong Cilik* (1994). His poem "Kemenangan Seorang Buruh Harian" won a prize in a poetry competition sponsored by Taman Budaya Yogyakarta (1994). He has also written several books about agriculture and Javanese culture. He is currently a freelance writer and lives in Yogyakarta.

Indonesia O'Galelano (Halmahera, North Maluku, November 17, 1940) studied communications at Ibnu Khaldun University in Jakarta. He was a member of the Central Board of the Himpunan Seni-Budaya Musyawarah Islam (HSBI), an organizer of the Badan Musyawarah Islam and a journalist for *Pelita* daily newspaper. His poetry has been published in *Mimbar Indonesia, Gema Islam, Horison, Pelita* and *Sastra*. Several of his poems were selected by H.B. Jassin to be included in the anthology *Angkatan '66: Prosa dan Puisi* (1968).

Inggit Putria Marga (Tanjungkarang, Bandar Lampung, August 25, 1981) graduated from the Faculty of Agriculture at Lampung University. She is active with Berkat Yakin Community and a member of the Lampung Arts Council. She is often invited to participate in various national and international literary events. Her poetry collection *Penyeret Babi* (2010) was nominated for the Khatulistiwa Literary Award in 2010. Her poems have appeared in various publications and anthologies, including *Traversing* (Utan Kayu International Literary Biennale) and *Suka Duka-Compassion and Solidarity* (Ubud Writers & Readers Festival, 2009). In 2008 and 2009 her poems were included among the best poems of the year and were awarded the Pena Kencana Literary Award.

(Raden) Intojo (Tulungagung, East Java, July 27, 1912–date and place of death unknown) studied at Hollandsche Indische Kweekschool (HIK) Teachers' College and Hoofdactecursus, a school for elementary school principals, in Bandung. He taught at Perguruan Rakyat School in Bandung, Mardi Siswa School in Blitar and Hollands Inlandse Kweekschool (HIK) in Rangkasbitung, Sumatra. His poems were published in *Puisi Baru*, compiled by Sutan Takdir Alisjahbana, and *Tonggak I* (1987), compiled by Linus Suryadi.

Isbedy Stiawan Z.S. (Tanjungkarang, Bandar Lampung, June 5, 1958) was literary editor of *Lampung Post* and *Trans Sumatra* and was active with the Lampung Arts Council. He was invited to participate in several national and international literary events. He has published more than fifteen collections of short stories and poetry, including *Darah* (1982) and *Dongeng Adelia* (2012).

Iskandar Leo (Dabosingkep, Riau, July 17, 1943) is also known as **Rida K Liamsi**, which is his original name, **Ismail Kadir**, spelled backwards. Currently he is the director of Riau Pos Group and PT Jawa Pos National Network. He founded the Sagang Foundation and has published *Sagang* cultural magazine since 1997. This foundation grants the Sagang Award to Melayu cultural activists. His poetry collections include *Jelaga* (1976), *Ode X* (1981), *Tempuling* (2003) and *Rose* (2013).

Isma Sawitri (Langsa, Aceh, November 21, 1940) studied in the Faculty of Letters and the Faculty of Law at the University of Indonesia without graduating from either faculty. She was a journalist for *Angkatan Bersenjata*, *Pedoman*, *Femina* and *Tempo*. Her poetry is published in *Seserpih Pinang Sepucuk Sirih* (1979), compiled by Toeti Heraty; *Tonggak 2* (1987), compiled by Linus Suryadi; and *Ungu: Antologi Puisi Wanita Penyair Indonesia* (1990), compiled by Korrie Layun Rampan.

Iwan Simatupang or Iwan Martua Lokot Dongan Simatupang (Sibolga, North Sumatra, January 18, 1928–Jakarta, August 4, 1970) studied medicine in Surabaya, anthropology at Leiden University (1954–1956), drama in Amsterdam and philosophy at the Paris-Sorbonne University (1958). His novel *Merahnya Merah* (1968) won the National Literature Award in 1970, and *Ziarah* (1970) won an award for Best Novel in ASEAN in 1977. His poetry collection is *Ziarah Malam: Sajak-Sajak 1952–1967* (1993).

Iyut Fitra (Nagari Koto Nan Ompek, Payakumbuh, West Sumatra, February 16, 1968) has written works that have appeared in various publications in Indonesia, Malaysia and Brunei Darussalam, including an anthology that received national recognition. Her poetry collections include *Musim Retak* (2006) and *Dongeng-Dongeng Tua* (2009), and her short story collection is *Orang-orang Berpayung Hitam* (2015).

J.E. Tatengkeng (Kalongan, Sangihe, North Sulawesi, October 19, 1907–Makassar, South Sulawesi, March 6, 1968) was a poet of the Pujangga Baru generation. He studied at Zendings Volks School in Mintung, a village elementary school where students were taught in the local Sangihe language. He was deputy minister for education (1948), prime minister of Eastern Indonesia (1949–1950) and head of the Culture Department of the Sulawesi regional office of the Ministry of Education and Culture (1951). He was one of the founders of, and taught at, the Faculty of Letters at Hasanuddin University in Makassar. His most famous work is *Rindu Dendam* (1934).

Jamal D. Rahman (Lenteng Timur, Sumenep, Madura, December 14, 1967) studied at Pondok Pesantren Al-Amien Prenduan boarding school in Madura and the Syarif Hidayatullah State Islamic Institute (Institut Agama Islam Negeri / IAIN) in Jakarta. He graduated with a master's degree in cultural studies from the University of Indonesia. He was editor of *Islam Islamika* journal (1993–1995), a journalist for *Ummat* magazine (1995–1999) and editor for *Horison* (since 1993). He was a member of the Jakarta Arts Council (2003–2006) and teaches literature at the Syarif Hidayatullah State Islamic University (Universitas Islam Negeri / UIN) in Jakarta. His poetry collections are *Airmata Diam* (1993), *Reruntuhan Cahaya* (2003) and *Garam-Garam Hujan* (2004).

John Waromi (Jayapura, Papua, August 6, 1960) studied law at the Faculty of Law at Cenderawasih University in Jayapura, Papua. He studied theater with Bengkel Teater (1987–2001). He has been invited to participate in various literary events, including the Ubud Writers & Readers Festival, Northern Territory Writers' Festival (2008), Writer's Journey Workshop, Backstage Bali (2011) and the Indonesia International Poetry Forum in Surabaya (2012). His poetry collection is *Sulur Sulur Sali* (2011). He also wrote a novel about the environment, *Anggadi Tupa Menuai Badai* (2015), which has been translated into English.

Joko Pinurbo (Pelabuhan Ratu, Sukabumi, West Java, May 11, 1962), also known as **Jokpin**, studied in the Department of Language and Literature at Institut

Keguruan dan Ilmu Pendidikan (IKIP) Sanata Dharma (now Sanata Dharma University) in Yogyakarta. He has taught at his alma mater and has also worked in publishing. He has been an editor for *Basis*, *Gatra* and *Sadhar*, a publication of IKIP Sanata Dharma. His work started to become widely known after he published his poetry collection *Celana* (1999), which won the Lontar Literary Award (2001) and was translated and published in English as *Trouser Doll* (2001). Another poetry collection, *Di Bawah Kibaran Sarung*, was published in 2001, when he won an award from the Jakarta Arts Council for Best Book of Poetry. He also won the Khatulistiwa Literary Award in 2005 for *Kekasihku* (2004) and in 2016 for *Surat Kopi* (2015). Several of his poems have been published in the BTW series (in Indonesian, English and German) as *Borrowed Body and Other Poems* (2015). He has won many other awards, including recognition by *Tempo* magazine as Literary Person of the Year 2001 and 2012.

Kirdjomuljo (Yogyakarta, January 1, 1930–Yogyakarta, January 19, 2000) was editor of *Budaya* and *Fantasi* magazines in Yogyakarta. His works include *Romansa Perjalanan 1* (1955), *Nona Maryam* (1955), *Penggali Kapur* (1957), *Dari Lembah Pualam* (1967), *Di Saat Rambutnya Terurai* (1968), *Cahaya di Mata Emi* (1968) and approximately twenty manuscripts of plays and poetry currently stored in the H.B. Jassin Literary Documentation Center in Jakarta.

Klara Akustia (Cibeber, Cianjur, West Java, March 7, 1924–Cibeber, February 7, 2007) was one of the pen names of Adi Sidharta. He studied at the Nationaal Handele Lallegiun (NHL) under the guidance of Douwes Dekker. He wrote poetry, essays, literary reviews and travelogues. His most famous works are *Saidjah dan Adinda*, a play adapted from the novel *Multatuli*, translated by Bakri Siregar, and *Rangsang Detik*, a poetry collection (1957).

Korrie Layun Rampan (Samarinda, East Kalimantan, August 17, 1953–Jakarta, November 19, 2015) grew up in Yogyakarta, where he attended university and was active in literary events, including the Persada Study Club. He was a member of the West Kutai subdistrict regional legislature in East Kalimantan (2004–2009) and was a journalist and editor of several publications. He wrote many poems, short stories and novels. His overview of Indonesian writers and anthologies of poetry and short stories have become important resources for literature studies. He also translated approximately one hundred children's stories and many short works of fiction.

Kuntowijoyo (Yogyakarta, September 18, 1943–Yogyakarta, February 22, 2005) wrote novels, short stories, poetry, plays, research articles and essays on culture and history. After graduating in history from Gadjah Mada University in Yogyakarta, he became a lecturer in history there and also continued his studies at the University of Connecticut (MA in American history) and Columbia

University (PhD in history) in the United States. His writings first appeared in *Sastra* and *Horison* magazines. His novels are *Khotbah di Atas Bukit* (1976), *Pasar* (1994), *Impian Amerika* (1998) and *Mantra Penjinak Ular* (2001); his short story collections are *Hampir Sebuah Subversi* (1999), *Dilarang Mencintai Bunga-Bunga* (1999) and *Waspirin & Satinah* (2003); his poetry collections are *Suluk Awang Uwung* (1975), *Isyarat* (1976) and *Makrifat Daun, Daun Makrifat* (1995); and his plays are *Rumput-Rumput Danau Bento* (1969) and *Topeng Kayu* (1973). Anthologies that include his short stories are *Pistol Perdamaian* (1976), *Laki-laki yang Kawin dengan Peri* (1995) and *Anjing-Anjing Menyerbu Kuburan* (1997). He received several awards for art and literature, including second prize in a script-writing contest sponsored by the Jakarta Arts Council for *Topeng Kayu*, the Award for Art from the Regional Government of the Special Province of Yogyakarta (1986), the Award for Literature from the Center for Language Advocacy and Development and the SEA Write Award for *Dilarang Mencintai Bunga-Bunga* (1999).

Kuslan Budiman (Sengunglung, East Java, 1935–date and place of death unknown) wrote in exile. He was a leader of Lekra (Lembaga Kebudayaan Rakyat; Institute for People's Culture) and a founder of Sanggar Bumi Tarung, which sympathized with the struggle of farmers. He studied and graduated from the Indonesian Academy of Fine Arts (Akademi Seni Rupa Indonesia / ASRI) in Yogyakarta (1962) and then studied at the Central Academy of Drama in Beijing and at the Stroganov Institute of Arts and Crafts in Stroganovskoye, Russia. In 1955 he began to write poetry, prose, reviews and essays in Indonesian and Javanese, which appeared in various publications. His work has also been included in publications by exiles. His poetry collection is *Tanah Kelahiran* (1994).

L.K. (Lesik Kati) Ara (Takengon, Central Aceh, November 12, 1937) is a poet from Aceh. He is a journalist with various publications in Medan, and he is one of the founders of Balai Pustaka Theater (1967). He is a prolific writer, focusing on Acehnese culture and literature. He was one of the editors for *Seulawah* (1995), an anthology of Acehnese poetry. His works include *Ensiklopedi Aceh I & 2* (2009–2012), two books on pantun Melayu (2004) and *Puisi Didong Gayo* (2006). He received an award for Achievement in Art from the regional government of Aceh (2009).

Leon Agusta (Sigiran, Nagari Tanjung Sani Maninjau, West Sumatra, August 5, 1938–Padang, West Sumatra, December 10, 2015) taught at the Sekolah Guru Bantu teachers' school in Bengkalis (1959), directed the Bengkel Teater in Padang (1972) and was a member of the Jakarta Arts Council. He participated in the International Writing Program at the University of Iowa in the United States (1976–1977). His poetry collections include *Monumen Safari* (1966),

Catatan Putih (1975), *Di Sudut-Sudut New York Itu* (1977), *Hukla* (1979) and a collection of children's poetry, *Berkemah dengan Putri Bangau* (1981).

Linus Suryadi (Kadisobo, Yogyakarta, March 3, 1951–Yogyakarta, July 30, 1999) studied English at the Foreign Language Academy (Akademi Bahasa Asing) and at the Institute for Teacher Training and Education (Institut Keguruan dan Ilmu Pendidikan / IKIP) Sanata Dharma (now Sanata Dharma University) but did not graduate from either program. In 1970 he was active with the Persada Study Club. He was selected to participate in the International Writing Program at the University of Iowa in the United States in 1982. His most famous work is the lyrical *Pengakuan Pariyem* (1981). He edited several important anthologies of poetry, such as *Tonggak*, volumes 1–4 (1987). Several of his works have been translated into English and Dutch.

M. (Muhammad Salim) Balfas (Krukut, Taman Sari, West Jakarta, December 25, 1922–Jakarta, June 5, 1975) was a member of the Angkatan '45 literary circle. He studied drama in the Netherlands (1954). He was editor of *Masyarakat*, *Gema Suasana* and *Siasat* magazines. With Sudjati S.A. he founded the literary magazine *Kisah*. He published several books, including collections of short stories, novels, plays, children's stories and a biography of Dr. Cipto Mangunkusumo.

M. Poppy Donggo Hutagalung (Jakarta, October 10, 1940) studied communications at the College of Communication Sciences (Sekolah Tinggi Publisistik) in Jakarta. She was an editor for *Sinar Harapan* and *Suara Pembaruan* daily newspapers. Her poetry collections include *Hari-Hari yang Cerah* (1970) and *Perjalanan Berdua: Kumpulan Sajak* (in collaboration with her husband, A.D. Donggo, 1999). She received an award for her poem that was published in *Sastra* magazine and an award from the Indonesian Women's Congress (Kowani) for her books of folk tales.

M. Taslim Ali (Painan, West Sumatra, June 16, 1916–date and place of death unknown) studied in the Faculty of Letters at the University of Indonesia. From 1948 until his retirement he was an editor with Balai Pustaka. His poems appeared in various publications. He was also known as an excellent translator. His most important translations were anthologies of world poetry, *Puisi Dunia I* (1952), which won an award from the Musyawarah National Board of Culture (BMKN) for best translation of 1952, and *Puisi Dunia II* (1953). He received commendation for his service in translating works of Dutch literature (1979).

M.A. Djoehana (Tanjung Balai, North Sumatra, 1925–date and place of death unknown) studied at Paris-Sorbonne University in Paris. He worked in the Ministry of Information, was the secretary for Sutan Sjahrir, was editor of *Opbouw* magazine (1948) and head editor of *Pembaruan* magazine, and worked at UNESCO in Paris. His poems have been published in *Vrij Nederland* and *Criterium*.

M.A. Iskandar (Montasik, Aceh Besar, 1936) taught at Tapaktuan, Blang Pidie, and in Lama Inong. His poems were published in *Mimbar Indonesia* magazine and were selected by L.K. Ara to be included in an anthology of literature of Aceh, *Seulawah: Antologi Sastra Aceh Sekilas Pintas* (1995).

M.D. Asien, the pen name of Mohamad Djoenasien, (Jakarta, December 20, 1920–date and place of death unknown) worked with Koninklijke Paketvaart Maatschappij (KPM, a Dutch shipping company), the Japanese navy (*kaigun*) and the Ministry of Information. His works were published in *Mimbar Indonesia*. Some of his poems were selected by H.B. Jassin to be included in *Gema Tanah Air* (1948).

Magusig O. Bungai (Kasongan, Central Kalimantan, September 25, 1940) or J.J. Kusni or Sulang Sahun, is an exiled writer. He studied at Gadjah Mada University, the School for Advanced Studies in the Social Sciences (École des hautes études en sciences sociales) in Paris and at New South Wales University in Sydney. He resides in Paris where, with Umar Said and Sobron Aidit, he runs an Indonesian restaurant.

Mahatmanto (Kulur, Yogyakarta, August 13, 1924) studied at Madrasah Muhammadiyah Darul Ulum Sewugalur boarding school in Yogyakarta. He also uses the names Ibnu Chalis, Sang Agung Murbaningrat and Sri Amarjati Murbaningsih. Several of his poems were selected by H.B. Jassin for the anthology *Gema Tanah Air* (1948) and by Linus Suryadi for *Tonggak I* (1987).

Mahbub Junaedi (Jakarta, July 27, 1933–Bandung, West Java, October 1, 1995) studied at the University of Indonesia. He was head editor of *Duta Masyarakat* (1960–1970); leader of Ikatan Putra, a youth group of Nahdlatul Ulama; vice chair of the central board of the Partai Persatuan Pembangunan (PPP) political party; vice chair of the advisory council of PPP; and a member of the Jakarta Arts Council. He received an award in a fiction writing competition organized by the Jakarta Arts Council for his novel *Dari Hari ke Hari* (1974). He has also translated several works of world literature.

Mardi Luhung (Gresik, East Java, March 5, 1965) studied Indonesian literature in the Faculty of Letters at Jember University. He was a teacher. His poetry is unique in its free use of words that tend to be avoided by other writers. His poetry collections include *Terbelah Sudah Jantungku* (1996), *Wanita yang Kencing di Semak* (2002), *Ciuman Bibirku yang Kelabu* (2007) and *Buwun* (2010), which received the Khatulistiwa Literary Award 2010.

Mas Ruscitadewi (Denpasar, Bali, 1965), whose full name is Anak Agung Sagung Mas Ruscitadewi, is active as a writer and in the theater. His play *Laki-Laki Serumah* won a Bali-wide scriptwriting competition (1985). His short story collection *Luh Jalir* (Naughty woman) addresses gender issues.

Maskirbi (Tarutung, North Sumatra, October 9, 1952–date and place of death unknown), whose original name was Mazhar, was active with Rendra's Bengkel Teater (1983) and Arifin C. Noer's Laboratorium Teater Kecil (1987). He was general secretary of the Aceh Arts Council (1995–2000) and taught theater at the Faculty of Dakwah at Ar-Raniry State Islamic Institute (Institut Agama Islam Negeri / IAIN) in Banda Aceh. His poetry collection is *Mataharikah Matanya* (1990).

Mathori A. Elwa, also known as **Mathori al Wustho** (Magelang, Central Java, September 6, 1965) studied Islamic law in the Faculty of Ushuluddin at Sunan Kalijaga State Islamic Institute (Institut Agama Islam Negeri / IAIN) in Yogyakarta and was active in Teater Eska Studio. He was an editor with several publishers in Yogyakarta before 2003, when he moved to Bandung and joined Nuansa Cendekia Publishers, where he continues to work. His poetry collections include *Yang Maha Syahwat* (1997), *Rajah Negeri Istighfar* (2001) and *Aku Pernah Singgah di Kotamu* (2005).

Md. Yati may be a pen name for **M.D. Yati** or **M. Dimyati** (Surakarta, Central Java, June 14, 1913–December 8, 1958), whose works include *Siti Nurjanah* (1935), *Student Sulaiman* (1935), *Ramona* (1940) and *Iwan Simatupang, Pembaharu Sastra Indonesia* (1985).

Medy Loekito (Surabaya, East Java, July 21, 1962) is the founder of Komunitas Sastra Indonesia literary community and Literary Multimedia Foundation. She is known for her short poems that are similar to haiku. She has represented Indonesia in various literary forums, including the Conference of Asian Foundations and Organizations, the North American Open Poetry Contest (2000) and the International Writing Program at the University of Iowa in the United States (2010). Her poetry collections include *In Solitude* (1993) and *Senja Hari* (1998).

Mochtar Pabottinggi (Bulukumba, South Sulawesi, September 1945) has a master's degree from the University of Massachusetts and a PhD from the University of Hawaii. He is a researcher with the Indonesian Institute of Sciences (Lembaga Ilmu Pengetahuan Indonesia / LIPI), focusing on developments in national politics. He was editor of *Mercu Suar* and *Harian Kami*. His poetry collections include *Dalam Rimba Bayang-Bayang* (2003) and *Konsierto di Kyoto* (2015).

Mohammad Diponegoro (Yogyakarta, June 28, 1928–May 9, 1982) wrote poetry, short stories, stage plays, radio plays and film scripts. He studied international law in the Faculty of Social and Political Sciences at Gadjah Mada University in Yogyakarta. He was assistant chair of the editorial staff of *Suara Muhammadiyah* (1975–82). His academic publications are *Kabar Wigati dan Kerajaan* (1977) and *Duta Islam untuk Dunia Modern* (with Ahmad Syafii Maarif, 1983). He also translated several foreign plays. He used the pen name Ben Hashem for several works that were broadcast on the government radio station (RRI) in Yogyakarta. His short story collection is *Odah dan Cerita Lainnya* (1986); his novel is *Siklus* (1975); and his most important play is *Iblis* (1961). His work appears in the anthology *Manifestasi* (1963). His book *Yuk, Nulis Cerpen Yuk* (1994) is about writing short stories. In 1973 he received an award from the International Book Year Committee for *Siklus*.

Mohammad Yamin (Sawahlunto, West Sumatra, August 23, 1903–Jakarta, October 17, 1962) earned a doctorate in law and was a pioneer of modern Indonesian poetry. He was chair of the Jong Sumatranen Bond, a semi-political organization of young Sumatrans. He actively promoted nationalism and participated in composing the Youth Pledge, which was issued in 1928. He served as minister of law (1951–1952) and minister of education and culture (1953–1955), as well as other important positions. He wrote many novels, plays, studies of history and nationalism, and biographies. His poetry collections are *Tanah Air* (1922) and *Bumi Siliwangi* (sonnet, 1954).

Motinggo Boesje (Kupangkota, Lampung, November 21, 1937–Jakarta, June 18, 1999) studied law at Gadjah Mada University. He was an editor for *Kartini* magazine and chief editor with Penerbitan Nusantara (1961–1964) and assistant chair of the Indonesian Artists Cooperative. He wrote novels, plays, short stories and poetry. Many of his works have been translated into various languages. His poems appear in *Antologi Penyair Asia* (1986) and *Antologi Penyair Dunia* (1990). His name is carved into a monument in a park in Seoul, South Korea, along with the names of one thousand poets from around the world.

Mozasa (Asahan, North Sumatra, October 10, 1914–Medan, North Sumatra, February 7, 1988) studied at the Malay School in Tanjung Balai; the Normal School in Pematang Siantar, a school for training teachers; and Landbouwonderwijzer agricultural school in Bogor. He taught at the Sekolah Rakyat people's school in Kisaran and at an agricultural school and was chair of the Medan Arts Council. Several of his poems appear in poetry anthologies, including *Puisi Baru* (1946), *Pujangga Baru: Prosa dan Puisi* (1963) and *Tonggak I* (1987).

Muh. (Muhammad) Rustandi Kartakusuma (Ciamis, West Jawa, July 21, 1921–place of death unknown, April 11, 2008) studied at the Faculty of Letters at the University of Indonesia and Muzieklyceum in Amsterdam. He was an editor for Mangle and for the national news agency Antara. He taught at Massachusetts Institute of Technology, Yale University and Harvard University. He received the

Satya Lencana Award for Culture (2004) and the Rancagé Literary Award (2005) for his contributions to Sundanese literature and culture. His poetry collection is *Rekaman dari Tujuh Daerah* (1951).

Mustofa W. Hasyim (Bantul, Yogyakarta, November 17, 1954) is known as a poet whose poems are "in tatters." Since the 1970s he has used humor to convey serious ideas. He is active with the Persada Study Club on Malioboro Street in Yogyakarta. He has been a journalist, editor and column writer for various publications. He also writes novels, essays and children's stories. His poetry collections include *Pohon Tak Lagi Bertutur* (2013), *Puisi-Puisi Maiyah, Telunjuk Sunan Kalijaga* (2013) and *Tanah Suci* (2013).

Nenden Lilis Aisyah (Garut, West Java, September 26, 1971) is a graduate of the MA program and a lecturer on Indonesian literature at Universitas Pendidikan Indonesia (UPI) in Bandung. She writes poetry, short stories and literary reviews and focuses on gender studies. She is the founder of the literary community Dewi Sartika and is an active adviser for the Community of Women Writers Indonesia. She has participated in the Southeast Asian Literature Workshop, the Winternachten Festival, INALCO (France, 1999), the Schamrock Festival of Women Poets and the Frankfurt Book Fair (Germany 2016), as well as various other national and international literary events. Her poetry collections are *Negeri Sihir* (1999) and *Maskumambang Buat Ibu* (bilingual, Indonesian and Inggris, 2016). She has also written short story collections and several nonfiction books. Several of her works have been translated into English, Dutch, German and Mandarin.

Nirwan Dewanto (Surabaya, East Java, September 28, 1961) has a degree in geology from the Bandung Institute of Technology and is known as a literary critic, art curator and actor. He is also an editor for the journal *Kalam*, editor of the literature page in *Koran Tempo* newspaper and program director of the Salihara Arts Community in Jakarta. His collection of essays is *Senjakala Kebudayaan* (1996). Both of his poetry collections, *Jantung Lebah Ratu* (2008) and *Buli Buli Lima Kaki* (2010), won Khatulistiwa Literary Awards. *The Origin of Happiness & Other Poems* (2015), published in Lontar Foundation's BTW series, features a selection of his poems translated into English and German.

Nursjamsu Nasution (Lintau, West Sumatra, October 6, 1921–Jakarta, 1995) studied in the Faculty of Letters at the University of Indonesia. He was a member of the Jakarta Arts Council (1973–1979). His poems have been published in several anthologies of poetry, including *Gema Tanah Air* (1948), *Seserpih Pinang Sepucuk Sirih* (edited by Toeti Heraty [Noerhadi], 1979) and *Tonggak 1* (1987).

Oei Sien Tjwan (Kudus, Central Java, February 8, 1947) studied law and philosophy at Satya Wacana Christian University in Salatiga. His work has been published in *Kompas, Sinar Harapan, Suara Pembaruan, Femina* and *Pertiwi*. His short story "Serantang Kangkungi" received the Bronze Reel Award in a short story writing competition organized by Radio Nederland Wereldomroep in Hilversum, Netherlands.

Oka Rusmini (Jakarta, June 11, 1967) writes poetry, short stories and novels. She has worked as a journalist for *Bali Post* and is active with Sanggar Minum Kopi in Denpasar. Her short story collection is *Akar Pule* (2012). Her poetry collections are *Monolog Pohon* (1997), *Patiwangi* (2003), *Warna Kita* (2007), *Pandora* (2008) and *Saiban* (2013). Her novels are *Tarian Bumi* (2000), *Sagra* (2001), *Kenanga* (2003) and *Tempurung* (2010). *Tarian Bumi* was translated and published in German as *Erdentanz* (2007) and in English as *Earth Dance* (2011). She has received several literary awards, including a Literature Award from the Center for Language Advocacy and Development in 2003 and the Khatulistiwa Literary Award in 2014 for *Saiban*. She is often invited to participate in national and international literary events.

Omi Intan Naomi (Denpasar, Bali, October 26, 1970–Yogyakarta, November 5, 2006) studied communications at Gadjah Mada University. She wrote several books of essays on social and political issues, including *Anjing Penjaga* (1996), *Gegar Gender* (2000), *Kata Kunci* (2001) and *Planet Loco* (in English, 2002) and a semi-autobiography, *Dog Days Eve* (2002). Her poetry collections include *Aku Ingin* (1986), *Sajak-Sajak Omi* (1986), *Memori* (1987), *Sebelum Tidur* (1987) and *Puisi Cinta* (1987).

Or. (Oemar) Mandank or Oemar gelar Datoek Radjo Mandank (Kotapanjang, Suliki, West Sumatra, January 1, 1913–date and place of death unknown) studied at Sekolah Guru Normal Teachers' College in Padang Panjang. His works were published in *Panji Pustaka, Pujangga Baru* and *Horison*. His books include *Nurmalina* (1939), *Pantun Orang Muda* (1939) and *Sebab Aku Terdiam* (1939). Several of his poems were published in the anthology *Puisi Baru* (1946).

P. Sengodjo (Gatak, Ungaran, Central Java, November 25, 1926–date and place of death unknown) studied at Gadjah Mada University and in the Faculty of Economics at Satya Wacana University in Salatiga. He was an editor for *Suara Muda* in Surakarta (1946–1947). His works were published in *Kisah, Siasat, Indonesia, Pujangga Baru, Roman, Budaya Jaya* and *Panca Warna*. Several of his poems were published in the poetry anthologies *Tonggak 1* (1987), *Pahlawan dan Kucing* (1987) and *Laut Biru Langit Biru* (1977).

Piek Ardijanto Suprijadi (Magetan, East Java, August 12, 1929–date and place of death unknown) was the principal of SMA Negeri Grogol High School in Demak, Central Java. Several of his poems were published in *Angkatan '66: Prosa dan Puisi* (1968), *Tonggak 2* (1987), *Dari Negeri Poci 2* (1994) and *Sajak-Sajak*

Perjuangan dan Nyanyian Tanah Air (1995). He also wrote short stories and novels.

Pitres Sombowadile (Manado, North Sulawesi, May 28, 1966) studied marine science at Minaesa Institute of Technology. He was a translator for *Manado Post* and special editor for *Maesan* magazine. His poems were published in *Sasambo* (1991) and *Mimbar Penyair Abad 21* (1996).

Putu Oka Sukanta (Singaraja, Bali, July 29, 1939) has been active as a writer since the age of sixteen. From 1966 to 1976 he was a political prisoner, following the military coup d'état that brought General Suharto to power. He has since been invited overseas for theater performances, poetry readings and literary conferences in Sri Lanka, Bangladesh, Australia, Malaysia, Germany and France. His works include children's books, three collections of poetry and two volumes of short stories. He works as an acupuncturist and has also written on alternative medicine.

Rachmat Djoko Pradopo (Klaten, Central Java, November 3, 1939) is professor emeritus of literature studies in the Faculty of Cultural Studies at Gadjah Mada University in Yogyakarta. He taught Indonesian language and literature at Hankuk University of Foreign Studies in South Korea. His works on the study of literature include *Pengkajian Puisi* (1987) and *Kritik Sastra Indonesia Modern* (2003). His poetry collections include *Matahari Pagi di Tanah Air* (1967), *Hutan Bunga* (1993), *Aubade* (1999) and *Mitos Kentut Semar* (2006).

Radhar Panca Dahana (Jakarta, March 26, 1965) studied sociology at the University of Indonesia (1993) and in France (2001). He writes poetry, prose, plays, studies and reviews about literature, culture and the humanities. He is the founder of the Indonesian Writers' Association and chair of the Indonesian Theater Federation. He was named one of the five Young Artists of Asia's Future by NHK, Japan's national broadcasting organization (1996), and Pusaka Bangsa's Ambassador of the Environment (2004), and he was awarded the Prix de la Francophonie Medal from fifteen French-speaking nations (2007). His poetry collections are *Lalu Waktu* (1994), *Lalu Batu* (2004), *Lalu Aku* (2011) and *Manusia Istana: Sekumpulan Puisi Politik* (2015).

Rahman Arge (Makassar, South Sulawesi, July 17, 1935–August 11, 2015) served as general chair of the Indonesian Journalists' Association (Persatuan Wartawan Indonesia / PWI) and the Makassar Arts Council. He was also a member of the People's Consultative Assembly. He founded and managed several mass media publications, including the South Sulawesi edition of *Duta Masyarakat*; magazines such as *Suara*, *Esensi* and *Timtim*; and newspapers such as *Harian Pembaharuan* and *Pos Makassar*. He received several awards for his contributions to the press, as well as the Satya Lencana Award from the president of Indonesia.

He wrote several books about social and political issues. His poems appear in various publications and anthologies.

Ramadhan K.H. (Karta Hadimadja) (Bandung, West Java, March 16, 1927—Cape Town, South Africa, March 16, 2006) studied at the Bandung Institute of Technology and at the Foreign Service Academy (Akademi Dinas Luar Negeri) in Jakarta. He was a senior journalist. He wrote poetry, four novels and several biographies and collections of essays, and he translated three books by F. García Lorca. His poetry collection *Priangan Si Djelita* (1956) was translated into several languages. He edited several bilingual anthologies of poetry, Indonesian-German and Indonesian-French. He received the SEA Write Award in 1993.

Raudal Tanjung Banua (Taratak, Pesisir Selatan, West Sumatra, January 19, 1975) studied theater at the Indonesian Institute of the Arts (Institut Seni Indonesia) in Yogyakarta. He founded the Rumah Lebah Community and Akar Indonesia Publishers. His poetry collections include *Gugusan Mata Ibu* (2005) and *Api Bawah Tanah* (2013). He received the SIH Award from *Jurnal Puisi* and an award for Best Short Story from *Horison* magazine.

Rayani Sriwidodo (Kotanopan, North Sumatra, November 6, 1946) has written many novels for children and young people, short stories, essays and poetry. She also translates. She participated in the International Writing Program at the University of Iowa in the United States in 1977. One of her poems won an award from *Horison* (1969), and her short story "Balada Satu Kuntum" won the Nemis Prize from the government of Chile (1987). Her poetry collections include *Pada Sebuah Lorong* (with T. Mulya Lubis, 1968), *Pokok Murbei* (1977) and *Percakapan Rumput* (1983). Several of her poems were published in an anthology featuring women poets from five continents, *Ik Heb Tien Benen* (1990), published in the Netherlands.

Remy Sylado (Malino, Makassar, South Sulawesi, July 12, 1945), whose full name is Yapi Panda Abdiel Tambayong, began his career as a journalist for *Tempo* magazine. He has also been a lecturer at the Bandung Academy of Cinematography, editor of the column "Puisi Mbeling" and director of the Bandung Cultural Center. He is a pioneer in the use of humor for social criticism in poetry. His poetry collection is *Puisi Mbeling* (2004). He is also known as a novelist, actor and musician. His novel *Kerudung Merah Kirmizi* received the Khatulistiwa Literary Award (2002).

Rendra (Surakarta, Central Java, November 7, 1935–Depok, West Java, August 6, 2009), whose full name is Willibrordus Surendra Bhawana Rendra Brotoatmojo and who is also known known as W.S. Rendra, studied English literature at Gadjah Mada University in Yogyakarta and at the American Academy of Dramatic Arts in New York. He founded Bengkel Teater in 1967. He was dubbed "the Peacock" for his flamboyant style of poetry readings. His works have been translated into several languages. His poetry collections include *Ballada Orang-Orang Tercinta* (1957), *Potret Pembangunan dalam Puisi* (1979), *Mencari Bapa* (1997) and *Megatruh* (2001).

Rivai Apin (Padang Panjang, West Sumatra, August 30, 1927–Jakarta, April 1995) was a member of the Angkatan '45 literary circle. With Chairil Anwar and Asrul Sani, he published *Tiga Menguak Takdir*. He was editor of several publications, including *Gema Suasana*, *Siasat*, *Zenith* and *Zaman Baru*. His poems appear in the anthologies *Gema Tanah Air* (1948), *Tiga Menguak Takdir* (1950) and *Dari Dua Dunia Belum Sudah* (1972).

Roestam Effendi (Padang, West Sumatra, May 13, 1903–Jakarta, May 24, 1979) graduated from the Hogere Kweek School teachers' college in Bandung (1924) and became a teacher at Perguruan Islam Adabiah II High School in Padang. He lived in the Netherlands from 1928 to 1947 and was a member of the Lower Council (Tweede Kamer), representing the Dutch Communist Party for fourteen years. His works include *Bebasari* (1926), *Percikan Permenungan* (1926) and *Van Moskow naar Tiflis*.

Rusli Marzuki Saria (Kamang, Bukittinggi, West Sumatra, February 26, 1936) was the cultural editor for the *Singgalang* daily newspaper in Padang. Known as "Papa," he was named Maestro of Literature by the West Sumatran Arts Council (2009). An active writer since the 1960s, he has written several books, including *Pada Hari Ini pada Jantung Hari* (1966), *Monumen Safari* (with Leon Agusta, 1966) and *Ada Ratap Ada Nyanyi* (1976). In 2014, at age seventy-eight, he published a bilingual anthology of poems, *One by One, Line by Line*.

S. Anantaguna (Klaten, Central Java, August 9, 1930–Jakarta, July 18, 2014) was given the name Santoso bin Sutopangarso at birth but later changed it to Sabar Anantaguna. He was one of the leaders of Lekra (Lembaga Kebudayaan Rakyat; Institute for People's Culture) from 1959 to 1965. His poetry collections include *Yang Bertanah Air Tidak Bertanah* (1962), *Kecapi Terali Besi* (1999) and *Puisi-Puisi dari Penjara* (2010).

S. Rukiah (Purwakarta, West Java, April 25, 1927–Purwakarta, West Java, June 6, 1996) was a secretary for the magazine *Pujangga Baru* and a member of the central council of Lekra (Lembaga Kebudayaan Rakyat; Institute for People's Culture) from 1959 to 1965. Her novel *Kejatuhan dan Hati* (1950) was translated into English and published as *The Fall and the Heart* (2010). She also wrote several children's stories. Her poetry collection *Tandus* (1952) won a Literary Award from the Musyawarah National Board of Culture (BMKN).

S. Wakidjan (date and place of birth and death unknown) wrote the book *Pita Biru: Kumpulan Sandjak-Sandjak* (1962). His poem "Menoedjoe Tjita" was published in *Asia Raja*, a newspaper published in the Dutch East Indies and in the early days of the Republic of Indonesia.

Saini K.M. (Sumedang, West Java, June 16, 1938) studied at the Institute for Teacher Training and Education (Institut Keguruan dan Ilmu Pendidikan / IKIP) in Bandung. He was a member of the West Java regional legislature, literature editor of the daily newspaper *Pikiran Rakyat* and a lecturer at the Indonesian Academy of Dance (Akademi Seni Tari Indonesia / ASTI) in Bandung. He was a translator and a prolific writer of plays, prose and nonfiction. His poetry collections include *Rumah Cermin* (1979), *Sepuluh Orang Utusan* (1989) and *Nyanyian Tanah Air* (2000). He has received several awards, including the SEA Write Award (2001).

Samar Gantang (Tabanan, Bali, September 27, 1949) also known as **I Gusti Putu Bawa Samar Gantang**, has been writing poetry since 1973. His poetry collections are *Hujan Tengah Malam* (1974), *Kisah Sebuah Kota Pelangi* (1976), *Aab Jagad* (2001), *Onyah* (2002), *Sagung Wah* (2002), *Puisi Modre Samar Gantang* (2003), *Kidung Dewata dalam Berkah Gusti* (2004), *Leak Kota Pala* (2012) and *Leak Jagat (Collected Works of Poetry: 1973–2013)*. His poetry has also been included in the anthologies *What's Poetry?* (2012) and *Sweep of the Violin* (2015). He is currently preparing a book of modre poetry, a type of poetry based on Balinese mantra. He received the Dharma Widya Kusuma Award for uncovering the roots of Balinese culture from Bali Province's Department of Culture (August 2015) and was the host poet for the Tabanan International Poetry Festival (November 2015).

Samiati Alisjahbana (Jakarta, March 15, 1930–Honolulu, Hawaii, August 15, 1966) was the oldest child of Sutan Takdir Alisjahbana. She studied literature and philosophy at the University of Indonesia in Jakarta and at Cornell University in Ithaca, New York. Her poetry collections include *Harapan dan Sangka* (1993).

Sandy Tyas (Semarang, Central Java, April 17, 1939–Jakarta, March 1, 2009) was a poet and radio broadcaster. He worked with the national television station in Jakarta from 1964. His poems have been published in *Sajak-Sajak* (1972), *Puisi ASEAN Buku III* (1978), *Hitam Afrika Hitam Amerika* (1977), *Tematis* (1981) and the anthologies *Tonggak 2* (1987) and *Angkatan '66: Prosa dan Puisi* (1968).

Sanento Yuliman (Jatilawang, Banyumas, Central Java, July 14, 1941–Bandung, West Java, July 14, 1992) was an editor for *Mahasiswa Indonesia, Horison* and *Aktuil* and a lecturer at the Bandung Academy for Theater and Film, the Faculty of Letters at the University of Indonesia and the Faculty of Visual Arts and Design at Bandung Institute of Technology. His poem "Laut" was praised by the editors of *Horison* (1966–1967). He wrote several books about visual arts.

Sanusi Pane (Muara Sipongi, North Sumatra, November 14, 1905–Jakarta, January 2, 1968) was an editor for *Timbul* magazine, *Kebangunan* daily and *Pujangga Baru* literary magazine. He lived in India between 1929 and 1930 and produced a book of poetry, *Madah Kelana* (1931), one year later. His year in India led to an exploration of his Eastern cultural roots, which nurtured a sense of what it was to be Indonesian. His poems, historical plays and essays reflect this perspective. His poetry collections include *Pancaran Cinta* (1926) and *Puspa Mega* (1927). In 1969 he received a literary award from the government of Indonesia.

Sapardi Djoko Damono (Surakarta, Central Java, March 20, 1940) was rector and is now a professor in the Faculty of Cultural Studies at the University of Indonesia. He was an editor for *Horison*. He is a translator and a prolific writer of poetry, essays, prose, short stories and novels. His works have received many awards and commendations. His poetry collections include *Mata Pisau* (1974), *Perahu Kertas* (1983), *Hujan Bulan Juni* (1994) and *Kolam* (2009). He has received the ASEAN Award for Literature (1986) and the Kusala Sastra Indonesia Award (2009).

Saut Situmorang (Tebing Tinggi, North Sumatra, June 29, 1966) is an editor and literary curator who graduated in English literature from Victoria University of Wellington and the University of Auckland in New Zealand. He is the founder of the Boemi Poetra community and journal, which provide a unique color to Indonesian literature. His works of literary studies include *Cyber Grafiti: Polemik Sastra Cyberpunk* (2004) and *Politik Sastra* (2009). His poetry collections include *Saut Kecil Bicara dengan Tuhan* (2003), *Catatan Subversif* (2004), *Otobiografi: Kumpulan puisi, 1987–2007* (2007), *Les mots cette souffrance* (Collection du Banian, Paris, 2012) and *Perahu Mabuk* (2014).

Selasih (Talu, West Sumatra, July 31, 1909–Pekanbaru, Riau, December 15, 1995) is a pseudonym for Sariamin Ismail, who also used the pen name Seleguri and many others. She was chair of the Bukittinggi branch of Jong Islamieten Bond (1928–1930) and was a member of the Riau regional legislature (1947–1948). She is known for writing about the meanings and implications of love and cultural traditions for women, particularly representing the perspectives of educated indigenous women. Her novels include *Kalau Tak Untung* (1933) and *Pengaruh Keadaan* (1937). Her poetry appeared in various literary publications.

Sides Sudyarto Ds. (Tegal, Central Java, July 14, 1942–Jakarta, October 19, 2012) studied Dutch literature at the University of Indonesia. He was a journalist for *Tempo* magazine and *Kompas* newspaper, an editor for *Jakarta Jakarta*, *Sinar Harapan* and *Media Indonesia* and managing editor of *Tiara* magazine. He wrote poetry, novels and children's stories. His poetry collections include *Kebatinan* (1975) and *Tiang Gantungan* (2002).

Sirikit Syah (Surabaya, East Java, 1960) earned a master's degree in communications from the University of Westminster in London and a doctorate from Surabaya State University. She has been a journalist for *Surabaya Post* and other publications, and she teaches. Her poetry collection is *Memotret dengan Kata-Kata* (2005).

Siti Nuraini (Padang, West Sumatra, July 6, 1930) studied law at the University of Indonesia. She translates and writes poetry, short stories and essays. She has been the secretary of *Gelanggang/Siasat* and editor for *Zenith*. Her poems have been published in *Mimbar Indonesia, Zenith, Gelanggang/Siasat, Sastra* and *Horison*, as well as in several anthologies, such as *Seserpih Pinang Sepucuk Sirih* (1979) and *Ungu: Antologi Puisi Wanita Penyair Indonesia* (1990). Her poem "Variation on a Theme" received commendation from *Horison* magazine in 1969.

Sitok Srengenge (Dorolegi, Grobogan, Central Java, August 22, 1965) was active with Rendra's Bengkel Teater. He writes poetry, novels, essays and plays. He is the founder of Kata Kita Publishers, which publishes works of literature, and an art venue, Senthong Seni Srengenge in Bangun Jiwo, Yogyakarta. His poetry collections include *On Nothing* (a compilation of four books: *Ambrosia, Nonsens/ Nonsense, Anak Jadah / Bastard* and *Persetubuhan Liar / Wild Coupling*, 2005) and *Trilogi Tripitakata* (a compilation of four books: *Kelenjar Bekisar Jantan, Anak Jadah, Gembala Waktu* and *Madah Pereda Rindu*, 2013).

Sitor Situmorang (Harianboho, Tapanuli Utara, North Sumatra, October 2, 1923–Apeldoorn, Netherlands, December 21, 2014) was a writer and journalist. He studied at the University of California (1956–1957) and taught Indonesian language at Leiden University (1982–1990). He was chair of the Institute of National Culture (Lembaga Kebudayaan Nasional / LKN) from 1959 to 1965. His poetry collection *Peta Perjalanan* received an award for poetry from the Jakarta Arts Council (1976). He wrote dozens of books of poetry, short stories, plays, essays and biographies. His poetry collections include *Surat Kertas Hijau* (1954), *Bunga di atas Batu* (1989) and *Rindu Kelana* (1994).

Slamet (Su) Kirnanto (Surakarta, Central Java, March 3, 1941–Jakarta, August 23, 2014) studied history at the University of Indonesia. He was chair of the executive committee for the student organization Kesatuan Aksi Mahasiswa Indonesia (KAMI), guest editor of the cultural pages for *Sinar Harapan* daily newspaper (1972–1973), a member of the secretariat of the Jakarta Arts Council and a member of the Film Censor Board (1978–1984). His poetry collections include *Jaket Kuning* (1967), *Kidung Putih* (1967), *Gema Otak Terbanting* (1974), *Bunga Batu* (1979) and *Luka Bunga* (1993).

Sobron Aidit (Tanjung Pandan, Belitung, June 2, 1934–Paris, France, February 10, 2007) wrote poetry and short stories. He began his writing career at age thirteen. He taught in Jakarta and was a journalist with *Harian Rakyat* and *Bintang Timur*. He was a lecturer at Multatuli Literature Academy (Akademi Sastra Multatuli) in Jakarta. He was known as one of the founders of the Senen Artists group. In 1963 he left Indonesia to teach Indonesian language in Beijing and then could not return after the anti-communist events in 1965–1966. He moved to Paris and became an active promoter for the alternative press in Europe for the rest of his life. He published four poetry collections: *Ketemu di Jalan* (with Ajip Rosidi and S.M. Ardan, 1956), *Pulang Bertempur* (1959), *Puisi* (1992) and *Mencari Langit* (1999). He has three short story collections: *Derap Revolusi* (including a novella, 1962), *Razia Agustus* (1992) and *Kisah Intel dan Sebuah Warung* (2000). He wrote two memoirs: *Gajah di Pelupuk Mata* (2002) and *Surat Kepada Tuhan* (2003). His short story "Buaya dan Dukunnya" won third prize from *Kisah* magazine in 1955, and "Basimah" won an award from *Harian Rakyat* in 1961.

Soeprijadi Tomodihardjo (Pare, Kediri, East Java, February 27, 1933) is a writer in exile who lives in Cologne, Germany. He began his writing career in the 1950s in Surabaya. He was editor of *Trompet Masyarakat* newspaper and *Brawijaya* magazine (which later became *Wijaya*). He was also a member of Lekra (Lembaga Kebudayaan Rakyat; Institute for People's Culture), the arts organization associated with the Indonesian Communist Party. After the events of September 30, 1965, he was exiled to China and worked as a journalist and translator for *Xinhua* in Beijing (1965–1967). Later he moved to Germany and worked at the Cologne University Hospital until he retired in 1998. He writes poetry, short stories, essays and journalism. His work has been published in *Kisah, Mimbar Indonesia, Siasat, Roman* and *Sastra*. He has published one poetry collection: *Suara Anak Semang* (1989); and three short story collections: *Saudara dan Seorang Anak Semang* (1988), *Kera di Kepala* (2006) and *Cucu Tukang Perang* (2011). Several of his short stories have been published in anthologies, including *Titian* (2007) and *Lobakan* (2009). His essay "Sumber-Sumber Kegiatan" was published by E. Ulrich Kratz in *Sumber Terpilih Sejarah Sastra Indonesia Abad XX* (2000).

Soni Farid Maulana (Tasikmalaya, West Java, February 19, 1962) was cultural editor for *Pikiran Rakyat* daily newspaper. He has written dozens of books of poetry, some of which have been nominated for the Khatulistiwa Award, such as *Telapak Air* (2013). He also writes poetry in Sundanese. His poetry collection *Arus Pagi* (2015) won the Poetry Day Award from the Poetry Day Foundation.

Sosiawan Leak (Surakarta, Central Java, September 23, 1967) is a poet who is active with the theater and has written several volumes of stage plays. His poetry collections include *Umpatan* (with K.R.T. Sujonopuro, 1995), *Dunia Bogambola* (with Thomas Budi Santosa, 2007) and *Kidung dari Bandungan* (with Rini Tri Purspohardini, 2011). He also devised the concept for the poetry anthology *Puisi Menolak Korupsi* (2013).

Subagio Sastrowardojo (Madiun, East Java, February 1, 1924–Jakarta, July 18, 1995) was a writer and educator. He was the director of the Indonesian Language Department B-1 in Yogyakarta (1954–1958) and lectured on Indonesian literature at several universities in Indonesia and abroad. He was also director of Balai Pustaka publishing company. He wrote poems and literary critiques. His poem "Dan Kematian Makin Akrab" won an award from *Horison* magazine (1967). He received an Art Award from the Indonesian government for his poetry collection *Daerah Perbatasan* (1970).

Sugiarta Sriwibawa (Surakarta, Central Java, March 31, 1932) is a writer and journalist. He studied in the Faculty of Letters at the University of Indonesia. He was director of the Tokyo branch of the Antara news agency and an editor with Pustaka Jaya publisher and the University of Indonesia publisher. He writes poetry and literary studies, and he translates. His poetry collection is *Garis Putih* (1978), and *Puisi Jepang Modern* (1975) is his study of Japanese poetry.

Suman Hs. (Bengkalis, Riau, April 4, 1904–Pekanbaru, Riau, May 8, 1999) was a writer and educator. He was a member of the Riau regional legislature. With M. Kasim he represents the first generation of Indonesian short story writers. He is known more for his novels and short stories. Several of his poems were included in the anthology *Puisi Baru* (1946).

Suminto A. Sayuti (Purbalingga, Banyumas, Central Java, October 26, 1956) is a professor in the Faculty of Language and Art and in the Postgraduate Program at Yogyakarta State University (Universitas Negeri Yogyakarta / UNY). He received the Kadaulatan Rakyat Award for Culture (2005) and the Literature Award from the Yogyakarta Literary Foundation (2014). He writes poetry and literary studies. His poetry collections include *Malam Tamansari* and *Semerbak Sajak* (2000).

Suparwata Wiraatmadja (Sragen, Central Java, July 22, 1938) studied at SMA-B High School. In 1959 he received first prize from *Basis* magazine for his poem "Soneta buat Adik." He published one poetry collection, *Kidung Keramahan* (1963).

Supii Wishnukuntjahja (Blitar, East Java, 1928–date and place of death unknown) graduated from Sekolah Guru Laki-Laki teachers' training school in Blitar and then continued his studies at SMA Sore High School in Malang. His works have been published in *Mimbar Indonesia* and *Panca Raya*. Several of his poems were selected by H.B. Jassin for the anthology *Gema Tanah Air* (1948).

Surachman R.M. (Garut, West Java, September 13, 1936) studied law at the University of Indonesia in Jakarta, Padjadjaran University in Bandung and Syracuse University in New York. He has served as a prosecuting attorney in Cimahi, Purwakarta, Karawang and Bandung and as a representative in the Bandung regional legislature. His works include *Surat Kayas* (1968), *Di Balik Matahari* (1974) and *Basisir Langit* (1976).

Sutan Takdir Alisjahbana (Natal, North Sumatra, February 11, 1908–Jakarta, July 17, 1994) was a linguist and important figure in Indonesian literature. He was editor of various publications, such as *Panji Pustaka*, and at Balai Pustaka (1930–1933). He co-founded *Pujangga Baru* with Amir Hamzah and Armijn Pane and managed it (1933–1942 and 1948–1953). He was instrumental in modernizing the Indonesian language and promoting it as the national language of the country. He wrote many books on grammar, linguistic studies and modern thought, as well as novels, short stories and poetry. His poetry collections include *Tebaran Mega* (1935) and *Sajak-Sajak dan Renungan* (1987). He also edited poetry anthologies that have become standard academic resources for literature studies, such as *Puisi Lama* (1941) and *Puisi Baru* (1946).

Sutardji Calzoum Bachri (Rengat, Indragiri Hulu, Riau, June 24, 1941) writes poetry, short stories and essays. Known as the "President of Indonesian Poets," he is considered to be one of the fresh voices of Indonesian poetry. His style of poetry and poetry reading is reminiscent of incantations in which words become mantras. He was formerly the poetry editor for *Horison* magazine and since 2013 has been the poetry editor for *Kompas* and *Indo Pos* daily newspaper. In 1974–1975 he participated in the International Writing Program at the University of Iowa in the United States. His collection of short stories is *Hujan Menulis Ayam* (2001). His poetry collection is *O Amuk Kapak* (1981), and his collection of essays is *Isyarat* (2007). Many of his poems have been translated into English by Harry Aveling and published in various anthologies, including *Arjuna in Meditation* (India), *Writing from the World* (United States) and *Westerly Review* (Australia). Some of his poems have also appeared in two Dutch anthologies: *Dichters in Rotterdam* (1975) and *Ik wil nog duizend jaar leven, negen moderne Indonesische dichters* (1979). He has received several awards, including the SEA Write Award in 1979 and the Chairil Anwar Literature Award from the Jakarta Arts Council in 1998.

T. Mulya Lubis (Muara Botung, North Sumatra, July 4, 1949) is a lawyer. He studied law at the University of Indonesia, Harvard Law School (Master of Law, 1980) and University of California at Berkeley (Doctor of Juridicial Science, 1990). He was director of the Legal Aid Foundation in Jakarta and has lectured in law at the University of Indonesia. His poetry collection is *Pada Sebuah Lorong* (with Rayani Sriwidodo, 1970).

Talsya (Aceh, June 23, 1925), whose full name is Teuku Ali Basyah Talsya, began his career as an editor for *Atjeh Sinbun* (1942–1945) and later worked for other publications and media outlets, including Antara news agency. He was the spokesperson for the governor of Aceh (1964–1968) and head of the Department of Information of the Aceh regional government. He has written poetry, short stories, novels, biographies and essays on culture and history. His collections of poetry include *Lambaian Kekasih* and *Musim Badai*.

Tan Lioe Ie (Denpasar, Bali, June 1, 1958) is a poet and musician who explores Chinese rituals and mythology through Indonesian poetry. His poetry collections include *Kita Bersaudara* (1991), which was translated into English as *We Are All One*, and *Malam Cahaya Lampion* (2005), which won a literary competition and was translated into Dutch as *Nach Van De Lampionen*. He was editor of the cultural journal *Cak*.

Taufik Ikram Jamil (Telukbetung, Bengkalis, Riau, September 19, 1963) graduated from the Faculty of Teacher Training and Pedagogy at Riau University in 1987. He is a writer and journalist. In 1991 he established Yayasan Membaca, a foundation devoted to supporting reading activities and that publishes the journal *Menyimak*, which features works of local writers. In 1999 this organization became the Pusaka Riau Foundation, which is active in culture, the arts and publishing. He also founded the Riau Malay Academy of Arts (Akademi Kesenian Melayu Riau). He served as general director of the Riau Arts Council (2002–2007). He writes fiction, poetry and historical studies. His short story collections are *Membaca Hang Jebat* (1995), *Sandiwara Hang Tuah* (1996), *Hikayat Batu-Batu* (2005) and *Hikayat Suara-Suara* (2016). His novels are *Hempasan Gelombang* (1998) and *Gelombang Sunyi* (2001). His poetry collections are *Tersebab Haku Melayu* (1994), *Tersebab Aku Melayu* (2010), *Tersebab Daku Melayu* (2015) and a trilingual edition of *What's Left and Other Poems* (2015). He has received several awards, including Best Cultural Achievement from the Sagang Foundation for *Sandiwara Hang Tuah* in 1997, Best Indonesian Short Story from the Jakarta Arts Council for "Jumat Pagi Bersama Amuk" in 1998 and Outstanding Artist from the Sagang Foundation in 2003.

Taufiq Ismail (Bukittinggi, West Sumatra, June 25, 1935) studied veterinary science as well as language and literature. He signed the Cultural Manifesto of August 1963 and was a founder of the Indonesia Foundation, which brought forth the literary magazine *Horison*, which he managed. He compiled anthologies of poetry and wrote dozens of books of poetry, many of which have become standard references for literary studies. He also wrote the lyrics for many songs for the musical group Bimbo. His collections of poetry include *Manifestasi* (1963), *Benteng* (1966), *Tirani* (1966) and *Malu Aku Jadi Orang Indonesia* (1998). A complete collection of his writings is presented in *Mengakar ke Bumi, Menggapai ke Langit* (four volumes, 2008).

Timur Sinar Suprabana (Surakarta, Central Java, May 4, 1963) has published poems, short stories and articles about culture in various publications since the 1980s. He manages the Gubug Penceng Cultural House, and he paints. His poetry collections include *Malam* (2005), *Matasunyi* (2005), *Dengan Cinta* (2007), *Sihir Cinta* (2008), *Dua Hati* (2008) and *Gobang Semarang* (2009).

Toeti Heraty (Noerhadi) (Bandung, West Java, November 27, 1933) studied philosophy at the University of Leiden in the Netherlands and earned a doctorate in philosophy at the University of Indonesia. She was chair of the Jakarta Arts Council (1982–1985). She participated in the International Writing Program at the University of Iowa in the United States (1984) and in various international literary events. Several of her works have been translated into foreign languages. Her poetry collections include *Sajak-Sajak 33* (1973) and *Mimpi dan Pretensi* (1982). She has compiled anthologies of poems written by female poets, such as *Seserpih Pinang Sepucuk Sirih* (1979) and *Selendang Pelangi* (2007).

Toto Sudarto Bachtiar (Palimanan, Cirebon, West Java, October 12, 1929–Paris, France, October 9, 2007) studied law at the University of Indonesia. He wrote poetry and translated works of literature. He was known as one of the pillars of Indonesian literature in the 1950s. His poetry collections include *Suara* (1956), which received a literary award from the Musyawarah National Board of Culture (BMKN), and *Etsa* (1958).

Trisno Sumardjo (Surabaya, East Java, December 6, 1916–Jakarta, April 21, 1969) was a writer, editor and painter. He was one of the first signatories to the Cultural Manifesto of 1963, one of the founders of the Taman Ismail Marzuki Art Center and the first chair of the Jakarta Arts Council. He received the Satya Lencana Award for Culture in 1969. He wrote poetry, short stories, plays and studies of visual arts. He was also a translator. His collections of poetry include *Kata Hati dan Perbuatan* (1952) and *Silhuet* (1965).

Umbu Landu Paranggi (Sumba, East Nusa Tenggara, August 10, 1943) studied at Gadjah Mada University in Yogyakarta. He was the founder and organizer of the Persada Study Club, a cultural community that has had an influential role in promoting and encouraging many writers. Centered on Malioboro Street in Yogyakarta, he became known as "President of Malioboro." Although he has mentored many young writers, he prefers to remain outside the spotlight and often lives on the street. His work has appeared in various publications and anthologies but has yet to be compiled and published in a book. He has retired to Bali where he writes the "Apresiasi" column in the *Bali Post*.

Upita Agustine (Pegaruyung, West Sumatra, August 31, 1947) was named Puti Reno Raudhatul Jannah Thaib at birth. She studied agriculture at Andalas University in Padang. Her poetry collections include *Bianglala* (1973), *Dua Warna* (with Hamid Jabbar, 1975), *Terlupa dari Mimpi* (1980), *Sunting* (with Yvonne de Fretes) and *Nyanyian Anak Cucu* (2000).

Usmar Ismail (Bukittinggi, West Sumatra, March 20, 1921–Jakarta, January 2, 1971) studied cinematography at the University of California at Los Angeles. He was a journalist, chief editor of *Arena* and chair of the Indonesian Journalists' Association (PWI). However, he is better known as a director and screenwriter. He is honored in the naming of the Haji Usmar Ismail Film Center, where Sinamatek, the first film archive center in Indonesia and Southeast Asia, is located. He wrote many plays and essays. His poetry collection is *Puntung Berasap* (1950).

Walujati (Sukabumi, West Java, December 5, 1924–date and place of death unknown) also uses the name Wiesye. She studied at Meer Uitgebreid Lager Onderwijs (MULO) junior high school in Sukabumi and at Hogereburger School (HBS) secondary school in Bogor. Her works were published in *Gema Tanah Air* (1948), *Pujani* (1951), *Seserpih Pinang Sepucuk Sirih* (1979), *Tonggak 1* (1987) and *Ungu: Antologi Puisi Wanita Penyair Indonesia* (1990).

Warih Wisatsana (Bandung, West Java, April 20, 1965) writes poetry and art reviews. He is the curator and manager of the cultural center Bentara Budaya Bali. He received the SIH Award in 2004 for his poetry. Several of his poems have been translated into foreign languages. His poetry collections include *Ikan Terbang Tak Berkawan* (2003) and *May Fire and Other Poems* in the BTW series (trilingual: Indonesian, English, German, 2015).

Wayan Sunarta (Denpasar, Bali, June 22, 1975), nicknamed "Jengki," graduated in cultural anthropology from Udayana University in Bali. He received the Widya Pataka Award from the governor of Bali for his contributions to the Balinese arts community. He writes short stories, novels and art reviews. His poetry collections include *Pada Lingkar Putingmu* (2005) and *Impian Usai* (2007).

Wiji Thukul (Kampung Sorogenen, Surakarta, August 26, 1963–kidnapped July 27, 1998, and presumed to have been killed sometime thereafter) was a laborer and was active in the Reformasi movement. A phrase from one of his poems, *"Hanya satu kata, lawan!"* ("Just one word, resist!"), was adopted by the demonstrators. He disappeared in 1998. He received the Encourage Award from the Wertheim Foundation in the Netherlands (1991) and the Yap Thiam Hien Award (2002). His poems have appeared in domestic and foreign publications. His works include *Puisi Pelo* (1984), *Kicau Kepodang* (1993), *Darma dan Lain-Lain* (1994), *Thukul Pulanglah* (2000) and *Aku Ingin Jadi Peluru* (2000).

Wilson Tjandinegara (Makassar, South Sulawesi, December 20, 1946) is a poet and translator of Mandarin. Many of his works have been published in the Mandarin newspaper *Harian Indonesia*. His collections of poetry include *Puisi Untukmu* (1996), *Cisadane* (1996) and *Rumah Panggung di Kampung Halaman* (1999). He compiled an anthology of classic Tang Dynasty poetry, *Antologi Sajak Klasik Dinasti Tang (Versi Modern) Mandarin-Indonesia* (2001), and has edited several anthologies of works by Chinese writers.

Wing Kardjo (Garut, West Java, April 23, 1937–Japan, March 19, 2002) studied French at Padjadjaran University and then was awarded a diploma for French literature from the Institute for Foreign Teachers of French (Institut des professeurs de français à l'étranger) in Paris. Later he returned to Paris to earn a doctorate at Paris Diderot University. He wrote poetry, essays, novellas and biographies. His poetry collections include *Selembar Daun* (1974), *Perumahan* (1975), *Fragmen Malam* (1975) and *Pohon Hayat: Sejemput Haiku* (2002). He also translated French poetry, in *Sajak-sajak Perancis Modern dalam Dua Bahasa* (1975).

Wowok Hesti Prabowo (Purwodadi, Central Java, April 16, 1963) studied chemical engineering at Syekh Yusuf Islamic University in Tangerang. He is the founder of the Roda-Roda Budaya culture group and the Gerakan Sastra Buruh labor movement. He was chair of the Indonesian Literature Community (1996–1999). His poetry collections include *Rumah Petak* (with Dingu Rilesta, 1996), *Trotoar* (1996), *Presiden dari Negeri Pabrik* (1999) and *Buruh Gugat (Lahirnya Revolusi)* (2000).

Yogi (Abdul Rivai) (Bonjo, West Sumatra, July 1, 1896–Jakarta, April 4, 1983) was the pen name of Abdul Rivai. He studied at a government school in Lubuk Sikaping and took a teacher training course before becoming an assistant teacher. His poems were published in *Gubahan* (1930), *Puspa Aneka* (1931), *Puisi Baru* (1946) and *Pujangga Baru: Prosa dan Puisi* (1963).

Yudhistira A.N.M. (Ardi Nugraha Moelyana) Massardi (Subang, West Java, February 28, 1954) began writing when he was in junior high school. He has been a journalist with *Tempo* and an editor for *Jakarta Jakarta, Editor, Humor, Indonesia Visual Mandiri* and *Tiras*. He was deputy head editor of *Lelaki* magazine (1976–1978). He writes poetry, short stories, novels, plays and literary essays. His short story collection is *Wawancara dengan Rahwana* (1982). His most popular novel is *Arjuna Mencari Cinta* (1977), which has two sequels, *Arjuna Mencari Cinta II* (1980) and *Arjuna Wiwahahaha . . . !* (1984); it won the Buku Utama Foundation Award for the Best Novel for Young People in 1977. His other novel is *Mencoba Tidak Menyerah* (1996), which was originally entitled *Aku Bukan Komunis* and won an award in the Jakarta Arts Council Novel Competition in

1977. He also has two poetry collections: *Sajak Sikat Gigi,* selected by the Jakarta Arts Council as the best book of poetry in 1976–1977 and later published by Pustaka Jaya in 1983; and *Rudi Jalak Gugat* (1982). His anthology *99 Sajak* (2015) won the Poetry Day Award in 2015. His plays *Wot* (1977) and *Ke* (1978) received awards in the Jakarta Arts Council Playwriting Competition.

Zeffry J. Alkatiri (Jakarta, August 30, 1960) studied and then taught Russian in the Faculty of Letters at the University of Indonesia in Jakarta. He earned a graduate degree in American Studies at the University of Indonesia (1997). His poetry collection *Dari Batavia sampai Jakarta 1619–1999: Sejarah dan Kebudayaan Betawi-Jakarta dalam Sajak* received first prize as Best Poetry Book from the Taman Ismail Marzuki Art Center (2000) and the best book from the Buku Utama Foundation (2002). His poetry collection *Postkolonial dan Wisata Sejarah* (2012) won the Khatulistiwa Literary Award in 2012.

Zen Hae (Jakarta, April 12, 1970) studied in the Department of Indonesian Language and Literature at Institut Keguruan dan Ilmu Pendidikan (IKIP) in Jakarta. He was a member of the Jakarta Arts Council (2006–2012). He also writes prose and reviews. His books include a collection of short stories, *Rumah Kawin* (2004), and a poetry collection, *Paus Merah Jambu* (2007), which won an award from *Tempo* magazine for the best book of the year (2007). His most recent book is another collection of short stories, *The Red Bowl and Other Stories,* published by By the Way Books in Indonesian, English and German (2015). Currently he is curator for literature at the Salihara Arts Community in Jakarta.

Publication History and Translators

(in alphabetical order by first name of author)

A. Kohar Ibrahim *Inspections (Pemeriksaan)*, translated by John H. McGlynn; *Kreasi*, 1998 (37). *You Appear (Nampaknya)*, translated by John H. McGlynn; *Kreasi*, 1998 (37).

A.M. Daeng Mijala *Laborer (Buruh)*, translated by Harry Aveling; *Pudjangga Baru*, June 1937 (IV/12).

A. Mustofa Bisri *If You Are Forever (Kalau Kau Sibuk Kapan Kau Sempat)*, translated by John McGlynn; *Ohoi: Kumpulan Puisi-puisi Balsem K.H.A. Mustofa Bisri*, Sapardi Djoko Damono (ed.), Pustaka Firdaus, Jakarta, 1991.

Abdul Hadi W.M. *Elegy (Elegi)*, translated by Harry Aveling; *Horison*, 2002 (XXXV/4). *Near God (Tuhan Kita Begitu Dekat)*, translated by Harry Aveling; *Horison*, 2002 (XXXV/4).

Abidah el-Khalieqy *My Yearning Is Queen (Rinduku Ratu)*, translated by Laura Noszlopy; *Selendang Pelangi: 17 Penyair Perempuan Indonesia*, Toeti Heraty (ed.); IndonesiaTera, Magelang, 2006.

Abrar Yusra *Unnamed Melody (Senandung Tak Bernama)*, translated by Harry Aveling; *Siul*, Abrar Yusra; Puisi Indonesia, Jakarta, 1975.

Acep Zamzam Noor *Kumbasari Market in Denpasar (Pasar Kumbasari, Denpasar)*, translated by John H. McGlynn; *Di Atas Umbria: Sajak-Sajak 1991–1997*, Acep Zamzam Noor; Penerbit Indonesia Tera, Magelang, 1999. *In Cipasung Town (Cipasung)*, translated by John H. McGlynn; *Jalan Menuju Rumahmu: Pilihan Sajak Acep Zamzam Noor*, Pamusuk Eneste (ed.); PT Grasindo, Jakarta, 2004. *A Poet Once More (Menjadi Penyair Lagi)*, translated by John H. McGlynn; *Menjadi Penyair Lagi*, Acep Zamzam Noor; Pustaka Azan, Bandung, 2007.

Afrizal Malna *The Running Century (Abad yang Berlari)*, translated by Andy Fuller; *Abad yang Berlari*, Afrizal Malna; Lembaga Penerbit Altermed Yayasan Lingkaran Merahputih, Jakarta, 1984. *Asia Reads (Asia Membaca)*, translated by Andy Fuller; *Arsitektur Hujan: Empat kumpulan sajak Afrizal Malna*, Yayasan

Bentang Budaya, Yogyakarta, 1995. *Nappies and an Infusion Bottle (Popok-Popok Bayi dan Botol Infus)*, translated by Andy Fuller; *Arsitektur Hujan*, Afrizal Malna; Yayasan Bentang Budaya, Yogyakarta, 1995.

Agam Wispi *Communist (Komunis +1)*, translated by John H. McGlynn; *Pulang*, unpublished collection of poems by Agam Wispi. *The Death of a Farmer (Matinya seorang Petani)*, translated by John H. McGlynn; *Matinja seorang Petani*, Agam Wispi et al.; 1961. *Going Home (Pulang)*, translated by John H. McGlynn; *Pulang*, collection of poems by Agam Wispi, not yet published.

Agus R. Sarjono *Fake Poem (Sajak Palsu)*, translated by Deborah Cole; *Horison Sastra Indonesia 1, Kitab Puisi*, Taufiq Ismail et al. (eds.); Horison Kaki Langit, The Ford Foundation, Jakarta, 2001. *Rendezvous*, translated by Deborah Cole; *Horison*, 2002 (XXXV/4). *Moving House (Syair Pindah Rumah)*, translated by Greg Harris and Nelden Djakababa; *Horison*, 2002 (XXXV/4).

Ahda Imran *Pidie*, translated by Joan Suyenaga; *Penunggang Kuda Negeri Malam: Kumpulan 70 Sajak Terpilih*, Ahda Imran; Penerbit Akar Indonesia, Yogyakarta, collaboration with Selasar Sunaryo Art Space, 2008.

Ahmaddun Y. Herfanda *Corn Seller (Gadis Penjual Jagung Bakar)*, translated by John McGlynn; *Tugu Antologi Puisi 32 Penyair Yogya*, Linus Suryadi (ed.); Dewan Kesenian Yogya and Barata Offset, Yogyakarta, 1986.

Ajamuddin Tifani *Red Henna Moon (Bulan Pacar Merah)*, translated by Annie Tucker; *Tanah Perjanjian, Antologi Puisi Ajamuddin Tifani*, Hasta in collaboration with Yayasan Bengkel Seni '87, Jakarta, 2005.

Ali Hasjmy *Beggar (Pengemis)*, translated by Marjorie Suanda; *Dewan Sajak*, Centrale Courant, Medan, 1940. *Regret (Menyesal)*, translated by Harry Aveling; *Pedoman Masyarakat*. 1954.

Amal Hamzah *The Sea (Laut)*, translated by Annie Tucker; *Panji Pustaka*, 15 April 1943 (14/XXI). *A Reflection of Life (Pancaran Hidup)*, translated by Annie Tucker; *Panca Raya*, July 1946 (17/I, 15).

Amir Hamzah *For You Only (Padamu Jua)*, translated by John H. McGlynn; *Nyanyi Sunyi*, PB/PR 1937, Amir Hamzah; Dian Rakyat, Jakarta, 1985 (first edition, 1937). *Swept Away (Hanyut Aku)*, translated by John H. McGlynn; *Nyanyi Sunyi*, Amir Hamzah; *Nyanyi Sunyi*, PB/PR 1937, Amir Hamzah; Dian Rakyat, Jakarta, 1985 (First publishing, 1937). *I Stand (Berdiri Aku)*, translated by John H. McGlynn; *Buah Rindu*, PB/PR 1941, Amir Hamzah; Pustaka Rakyat, Jakarta, 1959. *Object of Longing (Buah Rindu II)*, translated by John H. McGlynn; *Buah Rindu*, PB/PR 1941, Amir Hamzah; Pustaka Rakyat, Jakarta, 1959.

Anil Hukma *Abortion (Aborsi)*, translated by Deborah Cole; *Selendang Pelangi: 17 Penyair Perempuan Indonesia*, Toeti Heraty (ed.); IndonesiaTera, Magelang, 2006. *Poetry Suppressed by News (Puisi Tertindis Berita)*, translated by Deborah Cole; *Selendang Pelangi: 17 Penyair Perempuan Indonesia*, Toeti Heraty (ed.); IndonesiaTera, Magelang, 2006.

Aoh Kartahadimadja *Lost Love (Kehilangan Mestika)*, translated by Harry Aveling; *Gema Tanah Air 1*, H.B. Jassin (ed.); Balai Pustaka, Jakarta, 1948. *If You Knew (Kalau Tahu)*, translated by Harry Aveling; *Zenith*, June 1952 (6/II).

Apip Mustopa *An Old Dove (Seekor Burung Dara Tua)*, translated by Andy Fuller; *Budaya Jaya*, July 1976 (98/IX).

Ari Pahala Hutabarat *Love Story (Dongeng Cinta)*, translated by Marjorie Suanda; *Dari Bumi Lada*, Iswadi Pratama et al. (eds.); Komite Sastra Dewan Kesenian Lampung, Bandar Lampung, 1996.

Arifin C. Noer *Good Morning, Jajang (Selamat Pagi, Jajang)*, translated by Deborah Cole; *Selamat Pagi, Jajang: Sajak-Sajak Arifin C. Noer*, Puisi Indonesia, Jakarta, 1979. *A Hot Cup of Tea (Secangkir Teh Panas)*, translated by Deborah Cole; *Selamat Pagi, Jajang: Sajak-Sajak Arifin C. Noer*, Puisi Indonesia, Jakarta, 1979.

Armijn Pane *The Tranquility of Nothing (Tenangan Tiada)*, translated by Annie Tucker; *Pudjangga Baru*, August 1935 (III/2). *Diamond Eyes (Mata Berlian)*, translated by Annie Tucker; *Pudjangga Baru*, June 1936 (III/12).

Aslan Abidin *Religion, 3 (Religi 3)*, translated by John H. McGlynn; *Bahaya Laten Malam Pengantin*, Aslan Abidin; Ininnawa, Makassar, 2008. *Sun, Sand, the Beach, and Genitalia (Matahari, Pasir, Pantai dan Kemaluan)*, translated by John H. McGlynn; *Temu Penyair Makassar*, Dewan Kesenian Makassar, 1999.

Asmara Hadi *A New Vitality (Hidup Baru)*, translated by Harry Aveling; *Pudjangga Baru*, July 1937 (V/I). *Today's Generation (Generasi Sekarang)*, translated by Marjorie Suanda; *Pudjangga Baru*, May–June 1938 (V/11–12).

Badruddin Emce *The Spicy Sensation of Ma Sum's Food Stall (Rasa Pedas dari Warung Yu Sum)*, translated by Deborah Cole; *Dari Negeri Poci 3*, Adri Darmadji Woko et al. (eds.); Tiara, Jakarta, 1996.

Basuki Gunawan *The Train (Kereta Api)*, translated by Keth Foulcher; *Konfrontasi*, July August 1955 (7).

Beni Setia *Bomb's Feelings (Perasaan Bom)*, translated by Deborah Cole; *Dinamika Gerak: Sajak Beni Setia*, PT Pustakakarya Grafikatama, Jakarta, 1990.

Bibsy Soenharjo *Turtle in the Desert (Kura-Kura di Gurun Pasir)*, translated by John H. McGlynn; *Seserpih Pinang Sepucuk Sirih,* Toeti Heraty (ed.), Pustaka Jaya, Jakarta, 1979.

Binhad Nurohmad *Gigolo (Kuda Ranjang)*, translated by Marjorie Suanda; Binhad Nurohmad; Melibas, Jakarta, 2004. *Mattress Stud (Kuda Ranjang),* translated by Marjorie Suanda; *Kuda Ranjang,* Binhad Nurohmad; Melibas, Jakarta, 2004.

Budiman S. Hartojo *Waiting and Taking Leave (Menunggu dan Pamit),* translated by Deborah Cole; *Sebelum Tidur,* Budiman S. Hartojo; Dunia Pustaka Jaya, Jakarta, 1977. *Before You Were Late (Sebelum Engkau Terlambat),* translated by Deborah Cole; *Horison Sastra Indonesia 1, Kitab Puisi,* Taufiq Ismail, et al. (eds.); Horison Kaki Langit, The Ford Foundation, Jakarta, 2001.

Cecep Syamsul Hari *Anne,* translated by Harry Aveling; *Efrosina,* Cecep Syamsul Hari; Orfeus Books, Cimahi, 2002.

Chairil Anwar *Between Karwang and Bekasi (Karawang-Bekasi),* translated by John H. McGlynn; *Yang Terempas dan Yang Putus,* Pustaka Rakyat, 1949. *I (Aku),* translated by John H. McGlynn; *Aku ini Binatang Jalang,* Chairil Anwar, Pamusuk Eneste (ed.); Gramedia, Jakarta, 1986. *Prayer (Doa),* translated by John H. McGlynn; *Aku ini Binatang Jalang,* Chairil Anwar, Pamusuk Eneste (ed.); Gramedia, Jakarta, 1986. *Twilight at a Small Harbor (Senja di Pelabuhan Kecil),* translated by John McGlynn; *Aku ini Binatang Jalang,* Chairil Anwar, Pamusuk Eneste (ed.); Gramedia, Jakarta, 1986.

Cok Sawitri *prayer maker (tukang doa),* translated by John H. McGlynn; *Selendang Pelangi: 17 Penyair Perempuan Indonesia,* Toeti Heraty (ed.); IndonesiaTera, Magelang, 2006.

D. Kemalawati *Red Pools in Beutong Ateuh, Aceh (Kolam Merah di Beutong Ateuh),* translated by John H. McGlynn and Debra Yatim; *Surat dari Negeri Tak Bertuan;* Lapena, Banda Aceh, 2006.

D. Zawawi Imron *Tears Are My Ancestors (Nenek Moyangku Air Mata),* translated by Deborah Cole; *Nenek Moyangku Air Mata,* D. Zawawi Imron; Balai Pustaka, Jakarta, 1985. *I Am Your Blood, Madura (Madura, Akulah Darahmu),* translated by Deborah Cole; *Bantalku Ombak Selimutku Angin: Empat Kumpulan Sajak D. Zawawi Imron 1963–1995,* Abdul Wachid B.S. (ed.); Ittaqa Press, Yogyakarta, 1996. *Mother (Ibu),* translated by Deborah Cole; *Bantalku Ombak Selimutku Angin: Empat Kumpulan Sajak 1963–1995 D. Zawawi Imron,* Abdul Wachid B.S. (ed.); Ittaqa Press, Yogyakarta, 1996.

Dami N. Toda *Darmitea 10,* translated by Joan Suyenaga; *Penyair Muda di Depan Forum*, Dewan Kesenian Jakarta, 1976.

Darmanto Jatman *Testimony (Testimoni),* translated by John H. McGlynn; *Sajak-Sajak Putih*, anthology of work by Darmanto Jatman, Djadjak MD, and Darmadji Sosoropuro; Studi Sastra Kristen Yogya, 1965. *A Wife (Istri),* translated by John H. McGlynn; *Isteri: Pilihan Sajak 1958–1997,* Darmanto Jatman; Grasindo, Jakarta, 1997. *Honolulu Impressions (Impresi Honolulu),* translated by John H. McGlynn; *Isteri: Pilihan Sajak 1958–1997,* Darmanto Jatman; Grasindo, Jakarta, 1997.

Dhenok Kristianti *A Bowl of Red Beans (Semangkuk Kacang Merah),* translated by Thomas J. Sands; *Tonggak Antologi Puisi Indonesia Modern 4,* Linus Suryadi (ed.); PT Gramedia, Jakarta, 1987.

Dinullah Rayes *Metaphor (Metafora),* translated by Deborah Cole; *Jakarta dalam Puisi Mutakhir,* Korrie Layun Rampan et al. (eds.); Dinas Kebudayaan Provinsi DKI Jakarta, Jakarta, 2000.

Dodong Jiwapraja *Reading the Scriptures (Mengaji),* translated by Harry Aveling; *Laut Biru Langit Biru: Bunga Rampai Sastra Indonesia Mutakhir*, Ajip Rosidi (ed.); PT Dunia Pustaka Jaya, Jakarta, 1977.

Dorothea Rosa Herliany *Marriage of a Prostitute with No Body (Nikah Pelacur Tak Punya Tubuh),* translated by Harry Aveling; *Para Pembunuh Waktu*, Dorothea Rosa Herliany, Joko Pinurbo and Harry Aveling (ed.); Bentang Budaya, Yogyakarta, 2002. *Married to a Knife (Nikah Pisau),* translated by Harry Aveling; *Para Pembunuh Waktu*, Dorothea Rosa Herliany, Joko Pinurbo and Harry Aveling (ed.); Bentang Budaya, Yogyakarta, 2002. *Wedding Diary (Buku Harian Perkawinan),* translated by Harry Aveling; *Para Pembunuh Waktu,* Dorothea Rosa Herliany, Joko Pinurbo and Harry Aveling (eds.); Bentang Budaya, Yogyakarta, 2002.

Dullah *For 15 Friends (Kepada 15 Kawan),* translated by Marjorie Suanda; *Seniman,* 1947 (No. 1).

Eka Budianta *Reflection of a Teacher (Renungan Bapak Guru),* translated by Deborah Cole; *Sejuta Milyar Satu,* Eka Budianta; Penerbit Arcan, Jakarta, 1984. *Sangkuriang,* translated by Deborah Cole; *Sejuta Milyar Satu,* Eka Budianta; Penerbit Arcan, Jakarta, 1984.

Emha Ainun Nadjib *Mathematics (Matematika),* translated by Keith Foulcher; *Tugu Antologi Puisi 32 Penyair Yogya*, Linus Suryadi (ed.); Dewan Kesenian Yogya and Barata Offset, Yogyakarta, 1986. *An Ocean of White (Syair Lautan Jilbab),* translated by Keith Foulcher; *Syair Lautan Jilbab*, Emha Ainun Nadjib; Sipress, Yogyakarta, 1989.

F. Rahardi *Prostitute's Oath (Soempah WTS)*, translated by Deborah Cole; *Soempah WTS*, F. Rahardi; Puisi Indonesia, Jakarta, 1983. *Interview with Tuyul (Wawancara dengan Tuyul)*, translated by Deborah Cole; *Tuyul: Kumpulan Sajak 1985–1989*, F. Rahardi; Pustaka Sastra, Jakarta, 1990. *An Old Woman on Independence Day (Seorang Nenek di Hari Proklamasi Kemerdekaan)*, translated by Deborah Cole; *Tuyul: Kumpulan Sajak 1985–1989*, F. Rahardi; Pustaka Sastra, Jakarta, 1990.

Fakhrunnas M.A. Jabbar *Looking in on History (Menjenguk Sejarah)*, translated by Marjorie Suanda; *Dari Bumi Lada*, Iswadi Pratama et al. (eds.); Komite Sastra Dewan Kesenian Lampung, Bandar Lampung, 1996.

Frans Nadjira *Crazy Nyoman (Si Nyoman Gila)*, translated by Thomas Hunter; *Jendela Jadikan Sajak*, Frans Nadjira; Penerbit Padma, Yogyakarta, 2003.

Fridolin Ukur *Death and Resurrection (Kematian dan Kebangkitan)*, translated by Harry Aveling; *Darah dan Peluh*, Fridolin Ukur; Badan Penerbit Kristen, Jakarta, 1962.

Goenawan Mohamad *Husband (Suami)*, translated by John H. McGlynn; *Zaman*, 6–12 July 1980 (41/I). *Supposing We Were in Sarajevo (Misalkan Kita di Sarajevo)*, translated by John H. McGlynn; *Misalkan Kita di Sarajevo*, Goenawan Mohamad; Kalam, Jakarta, 1998. *About That Man Killed Sometime around Election Day (Tentang Seorang yang Terbunuh di sekitar Hari Pemilihan Umum)*, translated by John H. McGlynn; *Goenawan Mohamad: Sajak-Sajak Lengkap 1961–2001*, Goenawan Mohamad; Metafor Publishing, Jakarta, 2001. *Quartrain about a Pot (Kwatrin Tentang Sebuah Poci)*, translated by John H. McGlynn; *Goenawan Mohamad: Sajak-Sajak Lengkap 1961–2001*, Goenawan Mohamad; Metafor Publishing, Jakarta, 2001.

Gus tf *Malin*, translated by John H. McGlynn; *Daging Akar*, Gus tf, Kompas, Jakarta, 2005. *Scars of Metamorphosis (Luka Metamorfosa)*, translated by John H. McGlynn; *Sangkar Daging: Sajak-Sajak 1980–1995*, Gus tf; Grasindo, 1997. *Mythology (Mitologi)*, translated by John H. McGlynn; *Daging Akar*, Gus tf, Penerbit Kompas, Jakarta, 2005.

H.B. Jassin *Dreams and Life (Mimpi dan Hidup)*, translated by Harry Aveling; *Darah Laut Kumpulan Cerpen dan Puisi H.B. Jassin*, H.B. Jassin; Balai Pustaka, Jakarta, 1997.

Hs. Djurtatap *The Neck and the Tie (Leher dan Dasi)*, translated by Andy Fuller; *Parade Puisi Indonesia*, Pasar Seni, Jakarta, 1993. *The Sea in My Heart (Kini Ada*

Laut di Hatiku), translated by Andy Fuller; *Parade Puisi Indonesia,* Hamid Jabbar and Slamet Sukirnanto (ed.); PT Global Sarana Media Nusantara, Jakarta, 1993.

Hamdy Salad *Grief in the Timor Sea (Perkabungan di Laut Timor),* translated by Deborah Cole; *Sebutir Debu di Tepi Jurang,* Hamdy Salad; Penerbit Logika, Yogyakarta, 2005.

Hamid Jabbar *My Indonesia (Indonesiaku),* translated by Andy Fuller; *Indonesiaku: Sepilihan Sajak Hamid Jabbar,* Yayasan Indonesia and Majalah Horison, Jakarta, 2004. *Proclamation, 2 (Proklamasi, 2),* translated by Keith Foulcher; *Indonesiaku: Sepilihan Sajak Hamid Jabbar,* Yayasan Indonesia and Majalah *Horison,* Jakarta, 2004. *Song of a Colonized Land (Nyanyian Negeri Jajahan),* translated by Keith Foulcher; *Indonesiaku: Sepilihan Sajak Hamid Jabbar,* Yayasan Indonesia and Majalah Horison, Jakarta, 2004.

Hamidah (Fatimah Hasan Delais) *Parting (Berpisah),* translated by John H. McGlynn; *Pujangga Baru,* No 10 Th II, April 1935. *The Soul's Lament (Keluhan Kalbu),* translated by Harry Aveling; *Pedoman Masjarakat,* November 1936 (39/ II, 18). *Contemplating the Power of a Child (Merenungi Kesaktian Anak),* translated by Annie Tucker; *Pudjangga Baru,* July 1937 (1/V).

Harijadi S. Hartowardojo *Encounter (Pertemuan),* translated by Joan Suyenaga; *Siasat,* 2 December 1951 (V/242).

Hartojo Andangdjadja *Strong Women (Perempuan-Perempuan Perkasa),* translated by Harry Aveling; *Buku Puisi,* Hartojo Andangdjaja; PT Dunia Pustaka Jaya, Jakarta, 1973.

Hersri Setiawan *Notes on the Change of Years (Catatan Ganti Tahun),* translated by John H. McGlynn; *Inilah Pamflet Itu,* Hersri Setiawan; Yayasan Pondok Rakyat and Yayasan Tifa, Yogyakarta, 2007.

Hidjaz Yamani *Martapura River (Kali Martapura),* translated by Harry Aveling; *Tanah Huma,* anthology of work by Hidjaz Yamani, Yustan Aziddin, D. Zauhidhie; Pustaka Jaya, Jakarta, 1978.

Husain Landitjing *Bone Bay (Teluk Bone),* translated by Joan Suyenaga; *Basis,* December 1960 (3/X).

Ibrahim Sattah *Splash (Tempias),* translated by Marjorie Suanda; *Horison,* February 1972 (2/VII). *Dandandid,* translated by Marjorie Suanda; *Hai Ti Sejumlah Sajak Ibrahim Sattah,* CV Bumi Pustaka, Pekanbaru, 1981. *The Split Stone (Batu Belah),* translated by Marjorie Suanda; *Hai Ti Sejumlah Sajak Ibrahim Sattah,* CV Bumi Pustaka, Pekanbaru, 1981.

Iman Budhi Santosa *The Widow Who Peddles Vegetables between Yogya and Imogiri (Janda Penjual Sayur Imogiri-Yogya)*, translated by Deborah Cole; via *Horison Sastra Indonesia 1, Kitab Puisi*, Taufiq Ismail et al. (eds.); Horison Kaki Langit, The Ford Foundation, Jakarta, 2001. *Queen of the South Sea (Ratu Selatan)*, translated by Deborah Cole; *Matahari-Matahari Kecil: Pilihan Sajak 1969–2003*, Iman Budhi Santosa, Gramedia Widiasarana Indonesia, Jakarta, 2004.

Indonesia O'Galelano *Maritme Epic (Epos Laut)*, translated by Harry Aveling; *Sastra*, 1964 (IV/1).

Inggit Putria Marga *Before I Leave (Sebelum Aku Pergi)*, translated by Joan Suyenaga; *Surat Putih 2: 25 Perempuan Penyair*, Jamal D. Rahman (ed.); Risalah Badai, Jakarta, 2002.

Intojo *New Emotions (Rasa Baru)*, translated by Harry Aveling; *Pudjangga Baru*, April 1937 (10/IV).

Isbedy Stiawan Z.S. *You Say (Kau Bilang Tapi)*, translated by John H. McGlynn; *Ode Sajak-Sajak Reformasi Penyair Sumbagsel*, Ari Setya Ardhi (ed.); Jambi Independent Press, Jambi, 1998.

Iskandar Leo *The Sea I (Laut I)*, translated by Deborah Cole; *Menggantang Warta Nasib: Antologi Puisi Pekanbaru 92*, Dasri Al-Mubary (ed.); BTB collaborating with Departemen Pendidikan dan Kebudayaan, Pekanbaru, 1992. *The Sea (Laut II)*, translated by Deborah Cole; *Menggantang Warta Nasib: Antologi Puisi Pekanbaru 92*, Dasri Al-Mubary (ed.); BTB collaborating with Departemen Pendidikan dan Kebudayaan, Pekanbaru, 1992.

Isma Sawitri *A Mother's Heart (Hati Bunda)*, translated by Annie Tucker; *Indonesia*, July–September 1961 (3/XII). *North Coast (Pantai Utara)*, translated by John H. McGlynn; *Sastra*, 1964 (IV/3).

Iwan Simatupang *Rose Pink in Jasmine (Merah Jambu di Melati)*, translated by Joan Suyenaga; *Ziarah Malam: Sajak-Sajak 1952–1967*, Oyon Sofyan and S. Samsoerizal Dar (ed.); Grasindo, Jakarta, 1993. *What Does the Star Say in the Sea (Apa Kata Bintang Di Laut)*, translated by Joan Suyenaga; *Ziarah Malam: Sajak-Sajak 1952–1967*, Oyon Sofyan and S. Samsoerizal Dar (ed.); Grasindo, Jakarta, 1993.

Iyut Fitra *Here the Past Is Killed (Di Sini Masa Lalu Dibunuh)*, translated by John H. McGlynn; *Singgalang* Daily, 1997. *Lullaby from a Distant Point (Senandung dari Sebuah Tanjung)* translated by Annie Tucker; *Media Indonesia*, 20 February 2000.

J.E. Tatengkeng *Sangihe Fisherman (Nelayan Sangihe)*, translated by Harry Aveling; *Rindu Dendam*, J.E. Tatengkeng; Chr. Drukk "Djawi", Solo, 1934.

Sunday Morning Invitation (Panggilan Pagi Minggu), translated by Harry Aveling; *Rindu Dendam*, J.E. Tatengkeng; Chr. Drukk "Djawi", Solo, 1935.

Jamal D. Rahman *Children of Tobacco (Anak-Anak Tembakau)*, translated by Joan Suyenaga; *Reruntuhan Cahaya*, Jamal D. Rahman; Bentang Budaya, Yogyakarta, 2003.

John Waromi *Wawini in the Sound of Fire (Wawini Dalam Suara Api)*, translated by John H. McGlynn; unpublished manuscript, included and translated in http://www.whatispoetry.net/wp-content/uploads/2013/04/waromi.pdf. *Rats (Tikus-tikus)*, translated by John H. McGlynn; unpublished manuscript, included and translated in http://cordite.org.au/poetry/indonesia/rats-tikus-tikus/.

Joko Pinurbo *Trousers, 1 (Celana 1)*, translated by Linda Owens; *Celana*, Joko Pinurbo; IndonesiaTera, Magelang, 1999. *May (Mei)*, translated by John H. McGlynn; *Pacar Senja*, Joko Pinurbo, Pamusuk Eneste (ed.), PT Grasindo, Jakarta, 2005. *Patrol (Patroli)*, translated by Harry Aveling; *Pacar Senja*, Joko Pinurbo, Pamusuk Eneste (ed.), PT Grasindo, Jakarta, 2005.

Kirdjomuljo *Limestone Quarryman (Penggali Batu Kapur)*, translated by Harry Aveling; *Romansa Perjalanan*, Kirdjomuljo; Pustaka Jaya, Jakarta, 1979. *Wreath (Karangan Bunga)*, translated by Harry Aveling; *Tugu Antologi Puisi 32 Penyair Yogya*, Linus Suryadi (ed.); Dewan Kesenian Yogya and Barata Offset, Yogyakarta, 1986.

Klara Akustia *Between Thermopylae and Stalingrad (Antara Thermopylae dan Stalingrad)*, translated by Marjorie Suanda; *Rangsang Detik: Kumpulan Sadjak Periode 1949–1957*, Klara Akustia, Jajasan Pembaruan, Djakarta, 1957. *March to Socialism (Mars ke Sosialisme)*, translated by Marjorie Suanda; *Rangsang Detik: Kumpulan Sadjak Periode 1949–1957*, Klara Akustia, Jajasan Pembaruan, Djakarta, 1957.

Korrie Layun Rampan *Yogyakarta*, translated by Greg Harris and Nelden Djakababa; *Basis*, April 1982 (4/XXXI). *The Moon Rite (Upacara Bulan)*, translated by Greg Harris and Nelden Djakababa; *Dari Negeri Poci 2*, F. Rahardi (ed.); Pustaka Sastra, Jakarta, 1996.

Kuntowijoyo *The Universe's Mysticism? (Suluk Awang Uwung)*, translated by Andy Fuller; *Laut Biru Langit Biru: Bunga Rampai Sastra Indonesia Mutakhir*, Ajip Rosidi (ed.); PT Dunia Pustaka Jaya, Jakarta, 1977. *The Men (Lelaki)*, translated by Andy Fuller; *Tonggak Antologi Puisi Indonesia Modern 3*, Linus Suryadi (ed.); PT Gramedia, Jakarta, 1987.

Kuslan Budiman *The Plum Tree (Pohon Kedondong)*, translated by John H. McGlynn; *Bulan sedang Mati*, unpublished manuscript. *Beijing to Shanghai*

585

(Beijing-Shanghai), translated by John H. McGlynn; *Lembaran Pudar,* unpublished manuscript.

L.K. Ara *Kur Lak Lak,* translated by Harry Aveling; *Kur Lak Lak,* LK Ara; Balai Pustaka, Jakarta, 1982.

Leon Agusta *Meeting (Pertemuan),* translated by John H. McGlynn; *Horison,* No. 1 Th. X, January 1975. *Night (Malam),* translated by Marjorie Suanda; *Hukla,* Puisi Indonesia, Jakarta, 1979.

Linus Suryadi *Night Is Possessed by Grief, after Shouted Words. (Malam Dirasuk Duka Habis Diseru Kata),* translated by Annie Tucker; *Langit Kelabu: Sajak-Sajak 1971–1973–1974,* Linus Suryadi; Balai Pustaka, Jakarta, 1975. *Merapi at Twilight (Senjakala Gunung Merapi),* translated by Annie Tucker; *Langit Kelabu,* Linus Suryadi; Balai Pustaka, Jakarta, 1980.

M. Balfas *Seaman's Party (Pesta Kelasi),* translated by Joan Suyenaga; *Gema Tanah Air,* H.B. Jassin (ed.); Balai Pustaka, Jakarta, 1948.

M. Poppy Donggo Hutagalung *One Day in a Happy Month (Pada Suatu Bulan yang Cerah),* translated by John H. McGlynn; *Sastra,* July 1961 (2/I). *The Old Train (Kereta Tua),* translated by John H. McGlynn; *Sastra,* 1962 (II/4).

M. Taslim Ali *To the Wind, King Wanderer (Kepada Angin Raja Kelana),* translated by Joan Suyenaga; *Pujangga Baru: Prosa dan Puisi,* H.B. Jassin (ed.); Balai Pustaka, Jakarta, 1963.

M.A. Djoehana *Question (Pertanyaan),* translated by Joan Suyenaga; *Pembaroean,* January–February 1946, (I/1–2). *Serenade Interrompue,* translated by Joan Suyenaga; *Pembaroean,* April–May 1946 (I/4–5).

M.A. Iskandar *A Living Skeleton (Rangka Hidup),* translated by Harry Aveling; *Seulawah Antologi Sastra Aceh Sekilas Pintas,* L.K. Ara, Taufiq Ismail, Hasyim Ks. (eds.); Yayasan Nusantara in collaboration with the government of the Special Region of Aceh, 1995.

M.D. Asien *Gambang Semarang,* translated by Joan Suyenaga; *Mimbar Indonesia,* April 1951 (14/V, 7).

Md. Yati *At the Demak Mosque (Di Masjid Demak),* translated by Marjorie Suanda; *Pudjangga Baru,* March 1963 (1/9).

Magusig O. Bungai *Scatter Rice Salt and Ash (Tabur Beras Garam Berabu),* translated by Annie Tucker; *Sansana Anak Naga dan Tahun-Tahun Pembunuhan,* Stichting ISDM Culemborg, Netherlands, 1990. *In Vincennes Forest (Di Hutan Vincenne),* translated by Annie Tucker; *Arena,* 1991 (5).

Mahatmanto *Muhammadiyah Madrasah (Madrasah Muhammadiyah)*, translated by Marjorie Suanda; *Mimbar Indonesia*, 28 January 1948 (II/45).

Mahbub Junaedi *Girl Playing Piano (Gadis Main Piano)*, translated by Joan Suyenaga; *Siasat*, 1952 (383).

Mardi Luhung *My Father Has Gone (Bapakku Telah Pergi)*, translated by Deborah Cole; *Mimbar Penyair Abad 21 Dewan Kesenian Jakarta*, Taufiq Ismail et al. (eds.); Balai Pustaka, Jakarta, 1996. *Newlywed from the Coast (Penganten Pesisir)*, translated by Deborah Cole; *Mimbar Penyair Abad 21 Dewan Kesenian Jakarta*, Taufiq Ismail et al. (eds.); Balai Pustaka, Jakarta, 1996.

Mas Ruscitadewi *Before the Statue of Kwan Im (Di depan Patung Kwan Im)*, translated by Annie Tucker; *Hana Bira*, Mas Ruscitadewi; Yayasan Bali Anyar, Denpasar, 1999.

Maskirbi *Just Tell Her (Katakan Saja Padanya)*, translated by Joan Suyenaga; *Seulawah Antologi Sastra Aceh Sekilas Pintas*, L.K. Ara, Taufiq Ismail, Hasyim Ks. (eds.); Yayasan Nusantara in collaboration with the government of the Special Region of Aceh.

Mathori A. Elwa *Almighty Lust (Yang Maha Syahwat)*, translated by Marjorie Suanda; *Yang Maha Syahwat*, Mathori A Elwa; LKIS, Yogyakarta, 1997.

Medy Loekito *Woman Is the Earth (Wanita adalah Bumi)*, translated by Deborah Cole; *Jakarta Senja Hari*, Medy Loekito; Angkasa Bandung, 1998. *A Dragonfly and a Fish (Seekor Capung dan Seekor Ikan)*, translated by Deborah Cole; *Selendang Pelangi: 17 Penyair Perempuan Indonesia*, Toeti Heraty (ed.); IndonesiaTera, Magelang, 2006.

Mochtar Pabottinggi *For My Father (Kepada Ayahanda)*, translated by John H. McGlynn; *Dalam Rimba Bayang-Bayang*, Mochtar Pabottinggi; Penerbit Buku Kompas, Jakarta, 2003.

Mohammad Diponegoro *A Calligraphy Wall Decoration (Sebuah Kaligrafi dalam Lukisan)*, translated by Harry Aveling; *Panji Masyarakat*, June 1982 (363/21).

Mohammad Yamin *Language, Nation (Bahasa, Bangsa)*, translated by John H. McGlynn; *Jong Sumatra*, February 1921 via *Sandjak-Sandjak Muda Mr. Muhammad Yamin*, Armijn Pane, Firma Rada, 1954. *Shepherd Boy (Gembala)*, translated by John H. McGlynn; *Jong Sumatra* via *Pudjangga Baru*, 1963.

Motinggo Boesje *About Adams (Tentang Adam-Adam)*, translated by Joan Suyenaga; *Tugu Antologi Puisi 32 Penyair Yogya*, Linus Suryadi (ed.); Dewan Kesenian Yogya and Barata Offset, Yogyakarta, 1986. *About Women (Tentang Wanita-Wanita)*, translated by Joan Suyenaga; *Tugu Antologi Puisi 32 Penyair Yogya*, Linus Suryadi (ed.); Dewan Kesenian Yogya and Barata Offset, Yogyakarta, 1986.

Mozasa *My Language (Bahasaku)*, translated by Deborah Cole; *Pudjangga Baru*, April 1937 (10/IV).

Muh. Rustandi Kartakusuma *I Am a Grain of Sand (Aku Sebutir Pasir)*, translated by Harry Aveling; *Rekaman dari Tujuh Daerah*, Muh. Rustandi Kartakusuma; Balai Pustaka, Jakarta, 1952.

Mustofa W. Hasyim *Kindergarten Teacher's Testimony (Kesaksian Guru TK)*, translated by Lauren Zentz; *Republika*, 24 January 1993. *The Flag That Was Ashamed to Fly (Bendera yang Malu Dikibarkan)*, translated by Deborah Cole; *Republika*, Sunday 13 July 1994 (II/171).

Nenden Lilis Aisyah *Bee-Eaters (Orang-Orang Mengulum Lebah)*, translated by John H. McGlynn; *Selendang Pelangi: 17 Penyair Perempuan Indonesia*, Toeti Heraty (ed.); IndonesiaTera, Magelang, 2006. *Ode for Earth (Ode Bumi)*, translated by John H. McGlyyn; *Selendang Pelangi: 17 Penyair Perempuan Indonesia*, Toeti Heraty (ed.); IndonesiaTera, Magelang, 2006.

Nirwan Dewanto *My Childhood Floats on the Sea (Masa Kanak-kanakku Mengambang di Laut)*, translated by John H. McGlynn; *Buku Cacing*, Manuscript, 1986.

Nursjamsu Nasution *Crazy (Gila)*, translated by Annie Tucker; *Kesusasteraan Indonesia di Masa Jepang*, H.B. Jassin (ed.); Balai Pustaka, Jakarta, 1984. *Night Scream (Jeritan Malam)*, translated by Annie Tucker; *Kesusasteraan Indonesia di Masa Jepang*, H.B. Jassin (ed.); Balai Pustaka, Jakarta, 1984.

Oei Sien Tjwan *I Am Learning to Count (Aku Sedang Belajar Berhitung)*, translated by Joan Suyenaga; *Sinar Harapan*, Wednesday 14 July 1976 (5008). *Stars (Bintang Bintang)*, translated by Joan Suyenaga; *Sinar Harapan*, Saturday 22 January 1977 (5008).

Oka Rusmini *Men's Journey (Perjalanan para Lelaki)*, translated by Deborah Cole; *Patiwangi*, Oka Rusmini; Bentang Budaya, Yogyakarta, 2003. *Patiwangi: Renunciation (Patiwangi)*, translated by Deborah Cole; *Patiwangi*, Oka Rusmini; Bentang Budaya, Yogyakarta, 2003.

Omi Intan Naomi *Job Exam (Ujian TK)*, translated by John H. McGlynn; *Dari Negeri Poci 3*, Adri Darmadji Woko et al. (eds.), Tiara, Jakarta, 1996. *The City (Kota)*, translated by John H. McGlynn; *Angkatan 2000 dalam Sastra Indonesia*, Korrie Layun Rampan, R. Masri Sareb Putra (eds.); PT Gramedia Widia Sarana, Jakarta, 2000.

Or. Mandank *Humanity (Manusia)*, translated by Harry Aveling; *Pedoman Masyarakat*, April 1936 (13/II, 27).

P. Sengodjo *Day at MA (Siang di MA.)*, translated by Harry Aveling; *Zenith*, April 1952 (II/4).

Piek Ardijanto Suprijadi *Village Girl (Gadis Desa)*, translated by Harry Aveling; *Sastra*, July 1961 (I/3).

Pitres Sombowadile *Lion on His Throne (Singa Singgasana)*, translated by Joan Suyenaga; *Coelacanth Tak Pernah Mati*, Pitres Sombowadile; Komunitas Sastra Manado, Manado, 2007.

Putu Oka Sukanta *the lonely poems (sajak yang sepi)*, translated by Keith Foulcher; *Tembang si Jalak: Song of the Starling*, Putu Oka Sukanta; Wira Karya, Kuala Lumpur, Malaysia, 1986. *numbers (nomor)*, translated by Keith Foulcher; *Tembang si Jalak: Song of the Starling*, Putu Oka Sukanta; Wira Karya, Kuala Lumpur, Malaysia, 1986.

Rachmat Djoko Pradopo *Rectangular Sun (Matahari Segi Empat)*, translated by Deborah Cole; *Tonggak Antologi Puisi Indonesia Modern 2*, Linus Suryadi (ed.); PT Gramedia, Jakarta, 1987.

Radhar Panca Dahana *Dancing in the Void (Dari Kosong Menjadi Tari)*, translated by Deborah Cole; *Lalu Waktu*, Radhar Panca Dahana; Pustaka Firdaus, Jakarta, 1994. *Killing Coffee in the Morning (Pembunuhan Kopi di Pagi Hari)*, translated by Deborah Cole; *Lalu Waktu*, Radhar Panca Dahana; Pustaka Firdaus, Jakarta, 1994.

Rahman Arge *Bosnian Maggot (Ulat Bosnia)*, translated by Joan Suyenaga; *Malam Puisi di Bulan Puasa*, Slamet Sukirnanto and Hamid Jabbar (eds.); Dewan Kesenian Jakarta, 1994.

Ramadhan K.H. *Fire (Pembakaran)*, translated by John H. McGlynn; *Priangan Si Jelita*, Ramadhan K.H.; IndonesiaTera, Magelang, 2003. *Homeland (Tanah Kelahiran)*, translated by John H. McGlynn; *Priangan Si Jelita*, Ramadhan K.H.; IndonesiaTera, Magelang, 2003. *Song of Loving (Dendang Sayang)*, translated by John H. McGlynn; *Priangan Si Jelita*, Ramadhan K.H.; IndonesiaTera, Magelang, 2003.

Raudal Tanjung Banua *Reading the Map (Kubaca Peta)*, translated by Harry Aveling; *Embun Tajalli, Seikat Sajak dan Cerpen Penulis Yogyakarta*, Divisi Sastra Indonesia, Festival Kesenian Yogya (FKY XII), Yogyakarta, 2000.

Rayani Sriwidodo *Jakarta, Approaching May 21, 1998 (Jakarta, Menjelang 21 Mei 1998)*, translated by Deborah Cole; *Selendang Pelangi: 17 Penyair Perempuan*

589

Indonesia, Toeti Heraty (ed.); IndonesiaTera, Magelang, 2006. *There's Something I Love about Jakarta (Ada yang Kucinta Pada Jakarta)*, translated by Deborah Cole; *Selendang Pelangi: 17 Penyair Perempuan Indonesia*, Toeti Heraty (ed.); IndonesiaTera, Magelang, 2006.

Remy Sylado *Concerned in the New Order (Prihatin Orde Baru)*, translated by Deborah Cole; *Puisi Mbeling*, Remy Sylado; Kepustakaan Populer Gramedia, Jakarta, 2004. *Individualism in Collectivisim (Individualisme dalam Kolektivisme)*, translated by Deborah Cole; *Puisi Mbeling*, Remy Sylado; Kepustakaan Populer Gramedia, Jakarta, 2004. *Intimidation within Democracy (Intimidasi dalam Demokrasi)*, translated by Deborah Cole; *Puisi Mbeling*, Remy Sylado; Kepustakaan Populer Gramedia, Jakarta, 2004.

Rendra *Ballad of the Crucifixion (Balada Penyaliban)*, translated by Harry Aveling; *Kisah*, November 1955 (III/11). *Blues for Bonnie (Blues untuk Bonnie)*, translated by John McGlynn; *Blues untuk Bonnie*, Rendra; Pustaka Jaya, Jakarta, 1976. *Sermon (Khotbah)*, translated by Harry Aveling; *Blues untuk Bonnie*, Rendra; Pustaka Jaya, Jakarta, 1976. *A Pile of Corn (Sajak Seonggok Jagung)*, translated by John H. McGlynn; *Potret Pembangunan dalam Puisi*, Rendra; PT Dunia Pustaka Jaya, Jakarta, 1993. *Song of a Cigar (Sajak Sebatang Lisong)*, translated by Harry Aveling; *Potret Pembangunan dalam Puisi*, Rendra; PT Dunia Pustaka Jaya, Jakarta, 1993.

Rivai Apin *The Last Man (Orang Penghabisan)*, translated by John H. McGlynn; *Pudjangga Baru*, December 1948 (X/6). *Afro Asia in Tokyo (Afro Asia di Tokyo)*, translated by Marjorie Suanda; *Dari Dua Dunia Belum Sudah*, Rivai Apin, Harry Aveling (eds.); Indonesiatera, Magelang, 2004. *From Two Unfinished Worlds (Dari Dua Dunia Belum Sudah)*, translated by Keith Foulcher; *Dari Dua Dunia Belum Sudah*, Rivai Apin, Harry Aveling (eds.); Indonesiatera, Magelang, 2004. *Home from Vacation (Pulang Libur)*, translated by John H. McGlynn; *Dari Dua Dunia Belum Sudah*, Rivai Apin, Harry Aveling (eds.); Indonesiatera, Magelang, 2004.

Roestam Effendi *Not I, the Storyteller (Bukan Beta Bijak Berperi)*, translated by John H. McGlynn; *Pertjikan Permenoengan*, Rustam Effendi, 1926. *Tears (Air Mata)*, translated by Keith Foulcher; *Pertjikan Permenoengan*, Rustam Effendi, 1926.

Rusli Marzuki Saria *A Group of Stories (Sekelumit Riwayat)*, translated by Harry Aveling; *Ada Ratap Ada Nyanyi*, Rusli Marzuki Saria; Puisi Indonesia, 1976.

S. Anantaguna *Portrait of a Communist (Potret Seorang Komunis)*, translated by Harry Aveling; *Gugur Merah: Sehimpunan Puisi Lekra 1950–1965*, Rhoma Dwi Aria Yuliantri, Muhidin M. Dahlan (eds.); Merah Kesumba, Yogyakarta, 2008.

Too Many (Terlalu), translated by Harry Aveling; *Gugur Merah: Sehimpunan Puisi Lekra 1950–1965*, Rhoma Dwi Aria Yuliantri, Muhidin M. Dahlan (eds.); Merah Kesumba, Yogyakarta, 2008.

S. Rukiah *Life's Deceit (Pulasan Hidup)*, translated by John H. McGlynn; *Pudjangga Baru*, April–May 1948, (10–11/IX). *Unable (Tak Sanggup)*, translated by John H. McGlynn; *Pudjangga Baru*, April–May 1948, (10–11/IX). *The Light Will Die (Cahaya Mau Mati)*, translated by John H. McGlynn; *Indonesia*, November 1949 (10).

S. Wakidjan *Fallen Warriors (Pejuang yang Hilang)*, translated by Harry Aveling; *Pita Biru: Kumpulan Sandjak-Sandjak, S. Wakidjan*, Dinas Penerbitan Balai Pustaka, Djakarta, 1962.

Saini K.M. *House of Mirrors (Rumah Cermin)*, translated by Deborah Cole; *Rumah Cermin*, Saini K.M.; Penerbit Sargani & Co. Bandung, 1979. *Pilate (Pilatus)*, translated by Deborah Cole; *Rumah Cermin*, Saini K.M.; Penerbit Sargani & Co. Bandung, 1979.

Samar Gantang *Contradiction (Kontradiksi)*, translated by Deborah Cole; *Kabut Abadi: Kumpulan Sajak*, I Gusti Putu Bawa Samar Gantang & Diah Hadaning, Lembaga Seniman Indonesia Bali, Denpasar, 1979.

Samiati Alisjahbana *Calm Waters (Air Tenang)*, translated by John H. McGlynn; *Gema Tanah Air*, H.B. Jassin (ed.), Balai Pustaka. Jakarta. 1948.

Sandy Tyas *20 September 1966*, translated by Joan Suyenaga; *Angkatan '66 Prosa dan Puisi 2*, H.B. Jassin (ed.); CV Haji Masagung, Jakarta, 1968.

Sanento Yuliman *Battle at Dawn (Pertempuran Subuh)*, translated by Marjorie Suanda; *Horison*, September, 1967.

Sanusi Pane *Common Folk (Marhaen)*, translated by Joan Suyenaga; *Timboel* via *Poeisi Baroe*, S. Takdir Alisjahbana (ed.), Penerbit Kebangsaan Poestaka Rakjat Jakarta, 1946. *Lotus (Teratai)*, translated by Joan Suyenaga; *Madah Kelana*, Sanusi Pane; Balai Pustaka, 1957. *Poem (Sajak)*, translated by Joan Suyenaga; *Tonggak Antologi Puisi Indonesia Modern 1*, Linus Suryadi (ed.), PT. Gramedia, Jakarta, 1987.

Sapardi Djoko Damono *Who are You? (Siapakah Engkau)*, translated by John H. McGlynn; *Basis*, edisi "Semerbak Sajak," January 1965 (4/XV). *Walking Westward in the Morning (Berjalan ke Barat Waktu Pagi Hari)*, translated by John H. McGlynn; *Mata Pisau*, Sapardi Djoko Damono; Balai Pustaka, Jakarta, 1982. *Verses of Fire (Ayat-Ayat Api)*, translated by John H. McGlynn; *Ayat-Ayat Api*, Sapardi Djoko Damono; Pustaka Firdaus, Jakarta, 2000. *I Want (Aku Ingin)*, translated by John H. McGlynn; via *Horison Sastra Indonesia 1, Kitab Puisi,* Taufiq Ismail et al. (eds.); Horison Kaki Langit, The Ford Foundation, Jakarta, 2001.

Saut Situmorang *little saut talks with god (saut kecil bicara dengan tuhan),* translated by Deborah Cole; *Saut Kecil Bicara dengan Tuhan,* Saut Situmorang; Bentang Pustaka, Yogyakarta, 2003. *A Poet's Mother (Ibu seorang Penyair),* translated by Deborah Cole; *Otobiografi Saut Situmorang: Kumpulan Puisi 1987– 2007,* Saut Situmorang; Penerbit [sic], Yogyakarta, 2007.

Selasih *In Agreement (Bertemu Pandang),* translated by John H. McGlynn; *Pujangga Baru,* January 1940 (7/VII). *Hunger (Lapar),* translated by John H. McGlynn; *Seserpih Pinang Sepucuk Sirih,* Toeti Heraty (ed), Pustaka Jaya, Jakarta, 1979.

Sides Sudyarto Ds. *Today, the Birthday of the Gallows (Ini Hari, Ulang Tahun Sebuah Tiang Gantungan),* translated by Marjorie Suanda; *Sajak-Sajak Tiang Gantungan,* Sides Sudyarto DS, IndonesiaTera, Magelang, 2002.

Sirikit Syah *Jakarta,* translated by Annie Tucker; *Festival Puisi XIV,* PPIA Surabaya, Surabaya, 1994. *Broadway,* translated by Annie Tucker; *Selendang Pelangi: 17 Penyair Perempuan Indonesia,* Toeti Heraty (ed.); IndonesiaTera, Magelang, 2006.

Siti Nuraini *Light in a Glass (Cahaya dalam Gelas),* translated by John H. McGlynn; *Mimbar Indonesia,* 5 February 1949 (III/1–6). *A Woman (Perempuan),* translated by John H. McGlynn; *Mimbar Indonesia,* 12 November 1949 (46/III).

Sitok Srengenge *Osmosis of Origins (Osmosa Asal Mula),* translated by John H. McGlynn; *Nonsens,* Krassin Himmirsky (ed.); Yayasan Kalam, Jakarta, 2000. *Yin Yang,* translated by John H. McGlynn; *Nonsens,* Krassin Himmirsky (ed.); Yayasan Kalam, Jakarta, 2000.

Sitor Situmorang *La Ronde,* translated by John H. McGlynn; *Wajah Tak Bernama,* Sitor Situmorang; Dunia Pustaka Jaya, Jakarta, 1982. *The Eve of Idul Fitri (Malam Lebaran),* translated by John H. McGlynn; *Malam Sutera: Sajak-Sajak Sitor Situmorang,* Agus R. Sarjono (ed.); Mahatari, Yogyakarta, 2004. *Flower (Bunga),* translated by John H. McGlynn; *Malam Sutera: Sajak-Sajak Sitor Situmorang,* Agus R. Sarjono (ed.); Mahatari, Yogyakarta, 2004. *The Prodigal Son (Si Anak Hilang),* translated by John H. McGlynn; *Malam Sutera: Sajak-Sajak Sitor Situmorang,* Agus R. Sarjono (ed.); Mahatari, Yogyakarta, 2004.

Slamet (Su) Kirnanto *Deaf Man's Hill (Bukit Sibisu),* translated by Marjorie Suanda; *Ketika Kata Ketika Warna: Puisi dan Lukisan,* Yayasan Ananda, Jakarta, 1995.

Sobron Aidit *My Days (Sehari-hari),* translated by John H. McGlynn; *Zenith,* 1952. *Song of the Sea and the Mountain (Soneta Laut dan Gunung),* translated by John H. McGlynn; *Zenith,* 1952.

Soeprijadi Tomodihardjo *Not My Intention (Bukan Mauku),* translated by Annie Tucker; *Ilalang: Suara Seorang Anak Semang,* Soeprijadi Tomodihardjo, 1989. *Stone Wall (Dinding Batu),* translated by Annie Tucker; *Ilalang: Suara Seorang Anak Semang,* Soeprijadi Tomodihardjo, 1989.

Soni Farid Maulana *Gamelan Is Dead (Gamelan Mati),* translated by Deborah Cole; *Kita Lahir Sebagai Dongengan,* Soni Farid Maulana; IndonesiaTera, Magelang, 2000. *Two Quartrains about Love (Dua Kwatrin Tentang Cinta),* translated by Lauren Zentz; *Kita Lahir Sebagai Dongengan,* Soni Farid Maulana; IndonesiaTera, Magelang, 2000.

Sosiawan Leak *Bogambola World (Dunia Bogambola),* translated by Annie Tucker; *Dunia Bogambola,* Sosiawan Leak; IndonesiaTera, Magelang 2007. *Stud Pig (Pejantan Babi),* translated by Annie Tucker; *Dunia Bogambola,* Sosiawan Leak; IndonesiaTera, Magelang 2007.

Subagio Sastrowardojo *Nawang Wulan: Guardian of the Earth and Rice (Nawang Wulan),* translated by John H. McGlynn; *Sastra,* 1962 (II/8–9). *Symphony (Simphoni),* translated by John H. McGlynn. *Simphoni,* Subagio Sastrowardojo; Pustaka Jaya, Jakarta, 1971. *Motinggo Blues (Keroncong Motinggo),* translated by John H. McGlynn; *Laut Biru Langit Biru: Bunga Rampai Sastra Indonesia Mutakhir,* Ajip Rosidi (ed.); PT Dunia Pustaka Jaya, Jakarta, 1977. *And Death Grows More Intimate (Dan Kematian Makin Akrab),* translated by John H. McGlynn; *Daerah Perbatasan,* Subagio Sastrowardoyo; PN Balai Pustaka, Jakarta, 1982.

Sugiarta Sriwibawa *School (Sekolah),* translated by Marjorie Suanda; *Garis Putih,* Sugiarta Sriwibawa; Balai Pustaka, 1985.

Suman Hs. *Poisonous Words (Diracun Kata),* translated by Harry Aveling; *Pandji Poestaka* via *Poeisi Baroe,* Sutan Takdir Alisyahbana (ed.); Penerbit Kebangsaan, Poestaka Rakjat, Djakarta, 1946.

Suminto A. Sayuti *Kurusetra Drums of War (Genderang Kurusetra),* translated by Harry Aveling; *Tugu Antologi Puisi 32 Penyair Yogya,* Linus Suryadi (ed.); Dewan Kesenian Yogya and Barata Offset, Yogyakarta, 1986. *Prambanan Temple (Prambanan),* translated by Harry Aveling; *Tugu Antologi Puisi 32 Penyair Yogya,* Linus Suryadi (ed.); Dewan Kesenian Yogya and Barata Offset, Yogyakarta, 1986.

Suparwata Wiraatmadja *The Guard (Di Gardu Jaga)*, translated by Harry Aveling; *Kidung Keramahan*, Suparwata Wiraatmaja; Badan Penerbit Kristen, Jakarta, 1963.

Supii Wishnukuntjahja *Arrogance (Congkak)*, translated by Harry Aveling; *Panca Raya*, 15 June 1947 (II/15).

Surachman R.M. *Facing the Cemetery (Depan Pusara)*, translated by Marjorie Suanda; *Sastra*, 1962 (II/12). *Whoever It Is Who Comes (Siapa pun yang Datang)*, translated by Marjorie Suanda; *Sastra*, l962 (II/7).

Sutan Takdir Alisjahbana *Heading for the Open Seas (Menuju ke Laut)*, translated by Harry Aveling; *Lagu Pemacu Ombak*, Sutan Takdir Alisjahbana; Dian Rakyat, Jakarta 1978. *The New Humanity (Manusia Utama)*, translated by Harry Aveling; *Tonggak Antologi Puisi Indonesia Modern 1*, Linus Suryadi (ed.); PT Gramedia, Jakarta, 1987.

Sutardji Calzoum Bachri *Stone (Batu)*, translated by Harry Aveling; *Laut Biru Langit Biru: Bunga Rampai Sastra Indonesia Mutakhir*, Ajip Rosidi (ed.); PT Dunia Pustaka Jaya, Jakarta, 1977. *Herman*, translated by Harry Aveling; *O Amuk Kapak*, Sutardji Calzoum Bachri; Sinar Harapan, 1981. *One (Satu)*, translated by Harry Aveling; *O Amuk Kapak*, Sutardji Calzoum Bachri; Sinar Harapan, 1981. *Tragedy of Marriage and Live-Love-Lose (Tragedi Winka dan Sihka)*, translated by Harry Aveling; *O Amuk Kapak*, Sutardji Calzoum Bachri; Sinar Harapan, 1981. *Land of Tears (Tanah Air Mata)*, translated by Harry Aveling; *Antologi Puisi Indonesia 1997 Volume 2*, Slamet Sukirnanto et al. (eds.); Angkasa, Bandung, 1997. *And (Tapi)*, translated by Harry Aveling; *Horison Sastra Indonesia 1, Kitab Puisi*, Taufiq Ismail et al. (eds.); Horison Kaki Langit, The Ford Foundation, Jakarta, 2001.

T. Mulya Lubis *Bed (Ranjang)*, translated by Annie Tucker; *Basis* No. 9, Th. XX, June 1971. *A Gambler's Last Moment (Saat Terakhir Seorang Penjudi)*, translated by Annie Tucker; *Horison*, July 1971 (7/VI).

Talsya *Our Nation's Flag Is Red and White (Sang Merah Putih)*, translated by Harry Aveling; *Seulawah Antologi Sastra Aceh Sekilas Pintas*, L.K. Ara, Taufiq Ismail, Hasyim Ks. (eds.); Yayasan Nusantara in collaboration with the government of the Special Region of Aceh, 1995.

Tan Lioe Ie *Co Kong Tik*, translated by Thomas Hunter; *Mimbar Penyair Abad 21 Dewan Kesenian Jakarta*, Taufiq Ismail et al. (eds.); Balai Pustaka, Jakarta, 1996.

Taufik Ikram Jamil *Writing (Menulis)*, translated by John H. McGlynn; *Tersebab Haku Melayu: Buku Sajak Penggal Pertama*, Taufik Ikram Jamil; Yayasan

Membaca, Pekanbaru, 1995. *a letter from von de wall to raja ali haji (surat von de wall kepada raja ali haji)*, translated by John H. McGlynn; *Tersebab Aku Melayu: Buku Sajak Penggal Kedua*, Taufik Ikram Jamil; Yayasan Pusaka Riau, 2010.

Taufiq Ismail *A Bouquet of Flowers (Karangan Bunga)*, translated by Harry Aveling; *Tirani dan Benteng: Dua Kumpulan Puisi Taufiq Ismail 1960–1966*, Yayasan Ananda, Jakarta, 1993. *Ashamed to be an Indonesian (Malu (Aku) Jadi Orang Indonesia)*, translated by Amin Sweeney; *Malu (Aku) jadi Orang Indonesia*, Taufiq Ismail; Yayasan Ananda, Jakarta, 1998. *Dharma Wanita*, translated by Amin Sweeney; *Malu (Aku) jadi Orang Indonesia*, Taufiq Ismail; Yayasan Ananda, Jakarta, 1998.

Timur Sinar Suprabana *story for nin (cerita buat nin)*, translated by Joan Suyenaga; author's documents,1989.

Toeti Heraty (Noerhadi) *Postscript (Post Scriptum)*, translated by John H. McGlynn; *Nostalgi = Transendensi*, Toeti Heraty; Grasindo, 1995. *Cocktail Party*, translated by John H. McGlynn; via *Horison Sastra Indonesia 1, Kitab Puisi*, Taufiq Ismail et al. (eds.); Horison Kaki Langit, The Ford Foundation, Jakarta, 2001. *The Lone Fisherman (Nelayan Tunggal)*, translated by John H. McGlynn; *Selendang Pelangi: 17 Penyair Perempuan Indonesia*, Toeti Heraty (ed.); IndonesiaTera, Magelang, 2006. *Manifesto*, translated by John H. McGlynn; *Selendang Pelangi: 17 Penyair Perempuan Indonesia*, Toeti Heraty (ed.); IndonesiaTera, Magelang, 2006.

Toto Sudarto Bachtiar *The Beggar Girl (Gadis Peminta-minta)*, translated by John H. McGlynn; *Etsa*, Toto Sudarto Bachtiar, Pustaka Jaya, 1958. *Jakarta at Twilight (Ibukota Senja)*, translated by John H. McGlynn; *Suara*, Toto Sudarto Bachtiar, Balai Pustaka, Jakarta, 1985.

Trisno Sumardjo *Edge of the Rice Paddy (Pinggir Sawah)*, translated by Marjorie Suanda; *Gema Tanah Air*, H.B. Jassin (ed.); Balai Pustaka, Jakarta, 1959.

Umbu Landu Paranggi *Beloved Mother (Ibunda Tercinta)*, translated by Harry Aveling; *Manifes: Antologi Puisi 9 Penyair Yogya*, (no publisher), Yogyakarta, 1968.

Upita Agustine *A Thousand Memories Rise between a Thousand Mountains (Antara Seribu Gunung Menjulang Seribu Rindu)*, translated by Harry Aveling; *Laut Biru Langit Biru: Bunga Rampai Sastra Indonesia Mutakhir*, Ajip Rosidi (ed.); PT Dunia Pustaka Jaya, Jakarta, 1977. *Song of a Woman of My Country (Senandung Perempuan Negeriku)*, translated by Joan Suyenaga; via *Horison Sastra Indonesia 1, Kitab Puisi*, Taufiq Ismail et al. (eds.); Horison Kaki Langit, The Ford Foundation, Jakarta, 2001.

Usmar Ismail *From Dusk to Dusk (Dari Senja ke Senja)*, translated by Annie Tucker; *Kesusasteraan Indonesia di Masa Jepang*, HB Jassin (ed), Balai Pustaka, Jakarta, 1984. *I Hear the Azan (Kudengar Azan)*, translated by Annie Tucker; *Kesusasteraan Indonesia di Masa Jepang*, H.B. Jassin (ed.); Balai Pustaka, Jakarta, 1984.

Walujati *Pool of Youth (Telaga Remaja)*, translated by John H. McGlynn; *Gema Tanah Air*, H.B. Jassin (ed.); Balai Pustaka, Jakarta 1948. *The Country Awakens (Negara Bangun)*, translated by Annie Tucker; *Mimbar Indonesia*, April 1950 (15/15).

Warih Wisatsana *Proverb of a Statue (Amsal Sebuah Patung) Amsal Sebuah Patung*, translated by Joan Suyenaga; Warih Wisatsana; Yayasan Gunungan, Yogyakarta, 1997. *A Mouthful of Tears (Seteguk Tangis)*, translated by Joan Suyenaga; via *Horison Sastra Indonesia 1, Kitab Puisi*, Taufiq Ismail et al. (eds.); Horison Kaki Langit, The Ford Foundation, Jakarta, 2001.

Wayan Sunarta *Jimbaran 2 (Jimbaran II)*, translated by Harry Aveling; *Antologi Puisi Indonesia 1997 Volume 2*, Slamet Sukirnanto et al. (eds.); Angkasa, Bandung, 1997.

Wiji Thukul *Alive and Well (Aku Masih Utuh dan Kata Kata Belum Binasa) Aku Ingin Jadi Peluru*, translated by Richard Curtis; Wiji Thukul; Indonesiatera, Magelang, 2004. *A Reminder (Peringatan)*, translated by Richard Curtis; *Aku Ingin Jadi Peluru*. Wiji Thukul; IndonesiaTera, Magelang, 2004.

Wilson Tjandinegara *The Ballad of a Man in Nan Yang (Balada seorang Lelaki Hitam di Nam Yang)*, translated by Harry Aveling; *Cisadane Kumpulan Puisi Tangerang*, Ayid Suyitno PS., Iwan Gunadi (eds.); Roda-Roda Budaya, Tangerang, 1997. *Legend of the Tanjung Kait Chinese Temple (Legenda Klenteng Tanjung Kait)*, translated by Harry Aveling; *Cisadane Kumpulan Puisi Tangerang*, Ayid Suyitno PS, Iwan Gunadi (eds.); Roda-Roda Budaya, Tangerang, 1997.

Wing Kardjo *Snow (Salju)*, translated by Joan Suyenaga; *Horison*, March 1967 (3/II). *La Poète Maudit*, translated by Marjorie Suanda; *Selembar Daun*, Wing Karjo; Pustaka Jaya, Jakarta, 1974. *Sajak*, translated by Marjorie Suanda; *Selembar Daun*, Wing Karjo; Pustaka Jaya, Jakarta, 1974.

Wowok Hesti Prabowo *Wheels (Roda-Roda)*, translated by John H. McGlynn; *Mimbar Penyair Abad 21 Dewan Kesenian Jakarta*, Taufiq Ismail et al. (eds.); Balai Pustaka, Jakarta, 1996.

Yogi (Abdul Rivai) *Weeding the Rice Fields (Menyiangi Padi)*, translated by Harry Aveling; *Pandji Pustaka*, 1936. *Putting the Children to Sleep (Menidurkan Anak)*, translated by Marjorie Suanda; *Puspa Aneka* via *Pudjangga Baru*, 1964.

Yudhistira A.N.M. Massardi *Let it Go! (Biarin)*, translated by Deborah Cole; *Sajak Sikat Gigi*, Yudhistira ANM Massardi; PT Dunia Pustaka Jaya, Jakarta, 1983. *Toothbrush Poem (Sajak Sikat Gigi)*, translated by Deborah Cole; *Sajak Sikat Gigi*, Yudhistira ANM Massardi; PT Dunia Pustaka Jaya, Jakarta, 1983.

Zeffry J. Alkatiri *Batavia Centrum*, translated by Deborah Cole; via *Horison Sastra Indonesia 1, Kitab Puisi*, Taufiq Ismail et al. (eds.); Horison Kaki Langit, The Ford Foundation, Jakarta, 2001. *The Beloved Missionary (Habib)*, translated by Deborah Cole; *Horison* 2002 (XXXV/4).

Zen Hae *Kindergarten (Taman Kanak Kanak)*, translated by Annie Tucker; *Angkatan 2000 dalam Sastra Indonesia*, Korrie Layun Rampan and R. Masri Sareb Putra (ed.); PT Gramedia Widia Sarana, Jakarta, 2000.